The Midnight Letter

Selected Correspondence, 1950–2010

Edwin Morgan was born in Glasgow in 1920. He became lecturer in English at the University of Glasgow, from which he retired as Professor in 1980. He was appointed Poet Laureate of Glasgow in 1999, and received the Queen's Gold Medal for Poetry in 2000. In June 2001 he received the Weidenfeld Prize for Translation for *Phaedra*. In 2004 Edwin Morgan was appointed Scotland's Makar, or Poet Laureate. He died in 2010.

James McGonigal studied English at the University of Glasgow in the 1960s. Edwin Morgan was then his research supervisor in the 1970s. A school teacher and latterly Professor of English in Education, he has published in both disciplines. He is one of Edwin Morgan's literary executors, and his *Beyond the Last Dragon: A Life of Edwin Morgan* (2010, 2012) won a Scottish Saltire award.

John Coyle is Senior Lecturer in English Literature at the University of Glasgow. He has previously edited Ford Madox Ford's *It Was the Nightingale* and *Provence* for Carcanet Press.

EDWIN MORGAN

The Midnight Letterbox

Selected Correspondence, 1950–2010

Edited by James McGonigal and John Coyle

To Jean
with best wishes
John Coyle
J McGonigal

CARCANET

First published in Great Britain in 2015 by
Carcanet Press Limited
Alliance House
Cross Street
Manchester M2 7AQ

www.carcanet.co.uk

We welcome your comments on our publications
Write to us at info@carcanet.co.uk

A CIP catalogue record for this book is available from the British Library

ISBN 978 1 78410 079 7

The publisher acknowledges financial assistance from Arts Council England

Typeset by XL Publishing Services, Exmouth
Printed and bound in England by SRP Ltd, Exeter

Contents

Introduction

Edwin Morgan's correspondence is as wide-ranging as his poetry. The letters relate not only to current poems and translations but also to his ever-changing work in theatre, music, journalism, cultural politics and education. His literary correspondents were many and varied – here T.S. Eliot and Hugh MacDiarmid appear with W.S. Graham, Salvatore Quasimodo, Allen Ginsberg, Ted Hughes, Dom Sylvester Houédard, Ian Hamilton Finlay, Haroldo and Augusto de Campos, Eugen Gomringer, Alastair Gray, Laura (Riding) Jackson and more. There is helpful and long-term contact too with significant figures in the younger generation of poets, such as Veronica Forrest-Thomson, Tom Leonard and Richard Price. There are kindly letters to his readers of all ages, as well as sharper ones to publishers and editors from the 1950s onwards. And these letters take many forms, from verse epistles to newspaper correspondence, from editorial strictures to academic gossip, from calligraphy and postcards to email. How were we to pick and choose from such riches?

This book emerged from Morgan's own collection of letters, so in a sense the first selection was his. From the start, he seems to have kept most original communications and many of his own carbon- and, later, photocopied replies. He retained for the record much that a weaker personality might have concealed. Like his poetry, the letters reveal a determination to witness to the fullest range of human experience. From the late 1980s onwards, folders of this correspondence were sent in tranches with other material to the Department of Special Collections in the Library of the University of Glasgow. He had been a student there in the 1930s and lectured in English Literature from the late 1940s until 1980. From the many thousands of letters in these Edwin Morgan Papers (papers which also include manuscript drafts of poems and translations, his own and others' artwork pasted into striking scrapbooks, libretti and screenplays, essays, reviews, scripts, lectures and travel diaries), it is possible to trace a poet's response to, and active shaping of, a manifold life.

As editors we have attempted to map both that life and an age. In sequence the letters help recreate Morgan's intellectual biography, documenting his eager engagement with artistic movements such as constructivism, American and Scottish modernism, sound and concrete poetry, poetry in translation, gay and avant-garde writing – and with the writers and critics involved in these. We begin in the late 1940s, but focus mainly on the last six decades of his life, from 1950 to 2010. He had burned personal letters when leaving to serve in the Royal Army Medical Corps in 1940. He survived to return home, and appeared thereafter determined to keep a full record of whatever life presented to him. Thus personal and professional details emerge, with the charm and wit evident to all who met him.

Born in 1920, he tended to see his own long career turning quite radically with each decade – as it had suddenly changed from undergraduate studies to war service, and then from the narrow deprivation of 1950s Scotland to his 'second life' of cultural and emotional awakening in the 1960s, and again onwards into the darker 1970s, and so on. His letters reflect these changing contexts. We have followed his preference for a decade's-eye view in presenting the letters here.

There are constants throughout, of course. A central theme is his desire to extend Scottish culture through engagement with literature from other times and places – with avant-garde American writing, with international currents of sound and concrete poetry from São Paulo to Vienna, and with Eastern European poetry in translation, notably from Russia and Hungary. His correspondence reveals an increasing involvement with poetic theatre in the 1980s and 1990s, and other ensemble work in jazz and orchestral music. His love of science and cinema was life-long.

Amidst commissions and deadlines, his customary correspondence with artists, film-makers, composers, editors, academics and readers young and old seldom slackened. Into the midnight letterbox near his flat were posted late communications for early morning collection. Since he had a gift for warm and humorous contact at a distance, domestic details constantly illumine a working poet's life. Letters had the signal advantage of allowing him to retain the privacy essential for his poetic work while sharing enough of his alert creative self to make recipients feel that he wrote only for them. That self sometimes signed letters with six swift calligraphic strokes that resolved themselves into his initials, EM.

There are so many fine letters in the Papers that we did not need to prospect further into other literary archives in, for example, the National Library of Scotland. The present work is chosen from a much larger body of correspondence posted from Glasgow to – almost anywhere. It has been shaped finally by our and the poet's publishers, Carcanet Press, as the realism of price and production come into play. So these Letters are a selection of a selection of a selection. In order to present the maximum possible number, we did not attempt to produce facsimiles but instead saved space in the layout of addresses and salutations. Where only a date is given, the implication is that the letter was written from the same address as the last previously noted in full. Individual glosses were preferred to footnotes for similar reasons of economy. Asterisked names in these glosses mean that these individuals were also correspondents, with letters included elsewhere and page numbers noted in bold in the index. Together with introductions to each decade, we trust that enough detail is given to guide but not overwhelm the reader. Catalogue references refer directly to the Edwin Morgan Papers in the Department of Special Collections. A brief list of further reading is also included.

In the three years taken to complete these Letters, we have been helped by many people. This book would have been impossible without them. We would like to thank the poet's literary executors in The Edwin Morgan Trust for permission to publish; Professor Christian Kay and Dr Jean Anderson of Glasgow University for facilitating an early pilot project; and the Glasgow University Chancellor's Fund for supporting the costs of replicating the chosen letters. This formidable task was carried out with cheerfulness and accuracy by Dr Linden Bicket. Staff in the Department of Special Collections have been unfailingly helpful. Sarah Hepworth, Deputy of Special Collections, has been unstinting in her encouragement and advice. We are also grateful to Dr Sam Maddra, Project Archivist, for special help with the Veronica Forrest-Thomson letters; to Stella Halkyard of the the John Rylands Library in the University of Manchester for additional information; to Tom Leonard for guidance; and to Professor David Kinloch and Dorothy McMillan for copies of personal letters.

Lastly, we would like to thank Dr Helen Tookey at Carcanet Press for her positive support at every stage. And we are particularly grateful to the founder of the Press, Professor Michael Schmidt, for suggesting that two editors who had been taught by Edwin Morgan in different decades would work happily in partnership on the letters that ran vitally alongside that memorable teaching. He was correct.

Prologue

Alan Shearer, friend and fellow student
(handwritten postcard)

12 Albert Drive
Burnside
29 April 1947

Dearwisher

Tacks for pinning such
Fine-all washes
Your close holy
& mutch abbreechiated
Aha Mayday appropinquishes
liber-finnishgons re-odyssue
heimorganwards, by passthistime you
notes contentness by cor, I pense?
Tell laughter is animation

En Morg

1950s

(aged 30–39)

By 1950, Edwin Morgan was a young lecturer in English Literature at the University of Glasgow. He had returned in January 1946 to take up undergraduate studies interrupted by five years of war service in the Middle East. A conscientious objector at nineteen, he volunteered for a non-combatant role in the Royal Army Medical Corps, serving in Egypt, Lebanon and Palestine. Those years of open-air life, with a measure of sexual freedom within a military environment that was generally male, hedonistic and non-intellectual, had left him ill-prepared for the enduring austerities of post-war Scotland, and for the study of literature. Romantic poetry seemed particularly beside the point.

The army had taught self-reliance, however, and he gradually got back into the way of study, made friends among the younger generation of students (he was always a charming and interesting companion), and passed his Finals so confidently that he was immediately offered a post as Junior Lecturer. Classes were beginning to burgeon, with an unstable mix of ex-Forces mature students and youngsters who had been schoolchildren during the war years, so the work was demanding enough. His parents, with whom he lived until the early 1960s, would have preferred a 'safer' job in a bank for their only son.

The 1950s were difficult years for Morgan, a period of doubt and doubleness. He was assiduous in his teaching, thorough and attentive to detail, and yet the burden of term-time work constrained artistic ambition. The poetic life had to be postponed to university vacations, mainly, and a sense of frustration surfaces in his letters early and late. Yet progress in poetry failed to match this aspiration, with packed lines too often reflecting a conflicted life. In the late 1940s Morgan had sent Edwin Muir some poems to consider. 'You are too involved, in both senses of the word. You are in your own whirlpool', the older poet commented, and was never quite forgiven.

Translation offered relief, a range of different voices and languages – Lorca, Scève, Montale, Mayakovsky – and a schooling in technique. This range, however, could bring a different sort of frustration, as editors chose to publish the excellent translations and return his own poems with regret. Anglo-Saxon poetry offered a stoic and masculine world-view that appealed; later he came to see his successful late 1940s translation of *Beowulf* as his unwritten war poem.

Morgan's emotional life brought little satisfaction at this time. Although earlier he had been deeply and romantically attached to two heterosexual men (in his pre-war university years and in the RAMC) his 1950s relationships involved casual and risky encounters among the homosexual underclass of Glasgow – activities which, if discovered, could have led to social ostracism, prison and dismissal from his teaching post. Thus he came to value all the more his correspondence with those to whom he could unburden, sensing that they would accept him as he was. Two poets were particularly supportive, W.S. Graham and Michael Shayer. Elsewhere, letters half-reveal the tension, hidden beneath a camp or playful manner. We find him creating a persona in verse letters to match or mask the contradictions inherent in his daily life.

Britain struggled to emerge from a world of rationing and making-do. The post-war settlement entrenched a new sort of conflict – a Cold War of intrigue and intransigence fought out under the threat of atomic destruction. Morgan was radically left-wing and passionately interested in scientific and technological progress. The thought of human ingenuity being geared towards negation appalled him. That communism and capitalism each pursued such an end almost made him despair.

When he came to choose work for his *New Selected Poems* (2000), Morgan selected only two from this decade, from *The Vision of Cathkin Braes* and *Dies Irae* (both 1952, although a promised publication of the latter collection fell through). They represent the linguistically playful and the severely political aspects of his writing. The playful 'Verses for a Christmas Card' merges gay and literary dimensions, in a lexis that blends elements of late Joyce, Hopkins and the 'aureate' medieval Scots diction of Dunbar:

> [...] A snaepuss fussball showerdown
> With nezhny smirl and whirlcome rown
> Upon my pollbare underlift,
> And smazzled all my gays with srift [...].
>
> (*New Selected Poems*: 11)

The contrary vision of 'Stanzas of the Jeopardy' is a dark epistle to latter-day Corinthians that warns of the moment of atomic annihilation when all the itemised and precious particularities of the world

> [...] Shall craze to an intolerable blast
> And hear at midnight the very end of the world.
>
> (*New Selected Poems*: 10)

In the dark nights and uncertain days of the Fifties, at his most isolated, letters offered Morgan a lifeline to elsewhere, with the possibility and hope that his words might be answered by return of post.

Book and Pamphlet Publications

The Vision of Cathkin Braes and other Poems. Glasgow: William MacLellan, 1952.

Beowulf: A Verse Translation into Modern English. Aldington, Kent: The Hand and Flower Press, 1952.

The Cape of Good Hope. Tunbridge Wells: Peter Russell, The Pound Press, 1955.

Poems from Eugenio Montale. Translated by Edwin Morgan. Reading: The School of Art, University of Reading, 1959.

W.S. Graham, poet

12 Albert Drive
Burnside
Rutherglen
Glasgow
30 April 1950

My dear Sydney

Thanks for the postcard in two parts, the Shakespearian line, the looming and conception of an Epistle, and the news about your good self. You know, apart altogether from my natural desire to hear from you, I relish your communications as doves and ravens sent out from the Real, and they have I assure you plenty of waste rolling world to cross and cover, but when they do come, when they do reach me and knock on the glass of whatever half- or three-quarter-reality I am living in, I feel less like a forgotten survivor of godly flooding, with the Good Real packed away in their ark and those who were late for the queue or whose species was too indeterminate for invoicing or who couldn't be paired off left to scuttle for strange tors and listen to the bottom of the abyss rising. One of my triplex-plated howling ben-observatories is labelled 'Academic Pseudovivarium: Ark-Birds Keep Out' – yet I let them in by waiting for the night-watches and I read their messages by flashlight and I feed them with corn I have hidden behind the model of the new 400-incher and back they go over the wilderness to Life. You would hardly know how to describe the country I live in; Death certainly is not its image, but neither is Life. The crags and plateaux are incredibly recalcitrant to all good walking, hail and snow are frequent, the summits are high, and many of us are swept down by the avalanches that we know may any minute calve off from the shaggy icefields we roam over. Very remarkable are the visions we have of the moon, and of the stars, and of all the icy properties and manifestations; but something has been done to the sun, it never appears more than smouldering, an ochre, a snarling crimson, even a monstrous purple. The cold of our observatories can curl round our flesh like a lash; and then it is I often visit one of the centrally-heated brochs with double insulation to keep in its fieriness and windows of horn as thick and opaque as struggling lanternlight ever seeped through; the door says 'Half House: Communion for Incurables: Ark-Hawkers Not Wanted'. Even here, however, I have managed to lever out a few of the looser stones, and the birds soon learn to tap at the right place, and I can let them in (though they hate the smoke and heat and great press of bodies) and unscrew the tiny capsules and spell off their micro-messages. Sometimes hope is held out that the waters will eventually subside; sometimes we are urged to build an ark of our own and attempt to rejoin the Great Ark: but with what materials are we to make it? The truest messages warn me that I am not to hope, for myself or for those beside me, that things will ever be any better than they are; they even warn me against having unbounded faith in the buoyancy and oceanworthiness of the Good Ark; but it seems that nothing in heaven or earth can forbid them to enjoin love, and I have seen love even in these brochs, where so many people come to cast from them blindly and momentarily their knowledge either that they cannot love or that no one has ever loved them. As for me, I have made myself a new coat, which is of very strong material; my interest in astronomy is still keen; I neither scorn nor sell myself to the brochs; I hear snatches of our distinguished and piercing storm-music; and the petrels and frigate-birds which are messages in themselves equally with the fluttering pigeons that bring theirs attached to their bodies are my friends for whom I (with others) strain my eyes every evening through the familiar falling gloom and the accepted salty air.

I send you two more 'Sleights' – I think you already have one called 'Sleights of Darkness', which is appearing in Poetry London. Also there is a translation, I think a successful one. Have you seen the magazine Nine, edited by Peter Russell? Its next issue (should be May) is a 'Contemporary Poetry' number, and I have contributed a short (very short, too short) article on you and your Threshold. Russell thinks a lot of the WT volume.

All the best as ever | ∃|||

Uneasy in civilian and academic life, EM valued continued contact with W.S. Graham, with whom he had exchanged poems before the war. Born in Greenock, Graham now lived in Cornwall. 'Sleight-of-Morals' and 'The Sleights of Time' (*Collected Poems* [*CP*]: 28–29) were published in *Listen* 1:2, Summer 1954, and *The Poet* 12, 1955 – slow progress towards publication, as compared with Graham's success with Faber & Faber.

W.S. Graham, poet

13 May 1950

My dear Sydney

I've overstepped my 'week': forgive me. You chose just the most packed and hashed week of the year for me at the university – examinations, marks, class tickets, prize-buying, meetings, dinners – and so I have not been able to absorb the poem at all properly or to feel yet that I can make any very confident statement about it. I had better tell you <u>how</u> it has been read, so that you can discount whatever you want to discount for the improprieties of my methods – though forced, not chosen! Mostly, it was in bed from midnight onwards; and as a contrast today this hot and brilliant Saturday afternoon; twice completely through (you'll admit this is not often), to get the swing; and a great deal of leaning at rest on passages I liked or was worried about, and thinking about these, in intervals of the academic netcasting. From all this, what has so far emerged is, that the swing is there, the voyage completes itself, you have produced an <u>object</u>, and this reader atanyrate finds it a fine and moving experience (though I know myself so <u>near</u> many of the ideas that my liking is more of an expected identification than the quite objective comment you're after). What I thought most interesting was the way in which this poem sums up and picks out and clarifies all the hints and guesses of the earlier poems; reminded me of the Sibelius method in music. The only worry I had about the construction, and one which is not so strong as it was when I first read the poem, was that I thought its balance had a little topheaviness in the fact that the first three sections were the best, and by 'best' I mean too powerful for the more numerous but quieter closing sections. I don't know what you think about this; I am maybe looking for a greater 'simplicity' or even symmetry than I should be looking for, because I still feel there is a complication of the 'real' the 'remembered' and the 'creating' in the last four sections which may puzzle people considerably after the very clear physical/spiritual relationships of the first three. It is the time factor that upsets things, I think, and that is why I feel I know where (or 'when') I am except in Section V; when I read it first it read too much like a really <u>closing</u> section, and I thought that Section VII very nearly (taken with section I) rendered it unnecessary. But I am ready to admit that when I get to know the poem better I shall see the rightness of Section V. At present I cling to the slight dissatisfaction that comes from an early climax (the Ancient-Mariner-like return on page 11) followed by comments in different musical and psychological modes. I can't enumerate all the things I like about the poem, because there are so many details that would delight anyone with a heart for words; but I will mention the lilting Section II refrain you sent me before: the 'calm' in Section III stanzas 14–19: the homecoming in stanzas 35–38: the end of Section VII: and lines like 'The hauling nets come in sawing the gunwhale/ With herring scales' and 'The strident kingforked airs roar in their shell' and 'Sprigs of the foam and branching tines of water' and 'Springing teal came out off the long sand' and 'That wind/ Honing the roof-ridge'. The only point where I felt definitely let down verbally was the end of stanza 36 in Section III. I felt that 'And lay/ Like a mother' was flat and bathetic, partly because I objected to the introduction of the mother-idea which calls up a new and hoaxing series of associations but more because the stressing is too light – 'Like a mother' has really only one stress and you need two. And of course the short sentence and the final position throw all the light onto this idea and phrase. I felt something of that flatness at the end of the section too in 'My fruitful share', though this would be more of a criticism if the Section was in fact the last of the poem. There's a difficulty about 'unprised' and I don't know if you intend a double meaning. The 'harder reading' would be to take it as you spell it, meaning 'not pierced yet', 'not broken through'; but it could be 'unprized', 'not wondered at enough yet although it is ancient overhead'. I incline to the second because I have used the same image (with the word 'unconsidered') in the first stanza of my 'Midwinter'. You have 'siezed' for 'seized' on page 6, and 'amourous' for 'amorous' on page 4. Things I was reminded of may interest you: Section I ll 7–8 recalled immediately 'The Waste Land' ll 25–26 ('There is shadow under this red rock,/ (Come in under the shadow of this red rock)'); I often thought of Eliot's 'Marina' and 'this grace dissolved in place'; and of course the bells and wailing and gulls of 'The Dry Salvages'. 'The Wreck of the Deutschland' sometimes hissed and plunged through your starker rigging, but you have nary a nun on board, only chirpers and silver jerseys.

Now will these remarks be of any use to you? They're honest, but they don't come from a deep enough acquaintance with the poem. You must take from them what you can and couple them with your own feelings and whatever Eliot has said. One thing, I am glad I called my *Nine* article 'Graham's Threshold', for here you are cast off from the shore and sending back something brighter than herringshine. You become the sea bell, or the sea light, and there is something about both these things that fairly shakes the light in the blood and the tolled heart.

I would agree about Christopher Fry. What he should cultivate is his sense of humour, but it is a fantastic or exaggerative sense of humour and he intellectualizes it far too much (see 'Venus Observed'); he ought to collaborate with the author of *Titus Groan* and give joint and teeming birth to some gorgeous gingerococobread inanity that would keep all the pyrotechnophils and farcecrackers speechless for a golden year. Have you seen any Tennessee Williams or Arthur Miller plays in London? I like *The Glass Menagerie* and *Death of a Salesman*. Does the writer of *The Cocktail Party* approve of these tragedies of pity-without-terror?

This being a broch night, I had better put away the observatory typewriter and see which way the wind is howling. My thermometer is filled with californium; mercury by jove would explode. The Spirit Lamp is a greater invention than Davy's, and I keep mine bright. All my fur is pining marten.

Ever yours | ⊒||

Graham had asked for comment on 'The Nightfishing', the title poem of his 1955 collection from Faber & Faber. EM had reviewed *The White Threshold* (1949), in Peter Russell's Poundian journal *Nine* II:II (No. 3), May 1950.

W.S. Graham, *poet*

29 October 1950

To Sydney in Truro Ward, this dark Sunday evening
In a little frost, in a little fog, a verseletter.
– Nearly a month since I wrote you, and yes after
Promising better, but I am bitterly constrained
With lectures and work and the books growling around me
Hated, here, hellhounds, as I write: forgive me.
And first, how are you far away in that hospital?
Do you mend, and are you drugged still, can you
Hold a pencil yet for makarwork, for trobar
Close or frank? I am anxious to hear
And hope by this time you will have good news
To send me – by the merest line you like.
I mend, but slowly, it is an end that only
Will mend slowly! and I am sick of the discomfort
And the sour patience of a poor inactivity
But both should end soon. It is the poem
That has suffered, and its inactivity is
My main restlessness. Come back time and energy
And Christmas weeks come on, animators
Suspended, men not at work, till then!
(It was verse you requested, dear Joke Grim
From your Zennorward eyrie, and on eagle-wings,
Inked with inveigle-beak, immetriculable
Universe here like the sure iceman cometh –
Hereward Comesnatch Everyballadry.)

O it was gratitude welled for the verse of
Your letter when you said what I had confessed
Could make no difference to how you regarded me,
And if all the imagery and congestion and turgidity

Round a simple thing could have been swept away
I would have swept it away, but it is hard, hard
To say the simple things that involve a life and a friend,
And to me friendship is like others' love,
The most of life: and for this called, in pain, 'love'.

Aberration draws on rebuff, rebuke, contempt.
At thirty one has built a shell, or been beaten.
The shell is complex to guard a simplicity
Or hard to guard a reproved gentleness.
In penalty, sometimes like a live thing
Feeling unaccountable or at sight of a boy's face
In a city street stirs in me crying or
Trying rather to cry and to stretch outward
In a gesture twisting and bursting with yearning:

And I almost then stretch out my own hands
To the boy or the goading vision – almost speak;
Well, you might almost hear it, like sea's singing.
– It is only love trying to wail to be born,
The wailing of the never to be born.
If there are Hesperides, it is not heard there.
Wheesht, sleek silkie, wheesht in the Hert-Hebrides!
– You see how the images come, even here.
I rebuke their aberrant apparition.

You ask about the phrase of my 'friend in golden fell'.
It is one with whom I was naked and whose hair
And down were golden like a coat or fell
Or so exaggerated and word-romanticized
Since his was the golden hair in the dark and the
Down was compounded to him from a noonday
Recollection of a soldier at the beach in Haifa
Gold-felled like the Georgian epic hero
'The knight with the tiger's fell', for whom too I fell.

These things should be in prose (if this is verse)
But never mind; young men as well as old
Must be explorers. (And you must tell me
About the 'Morven maiden' and the 'limekiln Shony' – remember?

A few items, a long time back, I still want to know!)
'Cinderfall'? Well, not exactly a dream
But a halfawake full-imagination (fool imagination)
Nightmare one midnight as I watched the cinders fall.

Where now again they fall, inexpressible hour
Of the heart, when the sinking log hisses and the coal
With its faint crackle feeds the waning glow!
It will soon be twelve, and in the firelight darkness
I sit finishing fashioning this pyrotechnic
Glasgow-to-Cornwall Very-light, a Halloween
Hallowed Catherine-Wheel, a rocket of remembrance
And a poor aurora of northern thanks,
And send it all up, to flash for an hour on your sickness.

E.M.

Hospitalised in Truro after a serious leg injury, Graham was far from home in Zennor. EM lent money to help him cope with loss of casual earnings. 'Trobar clus' and 'leu' were the complex and accessible styles of troubadour poetry. EM was also suffering, from a complication of haemorrhoids, preventing work on 'The Cape of Good Hope', dated Aug.–Dec. 1950 in his poem folder. The images of 'golden fell' and 'cinderfall' are in 'The Sleights of Darkness' (*Collected Poems* [*CP*]: 27–28). *The Knight in the Tiger's Skin* is a twelfth-century Georgian epic poem by Shotha Rustaveli.

Vivien Linacre, friend and businessman

4 November 1950

You and your wires! – the centre
Will hold in our time (prepaid),
Vividest Lineament,
Centre hold, and I patient
To be mid-December-cured.
The doctor said hospital
Would not be needed, so I
Have just been struggling along

These long weeks with my fissure
Pretending nothing was wrong
And have now another month
Apparently to struggle
According to prediction.
This is called being patient
And I call miserable
The patience; my work suffers,
And the poem waits like doom,
And why should I write to you
Complaint and pity of self?
You rather write me tonic
Rx replication
Of some Vivid Liniment.
I would have written to you but
Fissure king gloom ow'rfret me
In the kingfisherless bounds.
My friend Sydney Graham is
In hospital in Truro,
Another poetry-shard
Another crock of a Jock,
And I worry about him
Since he is too drugged to write.
Tell me if you are working
Column-scanning or selling,
Coal-selling or saddening,
The diet crumbs and water,
Kebab, shashlik, fish-and-chips?
I am reading 'Ghormenghast'
And the 'Seventy Cantos';
Saw an aquarium fish
Exhibition yesterday;
And have put on a yellow
Pullover to knit up care
A little with its brilliant
Ravelment; such my poor news.
Haut les coeurs, kingfisher cries,
Haut les coeurs, O haut les coeurs!
– Endgloom Mornagain!

Linacre had been an active student debater at Edinburgh University and was now seeking employment. He had sent telegrams to EM. Rx on a 1950s medical prescription stood for 'recipe', meaning in Latin 'to take'.

F.W. Bateson, academic and editor

2 May 1952

Dear Mr Bateson

When you wrote to me on 28th March about my article 'Dunbar and the Language of Poetry' you said that you had 'accepted most though not absolutely all' of my proof-corrections. On looking through the article as printed in *Essays in Criticism* I find that the corrections you have in fact allowed are restricted almost entirely to mere typographical errors, and in none of the points to which I specifically referred in my letter of 19th February have you seen fit to be persuaded by the arguments I put forward to defend the way in which I had expressed myself. In your Editorial Note you announce your 'right to iron out the creases in contributors' English'. Whatever this figure of speech may precisely mean, it certainly implies a strangely autocratic attitude towards work submitted. I must say that I object strongly to the alterations you have made in my own article, but it is the general principle behind the alterations which seems to me (and I can assure you I am not alone in this opinion) so insulting and so scandalous. Prose is not so generically opposed to poetry that statements in it can be 'put in different ways' without change or loss of meaning; and this is especially true of good literary criticism, which presumably you want to encourage. 'Ironing out' an author's style is perhaps a legitimate device under an anonymity régime, to ensure perspicuity coupled with 'rightness of tone', but when an essay is signed, surely its writer is justified in asking that what he really wrote and intended should appear above his name? – otherwise, how easily will he reject criticisms of his article, by pointing out that 'these are the editor's words, not mine'! (This will certainly be my reply if anyone asks what I mean by 'the distillation of poetic situation' – a jingling and ambiguous phrase, but <u>not mine</u>.) Your policy will only help to perpetuate the mediocrity and timidity and 'stylelessness' which are the bane of so much present-day English scholarship. Why not renegue this censoring-right? I am sure the style of Matthew Arnold himself was 'creased', with the parallel ridges of repetition if by no deeper geologicoliterary faults; but 'ironing out' would have left him threadbare, if not naked. *Essays in Criticism* should try to win a lively integrity (and that is <u>an integrity of individuals</u>) quite distinct from the colourless though informative 'received standard' of *PMLA* or *RES* or *JEGPh*. Its title should not be understood as a synonym for *Critical Articles*. Let the authors take their style with them when they are exploring style: that is what Coleridge did, and Wordsworth, and Dryden, and Blake and Bacon too. And if this argument will not satisfy, there is a contrasting one which it seems to me is unanswerable: what could in the end be <u>less scholarly</u> than the practice of modifying other scholars' considered statements in such a way that they have no redress and the readers no way of knowing where the modifications occur? It really is not good enough, Mr Bateson! It is a policy which will neither make for 'gay and vigorous dissertations' nor accompany a scholarship that one can trust.

I have not yet, by the way, received my two complimentary copies. Could you please hasten these up? Also by the way: my name was misspelt (not, I think, by editorial principle) in the Notes on Contributors!

Yours sincerely | Edwin Morgan

'Dunbar and the Language of Poetry' was published in *Essays in Criticism*, II: 2, April 1952, edited by Bateson. This was EM's first substantial publication in literary criticism, and was reprinted in *Essays* (1974): 81–99.

Erica Marx, publisher

25 June 1952

Dear Erica Marx

These are the names for review copies: I'll include journals that you'll no doubt have thought of yourself, just in case we miss any obvious ones.

Essays in Criticism (F.W. Bateson)
The Cambridge Journal (Michael Oakshott)
Scrutiny (F.R. Leavis)
Arena (Jack Lindsay)
Colonnade (Iain Fletcher)
Review of English Studies (John Butt)
Archivum Linguisticum (Stephen Ullmann – The University, Glasgow W2)
The College Courant (George Brown – also Glasgow Univ.)
The Wind and the Rain (Neville Braybrooke)
The Month (Philip Caraman SJ)
World Review
Poetry Quarterly
The Poetry Review
The Adelphi
The Cornhill XX – don't have reviews, do they
Glasgow University Magazine (Ed., Pearce Lodge, The Univ.)
The Glasgow Herald (on a par with *The Scotsman*)
The Scottish Field (70 Mitchell Street, Glasgow C1)
The Universities Quarterly
Medium Aevum (pub. Basil Blackwell, 49 Broad St., Oxfd.)
Anglia (Max Niemeyer Verlag, Tubingen, Wilhelmstr. 18)
English Studies (Prof. Dr. R.W. Zandvoort, De Savornin, Lohmanlaan, Groningen, Holland)
Modern Philology (Univ. of Chicago Press, Chicago 37, Ill.)
Journal of English and Germanic Philology (Univ. of Illinois Press, 358 Administration Bldg., Urbana, Ill.)
Modern Language Notes (Johns Hopkins Univ., Baltimore 18, Maryland)
Comparative Literature (Univ. of Oregon, Eugene, Oregon)
Speculum (Mediaeval Academy of America, 1430

Massachusetts Avenue, Cambridge 38, Mass.)
The Times Literanonymary Shufflement!!

The transatlantic and continental journals listed above would
be almost certain to review a translation of *Beowulf*; so of
course would the British scholarly journals; and although
they're not widely read outside scholarly circles, their influence
is important as long as *Beowulf* is a recognized classic and a
prescribed text! (– Where I've mentioned an editorial name,
it means that I will already have been heard of or be known
personally.) – How about Beowulf on the Third Programme:
John Lehmann: 'Old Soundings'?! I remember when I
was listening to the Aeneid broadcasts I thought to myself
'Beowulf would sound at least as well as this, and probably a
good deal more heroic.'

I have seen *Colonnade* which I fear is going to be
too mediterraneany and broken-columny to be of great
contemporary significance (why does someone not bring out
a journal called *The Mushroom* or *Isotope*?); but it is at least
another journal for writers to write in, and that is something.
I.F. and his co-editors call themselves 'a splinter group' from
Nine, so presumably some split or splintering or sundering or
something must have taken place. 'Too many cooks' may have
been the cause of the relatively cliquey-look of the pre-fission
cookery-book.

I quite appreciate your remarks about punctuation. I have
always swithered myself between aesthetics and grammar in
the question of dashes-and-commas. Although I agree with
you that when the comma is omitted it <u>looks</u> better, I still feel
the sentence-reader is never quite quick enough in seeing that
the dashes are really taking over the omitted comma's duty, and
may think the sentence runs on rather loosely. In the other case
you mention, I had used dashes generally (instead of colons)
for the sake of consistency. I have of course no objections to
the changes.

I am glad to hear you say you think it reads well, now that
you see it in print. I do think myself that it should have a
fairly wide range of appeal; and certainly in the introduction
I have laid baits for the ordinary modern reader of poetry (if
such a person exists) as well as for the expert in Anglo-Saxon

versification. How can we interest the <u>Russians</u>, who admire the poem, and whom I refer to and quote at various points??!!

Sincerely yours | eadwine mhorghuinn

EM's *Beowulf* translation in hardback from Erica Marx's Hand and Flower Press was reissued in paperback by the University of California Press in 1962 and remained in print until 1999, selling over 50,000 copies. John Lehmann's* radio magazine was *New Soundings*. *Colonnade*, co-edited by Iain Fletcher, Ian Scott-Kilvert and D.S. Carne-Ross*, was soon subsumed in the arts journal *Adam*.

Alan Shearer, friend
(handwritten)

Dublin
23 July 1952

I think you would like this city. I've seen the Liffey and the docks and the book of Kells and been around the Guinness brewery and watched the Irish militia practise woodcraft in Phoenix Park. My kilt is a sensation – you'd think it was the first ever seen. Like this folksy card? I thought you'd be blasé about the Liffey so I picked up a spot of old boreen instead.
    Yours | Eddie

Shearer was a post-war friend and fellow student. EM often wore the kilt on holiday and special occasions at home and abroad during the 1940s and 1950s. A 'boreen' is Irish for a country lane, as illustrated on the postcard.

L.R. Lind, academic and editor

12 Albert Drive
10 June 1954

Dear Professor Lind

Your letter and the *Lyric Poetry of the Italian Renaissance* arrived almost together. I agree with you it is a very attractively produced book, and the poems and translations are nicely presented. Do not feel too desperate about the errors of page 47! It is most unfortunate, but it is the kind of thing that can happen to the most lynx-eyed reader of proofs. Curiously enough, only the other day we were complaining in the department about the inaccuracies that even the Oxford University Press have achieved of late, and I said, Indeed nowadays we tend to get fewer typographical slips from the American university presses! So this is my punishment for an unsupported generalization! Do you think that the publishers will be able to do anything at all about it, before there is a second impression or edition? There is, I should mention, one other small slip, on the same page: in the 7th song, the <u>comma</u> after 'Glisk o the burn' should be a <u>period</u>. If there is any chance of correcting this at the same time – ?

The two things that seem to me to stand out in the book are the Jacopone da Todi and the Michelangelo: for passion, and for strength. Perhaps this is a 'northern' or non-Italian estimate? At anyrate it struck me very forcibly. You have really got together quite a distinguished roll of translators, with Wordsworth and Shelley and Rossetti and Pound, and this gives the book a good variety of texture, variety of approach, which I think is useful.

My best wishes to you for the success of the book.

Yours very sincerely | ≡|||

Lind edited *Lyric Poetry of the Italian Renaissance* (1954) in which EM's translation into Scots of '13 Tuscan Songs' appeared, as well as translations of Michelangelo and Tasso. These appear in *Collected Translations* [*CT*] (1994). Not only was there inaccurate pagination in the Index and an incomplete glossary but whole lines had been omitted from Songs 3 and 4.

Ian Dallas, *dramatist and screenplay writer*

Dearest Ian, this being Saturday
It struck me this morning I might put on paper
The remnants of last night's brief and faulty
Conversation at Waterloo Street.
There were so many things I had still to say
But being so stuffed with sulfsuxidine
And feeling more gastro-enteritical
Than bright and critical I had to leave them
Sketched or unsaid. Here then are words
To suggest what I mean about patterned writing.
Divergence into freedom is still divergence,
Freedom is meaningless and self-destructive
Unless it is based on bondage and constraint
(And this is true for Marxist and Christian
As it is for poets!): the greatest of verse
In a Shakespeare or Milton presents the illusion
Of enormous liberty, but the liberties taken
Are variations within one frame,
Pleasure is never anarchic – daring
As daring as you like, but daring in design,
A vast counterpoint of speech and metre,
Not just metre – and not just speech.
Believe me there's no shortcut to impressiveness!
Speech is the very first problem to solve,
And those who would 'heighten' drama with words
(Rather than with stage or production techniques)
Will find in the end that poetry will do it,
Or prose will do it – but the choice must be made.
I do not say that dramatic poetry
Can never be written except by a poet,
But one who is not a poet must somehow
Encompass the disciplines the poet lives by.
And that, dear dramatist, is what I would say:
Put yourself to school, experiment more,
Extend your range, be flexible, not Fry,
Write farces, mysteries, masques, anything

To give you more patience with the varied subtleties
Of dramatic language and dramatic presentation –
And leave for a little while the ideas,
The mission, the contents, the hundredth element
Or the hundredth existential saint!
They will keep: they will! You don't believe me
But they will. And to find your own right form
They must wait till drama is itself heroic.
You search for the hero, but can that hero
Be a man or a woman? Can the playwright descend
Low enough, low enough, when the 'Depths' of Gorky
Or Blanche or the Salesman or Celia or Gettner –
Or Genet – or Jessie – are heights and happiness
Compared with the numbing anonymity

     Of even one of Hiroshima's dead
     With neither dust to go to the dust
     Nor ashes left to join the ashes?
     He is the hero and she is the hero
     And the burned child in her womb is the hero.
     What stage could – but I stop to remember
     That the Japanese theatre is a theatre of ghosts.

     – And what is your answer to the four-stress measure?
     You can write it easily and still give pleasure.
     And alliteration, make it massive,
     Sprinkle it with trickeries till it trips like Spring-
     Heel Jack or a flyblown trampoline:
     Or have it plain as plain can be
     With eight short words to each blunt line.

Experiment with blank verse too. 'Go on,'
He says; 'blank verse is dodo's food. Nothing
Can come of nothing.' Nevertheless, try!
Make things hard for yourself. Edith Evans
Must be put down, just like Edith Sitwell.
Flow must have point, liquidity a dam.
Hydroelectric epigrams! Dam Fry!
I use ten syllables in every line
Yet every line is capable of that

Fall into self-determination and
Late-Shakesperian ambidextrousness
Which might clothe any character you make.
'No good for the colloquial', you think?
Inversion's very useful – inversion
Of feet, I mean; it's more than surprising,
Indeed it's fair astonishing, how much
You can make its five feet speak: see
Bridges on Milton.
                            And for those pauses
Between the characters, a broken blank
Verse line is still
                      – Tops?
                                  – Well, tops if you like!

Even heroic couplets have their place –
They make you ponder at a cracking pace
– Heroic triplets too are no disgrace.

                    But joking apart, and without distress
                    Or undue stress in my four-stress dress –
                    Have I made the point? and can it help you?
                    The starting-points may be half-forgotten –
                    'Sweeney Agonistes' and Yeats's 'Purgatory',
                    Or a human Shaw or a thinking Synge.
                    Incision: bite: satire if necessary
                    But heroic clarity, the words like swallows
                    Cleaving a pattern of white and blue
                    In the sky of their rhythmic involvement.
                    Verse, or prose, is the choice I leave you.
                    And seek to be skilled, as words are weapons;
                    Waking, not sleeping, be Wayland the Smith!
                            Exit, with the morning,
                                    Edwin Morgan.

Dallas was a young playwright and actor from Ayrshire who had
trained at RADA in London and was now trying to make his way as
a writer. His *A Masque of Summer*, a high-society play in three acts,
was presented by Glasgow Citizens' Theatre in November 1952.
The 'discussion' here relates to the pre- and post-war trend towards

poetic drama, associated with Christopher Fry and also T.S. Eliot (in a plainer form of verse).

W.S. Graham, poet

15 November 1954

Dear Sydney:

Your pencilled carbon-copy letter, having been pressed folded in its envelope, opened up as a sort of shadowgraph, doublewrite, or pseudo-palimpsest, but it was really quite intelligible; nice, however, to think that your message was there backwards and upside down as well as forwards and upside up. I was glad to hear from you, as I was worried about where to send the pen. It's being posted separately in a box, the nib being protected by a rather absurd rubber thing which (if you don't mind the absurdity) you can keep using for that purpose. If you don't have a top, how do you not get ink everywhere? (This is one of about 365 questions I ought to be asking you.) Your photos, by the way, haven't been printed yet, but I should be able to let you have them soon. I had to finish off the spool, and the weather's been so bad that this was difficult, but on Sunday I went round by Cathkin snapping model aeroplane enthusiasts in a bing-bound field and lorries and tractors patterning the mud of the new Castlemilk housing scheme, with a wan wee free sun mourning over the shoulders of Sabbath labour and Sabbath play.

I'm sorry too that we didn't have more time together when you were up. It was exciting, as always. If it was too exciting, and I was a little on edge, and said things I shouldn't have said, I hope you'll forgive in the circumstances. A curious thing happened that night: when I went to bed I couldn't sleep, although I was tired, and in that pre-sleep state, with my eyes closed, I kept being startled by a succession of the most astonishingly vivid images I have ever seen either sleeping or waking. In the morning they had mostly gone, and I could only remember fragments, though in a vague way I still knew what sort of effect they had had. It was a series of bursts of energy: great curtains of rain coming suddenly down, rockets hurtling past, brilliant fusings and crystallizations, savage animals like tigers and leopards leaping out from caves – and in every instance there was an almost physical shock or punch as the image came into focus, making me open my eyes and think about it. I suppose my mind was very much awake, and yet there was no intellectual content in the imagery – at least, if there was, it had all been transformed into pictorial and kinetic terms. Have you ever had this sort of experience?

I look forward very eagerly to seeing how your next volume will appear. Although I have said that I 'got less' from your poetry than I did some years ago, I still find it more interesting than most of the poetry that is being written, and in a curious sort of way, because of the strongly continuing (no matter how superficially interrupted) involvement of each of us with the other (which I would never give up) I find myself wanting or willing you to make certain changes and developments, as if I was more concerned with poetry you have yet to write than with what you have written. So far, you are like harper in hall, goodly feres around, horns brimming, tables creaking, harp with fine tone, and you with 'Listen, all this companee!' give great swoop among strings, crouch to it, sweep and brandish, pick and knock and then again big swoop like a sweepskate: but guests grow restless, whisper from beard to beard: it is all prelude and no song, plectrum prances but voice is avoided: you say 'Listen!' but then you have nothing to tell us. – Is there anything in this that you would want to take? I think what I want to see you doing is assuming communication rather than speaking about it. This may involve some such thing as 'a return to subject-matter' – whether descriptive, narrative, or dramatic. One reason I liked *The Nightfishing* was, it had a definite physical subject, though still a highly romantic-symbolic one. Perhaps I am stupidly asking you to stand in Piccadilly Circus with a notebook? And yet, I did and do feel that the danger for your poetry is too much sea and too little pavement. – I merely throw you these strands, that are not necessarily lifelines, and you will see whether you require them as they are, or cut up for some other purpose – or whether they are to be thrown back to me.

Last week I saw not the best film I've ever seen but the

most beautiful: the adjective just slides out of it like hand
from glove. Japanese it was – a historical film, *The Gate of Hell*.
Recollection of it makes me think in exclamations. How lucky
to live in the 20th century when you can see so much beauty
for 2/6! What an impact, what meaning there is simply in
colour! Gorgeous robes and trappings and armour in gold and
purple and crimson and peach; rows of white-laundered monks
sitting like seagulls; a gamboge toril rising from the waves like
an ideogram; a blue moonlit garden where you could feel your
fingers stroking the glossy purring leaves..... The eye is some
sensualist.

You don't say in your letter, but I take it that your banns are
all gebunden, and that Nessie is Mrs G? My best wishes to you
both if this is so – and in any case.

I'll be having a poem in the next *Lines Review*, and my first
'Dialogue' (Joyce and MacDiarmid) will be in the *Saltire* –
sometime.

Write when you can. Love – | ≡\|\|

Graham came to visit EM in late September 1954, got lost and
arrived very late – to a cool reception. This letter and the promised
pen were by way of apology and explanation, an attempt to restore
friendship. 'Wee free' signals the austere Calvinism of the Free
Church of Scotland. Graham met Nessie Dunsmuir as a fellow-stu-
dent at Newbattle Abbey College.

Alan Shearer, friend
(handwritten)

Moscow
29 April 1955

Dear Alan

We arrived here today, and our hotel almost overlooks the
Red Square (and Lenin's mausoleum which you can see on
the other side). All is excitement and banners in preparation
for May Day. Warm sunny weather – though we had snow
in Stockholm and Helsinki and the ship couldn't go on to

Leningrad because the ice still blocked the Gulf of Finland (we took the Helsinki–Moscow train). I have a vast double room with private bath, telephone, and clear view of the Kremlin. More reports later I hope.

Yours | Eddie

EM's time as a delegate on a month-long study tour organised by the Scotland–USSR Friendship Society confirmed his commitment to socialism and Russian poetry. His translations of Mayakovsky appeared in *Lines Review* in 1954 and of Pushkin, Pasternak, Mayakovsky and Shevelyova in the *Saltire Review* and *Soviet Weekly* in 1955.

Odessa
11 May 1955

Dear Alan

Here is some modern Russian art – I hope to be able to show you more when I come back.

I've now been on the famous Odessa Steps, had a gargantuan meal with home-made wine on a collective farm, and read Burns at an open-air concert in Zaporozhe.

Very warm here on the Black Sea.

Yours | Eddie

EM's enthusiasm for Russian constructivist art was lifelong, and informed the design of his first Carcanet volume, *Wi the Haill Voice: 25 Poems by Vladimir Mayakovsky* (1972).

Bournemouth
28 June 1955

I have seen Egdon Heath, and I brought *Tess of the d'Urbervilles* with me but haven't read any of it yet – what with visiting Southampton docks to see the oceanic boats, inspecting the cliffs of Lulworth Cove (in company with a young man who has seen a flying saucer) and taking colour photographs (trying hard not to count the eventual cost!). I expect to be back Thursday night. Shall I see you Saturday at 11 (Station)?

Eddie

EM explored the poetic potential of both photography (*Insta-matic Poems*, *CP*: 217–29) and space travel (in *The Second Life*, *From Glasgow to Saturn* and *Star Gate* (*CP*: 196–98, 266–68, 383–94).

R.L. Lusty, publisher

12 Albert Drive
9 October 1955

Dear Mr Lusty

Thank you for your letter of 30th September addressed to me c/o the P.E.N. There are two things I should like to mention.

The first possibility is a collection of critical essays on poets and poetry, from various periods but mainly modern. Over the last six or seven years I have had a number of essays and articles published in magazines like *Essays in Criticism*, *The Cambridge Journal*, *The Saltire Review*, *Lines Review*, and *Nine*; and there are also some BBC talks. The essays wouldn't strictly speaking be connected, but most of them are related to ideas about 'purposefulness' and 'communication' in poetry, and I would write and add a general essay on this theme if you were interested.

The other suggestion is so far only a project. I paid a 6-week visit to the USSR recently as a member of a Scottish cultural delegation invited by V.O.K.S. I received various strong impressions, which I mean to write about, and I hope to produce something that will be not just another travel book about Russia. I took many photographs, in colour and black and white, and I would want to use some of these as illustrations.

I should certainly be very glad to know whether you might be interested in either of these two possibilities.

Yours sincerely | ≡‖ | (Edwin Morgan)

Lusty was Vice-Chairman of Michael Joseph Ltd, publishers of *New Poems 1955*, a PEN anthology in which EM's 'Northern Nocturnal' (*CP*: 564) had appeared. He enquired whether EM had any project ('not poetry') in mind for publication.

John Lehmann, editor

27 July 1956

Sir,

Mr Colin Wilson in his 'Writer's Prospect' shows a <u>concern</u> for the general literary situation which is refreshing, but his diagnosis is so incomplete that his concern can hardly be of much practical use. He betrays his own cause in the first sentence, when he speaks about 'Western Europe' and 'Western European literature' as if these were terms that needed no comment; as if it was possible, far less desirable, to cut off the western half of Europe from its eastern half, and as if nothing had been written on the far side of Bonn and Venice since Dostoevsky.

It is disappointing to see in Mr Wilson merely another Western European Provincial, dressed in a new suit of clothes but clinging resolutely to the same old threadbare ragbag of traditions. To offer us a new set of reverences, with Shaw and Wells in place of Eliot and Pound, may well produce a temporary enlivening effect, but the heart of our problem will remain untouched so long as we continue to try to perpetuate ourselves through this ceaseless cultural incest. Western European literature is starving itself because it has become afraid to go beyond its own boundaries for nourishment. Dread of political stigma compels us to remain ignorant or ignorantly contemptuous of literary values embedded in cultures opposed to our own. This ignorance is so shocking, and in the end will be so bad for our culture, that one must utter a protest when Mr Wilson says we can count on very few fingers 'the number of writers of the last thirty years who considered themselves actively involved in the destiny of their times', without mentioning the fact that if this is true it is because Western European writers had already severed most of their life-giving connections with the rest of the world, and had become enamoured of their own decline. There were plenty of writers, some of them very great and very human writers, who were 'actively involved in the destiny of their times', and from whom much might have been learned, by both novelists and poets: let me mention no more than Gorky, Mayakovsky, Sholokhov. Does Mr Wilson think that these writers belonged to a different race – or even to an incompatibly different culture? Is he aware of the fact that it is the USSR, and not Britain, which shares his high opinion of Shaw and his low opinion of 'Freud, Jung, Bergson, and Donne'? What is his view of another fact: that his 'sense of reality', search for pattern, 'diagnosis of the age', and necessity of affirmation, are all vigorously recommended by Soviet critics, and can indeed be found (allowing for natural shortcomings) <u>at the present time</u> by anyone who reads Russian or who even takes the trouble to look at translations of postwar Russian books. Leonov, Panova, Granin, Chukovsky, Ehrenburg: have they no relevance, Mr Wilson? <u>Can</u> we do without them – always?

I mention Russian literature not politically but because it is a foreign literature with which I have some familiarity and whose traditions and characteristics I respect. The point I want to make is simply that writers cannot afford at this time of day to dig themselves in within this little promontory of Eurasia and go on counting their treasures. We have all been doing that too long; the very coins will not clink as blithely as they did. I fully sympathize with Mr Wilson in his desire to revitalize the literary body, but I would suggest that his fashion of criticizing the 'writer's prospect' is like a man covering one eye with his hand and complaining of the wrongness of the scene.

≡‖ | (Edwin Morgan)

Colin Wilson, one of the Angry Young Men of 1950s British writing and author of *The Outsider* (1956), a study of modern alienation, had published 'The Writer's Prospect' in *The London Magazine*, edited by Lehmann. EM would later take part in a forum with Wilson at Glasgow's Athenaeum Theatre 'Trinity Celebrity Lectures' (14 January 1957), on the topic of 'George Bernard Shaw and the Decline of the Western World'.

Ian Dallas, *dramatist and screenplay writer*
(handwritten)

14 September 1956

Dear Sir

I read your letter in the *New Statesman*... Well, actually I
did, Ian, and having since that date also seen *Mother Courage*
I feel I must again <u>try</u> to correct that alarming tendency in
you to play down all production techniques in favour of ideas
and beliefs. I remember being shocked by your dismissal of
things like *Uranium 235* because 'people were doing that sort
of thing in Germany 20 years ago', and your clinging to all
the clichés of the British (oh so British!) drawingroom play.
Now that I've seen the Berliner Ensemble I am more than
ever persuaded that technique and presentation are of the
utmost importance. You deny the importance of the revolving
stage in your letter; but it is <u>precisely</u> this that stamps the
play and its meaning on your memory. The opening scene
with the cart going round and the song being sung shakes
you right out of the Eliot-Fry-Whiting continuum; it has an
astonishing effect, as also have the bare stage and the clear
unmelodramatized lighting. Certainly the ideas are important
in Brecht, and having the 'world-view' might solve the
question of technique, but the point you miss is that without
something fairly spectacularly new in technique <u>no</u> world-
view whether religious or political is going to revitalize British
theatre. If I may misquote you, 'It is not their holistic view of
drama, that makes them <u>lively</u>, it is their revolving stage.' Now,
does that not read much better? Be honest with me; after all,
I know you! This doesn't mean that <u>we</u> have to take up the
revolving stage, but we do have to find a revolving something,
even if it's only a revolver to shoot down all the designers of
living-room sets. The Berliners and the Peking Opera can
come and go, and people will still be unhappy unless they
get their three square walls and half a ceiling – and <u>you</u>, dear
friend, what do you do but encourage them? I despair of you,
I.D., so I do.

But anyhow, how are you? Does TV feed you reasonably?

Any plays in the offing – I mean real plays, not nom-de-ma-plume plays? Do drop me a line sometime.

Yours ever | Eddie

Dallas's *The Face of Love*, a tragedy set in a modern-day Troy, trans-ferred from Pitlochry Festival Theatre to the Vanburgh Theatre in London, and thence to BBC television. He then wrote screenplays in London and Italy, before converting to Islam in 1967, becoming a renowned Sufi teacher and spiritual leader. EM argues for Brechtian theatrical technique against the British tradition of 'the well-made play'. He saw Brecht's Berliner Ensemble perform *Mother Courage* in the Palace Theatre, London, in August 1956. In the following years, he wrote drama criticism for the *Glasgow Herald*, *Sunday Times* and *Encore* magazine.

Fred Woods, editor

4 May 1957

Mdear Mfred
	Assegai! (Zulu for wotcher)
	I'll bear in mind what you say about weekends and prospective in-laws. You seem, however, to have borne yourself with commendable sang-froid, savoir-faire, or whatever the right term is (not, perhaps, joie-de-vivre). I trust maternal bosom is opening gradually, as the light of understanding breaks (Charlie Chan).
	You're right about the sporran of course; I'll have to see about that. The stockings situation is a wee thing more obscure. I looked up photos I have in my scrapbook of HLI on parade (and therefore presumably correctly dressed), and although stocking height varied somewhat the general level was not only not lower but distinctly higher than mine – in fact much too high for aesthetic effectiveness, since the lower the better is almost a principle in this matter so long as sloppiness and doonhinginess are absent. Tell me, how in the army is the height of stocking regulated? I, being merely an ex-medic, could only tell you how high a Thomas splint goes (and that

would hardly be decent anyway). Thanks for returning the photograph.

Last week when your letter arrived I had just been twice to the opera (Sadlers Wells) and was feeling rather happy in a detached sort of way. I'm not really an opera fan at all, but some operas and some kinds of opera I do like, and I thought I would enjoy Puccini's *Trittico* and Chaikovsky's *Eugene Onegin*, went to find out, and came away highly pleased from both. To balance this emotional indulgence I also saw *Look Back in Anger* which was being played in Edinburgh. I was sorry I had read the text, as the blunted shocks began to fail to make contact – indeed they seemed often to be nearer literature than life (a kind of inverted 'fine writing', no more realistic or even 'contemporary' than the stage speech Osborne is out to replace). However, the play did undoubtedly make its impact as a piece of theatre. I didn't come away in a unified mood, and I'm not unified yet. Have you seen *The Entertainer* by any chance?

Yes, I suppose I ought to read *Room at the Top*. I have seen one instalment of it in a wellknown newspaper, and I have seen the author being interviewed on television; I certainly wasn't swep' off my feet by either, and from the instalment I received a strong impression tending in the direction of your opinion. No one seems to bother about the moral basis of a work of art any more. 'The atmosphere and accent of modern life have been brilliantly caught.' That's enough – no more is required. Of course, not having read the whole book I don't know how much moral condemnation of the hero is implied – any, much, or ambiguous?

Hope you have golden words from your Managing Director soon. If there's going to be a Channel Tunnel, and an H-bim (sorry!) – bomb on Christmas Island (fission and fusion beginning to affect Scottish typewriters already), surely there can be *Platform*. What is this new *Evergreen Review* (published by John Calder) like? The *Glasgow Herald* refers to its 'somewhat rarefied intellectual atmosphere', but knowing the GH I'd not assume that this meant it wasn't an unusually stimulating and meaty magazine!

We have painters in the house and a burst pipe in the garden, and I've just been trying to spring-clean my books by

Hoover plus various experimental attachments. Apart from that, all is quiet and well.

Best wishes to the Brontës: I like them. | And to yourself as ever | ≡Ⅱ

Wood edited *Platform* (Spring 1953–Autumn 1955), publishing some Scottish poets but not EM. The 'scrapbooks' were ledger-sized collections of pictures and texts, each page a collage of thematically linked material from the natural, scientific, political and artistic worlds. EM often wore a kilt in the 1950s, and his scrapbook pictures of kilted men and women reveal his fascination with the garment.

Alan Shearer, friend
(handwritten)

Eastbourne
31 July 1957

From the sea, quite an impressive chalk-fall. I hope you'll see it on a Kodachrome or two. Apart from Beachy Head, there is of course the front, and the bare backs. Sun has now burst forth after a few days vacillation. I saw some interesting plays in London, especially the *Summer of the Seventeenth Doll*. I'll be back on Saturday.
      Yours | Eddie

Summer of the Seventeenth Doll was a ground-breaking Australian play by Ray Lawler. First performed in Melbourne in November 1955, it went on a nationwide and then UK tour.

12 Albert Drive
21 August 1957

Dear Erica

I have been ploughing through hundreds of examination papers and have only now managed to get a moment to write to you about the *Whittrick*. I am enclosing copies of the dialogues as you requested, and I hope John Laurie will find the idea interesting. I expect the MacDiarmid one and the Brahan Seer one might appeal even if the others didn't. Thank you for thinking of this possibility.

Your *Company of Nine* sounds most interesting; one would expect perhaps John Buchan to be its president! Here are a few notes on the Whittrick, if you do decide to use any of the dialogues in your programmes – though please take them as hints and pointers rather than as a dogmatic account of the theme (the poet does well to leave that to others). The whittrick in general stands for truth or reality, but seen especially under its fleeting visionary relevationary aspect, which is in any case how it impresses itself on most people's minds (say when they fall in love or have some experience in wartime or just in everyday life have something happen to them which they cannot forget), and is also how it tends to appear in the arts, each work of art being like a 'flash' of something passing, whether a great sheet of lightning that lights up a whole tract of life (*Macbeth* or *The Canterbury Tales*) or a bright-eyed weasel running along a wall and darting across the country road in front of you in a striped flash of vitality and unexpectedness ('The Jolly Beggars' perhaps, or *The Whittrick*?). (I have been startled by a weasel myself in this kind of way, not far from Loch Lomond. And I should also mention that 'as quick as a whittrick' is or was a common expression in Scotland; my grandmother I remember was always using it, though I'm not sure she knew what a whittrick was!) – Each dialogue shows an aspect of this central idea; it probably comes clearest in the Japanese one and the Joyce one; Joyce's 'What is God? – A shout in the street' and his idea of epiphanies are very Zen-like, and it's in Zen that I

find the most exciting confirmation of my approach. II and
IV deal specially with the mysteriousness of experience: with
the role of imagination, and the doubt whether 'the real'
comes simply from outside. III and VI are a pair, dealing
with love and hatred respectively, and the impact of these on
experience of truth/reality. III shows the end of innocence,
and there the whittrick represents the (C E N S O R E D)!
Dialogue V mentions revolutionary 'mutant' truth under its
political aspect; the 1917 Russian spirit as opposed to Stalinist
monolithic gradualism, the quiet persistence of creative artists
like Shostakovich who during the oppressive days has 'kept his
whittrick' and now has been rewarded by the ability to write
the 10th Symphony and the Violin Concerto of recent years.
The obvious value of the relatively free society of the west is
that the daring, the unusual, the whittricklike, the tykish, is not
looked on quite so askance as under a more ordered régime.
The west, of course, has been too tykish; that's why I think it
is useful to keep facing it with Russia. The last (8th) dialogue
will deal with the future, and the question of possible efforts
to control and even create the whittrick, by man himself; the
science of cybernetics will rear its head. I hope to complete this
within the next month or so if I'm lucky, and will let you have
copies as soon as I can.

I appreciate what you say about Marilyn. It would mean,
of course, a full rewriting, and I don't know whether this
will be possible; I'll think about it. The sophistication, I felt,
would be bound to appear (a) relative to Ulanova and (b)
in the circumstances of two women talking freely together,
with no real necessity to produce naive Monroeisms! I'd say
it's true that Ulanova is naive in comparison; I'm not entirely
convinced that Marilyn is really naive. But as I say I shall
meditate on this point.

Good luck with my wee beastie. | All best wishes | ≡)||

After publishing *Beowulf* (1952), Marx now asked for a rationale for
The Whittrick, a sequence of eight dialogues between literary and
historical figures which EM worked on between 1955 and 1961. It
was published in 1973 by Duncan Glen* (*CP*: 79–116). A co-founder
of the Company of Nine, a group dedicated to poetry as oral enter-

tainment, Marx was trying to interest the Scots actor John Laurie in performing the Whittrick dialogues.

Alan Pryce-Jones, Editor, Times Literary Supplement

English Department
The University
Glasgow W2
16 November 1957

Sir,

Surely Robert Graves in your issue of November 15 has missed the point Dr Davie was making about translation? The greatest poetry does in fact survive translation better than we might expect, simply because it has so much to give – so much that cannot be destroyed, even by a relatively inept or a deliberately recast rendering. The Everyman's Library version of Mickiewicz's *Pan Tadeusz*, for example, by G.R. Noyes, is not even in poetic form, but in prose, and yet it must be clear to anyone reading it that he is in the presence of a major work of poetry. The power of a great poet stretches across language. This power resides not only, and not even mainly, in whatever is most inalienably personal to the poet or whatever is most peculiarly characteristic of the language he is using; his greatest power comes from what he shares (and has the insight and skill to express) with people of different skills, different manners, and different ages of history itself. Today we have such an inverted sense of values that we can hardly see this. We praise what is most 'interesting' – the stylistic or constructional distinguishing-marks – and profess to be bored by what is the most important thing – the moral and philosophical issues.

It is here that the translator's activity can become significant as well as useful. His duty is to present versions of foreign poetry which will convince his public of two things: (a) that the original was poetry, and (b) that the poetic message has been received, even though it was sent by an unfamiliar transmitting system. I suggest to Mr Graves that this has happened often enough now for us to be chary of denying the validity of translation. And not only that. The fact that Burns

and Byron have made a far greater impact on the world outside
Britain than Wordsworth and Coleridge does not mean
that it is the better poetry which is the less translatable and
exportable – though this may be what we like to think. It is
just possible – I extend the thought to Mr Graves on the end
of a stick – that Burns and Byron have qualities that readers
in England have been unduly loath to associate with poetry of
the highest kind? Translation, in this case, has perhaps proved
something that could not be shown in any other way.

≡‖| | (Edwin Morgan)

Pryce-Jones, editor of the *Times Literary Supplement*, declined to
publish EM's letter defending the critic and poet Donald Davie
against a complaint from Robert Graves that he had too brusquely
dismissed Robert Frost's dictum that 'poetry is what gets lost in
translation'.

Fred Woods, editor

12 Albert Drive
8 December 1957

Dear Fred
    What horrid bad luck. I do hope things are progressing not
too badly, and I'm relieved to hear you are able to look forward
to 'energetic exercises' and being on your feet again before
the hospital bed will have had a chance of really getting you
down. I expect, by the way, to be in London for a few days at
New Year, and might be able to look you up, if you're having
visitors. What are the days and times for visitors, do you
know? I am enclosing the current *Saltire* which probably you
won't have seen yet and which will provide an hour or so of
harmless reading. (What I should do is send you a copy of the
talk I gave at Erskine Hospital recently on 'Books for Hospital
Patients'!)
    The university term approaches its demise next week in a
flurry of examinations. Our literary society has had a meeting
discussing angry young men, at which both students and staff

contributed angry papers and answered angry questions. I
spoke about poetry (others were doing drama, sociology etc.),
and read bits (the few quotable bits – in mixed company)
of Allen Ginsberg whom I claimed as the only really angry
young poet. Ginsberg's 'America' went down well; I think,
in any case, it's good. Don't fancy it would appeal strongly
to Woodsberg, though – does it? I have the *Howl* volume
which has been made available over here, and of course the
second *Evergreen* had interesting stuff about the whole west
coast group. When I read Wilbur and Bishop and Merwin I
can't help feeling that Ginsberg is needed, if only to restore
balance. Well, the meeting was quite lively, and the anger
came chiefly from an angry young woman who denied that
she was an a.y.w. This was a crazy mixed-up ex-student of
ours with an outspoken and utterly tactless tongue and large
chips on both shoulders. She sat hunched up in an old pair of
slacks and dirty old belted raincoat and told us that since she
started teaching the working class in a school that perhaps
doesn't exemplify the best traditions of Scottish education she
had changed from radical to tory and was all for keeping the
working class in its place, it was the belt it needed, not Lindsay
Anderson's sympathy or John Osborne's hand outstretched
over the ashcan, and it was the establishment that should be
being angry with the lower orders etc.... So what do you think,
chum?

I was also present at a 65th birthday celebration given
to Hugh MacDiarmid in the Kenilworth Hotel. It was an
extraordinary affair, thick with the luminaries of Scottish
culture. Although organized, the evening held together
somewhat frayed at the edges. At one end of the room a hatch
to the bar buzzed and clinked continuously, while at the other
end distinguished figures such as the artist J.D. Fergusson were
endeavouring to make speeches or (like Joan Alexander and
William Noble) sing songs by Francis George Scott. Sydney
Goodsir Smith would utter very audible but half-pickled
hear-hears and bravos at not always appropriate moments,
and Michael Grieve (MacDiarmid's son) would try to restrain
him, and subside into his seat muttering 'Ignorant bastards!'
Telegrams were read from Abe Moffat and the Chinese
ambassador. Willie Gallacher made a rousing red speech

about the sputniks and the right course for Scotland. Cold chicken and cups of tea were served. There were knives but not many forks. We were all asked to sign a huge execrably-lettered presentation-memorial sheet of the occasion. The great man was presented with (the crowning touch) a blank cheque, to be filled in at some later date when everyone had paid up (everyone being loudly reminded at this point of their obligations – fortunately I had already given my mite) – and also a specially bound edition of his own works from the Castle Wynd Press in Edinburgh (with a further reminder that copies of his latest work were available for sale at the meeting). MacDiarmid made – or rather read – the usual long speech he goes in for on such occasions, ostensibly a speech of thanks in this case, but in fact an almost completely irrelevant harangue in which all feeling for the actual occasion disappeared, until he concluded by reading one of his most striking poems. – Now was this not a particularly Scottish evening? I think it was.

Well, I've got some work to do before the sands of Sunday run out – some essays to read for tomorrow; at least they are interesting essays, for I gave my Honours people William Golding to do this time (*Lord of the Flies*) and they have obviously enjoyed such a departure from academic necessity.

Do let me know if there's anything I can send you, or lend you. Some of my recent purchases include Dorothy Richardson, Cunninghame Graham, Kipling: any interest there??? Tell me how you get on with Hardy, who is one of my favourites (with all his faults, that is, I love him still).

And do get better every day. | Yours ever | ≡|||

The counter-cultural American quarterly *Evergreen Review* had just been founded, and would publish a wide range of avant-garde writing from Europe and America. Abe Moffat and Willie Gallacher were presidents respectively of the National Union of Mineworkers (Scottish area) and the Communist Party of Great Britain.

Maurice Temple Smith, *publisher*

Dear Mr Smith

Thank you very much for your letter (to my university address) and for your kind remarks about my *Twentieth Century* article. Curiously enough, I was about to send your publishing firm an entry for the *New Poets 1959* which Edwin Muir is editing.

I am not committed so far; I have only published in a small way with Peter Russell (a long poem), The Hand & Flower Press (a modern version of *Beowulf*), MacLellan of Glasgow (poems), and the Reading University Press who are to bring out a volume of my translations of the poems of Montale. I should certainly be very glad to discuss the possibility of future publications with you. I feel that I am one of those who tend to suffer from the range and scatter of their interests (howlers, Russia, translation, Scottish literature, abstract art, modern drama, etc!) and I should like very much to have something more substantial in book form.

Uncollected material I have at the moment (a good deal of it has been in various journals or has been broadcast) includes: (1) the group of original poems I was about to send in, (2) a large number of translated poems (French, Italian, Russian, Anglo-Saxon mainly) and a long essay on poetic translation which I read a university conference, and (3) essays on literary and allied (e.g. howlers) subjects, principally of contemporary interest but including Wordsworth, Dryden, and Dunbar, written or printed in the last few years. Perhaps you would let me know whether you might be interested in any of these? The translation of poetry is a thing I have made a special study of, and I think that in discussion of that and in my own examples of it I do have an original contribution to make. The various literary essays would be enough to make a book, but of course a unifying 'theme' might have to be searched for. My original poems are chiefly a group of dialogues between living and historical characters, on a common theme, the whole forming a poem of some length and I think a new type.

As for plans, I want to develop some of the East/West

literary relations and tensions which were suggested in my
Compleat Guide; I want to write a full-length study of how
far and in what way the poetry of our time has been reflecting
contemporary society and its aspirations – with the particular
aim of incorporating in such a study work by Russian poets
as well as English and American. This, of course, would be
a serious work; but the ironic, 'entertaining' mode of the
Compleat Guide I find very tempting and congenial, and
if given any encouragement I could apply the treatment to
other aspects of the cultural scene which are crying out for
comment! (To some extent I do this in my poetic dialogues:
one, for instance, is between Marilyn Monroe and Ulanova,
another between Cocteau and Dr Grey Walter.)

If there is anything in all this that interests you, I should be
pleased to hear from you and have your opinion. Or if you feel
that there is any sort of book that you would like me to write
(on my slightly odd qualifications), don't hesitate to mention it!

Yours sincerely | ≡||| | Edwin Morgan

Smith, a director of Eyre and Spottiswoode, had seen EM's 'Compleat
Writers' Guide USA–USSR' in *Twentieth Century* (163/973: 202–19).
Originally a talk to the Glasgow University Literary Society, this was
reprinted in *Essays* (1974). Smith wondered whether EM had any
projects in mind. (His poems, shortlisted for *New Poets 1959*, were
not in the final selection.)

Angél Flores, editor and academic

English Department
Glasgow University
5 October 1958

Dear Professor Flores

Here is the Heine which you asked for, and three poems of
Platen (one of them in Scots). I am also including a few others
(Mörike, Hölderlin, Eichendorff) which you may possibly
be able to use. The little poem by Bertolt Brecht I like, but I
expect it is rather out of your period.

If I have time to do other translations of the poets you mention, I shall let you have them. Is there a deadline date for contributions? I shall certainly look forward to seeing your anthology when it appears; I trust it will be available in this country? There are some very useful books in the Doubleday Anchor series.

I'm sorry I can't put you on to any other translations that I know of.

Sincerely yours | ≡)|| | Edwin Morgan

Flores taught modern languages in Queens College, New York, and edited anthologies of European poetry in translation for Doubleday. Hugh MacDiarmid* had recommended EM, particularly for his translations of Heine into Scots (*CT*: 402–405). Impressed by EM's translations of August Graf von Platen's sonnets, Flores kept asking for further work.

Alastair Dunnet, editor

12 Albert Drive
December 27, 1958

"Likely to corrupt"

Sir, – In support of Mr David Craig's remarks on pornography and literary merit, it is worth mentioning the recent case of the American poet Allen Ginsberg and his book *Howl*.

The publishers of *Howl* (which contains poems written in a violent and intentionally "shocking" style) were arrested in San Francisco in 1957 and put on trial for publishing obscene literature. Defence witnesses, who stated their belief that the poetry was seriously written and contained valid social criticism of certain trends in modern American society, included eminent writers and critics like Dr Mark Schorer, Kenneth Rexroth, and Dr Leo Lowenthal.

Essentially the defence was that although there were obscene things in the poems, there are even more obscene things in society itself, and the poetry was calling attention to these things in terms that no reasonable person would call recommendatory. The publishers won their case, and Judge Horn concluded by suggesting some rules which are, I think, well worth consideration. Here are a few of the more important clauses:

1. If the material has the slightest redeeming social importance, it is not obscene.

2. If it does not have the slightest redeeming social importance, it may be obscene.

4. The book or material must be judged as a whole by its effect on the average adult in the community.

8. Evidence of expert witnesses in the literary field is proper.

(A fuller report of the case will be found in *Evergreen Review*, Vol. 1, No. 4).

It seems to me that in the great majority of instances it is possible to distinguish between "well-written pornography" and outspoken literary works of serious intention. The exceptions, however, are sometimes important, and Mr Craig does not take into account the moral or educational problems posed by the writer who is both serious and yet "likely to corrupt."

The great test case here is M. Jean Genet, whose works were seized by the British customs in 1957 while on their way to Birmingham Central Library. Genet's writings – novels, plays, poems, autobiography – are undoubtedly obscene by any definition, and just as undoubtedly they have real literary power. They involve almost a complete reversal of the "respectable" world, and demand our (at least temporary) acceptance of values to be found only in the criminal underworld and in prison, in the characters of thieves, beggars, blackmailers, and murderers, most of them sexual inverts. These books certainly have what Judge Horn called "social importance." There might be a case for not putting them on general sale, but it seems quite wrong that they should not be available for consultation in Birmingham Central Library.

The criterion of "literary value" in cases like this does not help very much, and we have to consider not only the integrity of the author and the seriousness of his book but also the effects on society that his work would be likely to have. That is why the Victorian "tendency to corrupt" is an important (if notoriously vague) conception, and we cannot simply throw it overboard.

If we really worried about our society, perhaps we would be making less fuss over "Lolita," and be more concerned with writers like Nicholas Monsarrat and Ian Fleming, who make a deliberate and skilful appeal to the "average adult's" lowest emotions. Although it is necessary to try to clarify the pornography situation, it is even more important to remember that there are worse and more dangerous things in literature than pornography. – I am &c.

Edwin Morgan.

Dunnett was editor of *The Scotsman*, and interested in a wide range of cultural activities. EM's letter was in support of a piece by David Craig, 'Pornography and Art' (27 December 1958). He refers cautiously to two gay writers, Allen Ginsberg* and Jean Genet.

Angél Flores, editor and academic

English Department
Glasgow University
7 January 1959

Dear Angel Flores
Glad you got the Platen and correction all right. I don't feel terribly keen on Lenau and D-H, so if you don't mind I'll leave these for someone else to take care of!

I should be able, I hope, to help you with the other two anthologies, though I don't want to commit myself for too much at the moment, as I have a dozen articles to write for a new encyclopedia of modern literature Geoffrey Grigson is editing. I'd certainly like to contribute to the Spanish collection – and particularly at the modern end. I have some versions of Lorca, Cernuda, and Neruda (though here I trespass on your own territory!), whom I find very attractive. Let me know if I should send you such translations as I have done. If Petrarch comes into the other anthology, I can let you have some sonnets I have been doing for a Petrarch programme on the

BBC. I haven't tried the troubadors, and don't feel specially drawn to them, though they present interesting translating problems. If Jacopone da Todi is likely to be included, I'd like to have a shot at that. There's an intensity about him that offers a challenge.

I suppose you have the right address for Peter Russell (Fairwarp, Uckfield, Sussex)? Though actually I'm not surprised – he's a bad correspondent! Your most useful person, I think, might be D.S. Carne-Ross (Talks Department, BBC, Broadcasting house, London W 1), because he produces a great many programmes of poetry translation and is in touch with the best translators (he will know Iain Fletcher's address, by the way: he was at Reading University but I believe has moved).

May I ask you what the rate of payment is for the German poems?

Sincerely yours | ≡||

D-H is the German poet Annette von Droste-Hülshoff (1797–1848). Flores had mentioned two further anthologies: of Spanish poetry from Góngora to Lorca, and of medieval narrative poetry. EM contributed to both. Peter Russell, an English supporter and publisher of Ezra Pound, published *Nine*, as well as EM's long poem *The Cape of Good Hope* (1955).

Alan Shearer, friend
(handwritten)

Sunday   1959

I'm having an interesting time: heard Kenneth Rexroth playing tapes of American poetry & jazz sessions; and today at a huge Ban-the-Bomb demonstration in Trafalgar Square – Paul Robeson sang, and Christopher Logue had a poem read – art for the multitudes, eh?

Yours | Eddie

Some sixty thousand people took part in a CND march against atomic weapons, from Aldermaston to London, during the Easter weekend.

Angél Flores, editor and academic

12 Albert Drive
28 August 1959

Dear Angel Flores

I am enclosing a dozen poems by Rosalía, and perhaps you will let me know if this is sufficient. I have enjoyed doing them, and I hope they will appeal to you. All the poems are from her book *En las Orillas del Sar*. Most are without titles, so I have given the first lines. I have tried to keep her assonance and rhymes wherever I could.

I expect to fulfil what you have on your list: the Jorge Manrique 'Coplas', the Fray Luis 3 poems, the Rodrigo Caro 'Ruinas'; I'll let you know as soon as I can about the Garcilaso, though it will probably be based on your earlier suggestion (eclogue and sonnets); and I'd like to do one or two romances if I have time – again I'll let you know about this very soon.

If I do anything further, may it be from the modern period? I'm especially interested in Neruda. Could you take any more from him?

I'm back from a holiday up in the island of Skye and adjacent parts of the Highlands. A lot of mist and rain unfortunately! But impressive scenery for all that, and wonderfully beautiful in the sunny blinks. It was good to hear that your son Ralph has been having success in the by no means easy subject of analytical geometry; such an ability combined with literary interests is unusual and interesting.

I shall be writing to Peter Russell very shortly and I'll give him a jog for you.

All best wishes | Yours sincerely | EM

Flores had asked EM to translate a range of Spanish poets, including Fray Luis de León, Garcilaso de la Vega and the Galician poet Rosalía de Castro. Her work captivated EM most (see *Collected Translations*

[*CT*]: 383–89). Neruda's copyright fees proved too expensive. Flores's son was working towards a scholarship that would have allowed him to study at Glasgow University.

1960s

(aged 40–49)

> Slip out of darkness, it is time.
>
> ('The Second Life')

The 1960s fully established Morgan in his modernity. Many of his most celebrated poems emerged from that decade, while in a series of critical interventions he helped create the climate by which this work came to be judged. He did this through his advocacy of a poetry which was to be international as well as local, grounded in contemporary urban experience, open to technology and its innovations as well as to formal and linguistic experiment and collaboration with the other arts. His breakthrough collection *A Second Life*, published in 1968, speaks in its title as well as in its achievement of a new kind of Scottish Renaissance, one which was sceptical of the definition of national renewal proclaimed by Hugh MacDiarmid and the poets who followed him.

Personally, there were other new lives. His relationship with John Scott, an attractive opposite (Catholic, working-class), began in 1962 and was transformative in its influence on both life and work. He moved from the family home in suburban Burnside into a modern flat in Whittingehame Court, a short bus ride from the University. He was to live here for the next 40 years, the flat's spare minimalism offset by a growing collection of contemporary art, hi-fi equipment, poetry journals and first editions. In his professional life the expansion of the universities allowed for no let-up in his teaching and marking load. Yet he was more energised by the arrival of like-minded young colleagues than moved by the jeremiads of those who protested that more would mean worse. He travelled in Ireland, Germany, Austria and Hungary, and one of the remarkable things about the letters of this period is the expansive network of international connections which he established and sustained. Meanwhile radio recordings were made, a computer's Christmas cards composed, space-poems written. His projects to translate Hungarian and Russian poetry, his sympathetic interactions with Brazilian and other concrete poets, his championing of American poetry (then, inconceivably, a minority interest) and, slightly nearer home, of the Italian Salvatore Quasimodo and the Hungarians Attila József and Sandór Weöres in particular – all of this ran counter to a growing insularity and what Morgan saw as an increasing philistinism on the part of both Scottish and British literary establishments. His editorial role in the newly founded *Scottish International* offered a platform for resistance to these tendencies.

Correspondents offered stimulus in varying ways: the wit and dash of Dom Sylvester Houédard, the combative edge of Ian Hamilton Finlay, the dry canniness of Ian Crichton Smith, the brilliance of Veronica Forrest-Thomson or Haroldo de Campos. There is a mimic quality to his letters: while the voice is always his, it also bends to the frequencies of his correspondent. Meanwhile he was generous in offering guidance to local teachers and pupils, and encouragement to younger Scottish writers, while being necessarily astringent when required. Morgan was both a homemade and a cosmopolitan poet: his best-known poems of Glasgow life were composed in this decade. Ian Hamilton Finlay may have disapproved of their lack of experimental language, but these poems too were new and radical on a literary scene that hitherto had managed to discount the vitality of Scotland's busiest city. Glasgow was Morgan's scene and his subject – the place where letters and poems were written and posted out to the wide world, the place where replies were eagerly read.

In 1961 Morgan had published a review article entitled 'Who will Publish Scottish Poetry?'. This was a question to be resurrected with bitter urgency at the end of the decade, with prospects of publication for his own poetry receding at a time when his creative powers were at their peak.

Book and Pamphlet Publications

Soupoems. Worcester: Migrant Press, 1961.

Beowulf: A Verse Translation into Modern English. Los Angeles and London: University of California Press, 1962.

Collins Albatross Book of Longer Poems: English and American Poetry from the Fourteenth Century to the Present Day. Edited by Edwin Morgan. London and Glasgow: Collins, 1963.

Starryveldt. Frauenfeld, Switzerland: Eugen Gomringer Press, 1965.

Emergent Poems. Stuttgart: Editions Hansjörg Mayer, futura 20, 1967.

Poems by Alan Hayton, Stephen Mulrine, Colin Kirkwood, Robert Tait: Four Glasgow University Poets. Selected by Edwin Morgan. Preston: Akros Publications, 1967.

Gnomes. Preston: Akros Publications, 1968.

The Second Life. Edinburgh: Edinburgh University Press, 1968; paperback edn 1981.

Proverbfolder. Corsham, Wiltshire: Openings Press, 1969.

Royston Ellis, performance poet

English Department
The University
Glasgow W2
15 April 1960

Dear Royston Ellis

Many thanks indeed for your helpful and interesting
letter. It's nice to have people who cooperate like this, and I'm
fascinated by the account you give of your 'entertainments'
in Battersea Town Hall and elsewhere. I wish I could have
heard some of these sessions. You will have to try Glasgow
some time – Glasgow is mad keen on rock, and Cliff Richard
and his Shadows made a very successful visit here a week
ago at the Empire Theatre. If you got poetry across to a
Glasgow audience that would be really something! Though
strangely enough, the rock-loving teenage public has shown
an interest in Scottish ballads and folk-singers recently, and
will sometimes take poetry in that form without perhaps quite
realizing that it is poetry. We had a fine folk-singer, tinker
stock, Jeannie Robertson from Aberdeen, here a short time
ago, singing the old ballads to a spellbound teenage audience
in a Trongate café. It may have been partly the strangeness
that did it – and of course the Scottishness. We tend to react
best to either Scottish or American material – English is
less liked. When Tommy Steele was here people complained
they couldn't understand his cockney accent (he spoke &
joked between songs, and his talk didn't go down well at all).
Rocketry, however, we haven't yet tried.

In this talk I'm doing, I shall be saying quite a bit about
the American Beats like Allen Ginsberg and Jack Kerouac.
I wonder if you know the record Kerouac has made (called
Poetry for the Beat Generation) where he reads his poems
over a muted piano accompaniment by Steve Allen? It's very
effective, and I'd like to see more of that sort of thing done
over here. Christopher Logue's work with the Tony Kinsey
quartet doesn't seem to me to be quite right; the kind of poetry
Logue writes requires to be heard and understood and in their
interweaving of words and music neither the one nor the other

gets a chance – poet and quartet work together but the poetry subserves the jazz. And of course as you say jazz is by now a specialized appeal; Logue is not quite your generation!

I'll look forward to your next book – and I would be very glad to have any further comments or ideas you like to send me – or news of any changes and developments in your entertainment techniques. It is all of great interest.

With best wishes | Yours sincerely | ≣||| | Edwin Morgan

A performance poet, Ellis had described his own brand of 'rocketry' for teenage audiences, namely poetry accompanied by rock music. His Battersea event featured the Shadows.

Michael Shayer, editor and poet

6 June 1960

Dear Michael Shayer

I'm late in answering your letter because I've been in Germany – lecturing at Freiburg University on Robert Burns and on modern Scottish literature. It was an interesting experience in many ways, and I saw for the first time some of the attractions of the Black Forest.

First, may I just briefly say about the three poems you included that I liked them all, and it's not often that that happens when styles are so different (and when so many new poems make no impact at all). The Ginsberg one seemed more happily frank and easy than he sometimes is; though I am looking forward to seeing the whole of his *Kaddish* when it becomes available here. Parts of *Kaddish* are very fine, other bits seem to have run away with the author, in a sort of Jewish toomuchness. (Though I must say that Kerouac is beginning to appear more likable, more human, more moving to me than Ginsberg – at any rate I haven't enjoyed any Beat productions quite so much as the record Kerouac made reading his own poems over a piano accompaniment by Steve Allen: a most warm vibrant living document; I played an extract in a BBC talk I gave on modern poetry before I went to Germany.) –

Who is Matthew Mead, what does he do, do you know?

I am enclosing an announcement which may interest you, about a new Scottish magazine that appears this week. I think it shares some of *Migrant*'s preoccupations. Gael Turnbull has also been sent one of the forms. The journal has arisen out of the ruins of *Jabberwock*, the Edinburgh University magazine which often had very lively contributions; it now wants to cast a wide net and deprovincialize the slumbering Caledonian. We'll see, in due course, whether this can be combined with 'Scottish' writing. I think it's a useful venture at this stage. My own contribution to the first number is a short article on Genet – who is, I think one has to admit, a writer of importance, though little known yet in these puritanical islands.

Yes, it is really for Peter Russell that I am working on the Mayakovsky translations. I hope there will be a book of them some day. He hasn't seen them yet as I don't want to send them in dribs and dribs. The Pasternak images you ask about are closer in my version than in the <u>Zhivago</u> translators' version; indeed, they are surprisingly loose. Of course his earlier verse had more violent imagery – there has been a progressive simplifying of his poetry from about 1940. But it still kept a freshness and sharpness and the old Pasternakian pungence.

I've always been interested in the relation between a writer and his work, and I am sure there is a lot of truth in your suggestion that organic creative activity and wholeness of character ('acceptance of oneself as a sexual being') are connected. You are right about Eliot, of course; there is something there that has never been brought out into the open, and it festers on and on, giving his work its ingrown, withdrawing, joyless look, and distorting his entire outlook on human society and the human family and love, though this, like everything else, can be movingly & beautifully expressed. But I'm not happy about erecting this into a general statement, if only for the reason that going over the lives of great writers one would find quite as many maladjusted as well-adjusted, and probably more. A writer can overcome, in the actual production of his works, deficiencies and frustrations which are real enough – and perhaps criticizable enough – in his private or sexual life. He might 'have difficulties with women' and yet write an epithalamium. All depends on his attitude and spirit, his deepest desires and hopes. Even a greatly frustrated creative artist like the homosexual Chaikovsky or Michelangelo can make his artistic appeal and impact on a wide and universal and even popular level, although the tensions which lie at the back of the work are a matter for psychologists. Lawrence himself, whom you bring in as one of the healthy 'accepters', was far from normal, either in his half-acknowledged bisexual instincts or in his tortured overdemanding relationships with the friends he attached himself to. – Speaking as a human being, or as a sociologist, one would certainly like to think that there is a one-way correspondence between psychological and creative wholeness; and perhaps we are moving towards this; the Russians think so; but it's a slow process! And what about China – where the 'wholeness' of a man's character is being judged not by his relations to wife family relatives or friends but by his attitude to his <u>work</u>? Is work to be the future link between character and creativity? If this is so, then Williams is lucky being a doctor (though I have known some remarkably inhuman doctors in my time – even this profession gives no guarantee)! And science: science must somehow someday be brought into literature to a far greater extent than it has been; one of the real failures of 20th-century writing is simply that it has been <u>neither</u> a close reflection of an 'age of science and technology' nor a humanistic counter-balance to our supposed (though I don't agree) scientific hypertrophy. A 'beat' attitude to rockets and sputniks is easily understood and sympathized with, but it isn't my own attitude; in fact one of my strongest feelings is that of being on the threshold of a great epoch of history, and I only hope I live long enough to see some of the developments that are coming. I am very susceptible to the 'epic' feeling, to the idea of exploration, adventure, endurance, discovery, and I think that this feeling is very important to man as a species. It has languished since the days of the great terrestrial voyages, and it will soon be making a comeback when the nosecones turn skywards. In the epic early space voyages there will be that combination of science, technology, and human effort and frailty which could produce a new heroic art, sane, communicative, and majestic.

Looking at the last page of your letter I realize I have

unwittingly been commenting on your question about 'the next stage' – though I'm pretty certain it wasn't interplanetary poetry you had in mind! On the more mundane level, I think poets will and should be offering more direct and spontaneous testimony on our actual human situation (Neruda, Quasimodo, the American anti-academics, some of the younger Russians like Yevtushenko), instead of – as in the whole 'modern experiment' – trusting that their human concern will make itself felt <u>through</u> an interesting structure of images and words and allusions. I'll see if I have any copies of things to include with this letter – things that might have some bearing on these remarks. (Unfortunately I can't send you the Hart Crane poem at the moment; I have his Collected Poems but I'm working on them. I see by the way that there's now a paperback available, ed. Waldo Frank, pub. by Doubleday/Anchor, available here at 8/-.)

I'll be glad to have your comments any time. The questions you raise are interesting and important ones, and perhaps we can push these difficult contemporary issues out a little bit further into the light so that at least they can be clearly seen; though in the end action is needed too. (I like Cocteau's favourite image of pushing things out of their darkness into a sudden light; but once they are in the light, what then?)

Yours | ≣||

Shayer was the English editor of *Migrant*, produced in late 1950s California by the Scottish doctor and poet Gael Turnbull*, and succeeded by Migrant Press which published *Sovpoems* (1961). A secondary school science teacher, he later became a professor of applied psychology. Matthew Mead was another Migrant poet. The new magazine was the short-lived *Sidewalk* (1960), with an internationalist emphasis. EM's 'Jean Genet: A Life and its Legend' was in issue 1.

Nina Matveyeva, editor

4 September 1960

Dear Miss Matveyeva

I am glad you found the Mayakovsky translations interesting, and I quite understand that you might not want to inflict so much Scots on your readers – though in Britain at least, English readers are fairly used to seeing Scots in print, as most of the modern Scottish poets have in fact employed some degree of Scots vocabulary, and at the moment in Edinburgh (where I am writing this) the poet Sydney Goodsir Smith's new verse play *The Wallace*, which is in Scots, is drawing big audiences. I think that you (and Archie Johnstone, who has been writing to me) perhaps overestimate the difficulties – because although Scots is much less fully spoken than it used to be, it is still widely <u>understood</u>, and plays and music hall revues in Scots are popular in Scotland. The more Scots it is, of course, the less a purely English audience will get out of it; and in translating Mayakovsky I had to use a wide and even inventive vocabulary. I have no objection to your printing extracts, but I hope you won't be <u>too</u> apologetic about them, because I do think that there are certain of Mayakovsky's qualities which come across better in Scots than in English, and that was why I did the translations. I felt that Herbert Marshall's English versions missed something of the poet's pungency.

I don't mind there being no payment in English currency. If there is any payment due in Russian currency, would it be possible for me to buy, say, a Russian book or two with it?

Thanks you for sending copies to the Publishing House of Foreign Literature.

With best wishes | Yours sincerely | ≡‖

Matveyeva edited the English edition of *Soviet Literature*. It is unclear whether any of EM's Scots translations ever appeared there, but in this same year his Mayakovsky translations were published in *Migrant, College Courant, Sidewalk* and *Saltire Review*.

Ronald Bottrall, poet

12 September 1960

Dear Mr Bottrall

Thank you very much for your letter. It was good of you to take the trouble to write. I am glad to know that the I-have-been-here-before feeling I instantly experienced on reading your poem has some basis in fact! As you say, there are considerable differences as well as similarities in the two poems, and had I not been (as a translator of 'La Casa dei Doganieri') deeply and recently 'plunged' in the Montale, I might not have reacted so strongly. I had no idea, when I wrote the letter, that you had long been intimate with Montale. The fact that the similarities are purely unconscious argues, I suppose, a 'sympathy of minds' between you and Montale, in addition to the actual familiarity you must have with his poetry, and the points of contact there must have been in the initiating experiences behind both poems. What I find most particularly interesting is that it seems to be the most striking and powerful lines and images of the Montale (e.g. the breathing in the darkness) which have come forward again: as a kind of confirmation, through you, of their poetic value (or should I say, a confirmation of my own estimate of their poetic value).

I entirely agree that Montale is a challengingly difficult poet to translate. I got interested in his work a few years ago when I did one or two versions for the BBC, and eventually I translated about 40 poems. Since it might interest you to see what I have made of them, I am sending you under separate cover a copy of the volume I had published last year.

Again many thanks for your information on this curious and fascinating little episode.

Yours sincerely | ≡\| | (Edwin Morgan)

Bottrall had published a poem in *Encounter* (July 1960) in which EM noticed echoes of Eugenio Montale's 'La Casa dei Doganieri' ('The Custom-Officers' House'). It emerged that, as the then Director of the British Institute in Florence, Bottrall had known Montale since

1938. The Italian poet had asked him to translate his work, but its subtlety defeated him. Echoes of those now forgotten attempts had remained, he thought, in his own poem.

Michael Shayer, editor and poet

9 December 1960

Dear Michael Shayer

Thanks for sending the Finlay; my copy had arrived just the day before from America. It's quite attractive with the woodcuts. I'll be including it in a batch of poetry I have to review for the *Glasgow Herald* later this month. There will only be space for a sentence or two, but at least it will get a mention (and a favourable one). Do you want me to describe it as the first of a series of Migrant Pamphlets, or is Matthew Mead's the first? (I can possibly squeeze in both.) Is Mead's price also 2/-?

I'm perfectly agreeable to your Soviet-block translations idea, and you can put me down on your list, though I'm not sure what the pamphlet should be called. About how many pages, or poems, do you have in mind? And how long the introduction? I thought these, or some of them depending on space available, might be included: Pasternak – 7 or 8 poems, none very long (these are ready); Mayakovsky – perhaps only one long poem 'With the Whole Voice' (in Scots – I have this ready) since as you remember I promised Peter Russell I'd do him a 'Mayakovsky into Scots' volume; Tikhonov – one or two poems (ready); Tsvetayeva and/or Martynov (I've nothing of hers yet); a young poet Yevtushenko – perhaps one poem, to show that there's still something vigorous going on in Russia (still to do this); Neruda – 3 or 4 poems, including an extract from his epic *Canto General* (I'm working on this); and lastly Brecht – two or three poems (I have one done at the moment). That would make about 20 poems, one or two of them over 100 lines. Is this too much? Anyway, you can let me have your comments and suggestions; it's only a sketch of what I think is a grouping of the most important people (and things). I think

I (well, I hope I) feel what you're after; and I think there is a lifeline to be picked up.

Yours | ∃╢

Shayer had sent his own copy of *The Dancers Inherit the Party* by Ian Hamilton Finlay*, published by Migrant Press in the US. Planned volumes included work by Roy Fisher*, Anselm Hollo* and William Carlos Williams. Shayer had suggested a pamphlet of translations from Russia after Blok, also to include Communist poets such as Pablo Neruda.

T.S. Eliot, poet and publisher

12 December 1960

Dear Mr Eliot

I have received a letter from the Italian poet Salvatore Quasimodo, in which he says that Faber and Faber will probably be publishing a collection of his poems. He wishes to propose my name as translator of these poems, and has asked me to send you such versions as I have already done, mentioning his name and the name of Roberto Sanesi as recommendation. I am accordingly enclosing with this letter 14 poems which I have translated, from different periods of his work, and I shall be glad to cooperate in the proposed volume if these versions find favour. Some have appeared, or are due to appear, in magazines (*Critical Quarterly* and *Sidewalk*), and some have been accepted by Louis MacNeice for the BBC but not yet broadcast.

I might perhaps mention that I had a volume of translations from Eugenio Montale published last year by the University of Reading School of Art.

Yours sincerely | ∃╢ | (Edwin Morgan)

EM admired the Nobel prize-winner, Salvatore Quasimodo (1901–68), whom he had met briefly in Glasgow in March 1960, presenting him with some translations (*CT*: 212–21). Quasimodo now wanted him to be his translator, understanding that Faber & Faber intended to publish a selection. Eliot replied that Quasimodo had been 'over-optimistic', and that successful publication depended on the translator already being a well-known poet.

William Pratt, academic

12 Albert Drive
18 December 1960

Dear Bill

Our term has just finished, and at this highly artificial moment I begin to reply to your well-packed letter of nearly a year ago. And let me first thank you for your delightful photograph of Cullen and Stuart – what a dark-eyed little beauty is Cullen! I trust both are flourishing. I expect you will have had a busy time settling into your new house – unless your estimate of its completion was too optimistic.

There haven't been great changes here, though the university continues to expand. The new Modern Languages building contains an excellent little theatre, in which we have already seen Anouilh in French, Hofmannsthal in German, and Beckett (*Krapp's Last Tape!*) in English. The Modern Languages block was too small for its purposes even at the moment when it was opened; but at least the theatre will be a useful permanent addition to our not too startling amenities – especially as it is used too by our Film Society. Next month will see the official opening of what I believe is quite a luxurious gymnasium (there seems something wrong with that adjective, but – well, you know what I mean!). The church at the bottom of University Avenue has been taken over for transformation into a series of examination halls. One might say there is something very Scottish in being examined in a church? – However, it can be scented in the air that there are probably changes other than the merely physical awaiting us. A great amount of anguished discussion proceeds about the state of university education – especially entrance standards, failure rate during courses, large classes, further expansion – in Scotland, and while some of the problems may be solved by the proposed establishing of a fifth university (Inverness, Falkirk, Stirling, Ayr, and Dumfries have been suggested) others may involve us all in some rethinking about our teaching methods and our examinations. If a new university is established in Scotland, it will probably arrange its curricula very differently, as has already been done at Keele in North Staffordshire and as will be done at Brighton, in an endeavour to break down to some extent what many people feel is an unhealthy arts/science dichotomy. – In Glasgow, we also have the problem of the Tech, which in the more dignified singing-robes of its proper designation as the Royal College of Science and Technology is making a determined bid for full university status (over, of course, several eminent dead bodies in the Glasgow University senate), and would like to model itself on the M.I.T. How with such rage can Englit hold a plea?

No changes this year in our own department. Jim Arnott had an interesting year teaching drama at Wooster College Ohio, and I enjoyed a breath of fresh air in May when I was invited to give lectures on Burns and modern Scottish literature at Freiburg University. I hadn't been before to the Black Forest, and although I had little time to myself I managed to see quite a bit of that very beautiful and romantic countryside – largely because my visit happily coincided with the English Department's annual picnic, when they charter a bus and (singing 'Clementine' in very good English voice) drive to some attractive remoteness, on this occasion a dark tarn in the north of the Black Forest called the Mummel See. I also got across the French border to Colmar, and saw Grünewald's Isenheim altarpiece: these paintings are among the most impressive works of art I have ever seen. In Freiburg, as I suppose in most parts of Western Germany, there's a strong American influence. Several of the students spoke with an American accent and had had a year in the States; I asked one boy – opening a conversation in the bus – what English books he had read: 'Oh, *Moby Dick* and A *Farewell to Arms*... and Shakespeare.' Although Freiburg is quite a small town, it is fairly well off culturally in theatre, film, music. When I was there Ionesco's *Rhinoceros* and Tennessee Williams's *Suddenly Last Summer* were drawing the crowds. Indeed, looking at the cultural attractions on the month's programme I couldn't help smiling, it was all so deadlily expected, so determinedly avantgarde, so slavishly vowed to western fashion; nothing native, and not even much from the German classics. I felt strongly by the time I left, both from what I saw and from what people told me, that behind the prosperous economic façade there is a terrible emptiness somewhere, a spiritual numbness that no doubt shows itself in the absence of new literature. For all that, it was a very interesting experience, and I was sorry I had to hasten back for our Honours examination papers. I brought with me a fine bottle of Rhine wine and some cherry brandy – no spiritual numbness there!

To return to our 'dialogue' (is that the term these days?) on drama and poetry. At this year's Edinburgh Festival I saw two plays which were in different ways 'poetic' but which didn't cause me any violent reversal of views. One was *Vasco* by Georges Schehade, a fantasy with realistic touches, about an unwarlike barber who is unwittingly made the bearer of a dangerous military message; the other was Sydney Goodsir Smith's *The Wallace*, fairly straightforward historical chronicle, written in rather rhetorical verse. Neither play, I thought, just quite made it, though both had points of interest. The one had a genuine poetry, but only of atmosphere, and that more wistful than powerful, and the other had a sort of heavy false poetry in the language, which was disappointing considering what SGS has done elsewhere. – I also saw amateur productions of *Summer & Smoke* and *Orpheus Descending*, both of which I enjoyed. 'Williams, with all thy faults I love thee still!' More recently I have been reading Jack Gelber's *The Connection* – though it's really impossible to judge it without seeing it. I felt that it would be open to most of the objections you have brought against modern drama, and yet that the sort of gesture it makes towards society was worth making. It belongs nearly, though not quite, to the anti-art brigade, but perhaps one can distinguish between good anti-art and bad anti-art? Bad anti-art is Dubuffet and Ionesco and Robbe-Grillet; good anti-art is Kerouac and Corso and Ginsberg, and perhaps WCWilliams (whom I now begin to find a way into, well, part of the way, through some of the Beat writers who point in his direction)? If that sounds like nonsense, let me know. The distinction I see is between an anti-human(ist) anti-art and a human(ist) anti-art; in the latter case, the idea is that the time has come for one of those periodic mighty shifts of the hincty body of art OUT, out for a dipping in the mainstream, out for an admittedly dangerous reacquaintance with formless unclean and shocking life. I'm reminded of John Cassavetes' film *Shadows*. When I saw this I thought of your remarks on modern drama being 'so realistic that reality disappeared' – and here we are in Cassavetes and Gelber moving even farther in that direction. I wonder what you thought of that film if you happened to see it? I found it, for all that it was at times puzzling or abrupt, really very moving, and the material had been given just sufficient shaping to allow it to be called and judged as art. – Actually I believe our differences go quite deep here. It isn't only as regards modern drama that I find a salient 'reality factor' important and acceptable, but (as I now see from your last letter) even as regards the drama of the past. You say 'The play's the thing', and you say that you get so caught up in the action and its illusion that you don't have to 'make comparisons with real life at all.' Yet when I see or read Shakespeare this is exactly what I do, and what I feel I must do. I don't share your dislike of being 'made uncomfortable' by my playwright, and indeed I think the 'questioning' probe of the playwright, his ability not to wrap the audience up in a warm but unlucid emotional glow, is one of his greatest weapons. To my mind, a performance of *Hamlet* should bring out not only what causes the man to do this or that, or what will the man do next and isn't it exciting, but also and in fact mainly – what ought such a man to do? The play should give us feelings and thoughts not only about Hamlet and Claudius and Gertrude but also about murder and revenge and honour and love and remarriage. Without going so far as to re-ask how many children had Lady Macbeth, I can't help feeling that modern criticism has done Shakespeare a disservice in isolating his plays from life. I fully grant you that in the form of words which one uses the dramatist or the poet 'creates his world', but is the real interest and test of what he does not precisely in the relation between this golden world and the poor brazen one that we know?

How is your Russian coming along? Chitaete li vy *Doktor Zhivago*? I have just been reviewing Pasternak's last volume of poems, post-Zhivago, published here by Collins, with translations by Michael Harari. My own translating has centred recently on the Italian poet Quasimodo who beat Montale to the Nobel Prize. Faber and Faber are probably going to publish a selection of his poems in this country, and Quasimodo wants me to be the translator. I have sent a sample of 14 poems to T.S. Eliot but have not yet heard from him; of course he may have someone else in mind. But it is a job I would like to do. – I suppose by this time you will have heard definitely about your Imagist anthology? It would be a useful book; there is certainly a place for an Imagist paperback, as I know when I lecture on modern poetry. – I am ashamed not to have written earlier about your proposed radio programmes of Scottish poets. If it can be arranged, I think it's an excellent idea – though by now of course the opportunity may have passed or your plans changed. There are practical difficulties – I doubt if many Scottish poets have tape-recorders or even have easy access to one. It might be most easily done through someone like Maurice Lindsay, a poet who does a lot of work with the BBC, both sound and television; or George Bruce, another poet who is a BBC producer. I don't think 'sending tapes to poets' would do much good, in our still largely untechnical society! But I'm sure most poets would cooperate – I certainly would – if some scheme could be arranged.

Have you ever read 'Monk' Lewis? That is what I am reading this Christmas. That, and eecummingsselectedpoems-1923to1958. And I have bought a record of Pasternak reading some of his poems in Russian and speaking in Russian, German, and French: an interesting historical document.

But it is high time that this letter started off on its belated journey, so I'll close it with every best seasonal wish for 1961 to yourself and your family, and who knows, it may even reach you in time for Christmas!

Yours as ever | ≡|||

PS: I am fated never to meet your emissaries! Spiro Peterson wrote to me just as I was leaving for Freiburg.

Pratt taught English Literature in Miami University, Ohio, specialising in modern poetry. He had been a 'Rotary Foundation Fellow' at Glasgow University in 1951–52 when EM was a young lecturer, and shared his interests in modernism. They kept in touch for many years.

David Murison, lexicographer

21 December 1960

Dear Mr Murison
  Here are one or two comments on the questionnaire:

Lochgelly: This is current in Glasgow area, though the usage is generally semi-humorous, e.g. 'I gave him a bit of the old Lochgelly.'
losh: Would you not include this exclamation (from lord!)? It's still fairly common hereabouts, though oldfashioned: it was a favourite word of my grandmother's.
low(e): Quite frequently heard in Glasgow area, especially in phrases like 'a nice wee lowe', the idea being a small cosy fire, a warm glow.
lythe (the fish: pollack): There may be a quotation for this in W.S. Graham's *The White Threshold*, Faber, London, 1949, p.56, where the poet speaks of 'the lythed water' presumably meaning the water rich in lythe or thick with lythe.
magowk: I know this word in the 'huntmagowk' phrase (which you don't include under gowk). Children at school who had been 'had' on April 1st had 'Huntmagowk!' shouted at them.
maik: Still used in Glasgow area (halfpenny) (or rather, in a more indefinite sense, a small coin of little value – 'It's no wurth a maik').
mankie: Common in Glasgow area, though certainly 'vulgar' usage! Meaning: dirty, or unpleasantly dirty. A lad asks his china if he can loan him a comb – 'I don't want an old mankie wan but!' (Shouldn't this characteristic Glasgow use of 'but' also be recorded in the SND?)
man man: Gsw.1960.
mannie: Common, especially in phase 'my wee mannie', 'how's ma wee mannie today (or, the-day)?' (grownup speaking to

child).

map-map: Gsw.1960. (both meanings)

mask (infuse tea): Gsw.1960.

matlo: Sorry to be facetious, but this to me means only one
thing: 'sailor'! Services slang?

mauk: (meaning maggot, & pronounced like Eng. 'mock')
Gsw.1960. I know it as a housewife's term: 'I left the tin too
long, & when I opened it it was crawling with mauks.'

meh? – I don't know how to spell this, but it's the sound a
sheep makes [mɛ] – (not 'maa' or 'mae') – and a young child
will have a sheep pointed out to it as a 'sheepie-meh'.

ménage: Gsw.1960, but pronounced 'minodge'. For quotation
see short story by J.F. Hendry, 'Minodge' in *Sidewalk*, Vol.1,
No.2, 1960, p.9 (the word defined on p.15).

melt: Will you not include the vulgar but very characteristic
Gsw. usage, meaning 'bash, belt, beat up, annihilate' – the
famous phrase 'Ah'll melt ye!'

midden (dirty, slovenly woman) (or sometimes man):
Gsw.1960. I'm surprised your date for this is so far back; the
word is commonly used in this area. 'She's a right midden, that
yin!' Or, in kindly exasperation, wife to husband: 'Ach, look at
yir pipe all owre the clean cloth; ye're an auld midden, so ye
are.'

– Also, you don't seem to have the ordinary meaning of
midden: the rubbish-bin or place for rubbish or ashes at the
back of a tenement close.

minch: I've heard this, though not often; pronounced 'minsh'.
It's often used half-humorously, especially by Glasgow
comedians – references to 'minsh an totties' will get a quick
laugh. It's probably still fairly common, though maybe
obsolescent – except that the s/sh situation in Scotland seems
permanently unstable.

miss onesel: Gsw.1960. This, like a great many of your
Abd.1960s, seems to me to be 'general Scots' and widely
current. Why so much emphasis on Aberdeen? 'Ye fairly
missed yersel no coming to Glasgow!'

mither's bairn: Gsw.1960

mixter-maxter: Gsw.1960. 'It was an awful mixter-maxter.'

mony's the: Gsw.1960. But more usually 'many's the' – 'Many's
the time I've....'

<u>the morn's morn</u>: You don't have this form, but I have often
heard it used for 'tomorrow morning' or even just 'tomorrow'.
'I'll see ye the morn's morn.'
<u>mowdie-man</u>: Quotation in Albert D. Mackie's poem
'Molecatcher', line 2 or line 12 (in Maurice Lindsay's *Modern
Scottish Poetry*, Faber, London, 1946, p.42).
<u>lith</u> (segment of orange): wm.Sc.1960.

Best wishes of the season | Yours sincerely | ≡||| |
(Edwin Morgan)

As editor from 1946 of the *Scottish National Dictionary* (1931–76),
Murison was keen to expand the range of oral sources of Scots
vocabulary and had sent out a general request for information. EM
was equally keen that Glaswegian Scots should not be neglected by
lexicographers, because supposedly too 'debased' from traditional,
mainly rural, Scots.

Salvatore Quasimodo, poet and academic

English Department
Glasgow University
22 December 1960

Dear Quasimodo
    I am sorry to say that T.S. Eliot has returned the
translations of your poems which I sent to him. He makes
no comment on them as translations, but simply says: 'I told
Mr Roberto Sanesi... that we could not make a success of
translations of poetry here unless the translations were made
by a poet already very well known and with a considerable sale
of his works in England...'
    This is perhaps a question of the economics of publishing,
but I think it is very unfair, and it shows no sense of
responsibility towards the poet who is being translated, as
there is no guarantee that the 'very well known' poet (when he
is found) will produce better versions than these ones which
Mr Eliot has rejected – apparently without bothering to
examine them at all, and without taking into account the fact

that you yourself thought them good enough to propose my name.

I thought I had better let you know right away, in case you or Roberto Sanesi should want to write to Mr Eliot and carry the matter further. I do not see what else I can do, unless you want to try some other publisher. I am sorry about this disappointment, because I feel that my translations are worth considering – even by Faber!

With all best wishes | Yours sincerely | ≡||

Roberto Sanesi had written to Faber & Faber on Quasimodo's behalf. Quasimodo replied that if England was proving deaf to foreign voices then perhaps Scotland, 'una "nazione" viva poeticamente', might take up the project.

Angél Flores, editor and academic
(airmail)

GU
8 January 1961

Dear Angel Flores

Yes, I can see that your Middle English pieces are a real problem. Of the three possible solutions, I think that close rephrasing of the original text is least satisfactory, as it ends up neither fish nor flesh, neither antique nor truly modern. Best is either the original text with a footnote glossary, or a complete 'translation' into modern English. For Chaucer, I'm inclined to believe that he is not all that difficult if there is a good running glossary on the same page as the text. Do you know Nevill Coghill's modern translation of Chaucer in the Penguin series? It's not terribly well done, but I suppose it is one solution. I'm including Franklin's and Nun's Priest's Tales in my own anthology of long poems, and am making up a running glossary which will be at the foot of each page (with the original text); so if you do decide to use this method, I could pass on the glossary to you for these two poems. As I have so many other things on hand, I don't think I could undertake to gloss the other Chaucer poems. – Would you not follow the same method with *The Bruce*? Giving the original text (with perhaps a few simplified spellings) plus glossnotes? If you do decide to do this, I could send you a glossary for the passages you suggest (your prose selection: Book XIII, lines 152–381, 631–50). – If you want any more *Beowulf*, there is my own verse translation into modern English (Hand and Flower Press, 1952) (the University of California Press are negotiating to bring it out in a paperback at the moment). – Dent's Everyman's Library have a good new version of the *Mabinogion* by T. and G. Jones, which probably you might be able to use.

In some haste – our term restarts tomorrow!

Yours sincerely | Edwin Morgan

Flores's publishers were unwilling to have a selection from John Barbour's medieval epic *The Brus* in the original Scots, and he enquired whether EM could either 'rephrase' it or supply marginal glosses. Similar problems applied to the Chaucer selections. The book appeared as *Medieval Age* (New York: Dell Publishing Co., 1963), and EM's final contributions were his Anglo-Saxon 'The Seafarer' and 'The Wanderer' (*CT*: 246–51), 'Romance of Count Arnaldos' (*CT*: 455), and Canto V of Dante's *Inferno*.

Salvatore Quasimodo, poet and academic

English Department
Glasgow University
20 May 1961

Dear Quasimodo

I know that it must be very disappointing for you that Eliot and Faber have not gone any further into the possibility of publishing your poems. I am not so sure that I can flatter myself that in Scotland we are less philistine or provincial than the English, though I believe we have more interest in Continental writers. At any rate, I can offer you a hope – it is no more than that at the moment – of a collection of my versions being published by a new Edinburgh publisher,

Kulgin Duval, who is anxious to bring out your poems if this
can be arranged and you are agreeable. A new publisher always
includes an element of risk, and you might prefer to wait until
Faber or another well-established house takes the plunge. On
the other hand, the Scottish proverb says, He that will nocht
when he may sall have nocht when he wad! Duval will do a
good job of layout and printing (he has done some splendid
catalogues), and he has an extensive mailing list, here and
in America. His first books are to include a new selection of
Hugh MacDiarmid's poetry (with an introduction by me),
and a tribute volume of essays next year on the occasion of
MacDiarmid's 70th birthday. He wants to publish mainly
Scottish and Continental, rather than English, authors. If you
feel interested in this tentative proposal, we can discuss the
matter further. At the moment I am thinking of about 30–40
poems with facing Italian text and a short introduction; and it
would be an added interest if I could include a new translation
of your Nobel address, which I consider to be an important
and remarkable document.

With all kindest regards | Yours sincerely | ☰||

EM believed he had persuaded Duval*, an Edinburgh-based book-
seller, occasional publisher, and life-long friend, to bring out a selec-
tion of Quasimodo translations. Hence his annoyance in the letter of
21 October 1961 below, when the work failed to proceed.

Angél Flores, editor and academic

31 May 1961

Dear Angel Flores
It was good to hear from you again – and quite a surprise
to hear from Italy. I hope you are having an agreeable trip.
We are in the midst of our end-of-term examinations here
at the moment, and then my next chore will be a summer
school (in a mansion house near Glasgow) in July. I am at
present editing an anthology of longer poems (Chaucer to
contemporary) for Collins, and I have also undertaken to

write a book on the translation of poetry for Routledge, so I have no shortage of work in the near future! However, I'd like to give you some translations for your new project if I can. I think perhaps I ought to restrict myself to your first suggestion of some Spanish ballads (I know from previous tryouts that Villon with his rhyme-schemes is a very hard nut to crack), and I might do <u>Alora la bien cercada</u>, <u>Durandarte</u>, <u>Julianesa</u>, <u>La linda Melisanda</u>, <u>La Constancia</u>, and the <u>Conde Arnoldos</u>. If this is too many, you can pick out the ones you prefer. I wonder whether you will go back as far as Anglo-Saxon poetry? Possibly not; but if so, I have versions of <u>The Wanderer</u> and <u>The Seafarer</u> which might fit in with your scheme. Let me know if you would like to see them. As you ask for suggestions – will you include some of the Scottish ballads? Robert Henryson (one of the fables, perhaps the delightful <u>Two Mice</u>)? Barbour – an extract from the <u>Brus</u>?

I am glad to hear the other anthologies are progressing and I look forward very much to seeing them in due course.

All best wishes | Yours sincerely | ≡\|\|

Travelling in Europe, Flores continued to plan a *Medieval Age* anthology, emphasising narrative art, and had asked for suggestions. Three Spanish ballads are in *CT*: 453–55. EM's *Collins Albatross Book of Longer Poems* was published in 1963.

Lee Holland, editor

31 May 1961

Dear Lee

Sorry to be so long in replying to your mississipive; our term here is just weltering off in a flurry of examination-papers. New Orleans seems to be a perfect hive of beeing and becoming. What I send you here is not much, but you are welcome to use it if it is of interest. I have been sending a great deal out recently, and until some of it comes back my cupboard is rather bare. I hope to get down to some new things now that the academic grindstones are grinding more faintly. Have you

written to Glasgow poet W. Price Turner who is this year's
Fellow in Poetry at Leeds University? He may contribute, and
also put you on to others, especially poets. (The students at
Leeds produce a regular poetry broadsheet.) When you get
to the selling stage, the bookshops most likely to take your
outcry (I mean those that I know of): Paperback Bookshop,
Charles Street, Edinburgh; Better Books, Charing Cross Road,
London; Zwemmers, Charing Cross Road, London. There are
bound to be others, but these spring to mind.

If new thoughts, poems, etc. break into consciousness I'll
transmit them your way later. Meantime all best wishes for the
venture.

Yours sincerely | ≡川 | Edwin Morgan

Based in New Orleans, Holland was starting up a new quarterly
magazine, *The Outsider*, and was looking for material and also
possible sales outlets in the UK. EM sent him 'jean genet: "a legend
to be legible"' (*The Outsider* issue 2, Summer 1962).

Jessie McGuffie, *teacher and editor*

12 Albert Drive
28 July 1961

Dear Jessie
   Yes, I'll write to Arthur Koestler. Do you think about
1000 words would do for an introduction? Or more? I think
it should be mostly about the man, since the poems really
speak for themselves, and anyone can see their quality even in
translation. I won't write to him until I have decided just which
poems are going to be included. Did you like the short piece I
sent to Ian? What 'life' it has in it!
   'Poets of the Cuban Revolution' is a fine idea. If you get
a 'Letter from Fidel Castro' that is almost a poem in itself.
If you don't get any reply, by the way, all is not lost. We have
in Glasgow a brand-new young nice Cuban consul, Dr
Cesar Lopez, temporarily residing at 192 Wilton Street till
his consulate is established; I met him last week at a Polish

National Day reception and he was introduced to me as being 'more interested in literature than diplomacy'; he is a son of the revolution, and a writer, and although he is still busy perfecting his English I'm sure he'd be glad to help. So: do write to him if you want to, and mention my name.

L. Niedecker: I'd like to help, but I really do have a lot on hand at the moment, and Ian has asked me if I'm interested in translating Henri Michaux, which I am (I've done 3 or 4 of his poems) and would enjoy doing if you decide to bring out a volume of him. If it comes to a choice, I'd rather do the Michaux; it's also more worth-while I think. Now that Tom Scott has a First Class Honours there will be no holding him, will there?

When I saw that letter in the *Scotsman* I said to myself, Surely I know J. McGuffie at that address, but why is she disguising her sex? Somehow I thought the letter – both letters – sounded like you; but then I thought, No, she must have a brother Johnnie whom I haven't met! Did you notice that Sydney Goodsir Smith came in with a piece in the *Weekly Scotsman*, claiming bafflement at the idea that *Renascence* implied Establishment?

I hope you have recovered from the turquoise roses. With that spot of colour you should have been at the wedding where I acted as what the papers call a kilted usher and where the whole proceedings was given everlasting remembrance on a cine camera (expense no object, the groom being Mr Charles Gordon of Grants Whisky – Stand Fast there, just behave quite naturally, keep smiling, keep chatting with one another, don't stand too long in the one place, now would the kilted gentleman – that's lovely, quite natural now, thank you –)!

Well, I must pack a bag. I am away for a week. I'll be thinking of you both on Oliver's Mount – now where's that? For answer see next postcard.

I told Ian most folk called me Eddie, except my professor who says Yedward; Ian of <u>course</u> gives me Yedward. Well, if he likes it that way –

But anyhow: all the best – | Eddie

McGuffie, an early partner of Ian Hamilton Finlay* in the Wild Hawthorn Press, was keen to publish EM's translations of Attila József, with an introduction by Koestler. Other projects were 'Poets of the Cuban Revolution' (with an Introduction by Fidel Castro), and work by Louis Zukofsky and Lorine Niedecker. Tom Scott had shown interest in translating the latter into Scots. McGuffie had recently been a bridesmaid with three artificial roses in her hair.

Kulgin Duval, bookseller and editor

21 October 1961

Dear Kulgin

I am deeply disappointed that you have given up the idea of publishing – especially as I have just been writing an article on the difficulty of getting poetry published in Scotland. Your venture was about the only ray of hope at the back of my mind – though I didn't mention it in the article, perhaps prophetically. In fact I always doubted whether you were really serious about publishing, and it was with some misgivings that I gave you the manuscripts I did. You shouldn't have gone so far into this business, Kulgin, and raised so many expectations. You will have disappointed and angered a number of people besides myself. What am I to say to Quasimodo, for instance? You accepted the idea, even though it was a fairly distant one, and you yourself gave publicity to it in Scotland as recently as August. But it is I who will have to write to Quasimodo and tell him the project is off, and I dislike treating a man of his distinction in this way.

Can anything be done with my own poems? If you are trying to negotiate the other two books with McGibbon & Kee, will you try them with *The Whittrick* as well?

I feel bad about the whole thing. I think it is terrible that you should sink back into that artificial rackety world of fine bindings and t.e.g. when you might have been launching out into something that would have been of service to Scottish literature, if you had made up your mind to do it.

Yours | ⧮‖

PS: If you are writing to McGibbon & Kee, could you ask them if they'd be interested in Quasimodo?

Duval had been involved in two volumes to mark Hugh MacDiarmid's* seventieth birthday. EM's disappointment over the failed Quasimodo project spills over into anxiety about his own lack of headway.

Brian Cox, academic and editor

English Department
Glasgow University
31 October 1961

Dear Cox

Thanks for writing about Quasimodo. I quite agree it would be good to have some sort of plan for translations – perhaps making one country a main 'theme' for some particular issue. I think it would be very useful if without attempting any systematic coverage you could introduce people now and again to interesting developments in Europe (including Russia). The British are in another of their provincial/philistine moods, and Arnold thou shouldst be living at this hour etc! Fresh currents of ideas are badly needed to dispel accidie, apathy, atony and other bad things that pervade. I enclose a few more Quasimodo poems, and also some of Montale (these ones are not in my Reading University volume); I suppose that although the former won the Nobel prize most critics would place Montale higher; certainly his work vibrates and bites. You may be interested too in my pamphlet of *Sovpoems*; would it be possible to give it a review, do you think? The introduction throws out some ideas about English and American poetry that I'd be glad to see discussed.

Yours sincerely | ☰‖‖ | Edwin Morgan

Cox and Anthony Dyson (later widely known as editors of the conservative Black Papers on education) taught at the University of Hull and edited *Critical Quarterly*. Cox had apologised for a lengthy

delay in publishing EM's Quasimodo translations, arising from lack
of a journal policy on translations. Later at Manchester University,
Cox was instrumental in bringing Michael Schmidt* to teach and
edit there, helping to set up *Poetry Nation*, later *PN Review*.

Anselm Hollo, poet and translator

6 March 1962

Dear Anselm

How nice to hear from you. I wish I could help you with
Voznesensky, but I don't have his book, and the Russian
Department here does not show any eagerness to keep up with
Soviet developments. Do you see the *Paris Review*? In the
Summer/Fall number of 1961 (No.26) there is a 'Portfolio of
Russian Poetry' collected and edited by Olga Carlisle which
includes one poem by Vozneisenski (described by her as 'a
lighthearted poet') called *From the Window of a Plane*, taken
from the *Mosaic* volume and dated 1960. It is translated by
Rose Styron and Olga C. I wonder if it might be worth while
for you to write to her/them c/o the review, since presumably
she/they will have the *Mosaic* volume? I was interested too
to notice that Voz is mentioned with enthusiasm by the
liberal Soviet critic Korneli Zelinski in an article reprinted
in *Survey* (No.40, January 1962): he calls him 'characteristic
of the generation of the cosmonauts' (whether this is the
same as being lighthearted?? who can say). All this is merely
tantalizing, and I know from previous experience how very
difficult it is to get such books out of Russia (it took me a
long time to get hold of Yevtushenko even). I have no special
contacts myself and have to rely on Messrs Collets who are all
right within limits. I expect you will have tried their Russian
Bookshop in London? I would like to get hold of Vozne(i)
sensky myself, as I am doing three programmes for the BBC
(Third) on modern Russian poetry – a sort of anthology with
linking script. (I aim to include, by the way, a part of your
version of *The Twelve*, which I find a fascinating transposition.)

Red Cats after the Red Birds, dancing on hot ivory… or a
hot tin curtain. Yes, it's a good title.

Another faint possibility has just struck me: the Society for Cultural Relations with the USSR – they are sometimes helpful, they have a library, and even if they had no Voz they might put you onto something. – If you do have any luck would you let me know, as I might have space to include a Vozpiece in my last programme. (I shall have some Yevtushenko, Kirsanov, and Martynov.)

At the moment I am considerably excited by Attila József, whom I'm translating for the Wild Hawthorn (through the medium of versions in other more accessible European languages – but even by this method the extraordinary force of the man comes through). A Magyar Cat if ever there was!

All best reminiscences, regards, and powers – | ≡∥ |
    Edwin Morgan

PS: If you have a version of <u>Goya</u>, perhaps I could use it in my programme? Could you let me see it sometime?

Born in Helsinki, Hollo translated Finnish, German, French and Swedish poetry, and was influenced by the Beat poets. He was in search of Andrei Voznesensky's *Mozaika* (1960), for 'Poems of the Thaw', translations of Yevtushenko, Kirsanov and Voznesensky (City Lights Pocket Poets, 1962). Allen Ginsberg* had suggested *Red Cats* as the title.

Alasdair Gray, painter and novelist

12 Albert Drive
18 March 1962

Dear Mr Gray
    I wonder if you would be interested in doing some illustrations for a couple of booklets of poetry? I was speaking to James Morrison on Friday and he suggested that you might be. Ian Finlay (the poet) and Jessie McGuffie have started in Edinburgh a small publishing venture called the Wild Hawthorn Press. Their first two books were Ian Finlay's *Glasgow Beasts, An a Burd* (illustrated with papercuts by John

Pickering and Pete McGinn) and Lorine Niedecker's *My Friend Tree* (illustrated with linocuts by Walter Miller). They are proposing to bring out some of my poems (*The Whittrick*, a series of imaginary dialogues) and a volume of translations from the contemporary Italian poet Quasimodo, and these are the two volumes I am looking for someone to illustrate. Of course the Wild Hawthorn is still working on a shoestring and I don't suppose there would be much monetary reward in this for you; but you might find it an interesting thing to do, and I think the whole series of books will eventually make its mark.

I'd be very glad if you could tell me, as soon as you can, whether you find the idea at all attractive. If you do, we can then go into more detail and I can let you see the poems.

Yours sincerely | Edwin Morgan

Both James Morrison and Alasdair Gray were keen to illustrate these Wild Hawthorn publications but neither collection transpired, presumably because of financial problems.

Anselm Hollo, poet and translator

English Department
Glasgow University,
18 March 1962

Dear Anselm

I am glad to have the Goya poem, and I certainly hope to use it. I can't tell you yet when these programmes will be coming on, but it won't be just in the immediate future as I have still to finish the scripts. I expect I shall be recording them later this month, this unfortunately <u>not</u> involving a flying visit southwards; when I have done this sort of thing before it has usually been recorded in Glasgow straight through to London (science etc wonderful etc). – Your point about the explanatory dedication to Blok noted.

I haven't tried the flu-flu-flicker machine yet. Does it really give one an Experience?

Am busy today with another BBC script, a short talk on

the current literary scene in Scotland which is to be broadcast on the Scottish Home Service on All Fools Day (no cracks by request).

Hope you have some luck with Voznesensky.

Yours | Eddie

PS: Do you like my old beat writing-paper? (Hand beat, of course.)

EM wanted Hollo's translation of Voznesensky's 'I am Goya' for one of his three BBC radio programmes on Russian poetry since 1917, due for broadcast in June 1962. His own translation is in *CT*: 191–92. The Flicker machine was 'a hallucinating gift to the reader' in a poetry magazine.

Ian Hamilton Finlay, poet and artist

12 Albert Drive
10 April 1962

Dear Ian

Here's the carbon copy of the letter which as Jessie has no doubt told you seems to have been sunk without trace between G and E. Hope it is legible.

I am glad you liked the broadcast. I had no control over the reader (or the choice of him) of course. Actually I had recorded your poems myself (I asked if I could do this) but the BBC got Duncan McIntyre to read them too, reserving the right to substitute his readings if they seemed better. My reading, I was told, lacked 'breath control', so D. McIntyre won. Possibly the BBC were right – I'm not a professional reader – but I agree with you that D.M.'s versions could have been improved on. George Bruce likes the 'grave' timbre of his voice, but there are other things than gravity (as Nell Gwynn said to Newton).

Sorry if I misinterpreted you over 'Scots'; I was judging by general impressions and by what you have written and said about the Scottish Renaissance; I took it for granted that you weren't in favour of <u>synthetic</u> Scots. If you are, you had better put me (as they say on the telly) in the picture as soon as possible, and tell me what your attitude to the language situation really is.

You shouldn't worry so much about 'gauche and sly'. It is one of the first principles of journalism that even a critical mention is better than no mention at all! In any case, further down the same page was a highly appreciative review of your other book, and it is the final impression the reader would be left with. Your battle with WPT – well, there would be no point in a third party stirring up the broth even further. I agree that 'gauche and sly' is a wrong phrase, and probably loaded personally as you suggest, but do you think it really is so derogatory in <u>effect</u>? The gauche can be attractive – I rather like it myself; a faun can be both gauche and sly and yet fascinating; I like fauns, faun-like people. All this is not an attempt to justify a wrong descriptive phrase, merely to suggest to you that publicitywise WPT's remarks will not do you as much harm as perhaps he thought they would.

Tell me, what address do you want me to send my letters to? You have been using Fettes Row in all your recent missives. Are you not using the Northumberland Street address? For safety's sake I shall enclose this letter in my letter to Jessie.

Long life to the p.o.t.h. How is it selling?

Yours ever | Eddie

EM's missing letter raised concerns in IHF's anxious mind. EM had broadcast on contemporary Scottish poetry for George Bruce* at the BBC. WPT was William Price Turner, editor of *The Poet* (1952–56), and IHF was suspicious of EM's seeming reluctance to join (on his side) in an ongoing literary quarrel.

Jessie McGuffie, *teacher and editor*

22 April 1962

Dear Jessie

I've asked Alasdair Gray to let you see some samples of his work. He has different styles; some I like, some I don't. He is strong on line, and decorative effects; he has learned something from Beardsley. This might not particularly fit the general conception you have of your series of books, and of course I have no wish to 'push' him if you don't take to his work. What interested me was his enthusiasm for *The Whittrick*, which I thought might spark something off. Have you anyone else in mind? Do you want me to send you the typescript of *The Whittrick* now, or wait till later? – I have had a letter from Quasimodo and he is pleased at the prospect of coming out in your series; the only stipulations he makes are that he wants the Italian text facing the translations (which is fair enough) and that we must get his publisher's permission to reprint this text (Mondadori – I shall write to them). I still have something of an anxiety feeling about this particular project (this is a sort of Kulgin-Duval hangover) which I know you will understand; I realize you are not in a position to make any promises about when the book might appear, but before I write definitely to Mondadori would you just give me the final okay in the sense that barring accidents wars floods volcanoes and so on you do really and truly intend to do the book; I would feel terrible if it fell through again.

What did I do on the Dunera? Well, I got a thick ear for one thing, being pitched backwards across the cafeteria in company with my chair, a cup of coffee, and a copy of *Sister Carrie* in a great roll off the Mull of Kintyre. Apart from that I watched the fulmars, listened to Jack House, saw *The Maggie*, went to a ceilidh in Stornoway, and photographed St Kilda. Oh yes, and talked to Charlie Senior, who also happened to be on the ship. And ate, as you say.

Do you know that after you mention Douglas Young you call our artist Alasdair Young? This Freudian slip makes me fear for the poor man!

As ever | Eddie

McGuffie had reservations about Alasdair Gray as an illustrator. EM had been on a sea trip on the *Dunera*, a former troop carrier turned educational cruise ship (see also 27 March 1969). *The Maggie* was a 1954 Ealing comedy featuring a Clyde puffer; Jack House was a Glaswegian journalist and broadcaster; and Charles Senior was a Scottish poet whom EM would later support (see 2 September 1968). Douglas Young was a stalwart of the twentieth-century 'renascence' in traditional Scots-language poetry, which McGuffie and Finlay* opposed.

Ian Hamilton Finlay, poet and artist

7 May 1962

Dear Ian

Here are *Sovpoems*. Could I in return ask you to send a Lorry Knee-Decker which I want to send to someone. Michael Shayer tells me he has just about 25 of the SOVs left from the 300, which is not too bad. There still seems to be a demand for it; I don't know whether he'll want to print more. It's disappointing that there's been so little reaction to it, though (in reviews, I mean). But that's an old story.

Yes I have the second P.O.T.H which I shall guard as a bibliographical raritee and await with interest the replacement. Rather agree with you about the layout, though I enjoyed the contents. Wish I could have seen Yevtushenko for poems for P.O.T.H and other things, but my only chance of seeing him was Friday and I had already arranged to be up at Stonehaven for the weekend (I was at Catterline, staying with James Morrison; I showed him the Quasimodo poems and it's possible he might want to illustrate them; I like his work – do you?). Some of Alasdair Gray's illustrations to Scottish ballads are extremely good I think; I hope he has sent Jessie something which will appeal to her. He's interested mainly in the *Whittrick*, not the Quasimodo). – And thanks, by the way, for the reassurance about doing the books! I shall write to the Italian publisher to get the necessary permission.

I like Margot Sandeman's illustrations <u>very</u> much; – no, I don't know her. As soon as I can hack myself a little time-space out of the present exam-marking flux I shall do you a new wee introduction; and I'll also let you know if I have any suggestions about the choice of poems – I haven't looked at them properly yet. All things will be guarded and returned safest earliest as the telegraph man said.

Thanks for your *New Saltire* letter and the cutting. More about this when I have more time for a proper letter. Did you see W. Pride-&-Passion Turner's attack on me in the *Scottish Field*? I feel like the man who gave the bear a bun and got his hand taken off. It was quite unnecessarily offensive, as he must have known very well that my talk was the third in a series and that I <u>had</u> to mention the Renaissance (a term which I don't enjoy using any more than he does). He wants in any case to claim far too much of the credit for himself, as if he singlehanded had turned Scotland's poetry into a new channel; one can't really accept this. I have sent in a reply. I suppose I can expect nasty Christmas cards too now?

Good old football, *Concertina*, etc. Still, you'll have to be careful. I read that 'intellectuals are "taking up" football', having tired of the jazz fad.

And you a <u>Fettes</u> man, too.

Looking forward very much to seeing the Robert Frame cuts.

As ever | Taffy | Taff Morgan, Docker
(and thanks you for sending back | his other face)

Wild Hawthorn Press published Lorine Niedecker's *My Friend Tree* (1961). The second issue of *Poor.Old.Tired.Horse* had been designed by Paul Pond (an Oxford student, later Paul Jones of the Manfred Mann band), and IHF insisted on a reissue. W. Price Turner wrote a negative review of EM's BBC broadcast on contemporary Scottish writing. IHF was living in Fettes Row, and the reference is to the rugby-playing tradition of Fettes College.

Alan Boase, academic

12 Albert Drive
7 May 1962

Dear Professor Boase
    I am sorry that my absence in Stonehaven at the weekend made me miss the *New Saltire* meeting on Sunday. I have, however, been thinking over what you said. The conclusion

I have come to is that while I would be agreeable to join the editorial board and give what help I could in that capacity, I really have too many things on hand to consider the editorship; I don't feel I could give it the sort of wholehearted attention it ought to have. The book on the translation of poetry which I mentioned to you will be taking up most of my spare time for quite a while; it has been held back because I have been engaged in editing an anthology for Collins. In addition, I am involved in editorial work for the *Review of English Studies*, and I have several translation projects on hand. Looking ahead, I see little respite in the near future, and I feel that I must, with some regret, decline your suggestion.

I think that the proposal in the third paragraph of the draft ('to deal with literary and artistic problems over a much wider field and to publish contributions of interest from other countries') is an excellent step in the right direction, and if I can give any help in this regard I shall be glad to do so.

Yours sincerely | Edwin Morgan

Boase, Professor of French in Glasgow University, was on the board of *New Saltire*, a continuation of *The Saltire Review* (1954–61). EM eventually became its Poetry Editor. He was also editing the *Albatross Book of Longer Poems: English and American Poetry from the Fourteenth Century to the Present Day* (Collins, 1963), and, for *Review of English Studies*, co-writing the thrice-yearly 'Summary of Periodical Literature' from the research journals.

Ian Hamilton Finlay, poet and artist

15 May 1962

Dear Ian

Here are the poems and engravings, with a new introduction which is shorter and I hope will suit. The only poem I'm not too happy about is 'A Wee Worry' – I liked the 'City Thistle' one better.

Many thanks for your C-O-N-C-E-R-T-I-N-A- – delightful thing. I showed it without saying anything to my colleague Jack Rillie at the university, and he smiled and said, Surely this is Ian Finlay? So you see the fingerprints are there, in the Great File… I felt, by the way, that your note at the end spoiled it a little – it was like rubbing it in after the effect had already been gained. I think I'd have preferred a purely factual note on Barley and Keys, and I don't know if even that was needed, except I suppose for furrin readers? Anyhow, splendid thing! When you're writing would you include two more, and I'll send a postal order in my next letter.

I am glad you saw Yevtushenko, as I missed him. Yes, I shall look forward to the chance of translating any poems he sends you. We might eventually make a book of it? I agree with you that he is a very lively and worthwhile character. I shall be going down to London at the weekend to record my Russian poetry programme with George MacBeth.

James Morrison has done a lot of Glasgow tenement paintings which are remarkably 'atmospheric'. Up at Catterline he has been doing landscapes, boats, and so on. He lives just beside Joan Eardley. I shall try, as you urge, to urge the artists (though artists, as you will well know, are not particularly urgeable or letter-prone beings). Alasdair Gray <u>says</u> he has sent some of his prints to Jessie. Has she had these now?

> Yours from the grassless fields
> – where the concertina yields
> to bushes telly-bields
>   and stony burns!

Eddie

EM wrote an introduction to IHF's *Whistling in the Dark* (1962). Because some early readers expressed puzzlement, IHF had added a note to his fold-up poem. Yevtushenko had agreed to send poems to *Poor.Old.Tired.Horse* for EM to translate. EM owned one of James Morrison's paintings, *The Window* (1961).

Michael Shayer, editor and poet

25 May 1962

Dear Michael

I've duly sent off a photograph and some biographical details to the Writers Conference people. What this jamboree will amount to I don't know, though it is interesting to see literature getting some recognition as a festival art! I'm not fond of conferences myself but have been roped in (in Scotland one can hardly escape).

Thanks for the figures about *Sovpoems*: it has really done quite well, though like you I was disappointed by the lack of reviews. Still, it has made its way quite widely about (even Yevtushenko is away back to Russia with a presentation copy), and the other day Gael Turnbull forwarded to me a letter from Walter Lowenfels (of *Mainstream*) who wants to have it reviewed and he says 'help to get it distributed'. I expect we shall sell our last 2 dozen, either in Ian Finlay's new shop to be opened soon in Edinburgh, or elsewhere. Which makes me wonder if you have thought at all of printing more copies, a 'second edition', either of this or any of the other pamphlets? There does still seem to be some demand.

I am enclosing a copy of the BBC talk, but I'd be glad if you would let me have it back when you've finished. I agree with a lot of what you say, though I think the Irish parallel is not really very close to the Scottish situation. In Ireland there was only Irish Gaelic, and English; but we have Scottish Gaelic, English, and Scots, three traditions, and although Gaelic is dying and Scots is debased they are still both fairly tenaciously <u>there</u>, as complicating factors. I think most writing in Scotland will increasingly have to be in English, but it's difficult to be <u>happy</u> about this! – Hence so much simmering and unprofitable discontent – we are unable to move towards independence, we are unable to assimilate to an unquestionably alien ethos (the England of monarchy, Church, 'society', public schools, and general imperturbability). Although I can't 'see' any political solution to this state of affairs, I don't feel that the political history of (as they say) these islands has stopped.

I've been recording three programmes of Russian poetry

(post-1917) to be broadcast on the Third in June. It will include some of the *Sovpoems*, and quite a number by other translators.

All the best – | Yours – | Eddie

Yevtushenko had been given *Sovpoems* by the area representative of the British Council. EM's translations of Yevtushenko are in *CT*: 53–55, 201–204, 483–86. Shayer had been considering parallels between Scottish and Irish nationalism.

Ian Hamilton Finlay, poet and artist

27 May 1962

Dear Yan

I am safely back from the padded cells of Broadcasting House W1. I think the programmes should be quite interesting – the broadcasts are to be on 4th, 11th, 18th June. I didn't have time to see much else of London, though I managed to go to the Chekhov film *The Lady with the Dog*, very charmingly done. Visited Anselm Hollo in his new flat in Kensington (87 Cornwall Gardens SW7); he hopes his City Lights volume of *Red Cats* will be out in June – and it looks as if it will be interesting – it overlaps on your Thaw idea, at least as far as Russia is concerned. I think the thaw idea is a good one (though it will take a little thinking out if it is going to be really effective – there will be pens poised in different camps to attack it). (What I mean is that one doesn't want to be too vaguely 'universal' – there may be special and varying circumstances in different countries for a particular 'thaw', apart from a general post-atomic situation which all share, and I think the introduction would have to tread with care, and the poems would have to be chosen with care too. You can see some of the pitfalls in Conquest's anthology *Back to Life*, which is something of the same thing but has not been fairly or properly thought out – do you know it? I'd be willing to have a go, however. I think I can interpret what you have in mind.) Some thoughts that immediately strike me: France (Yves Bonnefoy?) and Germany (??? – most of the younger poets seem to be too nihilistic for your purposes, though interesting enough in themselves) may prove difficult. Italy has perhaps Pier Paolo Pasolini (and one might include Quasimodo who though older has been one of the leaders of the postwar revival in Italy). There ought to be a Polish representation, I think (see Conquest for this?). England: are you really stuck on Kops? I wouldn't mind having him if there was also something a bit stronger to offset him; in Kops the thaw has really gone somewhat soft, don't you think? What about Logue (if carefully selected)? Pete Brown (if ditto)? USA: it would be hard to avoid Ginsberg and Corso, and maybe Ferlinghetti; and the introduction could mention Rexroth, Kerouac, Williams, Creeley... USSR: Yevtushenko, Bella Ahkmadulina, Martynov, Voznesensky (you can hear a Voz. in my third radio programme). And what about the Hundred Flowers? Would it be worth while writing to someone like Hugh Gordon Porteous to see about the Chinese situation? I am sure that the thaw of Chinese classical poetry must have produced some striking results. And oh, an afterthought for England: D.J. Enright, surely? Scotland is ticklish. Michael Levy, perhaps? Alan Jackson (or has he turned to politics?) George Mackay Brown? I have been writing some poems about Glasgow, which might be worked in. Your 'Optimist' as well as 'Writer & Beauty'?

I shall let you know if further thoughts emerge. But do go ahead with your plans. I think *Thaw* is not the best word to use, perhaps, since it has rather narrow associations (chiefly political) with the mid-1950s, and I take it that you don't want to restrict yourself too much to the Dudintsev/Ehrenburg/ Pasternak post-Stalin 'thing' which is only one element in a wider picture? We must see if there's some other word or image that could be used. The image of 'thawing' is perfect, but the noun itself has become a stale sort of cliché at the present time, don't you feel? A sort of Kremlinological inexactitude?

I am glad you and Jessie wrote to the *Scotsman*. I think you were wise to stop where you did. It really is impossible to puncture these amorphous attacks, and a time-wasting correspondence would go on and on without settling anything. It's more important to write, and produce your books. The evidence itself will speak.

Will *Cool Ossian* include cut-ups (e.g. Gysin)? Wordplay by Michaux? My lips, as requested, are sealed; my ears are a wee gog.

I am enclosing with this letter some sample drawings which James Morrison has sent me for the Quasimodo poems. I'd like to know what you and Jessie think of them. They seem to me to capture the atmosphere very well. He's not sure how they could be reproduced – whether they'd have to be simplified first; these are just his first reactions to the poems. But I like them.

Thank you for the two concertinas. I look forward to the Zukovsky.

Yours | Eddie

EM's broadcasts on Russian poetry were produced by the poet George MacBeth. IHF suggested that EM and himself co-edit an 'Anthology of the Thaw', celebrating a new life-affirming spirit in international poetry, and an easing of the Cold War. *Cool Ossian* was a planned anthology of sound and Dada poems, ultimately unrealised. EM had bought two of IHF's 'concertina' fold-up poems.

P.A. Casimir, Further Education lecturer/librarian

13 June 1962

Dear Mr Casimir

Thank you for your letter about my *Sovpoems*, which has just been forwarded to me from the Migrant Press at Worcester. I share your interests in 'poetry that looks as if life had some say in its making' – I think that's why English poetry at present doesn't make much impact. I have published some poetry (*The Cape of Good Hope*, Peter Russell, 1955; poems in PEN *New Poems* 1954, 1955, 1961; a forthcoming volume of poetic dialogues, *The Whittrick*, with the Wild Hawthorn Press, Edinburgh), and translations of *Beowulf* (Hand & Flower Press, 1952) and *Poems of Eugenio Montale* (University of Reading, 1959). The Wild Hawthorn Press will be bringing out a volume of versions of Salvatore Quasimodo (whom I find very interesting) and also of Attila József (translated not directly from the Hungarian but through other European versions). I haven't done any German 20th-century poetry except the Brecht you have seen in *Sovpoems* – largely because my German is somewhat laboured and means slow going. Polish I don't know except in so far as it resembles Russian and one can often guess meanings here and there; but what I have seen of modern Polish poetry (e.g. in Conquest's *Back to Life*) is sharp and real and exciting (like some of the Polish films) and has made me want to know more about it. I have also a lot of unpublished Mayakovsky done into Scots. Curiously enough, I saw a copy of *Unicorn* very recently; I sent for the number with Pasternak poems by Lynda Slater (despite her self-defence she is not really a good translator of Pasternak!). *Migrant* is/was a little mag which is now defunct, but Michael Shayer its editor has brought out a series of 'Migrant Pamphlets' of poetry and translations by Ian Finlay, Anselm Hollo, Roy Fisher, Matthew Mead, myself, and others.

Yours sincerely | Edwin Morgan

Casimir, who worked in a college in Hemel Hempstead, had received *Sovpoems* (1961) from his County Library service and written to enquire about EM's work. He was connected with *Unicorn* (1960–63), a magazine of poetry and criticism.

Ian Hamilton Finlay, poet and artist

29 July 1962

Dear Ian
    I don't know just what stage the József is at, but looking over it I thought it looked a bit thin (especially when we're introducing a virtually unknown (in the English-speaking world) poet, and if it is possible to include a few more poems I'd like you to put in the ones I have enclosed here, making the total up to 20 (same as Quasimodo). I have also typed out a slightly altered introduction, and I have made a few changes in the second page of 'Ode' – I thought typing out the whole page

(for you to substitute) would be the easiest way of giving you the changes. I hope all this is not too complicated, and not too late. Have you had the József illustrations?

The CBC address which you asked for is: National Script Department, P.O. Box 500, Toronto, Ontario.

Yes, the *Ugly Birds* is well off the beam. I can see that the *Thaw* collection will <u>have</u> to be produced, if only to set some facts before him. (Let's hope some more <u>Scottish</u> youngpoets make their appearance by the time I really get down to compiling; are you not getting anything interesting sent in to POTH??) I sent in a little 'reply' to MacD's 'letter' to me in *New Saltire* 4 but I was too late – NS5 is already printed. However, here it is:

Sir,

Candymill may sweer and bock,
It's stawed wi its ain stick o rock.

Maybe there's noo mair virr and vigour
In Beats, nor in the Square o Biggar?

Dinna fret, man, dinna rage!
Your answer's on anither page.

Yours, etc...

– Actually – accidentally – I <u>have</u> given him an answer, as NS5 is printing an article on some American Beat ideas which will no doubt infuriate him farther. It's a fairly general article, which I hope to follow up later with more detailed aspects of some writers.

I didn't think the little *Spectator* thing was in itself worth writing about, but I am, as they say, keeping my eye on the situation.

But I must get on with my review of H-gh M-cD--rm-d's *Collected Poems*. Would you like to lend a hand, help me out, add a rider, stitch on an appendix? 'I can only regard Mr Morgan's interest in the later poems of MacD as an unaccountable aberration.'

As ever | Eddie

The Attila József translations were not published. EM's *Beowulf* had been dramatised by the Canadian Broadcasting Corporation. *The ugly birds without wings* was Hugh MacDiarmid's* spirited riposte to newspaper complaints from IHF and others about an 'Establishment' of older poets favouring writing in Scots – a quarrel noted in the *Spectator*. EM kept a foot in both camps, reviewing MacDiarmid's *Collected Poems* in *The Review* 3 (August–September 1962) and praising his later 'poetry of fact', which few critics did, while also publishing 'The Beat Vigilantes' in *New Saltire* 5.

Magnus Magnusson, editor and journalist

28 September 1962

Dear Magnus

Thank you for your letter. I regret this a lot. I am very
sorry that I couldn't go to the Edinburgh meeting where
presumably some of the points in Boase's letter were being
made. (I had to invigilate the degree re-sits that day.) When
I read through NS5 I was certainly a bit uneasy about it, and
when Boase phoned me to give me <u>his</u> opinion I couldn't but
agree that some things in it were not up to the mark. I said
in particular that it <u>began</u> badly: the first three articles being
the weakest, this could act as a quick deterrent to would-be
purchasers flipping through the opening pages. But as far
as I was concerned this was merely a matter for ventilation,
discussion, and improvement, and Boase has clearly made a
more sweeping condemnation than I understood he intended
to make. Your resignation (which I agree was forced by his
letter) is therefore no 'welcome relief' to me, though I would
have liked to persuade you that <u>some</u> of the contents were
on the wrong lines. Much of Boase's criticisms I either don't
agree with or think exaggerated, but I do concur on two
points: the articles by Hanley and Watson. Hanley's really is
a wretched piece, and I think it was a major mistake to give it
pride of place. It, if nothing else, merits Boase's words 'cheap
and vulgar'. I think you know that I am not a pedant, and I
believe it is possible to write both interestingly and popularly,
but that sort of matey facetiousness just gets us nowhere. You

could have done a far better piece on the same subject yourself, and so could I. So could Hanley, for that matter. As for the 'Sugar-Plum Pundits', that seemed to me the worst kind of anti-intellectualism, and once you allow it to creep under the door you are mined from within – it would be death to any magazine that claimed to discuss ideas as well as facts and events. Both these articles are a sort of <u>trahison des clercs</u>.

However, all this will be of little interest to you now. What will happen next I have no idea. I wanted at least to let you know that such criticisms as I would have made would have been far from the vote of no-confidence which Boase's letter seemed to suggest you were in fact receiving.

Yours | Eddie

Professor Alan Boase* chaired the Saltire Society sub-committee overseeing *New Saltire*. He had written a scathing critique of the latest issue edited by Magnusson, who felt he had no option but to resign. He was later persuaded to continue as Editor.

U. Grant Roman, book dealer

English Department
The University
16 October 1962

Dear Mr Roman
Thank you for your letter of 9 October. It is true I have some William Burroughs first editions but I need these for my own use; however, if any other copies come my way I shall let you know.

Of the Wild Hawthorn items you mention, I could sell you the Number Two issue of *Poor. Old. Tired. Horse.* What I have is indeed something of a rarity as two different 'states' of this issue were printed, the second one 'correcting' and superseding the first (which the editor Jessie McGuffie thought had been badly put together by her co-editor Paul Pond – Paul Pond's name is omitted in the second printing). I can let you have both states of Number Two, in very good condition apart from some creases (almost unavoidable in a broadsheet of this kind.). Published price 9d.

I can also let you have Ian Finlay's *The Dancers Inherit the Party*, with the author's corrections in ink, inserted 'Note' by Michael Shayer, and of course the original woodcuts by Zeljko Kujundzic. Excellent condition, published price 2/-.

The Migrant Press which published Finlay's *Dancers* has also published my pamphlet of Russian translations, *Sovpoems*, 1961, 3/6, and I can let you have a mint copy of this, signed, if you are interested. (I should perhaps mention that the other items above also have my signature on the fly-leaf.) I can also let you have, in very good condition, an earlier volume of my poetry, *The Cape of Good Hope*, Peter Russell, 1955, 5/-.

I expect Ian Finlay in Edinburgh may be able to help you with the other items you refer to in your letter. I shall drop him a note. I shall myself be very glad to see your 'Outsiders' catalogue when it appears, as there are a number of books of this type which have been practically impossible to get over here.

Yours sincerely | Edwin Morgan

PS Would you be interested in a signed duplicated copy of my article 'The Fold-In Conference' (dedicated to William Burroughs) which is to appear in the next number of *The Outsider*?

Roman was a rare book collector, especially of modern first editions. He had heard of EM's interest in Burroughs through the editor of the *The Outsider*, Jon Edgar Webb, who published EM's article on Jean Genet. EM suggested to Ian Hamilton Finlay* that he might raise funds by selling some Wild Hawthorn editions to Roman. On 'The Fold-In Conference', see 8 January 1974.

Allen Ginsberg, poet

12 November 1962

Dear Allen Ginsberg

Miss Ross of Collins sent me your airletter, and I'm
very glad we can include your poem in the anthology. I am
enclosing a proof, and would be obliged if you can let me have
it back with your corrections as soon as you possibly can. It
would also be very helpful if you don't make too many changes
in the text of the poem! – the reason being that each poem has
explanatory footnotes for any difficult words and the footnotes
have already been set. Would you let me know if you would
like the Latin words to be normalized – to Annuit Coeptis,
Novus Ordo Seclorum.

Yes, I admire Gregory Corso's poems and would have liked
to include one – possibly *Marriage* – but for reasons of space
I had to choose between him and yourself. The anthology is
from Chaucer right on to the present.

I'll be looking out for your next book. I hope India has been
fruitful and strange.

Two poems enclosed for your interest: one was in the
New Statesman recently, the other is for a little anthology of
rhinoceros poems which Anselm Hollo is doing for (probably)
City Lights. Although India is elephants, I thought the white
rhinoceros might appeal to you in your present situation.

With thanks, and all best wishes | Yours sincerely | ≡|| |
Edwin Morgan

EM had tracked Ginsberg to Calcutta for permission to include
'American Change' in his *Collins Albatross Book of Longer Poems*
(1963). Ginsberg had pointed out that the source copy in *Nomad*
9/1961 was out of alignment. The Latin mottoes from the US dollar
remained as originally printed, glossed correctly in a footnote. The
two poems sent were 'The Death of Marilyn Monroe' and 'The White
Rhinoceros' (*CP*: 146, 150).

Augusto de Campos, poet

8 August 1963

Dear Augusto de Campos
Many thanks indeed for sending *Invenção* No.2 and *Noigandres* 5 which reached me safely, also for your letter of 8 July. Your little vocabulary was helpful, and I have too a small Portuguese dictionary and am at present working my way through some of the poems. I am struck by the great variety of approach, from the most abstract and 'patterned' to the committed (I like very much your *Cuba Sim Ianque Nao*). It is good to keep the concrete method capable of doing different things, from effects of pure place, relation, and movement to effects of satire, irony, and direct comment. The American poet Jonathan Williams, who has been in this country recently, has done some interesting work (you may know it) which uses certain aspects of concrete technique to comment on the Negro problem in the American South.

I am enclosing a few poems and translations in the hope that they will reach you this time! Two translations of poems by yourself – which I am trying to get into print, together with some other versions, in our *Times Literary Supplement*, a somewhat conservative organ – but we shall see.

I shall look forward very much to seeing the translations of Pound and Cummings you refer to – particularly as I am gathering material for a book on the translation of poetry.

With all best wishes | Yours sincerely | ≡||| |
    Edwin Morgan

An enthusiastic sharing of texts and translations was a feature of the concrete movement at this stage. The Brazilian poets had figured in Issue 6 of *Poor.Old.Tired.Horse* (March 1963). EM's review and translations appeared almost a year later in the *TLS* of 3 September 1964, in a special number on the avant-garde: 'Any Advance? The Changing Guard – 2'.

Ian Hamilton Finlay, *poet and artist*

Glasgow 22 August 1963

Dear Ian

Many thanks for your letter, *Tug*, and P.O.T.H. I think the *Tug* is perfect: the dark background and growing type-size make it loom up with admirably snorting perkiness. Coming back to Grangemouth from Stavanger – the tug had a grand time turning the ship right round so that we came in like a ship of the dead: it visibly and audibly enjoys such operations. I thought the link-up between old and new in P.O.T.H. came across well, though the Tvardovsky is rather out of place (nice though it is in itself). "Spike's Pig (<u>Porcus spicatus</u>). This newly discovered species of pygmy pig, which breeds rapidly in the marshes near Tilbury, is thought to be a strontium mutant. Sandwiches filled with Spike's Pig Paste must <u>never</u> be given to children under 12. The Ministry of Health are investigating." Seriously though, I liked the whole 'tribute'. Doubtless it will become a collector's piece (better send a copy to Fort Lauderdale!).

The oboe poem is much clearer now, thanks. Actually when I wrote about it I had stupidly forgotten the title you had given it; and in this case the title is an essential part of the poem's information.

Did you get from Augusto the new *Invenção* with our poems in it? The whole magazine is interesting and well-documented too. They're a go-ahead lot in Saõ Paulo. Concrete poetry should be published and discussed, but how is it to be done in this country? I sent translations of the Brazilian concretists to TLS many months ago, but have had no reply. A pity you couldn't bring out a little collection of British concrete poetry – if only to show the rest of the world that these islands are not entirely fogbound. I hope I shall see your concrete show at the MacEwan Hall – and you too – sometime during the last week of the Festival.

Avanti, etc. | Yeddie

EM had been on a cruise to the Norwegian fjords. 'Spike's Pig' refers to a poem in *Poor.Old.Tired.Horse* by Spike Hawkins. Augusto de Campos* had got in touch after seeing EM's work in *Poor.Old.Tired. Horse*. IHF was trying to arrange an exhibition of concrete poetry during the Edinburgh Festival. On the origin of 'Yeddie', see letter of 28 July 1961.

Ian Hamilton Finlay, poet and artist

19 Whittingehame Court
Glasgow W2
11 September 1963

Dear Ian

Here are some things for you to look at for P.O.T.H: would you just send back anything you don't want?

I have read Pierre Garnier's projet de plan-pilote and am in general agreement in so far as I would like to see experiment going on along the lines he indicates though I doubt if his use of the word cosmique is really very helpful (it's like those competitions for Miss Universe instead of Miss World), and also I don't think it is true to say that 'la langue est une partie autonome du monde', it seems to me that it shades off only too readily into other things, into music (a language without a Rosetta Stone – yet), into noise (thunder, the sea, a train can obviously 'speak' to us), even into silence (a look, a gesture can 'say' very complex things that we understand yet cannot put into verbal language); there is the animal world too: are we sure that the chatter of monkeys or starlings is different in kind from human communication, or only in degree of sophistication? The usefulness of musique concrète is that it reminds us that music is basically 'noise' and that music's vocabulary may be widened (if it seems to be becoming attenuated or overworked) by re-relating it to the noise that fills the world itself. If there is to be any analogy with poetry, poésie concrète would imply a double search: for an extension of the musical-semantic possibilities of language, and for an extension into life, embodying perhaps noise, or pictures, or things (cf. some of Joan Eardley's landscapes in which blades of grass blown by the wind onto the canvas have been embodied in the picture). Such a <u>double</u> search is indicated because language must combine musical and referential elements; indeed I would go so far as to suggest that it is impossible to use langage-matière libéré de <u>toute</u> charge représentative. As existing examples of poésie concrète show, there is a wide range of possible effects from the most engagé and satirical down to the most nearly purely abstract, but in very few cases (if any) can we really say that there is no charge représentative (whether intended by the poet or not). This would be my qualification of M. Garnier's <u>1st</u> kind of poésie spatiale. As for No.2 (visuelle): I am not too happy about the phrase centre d'énergie, which suggests to me a very different kind of poetry – a rough, shaggy, flawed, but emotionally charged language which casts its seeds in future minds and (to be Irish) means more than it is worth (e.g. some of Hart Crane's poems, one or two of Emily Dickinson's). But this is due to the associations of the phrase; others may not feel this particular objection. A more general objection to it might be simply that any poem, or vital part of a poem, is (and has long been thought of as) a centre d'énergie. Comment on No.4 (mécaniste): I am not sure whether this refers to humanly composed poetry using permutations or to poetry composed by (or with the help of) computers. Computer poetry would not necessarily be mécaniste to look at. What place does M. Garnier envisage computers as having in the general field of poésie spatiale? No.5 (phonique): I am not clear about this either. Does it mean simply something like the Gysin/Burroughs cut-up technique, words spoken onto tape and then the tapes cut about, or is it something nearer electronic music, with no 'words'? No.6 (phonétique): This presumably differs from No.5 but the difference should be made clearer.

Would you like to pass these remarks on to Garnier, and add your own? I think we can support him on general lines, for what might come of it, even if we don't feel quite cosmic about the centres of energy. I am returning the pilot-plan-project-presented-py-Pierre.

I have received a mad book on Krishnamurti by and from the Raja of Bhor, who requests any kind comments. Have you any experience of addressing Rajas?

It was nice seeing you and Jessie again. Más allá.

Yeddie

EM had moved into his own flat, home for the next 40 years. Pierre Garnier, the 'spatialist' poet, aimed to conceptualise the various lines of experimentation in concrete and sound poetry by having such poets affirm a commonality of purpose. The poems sent included recent Glasgow poems such as 'King Billy', which Finlay found rather 'didactic' and lacking the precision of language found in EM's concrete work.

Augusto de Campos, poet

13 September 1963

Dear Augusto

Very many thanks for your letter of 25 August and for the three books which have now reached me safely: *Invenção* No.3, Pound's *Cantares*, and Cummings's *10 Poemas*. It will take me more time to look more closely at the latter two translations, but my first eager glance has found both of them a remarkable achievement; the Cummings poems in particular seem to bear out my belief that there is much less in poetry that 'cannot' be translated than most people like to suppose. I like best so far the 'grasshopper' and 'fog' poems, which you have done brilliantly.

I am glad you liked my versions of your two poems, and I am enclosing a version I have just made of 'ovonovelo' (from *Poesia Concreta*). If it meets with your approval you are welcome to use them all in *The Plumed Horn* (a magazine which I have seen recently for the first time). I quite agree with you about the better spacing of r a i n y/ b r i n y . And also about the 3rd-dimension look of tintinna/bulation.

Yes, my Russian translations are made direct. I can't really speak Russian but studied it at Glasgow University. I shall try to get you a copy of Voznesensky's *Triangular Pear* but I'm afraid it will be out of print, as books in the USSR go out of print almost immediately. I had great difficulty in getting my own copy. If I had time I would copy it out for you, but I have no Russian typewriter! Anyway, I am sending you the text of one section, and also the poem by Pankratov, in case you or Haroldo want to have a go at translating them.

Jonathan Williams has just published *Lullabies Twisters Gibbers Drags* (Nantahala Foundation, Highlands, North Carolina, 1963, $1.00); these are poems I think you would enjoy. They are semi-concrete poems about segregation. I liked your own *Bhite & Wlack* – as also the *Bestiary* (you certainly don't need to apologize over the 'English'; on p.2 your query on or upon the thin stripe… I would put upon as it goes better with thin; further down on the same page, you couldn't make your chameleon a salamander? since salamanders lived in flame).

I forgot also to thank you for the *Cubagramma*. I look forward to the *Finnegans Wake* translations and Haroldo's Mayakovsky.

All best wishes | Edwin | Edwin Morgan

With his brother Haroldo de Campos* and Décio Pignatari, Augusto de Campos was a member of the Brazilian Noigandres group of concrete poets, who translated such experimental writers as Mallarmé, Mayakovsky, Khlebnikov, Joyce and Cummings. *The Plumed Horn* (*el corno implumado*) was a Mexican journal in which their poetry appeared. Augusto de Campos had seen EM's versions of Voznesensky in *Poor.Old.Tired.Horse*. Haroldo de Campos was learning Russian.

Ian Hamilton Finlay, poet and artist

Glasgow 10 November 1963

Dear Ian

Many thanks for your letter and lettercard. The l/c was somewhat cryptic but I think I have got it. Anyway I shall write to Dom Thing, and if I have time to type anything out I shall also send something to Camilla for transmission. (Time is the bugbear; before Thursday I have to write the script for a 20-minute film about Glasgow which the Corporation has sponsored from Templar ('Seaward the Great Ships') Films.) I'll also write a brief 'yes' (not going all the way) to Garnier and return you his document when I've got it typed for my own use. I've now had *Labris* (with some of your pieces in it) and a letter saying they will print my Chunnel Tannel and probably some other things.

Yes, I am keenly aware of the language problem, the 'lack of precision' etc which you mention. But I still think something can be done on those lines, and I am going to keep trying. I like your term 'off-concrete'; I shall keep doing this too… Your own r a p e l I shall certainly try to review somewhere, though it will probably not be *The Scotsman*, as they've never asked me to review anything. I may be writing to George Bruce soon, and can suggest Arts Review. I have just had a disappointing letter from the California Press; they aren't doing <u>any</u> of the projects (József, Quasimodo, Montale, Mayakovsky) they seemed to be so enthusiastic about a year ago. The Italians they can't do because they can't get copyright; for the József they don't even give a reason, and they rub salt in by saying they trust the Wild Hawthorn selection safely appeared… So I am back where I started. The California experience is particularly galling because it was they, not me, who suggested these projects in the first place, and they didn't even have the courtesy to tell me the projects had been dropped, I had to write and ask them. I needn't ask you (with your sailor trouble, among other things) whether your own publishing programme is likely to pick up. Nailing one's József to the trees seems to be about the only method left. The mood will pass, but at the moment I feel like just locking everything up in a drawer.

I liked your joint letter about Kerouac in TLS – short and
to the point. I was glad to see them printing Robert Garioch's
poem this week. But why did they give him two arrs?

Best as ever | Eddie

Dom Sylvester Houédard* had written that Camilla Gray of the British
Museum (who was in touch with Russian experimental poets such
as Khlebnikov) could send poems or letters from EM. The Templar
film concerned social and town planning issues in Glasgow. *Labris*,
a Belgian poetry magazine, published 'O Pioneers' (*CP*: 189). Paul
Garnier was circulating a letter to be signed by Scottish concrete
poets. IHF thought that EM's recent Glasgow poems lacked sharp-
ness. The 'sailor trouble' was that Jessie McGuffie* had fallen in love
with an American sailor visiting on behalf of Louis Zukofsky, and
had followed him to New York.

Dom Sylvester Houédard, monk and poet

19 Whittingehame Court
27 December 1963

Dear Silvester

Here returned with many thanks are the Indecorous Tract
and the Malevich miniatures. Hope I have not kept them
too long. Do tell me if you want me to return the journals etc
you sent; Ian F has *Cuff You* at the moment, he hadn't seen it
before. I am also grateful to you for sending the offshoot from
Typographia with your valuable article which I hope people
will read: you have a net with a thousand rays. Thanks too
for the Corvo offpull. I had read this when it appeared in the
Review. I've always been interested in Corvo; I think *The Desire
& Pursuit of the Whole* is a remarkable, even great book. Your
piafstract is fine.

I wonder of the enclosed poem is any use for your
unfolders? Or would you prefer something more strictly
concrete?

No I don't know of other poets than the ones you mention.
The Scottish BBC is holding a competition for student poets

(at the Scottish universities) which I and Norman MacCaig have to judge. I shall let you know if anything interesting emerges from this...

Nothing happened, I am afraid, about Artaud; I had too much on hand to follow it up properly.

What do you think the Pope will bring back from Jerusalem? It certainly requires the eye of faith to see anything holy in the holy places as at present constituted – or so I found when I was there. I trust he will take his bare feet with him? He will surely not be <u>carried</u> along the via dolorosa?? – Will he someday go to Moscow, Peking???

Balafong
dong
dom

Love – | Eddie

<u>JAPANESE PLAY</u>

– Give me your hand.
<u>Chop</u>. – Here.

Although his first name came to be spelled with a 'y', Houédard's early letters to EM used 'Silvester'. Networking for the avant-garde, dsh had sent photostats of the work of Kazimir Malevich, the Russian pioneer of abstract art, together with a 'Tractate on Indecency' (whether secular or religious is uncertain) and material from journals, including from *Typographia* No. 8 (Dec. 1963) his article 'Concrete Poetry and Ian Hamilton Finlay'. *Cuff You* probably refers to *Fuck You: A Magazine of the Arts*, founded in New York in 1962. EM enclosed 'Canedolia' (*CP*: 156) for dsh's planned series of artist and poet folder collaborations that would develop into Openings Press productions with John Furnival. Experimental poets mentioned by dsh in his earlier letter included Finlay*, Hollo*, Raworth, Shayer*, Horowitz* and Brown. Pope Paul VI visited Jerusalem in January 1964. EM's poem on Edith Piaf, 'Je ne regrette rien' (*CP*: 146) had drawn a positive response from dsh. The 'balafong' refers to a poem sent by dsh, 'homage to leopold sedar senghor', that echoes the balafong's wooden sounding bars.

Michael Shayer, editor and poet

3 January 1964

Dear Michael

Many thanks for *Poems from an Island* – these are your best yet. I thoroughly enjoyed the sequence – though I read it as a kind of dialogue of disagreement! In fact I have just finished it, and these 'instant comments' may be of interest –

'When you give a man a promise he expects you to fulfil it' – And why not? Without trust is anguish; or a sub-life. Either you sit watching the trains go by – or 'it is the missing dates at which the heart expires'...

'You could starve here easily if....' THE NECESSITIES OF LIFE SHOULD NOT HAVE TO DEPEND ON PERSONAL RELATIONS.

It should not be necessary to go 'drinking' in order to be intimate with people? Anyway, long live tea.

'No sermon' – Yes, that's what's wrong with Ireland!

'Bofin needs its monks again' – NO! More monks, <u>more</u> bachelors. It wouldn't be 50, it would be 75, 100... See Mongolia, Tibet, 40% celibates pre-revolution, plenty of god but what about hospitals, schools, universities... poor roads, poor crops... fine prayerwheels, fine bells. You want bells and ignorance??

'Love is source of evil when it overruns' – No! Let it brim over, let it shower the world. I know what 'justice' means. Use every man according to his deserts and who would escape whipping.

'Martha was angry with Mary as usual' – and damned right she was! I have always disliked Christ's words to Martha, and I think it wouldn't be going too far to say that the world has suffered for them.

'The basic life from which if it was destroyed civilization would have to begin again' – This reminds me of Edwin Muir. Civilization <u>will</u> be destroyed if people keep talking like this. I do not like a catastrophism which seems to be hankering after the thing it deplores.

HUMANITY – VIGILANCE – STUDY – WORK – HOPE

(Mind you, I love Ireland. I stayed there, in the Wicklow mountains, some years ago. But were there never moments when you said yourself, 'O a hopeless country – like India'????)

I have been writing quite a few poems myself recently. You are not thinking of bringing out any more pamphlets?

Thanks for sending the 'cellar' poems. <u>That</u> seems a long time back.

All the best for 1964 | Eddie

Shayer had written some poems while on holiday in Ireland. The 'cellar poems' probably relate to late 1950s Festival readings in Edinburgh basements by EM and other young poets.

William Buchanan, *Arts Council Exhibitions Officer*

4 January 1964

Dear Mr Buchanan

Thank you for your letter about the Joan Eardley Memorial Exhibition. I am returning the completed questionnaire.

I thought the enclosed poem might be of interest, as I wrote it about the picture in question. I have always been particularly attracted by Joan Eardley's work and have felt a certain affinity: I think she was perhaps finding parallel solutions in paint to some of the problems that I have come up against in poetry. The poems might conceivably make a tribute somewhere in the catalogue?

I have two other Eardley paintings: 'Setting Sun & Stacks'

(1956) and 'Stacks at Evening' (1957). These can be seen, if
desired, at the same address.

Yours sincerely | ☰||| | (Edwin Morgan)

PS: If you are telephoning and cannot contact me at my home
number, try the University – English Department – WEStern
8855 Ext. 226.

Joan Eardley had died unexpectedly in the autumn of 1963, and the
Scottish Committee of the Arts Council of Great Britain organised
an exhibition in Glasgow and Edinburgh. EM owned *Sweet Shop –
Rotten Row*, and, allowing it to be borrowed, he included 'To Joan
Eardley' (*CP*: 163) which describes it.

Magnus Magnusson, editor
(handwritten)

19 WC W2
11 1 1964

My dear Magnus
   Thank you for the py [poetry], which didn't amount to so
much in the end. I hv kept abt 3 poems, wh I shall pass on to
B. Hook.
   I think you underestimate yr own qualities, though I agree
that there is still something wrong w/ the magazine. I am quite
willing to work w/ B.H. as you suggest, but I wd be dishonest
if I didn't say that there are limits to my own enthusiasm in
participating. The whole 'Saltire' background, serious though it
may seem, has I think been subtly influencing and moulding
the magazine, & both the influence & the mould are really
not my cup of tea. We produce gd solid unexciting articles;
there is still a heavy Scottish emphasis; the tone and image
are innocuous & middlebrow. I'm not saying that all these
things are <u>wrong</u>, bt they are not what I cd feel myself to be
deeply identified w/; they are not what I think is <u>needed</u> most
at the present moment. Is it not a case of aabody being out of
step except Jock? When the mood is, above all, international,
synthesizing, spatial – we go on hoeing our little dim northern

row, wh is likely to prove our grave if we don't wake Jock up. I think I wd like to found an *Anti*-Saltire Socy …

I'll do what I can, bt – I feel I ought to end on a but.

Yours aye | E

This is a draft reply to Magnusson, who had lost confidence in his own role as Editor of *New Saltire*, and suggested that EM work more directly with William (Bill) Hook, the production editor, while he himself concentrated on writing as a journalist for the review.

Alan Bold, poet and biographer

19 Whittingehame Court
25 January 1964

Dear Alan Bold

No, I have not changed my mind. But you have little cause to be bitter. You have, as far as I know, submitted only one group of half a dozen poems to *New Saltire*. If you had been receiving rejection after rejection from one magazine over a period, you <u>might</u> have some grounds for bitterness. In one respect you have been unfortunate – though the fault is not mine – in that by the time I first received these poems at the beginning of January you had already published the best of them in *Gambit* and I was therefore unable to take one or perhaps two that I would certainly have considered (<u>Sir Humphr[e]y Davy</u> and <u>Rich and Strange</u>); of the non-*Gambit* ones, <u>Trafalgar Square</u> seemed the best, but I thought it didn't come up to the other two I have mentioned, and I still think so, having looked at it again. So don't let's get our lines crossed on this. If you send poems as attractive as <u>Sir H.D.</u> I shall certainly be considering them seriously for publication. Your remark that I 'take no account of the content' is nonsense, as I am sure you know it is. I imagine I am more favourably disposed towards your content than anyone else you could send your work to. But someone has to remind you, and that's what I want to do, that content by itself won't carry you through. Byron wrote quickly and sometimes carelessly and badly, but for all that he took care to give his readers pleasure and entertainment and excitement. If your *Triumph of Death* had been written in the difficult rhyme-scheme of *Don Juan* you would have had some excuse for writing badly, but as it is it gives the impression that form was not considered at all, and it is unsatisfactory (I admit its 'ambitiousness' – that's all right) in the same way as Hugh MacDiarmid's *The Battle Continues* is unsatisfactory: the bullying tone drives poetry out of the house, for there are some things that poetry for all its toughness will not stand – it just quietly melts away and leaves you with the soap-box. It seems to me that since you have expressed admiration for Brecht and Mayakovsky, you should begin to learn something from their poetry, and above all from their attitude towards their art. There have been few more committed poets than Brecht, yet he sweated as many tears of blood over form as he did over content. He mastered every form he took up, from ballads to free verse, and his freest-verse poems are as tight, sinewy, and beautiful in their movement and accurate placing of words as the most formal poem ever was in the past. And Mayakovsky, though he was a civic and political poet through and through, was also a virtuoso of vocabulary, rhyme, and metric. I say this to you because I am entirely in agreement with you about the place and significance of content, especially at the present time. But the rhythm and movement of poetry are so important that they are almost basic; when they break down, the poem breaks down. Your scornful reference to 'elegant expression' seems to show some misunderstanding of this. I am not talking about elegant expression. I am talking about the inner 'song' by which the poem must either convince or fail to convince its readers or hearers. This applies quite as much to a poetry of ideas as to a poetry of feeling or imagination – perhaps even more. I hope you'll think about it. It's no use saying in a blustering fashion that you 'don't give a damn'. You <u>must</u> give a damn, and more than that too. Anyone who has talent has responsibility.

If you are submitting further poems for *New Saltire*, send them direct to me so that there won't be a hold-up as there was the last time. Many thanks for the copies of *Student*.

Yours sincerely | Edwin Morgan

Bold was a young working-class Scottish poet and journalist who went on to edit the *Penguin Book of Socialist Verse* (1970) and wrote *MacDiarmid: A Critical Biography* (1988). He featured along with Edward Brathwaite and EM in *Penguin Modern Poets 15* (1969).

Christopher Murray Grieve (Hugh MacDiarmid), poet

25 February 1964

Dear Christopher Grieve

The letter is from the pupils and teacher of School No.109 in Kuibyshev, on the Volga. It's really a kind of circular, addressed to distinguished people in various countries who are thought to be 'fighters for peace'. This school has apparently started what it calls 'Mailbox of Peace, USSR/Scotland', and this is part of the wider 'Second Inquiry into Peace, with the Theme of "Peace and Happiness to all Children", 1964' which follows a previous 'Inquiry into Peace' held in the USSR in 1963. A good deal of the letter is taken up with this earlier inquiry, and especially with the reply they received from Bertrand Russell (he sent them his book 'The History of Peace'). Most of it is routine rhetoric on the need for peace, the cold war, the test ban treaty, the situations in Cyprus, Vietnam, Panama, etc... When the letter gets down to business (not till the third page!), it addresses you more directly and says: 'We turn to you with this appeal, to act for the preservation of peace on earth, to confirm and manifest your determination to struggle for the happiness of the children.' It goes on to beg you to answer the letter by sending a message, together with your photograph, and some of your books (autographed) for the school's Peace Fund. It also asks you to tell your friends and colleagues to do the same, and to send letters, books, postcards, stamps, badges, toys, etc. to strengthen ties between Scottish and Russian children. The postscript asks you in addition to send a short 'literary biography' in your own handwriting for the school's literary museum. The post-postscript says that the letter had already been sent in January and been returned; it's being sent now for the second time. All the children (both boys and girls) have signed the letter, and the teacher's name is Alexander Kisel. The return address is: Alexander Kisel, Teacher, School No.109, Kuibyshev (Volga), USSR.

I hope this will be of help to you. I can see that you are going to be kept busy!

With all best wishes | Edwin Morgan

MacDiarmid had sought EM's help as a translator. They had known each other since the mid-1950s, through the Glasgow University Literary Society, the Scottish–USSR Society and a shared interest in Attila József.

Ian Hamilton Finlay, poet and artist

19WCGW21471964

Dear Ian

So sorry you have been unwell; I hope that things are picking up again? I enjoyed POTH10 – I think especially the Robert Lax and that gawcy Guernsey dom or don's lovely/ lonely. I thought there must be something wrong with the Brazilian football poem but I couldn't see what: would you please throw light? Would you also tell me why Canal Stripe Series 4? What are the other 3? I thought this was very nicely executed – and true too, though I wonder if you really believe it? If little fields long for horizons, should writers of little poems not long for epics? Somewhere, underneath, deep down?? Finally's DV Coamedy?

I haven't written my concrete talk yet, but I have a sort of plan, and I shall be getting down to it soon. I've just been recording (for the Third in the autumn sometime) two half-scripted half-spontaneous dialogues (with my colleague Jack Rillie) on 'The Computer & the Critic' and 'The Computer and the Creator'. These I think will be quite interesting, if you happen to have a chance of listening in – I don't know yet when it'll be, possibly October. The dialogues will link up to some extent with the talk on concrete poetry and also with the special numbers on the 'vanguard' which the TLS plans for the autumn and which Dom Sylverstarre and I are both involved in. I've also had a letter from Mike Weaver about his proposed Kinetic Poetry Exhibition in Cambridge at the end of the year (you'll know about this), and I hope something comes of this idea, though I gather it will largely depend on the money situation, as usual. I have sent him my Persian cats poem (copy enclosed) (I didn't send you it before, did I?) which is a kind of 'moving' poem and which I thought might interest him. I'll enclose also (forgive me if I've sent these before) an example of 'committed concrete' which is another possibility (as of course some of the Brazilians have shown). Eugen Gomringer is going to bring out a pamphlet of my concretes (24 poems); I've sent him the typescript and he hopes to start the printing quite soon, so it may be out this year. I am impressed and heartened by the <u>friendly interest</u> and <u>immediate reaction</u> of Eugen and Augusto de Campos – what a change it is from the dead hand or polite smile of literary England which wonders what you are up to but hardly thinks it is worth while to find out! Do you not find this?

Tell me – in Dom Silvo's last letter he mentioned Margaret Lothian – does she write concrete poetry? and if she does can I see any of it? (I'm thinking of my BBC talk.) And also can you tell me anything about Robert Lax?

The kettle boils – for my tame tea – | Yours aye | Eddie

Robert Lax was an American poet, both meditative and minimalist. Dom Sylvester Houédard* was born on Guernsey. Mike Weaver would later co-edit *Form* with Stephen Bann*. EM's 'French Persian Cats Having a Ball', and his committed 'Starryveldt' on the Sharpeville massacre of black protesters by South African police, are in *CP*: 161, and 157–58.

Glasgow 14/15 July 1964

My dear Silvas Terras
    I had just begun to write you when your second package
arrived today (no mailstrike in prinknash) so I am beginning
again. You shower me with goodthings, typestracts: I loved
your M U G A, very interesting to see the back of the <u>organic</u>
being broken in this medium; when the non-square one in
your second letter fell out and I picked it up I said, Ah, a tree,
but then your signature made me turn it up the other way and
it looked like a stream of donations pouring into a piggybank,
or the bottom half of an eggtimer in full sift, so that (these
interpretations being a wee thing improbable) I am now at a
loss and have to ask you whether you did sign it the wrong way
up??? Your BURNT KA-O was a nice idea too, though I agree
ill reproduced in the Bulletin. Anyhow – let me add my voice
(would I could add money too) for you to publish these stracts
somehow/time/SOON; at least blown-ups in Cambridge
will be something. Yes, I have recently heard from Mike
Weaver and have replied very glad to cooperate etc any way
I can – sent him a couple of conceivably motorizable poems
for his comment and will do some thinking about the whole
matter when I can. <u>Many</u> thanks for all your addresses and
documentations. I must write to *Link* to get a copy of the issue
that will have your article; it's a magazine I have never seen. I
am enclosing first copy of *The Insect Trust Gazette* though of
course your wide web may already have snapped it up; it has
features – Burroughs, Gysin, Artaud, computer prose poems,
Jackson MacLow, Robert Basara – that will interest you, and
two quite non-concrete bits of Genet translated by me. – I
am sorry not to have commented on your EYEAR 1 but then
you didn't <u>ask</u> for comments and your documentation was so
full that I couldn't honestly say you had omitted anything, nor
could I disagree with your analysis and your First Nine Things
except that I think your point 9 (concrete non-mimetic) is a
somewhat <u>severe</u> reading of the situation since art of any kind
is and must be in <u>some</u> way mimetic and I find no disgrace
or contamination in this – or should I put it this way, that

the further concrete moves away from some sense of mimesis the less interesting it becomes (e.g. Emmett Williams), and I might add of point 7 that again I feel this as too rigorous and definite, since <u>some</u> concrete is didactic or satirical and this is as it should be, since I look on concrete as a medium in which <u>different</u> things can be done – a Brazilian poem on Castro's Cuba as well as a pattern of exclamation-marks by Diter Rot. I wondered if in finding as <u>many</u> points as 9 you were in danger of narrowing down the valuable openness and potentiality of spatialism???? The only point of documentation that strikes me, and it is very minor: when you were describing the beginnings of concrete in GB you said 'thru eg & the brazilians' – which is loosely correct, but in my own case the initial knowledge and impetus came from the <u>Portuguese</u> concretist E.M de Melo e Castro in Covilha to whom I wrote in May 1962 after he had a letter in TLS about concrete poetry; he sent me the anthology of *Poesia Concreta* published in Lisbon through the Embaixada do Brazil and containing of course the Brazilians' work: that was what set me off. That letter in TLS is worth mentioning as presumably the first definite British reference in print to international concrete movement? I told IHF about the letter, and I also sent a copy of it to Augusto de Campos who later asked to see it... – My BBC talk (short, 20 minutes) is not yet written but I hope it will be very soon; it has been accepted in skeleton outline by the Third but of course I don't know when it will be broadcast – sometime in autumn presumably. There may be a tieup with two dialogues I have just recorded (the other voice is my colleague Jack Rillie at GU) for the Third on 'The Computer & the Critic' and 'The Computer & the Creator' – these are half-hour talks which will be going out with the autumn leaves, I believe as part of a series of similar discussions of electronic music etc – SO possibly TLS & BBC will have a grand joint vanguard ball which will itself lead up to the Cambridge manifestation. I'll certainly send you a copy of my concrete talk when I have it done, and perhaps you will be able to work in a mention of it at some point. The talk of course will be simple and vastly selective, since one can't shower names dates titles etc in a broadcast talk of this kind.

I am sending this off now, and I shall try to return and comment on with all alacrity your TLS piece which many

thanks let see (though I am busy reading scripts as member of
Play Panel for Arts Council: thus the summer passes!) – May
see you October then? (unfortunately busiest month with
university new term, and in our case new professor too!) –

All best wishes as ever | eadwine

Prinknash Abbey in Gloucestershire is where dsh served as a Bene-
dictine monk. 'Typestract' was EM's invented term for dsh's exper-
imentations with the vertical and horizontal axes of typewriting,
creating intricate patterns for contemplation. MUGA was the title
of one such typestract sent previously. EM's 'Construction for I.K.
Brunel' (CP: 190) appeared in Link (Nov.–Dec. 1964). The Insect Trust
Gazette, a counter-cultural magazine, was co-edited by Belasco,
Levy and Basara* in 1964–68. EYEAR 1 was a talk given by dsh at the
RCA, London, soon to appear in Evergreen Review. He had also sent
a draft of his article on concrete poetry for the TLS special avant-
garde issues 1 and 2 (Aug.–Sep. 1964).

Iain Crichton Smith, poet and novelist

19 Whittingehame Court
10 September 1964

Dear Iain

Many thanks for letting me see the essays, which I have
enjoyed reading. I think they say some penetrating and
important things both about individual writers and about
Scottish literature in general, and for that reason I would very
much like to see them published; but I also think you will find
it not too easy to get them published in their present form.
Would you not consider doing a spot of rewriting or going
over? To me, they bear signs of haste which detract from their
value. The presentation is too offhand to do your ideas justice.
Often you strike up some interesting train of thought and then
drop it just when it is developing, and go on to something else;
you seldom think an idea through, and this leaves the reader
with tantalized, disappointed feelings – the final impression
being that these were more like sketches for critical essays

than the actual essays themselves. I know you more than once disclaim any 'scholarly' intent, but I don't think this will cut much ice with publishers at the present time, when literary criticism has become so professional. Is 'scholarship' in this context not simply a greater desire for the reader's help and convenience? (E.g. you don't say where your quotations come from, so that people can't look them up in their context; you have a lot of misspellings, wrong names, wrong titles, etc.) – I mention these things only because I'm trying to put myself in the place of a publisher's reader with your MS on his lap, and reading between the lines of Temple Smith's letter I suspect that the rather 'unprepared' and provincial look of the typescript (with even the pages not numbered) may well have put him off. It shouldn't make any difference how a thing is presented, but I think in practice it does. I am sure that if you had sent the essays one by one to magazines, many of them would have come back not with rejection slips but with requests for tidying up and would-you-not-make-this-paragraph-clearer! If you can be bothered to do this, I suggest you carefully and ruthlessly work them over before you send them out again. It really wouldn't be time wasted, because they are very much worth publishing.

Your essays on the novelists are much superior to those on the poets, which is strange but undoubtedly true. You seem to me to have a real insight into what has been wrong with the Scottish novel, and you are bang on in what you say about Brown, Gibbon, Hogg, and Scott. Bringing in *Young Adam* was a brilliant stroke too. I thought the essays on Carlyle and Stevenson weren't as convincing as they might have been – they were not close enough to the text, and the final impression was a little lightweight. I'm afraid I can't share your (and MacDiarmid's) admiration for le beau David! And I think you are well off the mark with 'Holy Willie's Prayer'. Both Dunbar and MacDiarmid really need a more extended consideration than you give them. In your last essay you lament 'no serious playfulness' – what about Edwin Morgan and Ian Hamilton Finlay? (Seriously, though, some of your generalizations, stimulating through they are, could do with more evidence; when you write a book, you have a case to prove, you are not Moses with tablets as perhaps you are when

you are writing a poem…) – These are just some random notes
that occur to me as I think back over the essays. But let me
reiterate that the general impression was one of great interest
and considerable agreement, and I hope what I have said will
not seem presumptuous or unhelpful.

It might be worth trying Oliver & Boyd or Edinburgh
University Press, do you think?

I expect you will be back in the thick of your classes now.
We have a new professor to look forward to (though he won't
be fully with us till 1965) – Peter Butter from Belfast (you may
have seen his little book on Edwin Muir?). I have been asked
to address the Aberdeen University society 'Poetry North' in
October – I expect you will know about it. I think there is
some quite good poetry being written by students at Aberdeen
just now, so the visit might be quite interesting. I hope your
mother is keeping better. My own father is out of hospital and
reasonably well again now, though pretty weak on his feet. My
'holiday' this year was a week at Edinburgh – fortunately a hot
and sunny one; it's a nice place and area to wander about in.

All the best as ever | Eddie

The carelessness of his friend's approach to presentation was a
source of wonder and exasperation to EM, who was fastidious in
matters of proof-reading. Maurice Temple Smith* was a director of
Eyre and Spottiswoode. Among the young poets in Aberdeen were
Rory Watson and Alexander Hutchison*.

Alexander Hutchison, poet and academic

14 September 1964

Dear Mr Hutchison

Dr Gorrie of the Saltire Society has just passed on to me
your letter and pamphlet of poems and asked me to reply. As
you may know, the Saltire Society is not publishing poetry at
the moment (I think it would like to, if it had more funds)
and the *New Saltire* magazine has also unfortunately had
to suspend publication. Your problem is really part of the

general difficulty which everyone experiences of getting poetry published in Scotland. I enjoyed your pamphlet and I think the poems are interesting and promising, though if you were submitting them to a publisher the collection is a bit on the thin side and should be added to if possible, as it's hard to make a firm judgement on ten short poems. As far as Scotland is concerned, the main publishers don't seem to be interested in contemporary poetry and it would probably be a waste of your time trying them. The most likely publishers would be William MacLellan in Glasgow and M. Macdonald in Edinburgh, both of whom as I expect you will know have done a good deal of poetry. MacLellan has a new paperback poetry series just now and might be the best to approach. I am wondering if, since you say there are four or five of you writing at Aberdeen, some sort of group publication might not be best proposition? Young painters usually begin with group exhibitions but young poets haven't much tried the same method; perhaps they should. I knew that some promising poetry was being written at Aberdeen when I judged the BBC universities poetry competition with Norman MacCaig recently. James Rankin and Rory Watson in particular are names that struck us both, though no doubt there are others. Have you had much published in magazine/newspapers? In some ways it's a good idea to build up magazine publication before you take the plunge of a book, if only because it lets you see your poems in cold print and receive comments! There's the *Glasgow Review*, *Lines Review*, *Cleft*, *Extra Verse*. And there's no harm trying the BBC (send them to George Bruce in Edinburgh) for 'Scottish Life & Letters'. But in general it's a case of plugging away and exploring as many avenues as possible.

Let me know if I can help you more specifically, for example with addresses of any of the things I've mentioned. I shall be coming to Aberdeen to address the Poetry North society on 30 October so possibly I may see you. In any case I shall be glad to hear from you.

Yours sincerely | Edwin Morgan

Hutchison was born on the north-east coast of Scotland, later lecturing in British Columbia and Scotland. Returning from the

Poetry North visit, EM wrote 'Aberdeen Train' (*CP*: 152) and sent it to them.

Ian Hamilton Finlay, poet and artist

de mon moulin à
19 Whittingehame Court
20 October 1964

Dear Ian
    So many thanks for City Poem, Telegrams, and Lollipoth.
The Lollipoth issue was a nice idea – though perhaps you
should follow it up with a stern masculine Quidchewing
number to counter the suggestion of Infantile Regression.
I must confess I'd like to see a bit more Hairy Knee in the
magazine. Am I alone in this request? Does it sound daft? Or
do you see what I mean? Gritty is usually a term of dispraise
but I think what I want to feel is more grittiness, more bite,
more friction... I notice, by the way, that tonight's 'Evening
Times' quotes the dromedary poem – ironically, but still. I
liked the bold type on Augusto's poem – just right, I thought.
(I'm also very fond of black and yellow, I think it's my favourite
colour combination – [The Bumbee of Whittingehame,
bz] –. LANG MAY YOUR WINDMILL REEK STOP
MUCH PREFER COMIC GIRL AU PAIR TO ROSES
SENTIMENTAL QUERY LONG LIVE COMEDY
X MARKS THE SPOT STOP YOURS ALL ALONG
EMILY BRONTË. It would be nice to have some revolving
poetic telegrams on the revolving restaurant of the new
London post office tower 600 feet up which I see Billy Butlin
is getting ready to open in January 1966 – apples and cables/
capable apples/applicables... all round the walls. Anyhow,
I enjoyed your telegrams very much. – I don't see why you
shouldn't print a part of Eugen's poem, as the whole thing
seems in any case to be an extract from something longer. I
have just had a request for some Gomringer from Bob Basara
of the *Insect Trust Gazette*, so if you can decide perhaps which
half of that poem you'd like to print I could send Basara tother
half? Could you let me know about this? – I met on Saturday

the editor of the *New Hungarian Quarterly* who is visiting this country and I agreed to do a little poetry article for him; reciprocally he will get someone in Budapest to write a piece on modern Hungarian poetry for the *Glasgow Review*. He was interested in my Attila József and will probably print some of them in his magazine. He says poetry is a national passion in Hungary; the novel and drama are nowhere in comparison. He said – and I believe him – that some Hungarian poetry is among the best in Europe. What anguish it must be to write in a language that the rest of the world will never learn! He was quite touched to discover that someone in remote Scotland had had a go at József, even through indirect translation. He told me there is a vanguard poetry in Hungary too (not mentioned by TLS), and he promised to send me some apparently concrete poetry by a man called Sándor Weörös which he thought I'd be interested in. Hungarian, because of its elaborate affix system, seems to be well suited to concrete. The editor was a most cultivated man, and I got the impression of a most cultivated country too, isolated but sending out its feelers to the world... These 'conversations with another place' are always moving and illuminating; they make the rest of the day they take place in seem drab.

Yes I know, Tom Scott should be answered, and I wish you would do it. I am absolutely too busy with university things at the moment to do it myself. This letter is just being rattled off, as you will no doubt find when you skelter through it. Forgive its inadequacies.

Yours at midnight | Yeddie

IHF's *Telegrams from My Windmill* appeared in 1964. EM's translation of Eugen Gomringer's* long poem 'The Book of Hours II' ('das stundenbuch II') is in *CT*: 296–300. The editor of *New Hungarian Quarterly* was Miklós Vájda, who admired EM's Hungarian translations. Unfamiliarity leads to a misspelling of the surname of Sándor Weöres*.

Martin Bax, editor and paediatrician

19 Whittingehame Court
25 October 1964

Dear Martin Bax

Thank you for your letter. I am returning 'In Sobieski's
Shield' in a version that I hope will be easier to read. I've
divided it into five blocks (each ending with a short line). I
don't want to divide it any further than this, or it will lose the
interior monologue feeling and flow. Does this meet the case
do you think?

I am also enclosing some other poems and translations as
you request. 'In the Snack Bar' and 'From a City Balcony' are
among a batch of poems I sent to Anselm Hollo for the new
magazine *Horde*; I don't know yet whether he is going to take
them, but I thought I'd let you see them anyway.

I don't know how the rumour started up that I was going
to organize a poetry festival next year at Edinburgh – it's the
first I've heard of it! I suppose because I took the chair at two
of Jim Haynes's unofficial poetry get-togethers at the Traverse
Theatre this year, someone has been putting two and two
together and getting a lot more than four. Actually the Festival
authorities are not too keen on any more literary conferences,
and it's very uncertain what will happen next year. However,
if I hear anything I'll let you know. It would be good to have
some *Ambit* readings.

With best wishes | Yours sincerely | Edwin Morgan

EM had sent 'In Sobieski's Shield' (*CP*: 196) to *Ambit*, edited by Bax,
who said that the poem's original lack of punctuation had created
problems for some of the editorial staff.

Ian Hamilton Finlay, *poet and artist*

22 November 1964

Dear Yian

Do you still have copies of Nos.1 & 2 of *Signalz(s)*? Silvester tells me you are a sort of distributor of it, and I'd like to have the first 2 numbers. Can you send me a copy of each, and I'll send you a postal order?

I was sorry I couldn't see more of Silvester who was in Glasgow for a couple of days. He was at my place one afternoon and then I saw him again at Robert Tait's the following evening together with David Irwin and a few others, where we spent most of the time going through his portfolio of tres riches heures du duc de typestract. He has done some things with the typewriter which I wouldn't have thought possible, and I have always had a soft spot for human ingenuity and patience (Chinese concentric ivory balls weren't just sweated labour); but he wasn't giving anything away – there is an interesting sort of Mata Hari element in him which goes with his having been in intelligence during the war. Remarkable man – I hope somebody will someday write his biography.

About the Gomringer; I think it will be all right to keep the second half of the poem until you are ready to use it. I'm sure Eugen won't mind. I shall send the first half to Bob Basara. No word yet of my own pamphlet from Eugen. I hope the second printing hasn't had to be scrapped as well as the first!

Charm. Yes, I love the 'mite of charm' as you call it and I think it is a valuable counterpoise to what one finds in some other quarters. At the same time it's important to recognise the limitations. There are too many things in human experience which are neither charming in themselves nor can they be talked into any kind of charming expression. Like Jane Austen, you might reply that you left such things to 'other pens'. Still, it worries me a little that you should be so little worried about this, and that you should assume that a concern with violence is only 'fashionable' or 'easy'. It seems to me that on your view of the matter it would be impossible to write any poem on such a subject as Sharpeville, no matter what one felt about it. Well, I'm sure Jonathan Williams wouldn't accept this any more than I do. One must at least <u>try</u>. It is no use being ashamed of a simple reaction to a bloody event just because the reaction happens to coincide with the perhaps conventional and naive response of a group of leftwing liberals. My own poem tries to guard against the charge you bring, how successfully I don't know. What does Vae victis mean in the last line? Is that 'easy' or 'sentimental'? I don't think so.

Where I agree with you is that it is very <u>difficult</u> to avoid the sort of traps you mention, in writing any kind of Sharpeville-type poem; certainly I'm not claiming I've escaped them; but I strongly believe such poetry must be attempted (as the Brazilian poets do also) if we are to avoid formalism and (in the end) triviality. This has nothing to do with being in or out of fashion, it is just a question of the human centrality of what one is doing. Even Emily Dickinson, it seems to me, had a hairier knee than Lorine Niedecker... recluse or no recluse.

However – I must fly to the post. May your lollipop become an Electric Eel.

Yours aye | Yeddie

Signalz (the first issue featured this spelling) was the bulletin of the Centre for Advanced Creative Study, an alternative 1960s arts organisation founded in London by David Medalla. Bob Basara* edited the *Insect Trust Gazette*. Eugen Gomringer* published EM's *Starryveldt*. Its title poem reflects the Sharpeville massacre and ends: 'VAE VICTIS' (in Latin, 'woe' or 'alas' for the conquered ones) (*CP*: 158).

Ted Hughes, poet

English Department
The University
25 November 1964

Dear Mr Hughes
    Recently we set your poem 'A Woman Unconscious' as a class essay in interpretation. Those of us who were marking the essays had a great tussle and a good deal of disagreement over one of the lines, and it is because none of us came up with a solution satisfying to all the others that I am writing to ask you if you would like to comment on the line as you see it. The essays have all been marked and handed back, so you need have no fear about having to 'supply an answer' which would commit you to 'the' interpretation! But purely as a matter of interest on a puzzling point, I'd be delighted if you could say something about it.
    It is line 20, and the problem is really one of syntax. Is 'Did a lesser death come' a question (but you have no question-mark), or a statement meaning 'a lesser death did come' (but this involves an odd and unidiomatic sort of inversion, and in any case the past definite tense seems not to follow from the concessive future of 'though bomb [should come to] be matched against bomb…'), or possibly even something itself concessive ('if a lesser death should come') (but then where is the main verb?).
    Do forgive this intrusion. It's really very improper to plague living poets about their 'meaning'. But it would be of great interest if you felt a comment was in order.

Yours sincerely | ▤❘❘ | Edwin Morgan

Hughes replied that there should in fact be a question mark at the end, but that this would have forced 'undesirable overtones on to the last three lines, which more or less assume that the question has already answered itself No'.

Bob Basara, editor and poet

19 Whittingehame Court
23 December 1964

Dear Bob Basara

    Sorry I haven't replied sooner – it has been a busy
term at the university. Now shaken off the coils of
lectures into the coils of Christmas – but trying to
catch up with letters. I am enclosing a few things,
two poems of my own and some translations of the
Brazilian concretistas and Gomringer (a new poem
he sent me recently). Use any of these if they
appeal. I hope when I have a moment to get down
to some further work in this line and will send
you anything that seems interesting. I suppose
you will have seen recent concrete number of
Ian Finlay's *Poor.Old.Tired.Horse*? By the
way, Ian Finlay (you know his address – 24
Fettes Row, Edinburgh) will advise you
better than I can about possible
printers in Scotland as he himself
has shopped around quite a bit.
I am about to shop myself
for a shirt for my
father's Christmas
stocking if that
makes sense so
must run with
a best wishes
wave here to-
wards Point
Pleasant
Pa
I   am yours dear sir etcetera

Basara was editing Issue 2 of *Insect Trust Gazette*, based in Point

Pleasant, Pennsylvania, and had asked EM for contributions for an issue of concrete, kinetic and phonetic poetry.

Kulgin Duval, *bookseller and editor*

24 January 1965

Dear Kulgin

Many thanks for the SGS book – cheque enclosed. Isn't it a pity this wasn't published properly in 1947? It comes rather late now to make much of an impact, since the mood is so different, and Joyce has been taken over by the scholars & academies... I have been reviewing it for *New Statesman*, I suppose it will be in this week if they have space.

My other enclosure is a pamphlet hot from the press of Eugen Gomringer in Switzerland. I hope it will entertain you even if it fails to convert you to concrete poetry!

I liked your anti-Craigiad. Yes, I had seen SSL. I haven't written for them except that they have now asked me to review Kenneth Buthlay's book on MacDiarmid. The annoying thing about Craig of course is that he is one of the few serious critics of Scottish literature – if he didn't just see everything through the narrow slits of his iron mask. Like Leavis, he is full of interesting analysis but wrong judgements.

Speaking of collecting paintings, I must admit I have a watercolour of a Motherwell steelworker in an open-necked (open-chested indeed) red shirt, but the choice wasn't based on political motives! Certainly I wouldn't object to a Newmarket scene. Perhaps you will take up painting in your odd moments at Falkland?

All good wishes, books, bindings, etc. for | 1 9 6 5 | Eddie

EM's review of Sydney Goodsir Smith's *Carotid Cornucopius* appeared in *New Statesman* LXIX: 1769, 5 February 1965. *Studies in Scottish Literature* ('SSL') had been launched by G. Ross Roy in 1963. David Craig's *Scottish Literature and the Scottish People* (1961) followed the model of a 'Great Tradition' in literature posited by F.R. Leavis. The pamphlet was *Starryveldt*. *The Red Shirt* (1952) by William Baillie was later gifted to the University of Glasgow's Hunterian Gallery. Duval moved his rare book business from Rose Street in Edinburgh to the more rural Falkland.

Cavan McCarthy, editor and librarian

26 January 1965

Dear Cavan McCarthy

Many thanks for flow of letters and *Tlaloc*! No I didn't at all mind your comments on the spacepoem, I wasn't by any means entirely happy about the presentation myself, and I agree with a lot of your criticism. I don't think however that the answer is John Furnival's letter-pictures (which incidentally I like very much), as I am doing something different: to me the words and sounds are important and must emerge clearly, to JF they are more like bricks with which he builds and often they are set askew or overlaid so that they cannot be read, and this is not what I am after. I think what I am doing can be done on a (horizontal rather than vertical) page. I knew the mixture of different types of poetry which you refer to was a risk, but it was a calculated one. Be not afeard, the isle is full of voices (or noises) – I wanted a succession of different noises/voices mechanical/human scrambled/clear all the way through; perhaps the answer is simply different type faces. And better spacing. Anyhow I shall have further thoughts about the whole piece, so do just keep the copy I sent you at the moment.

Yes, I think probably a mixed group of poems as in No.3 is best for *Tlaloc*, unless you become so interested in the spatialist thing that you feel you must run it exclusively. By the way, should Dom SH's SATISAKI at the bottom of his first rhopal not be ASITASIK?

I liked your blokpoem. There is so much sound-effect in the original poem itself that this treatment seems quite in keeping, and the mesmeric melancholy, though floating about uprooted, is still there, like a series of echoes, or things half-recognized in flickering light. Uch and foch are a nice pair, and so is aptitsa the chemist-bird? The Kruchonykh piece is as you say hard to translate in any real sense except on a scientific basis of sound-frequencies and/or associations. It would be a real test for a translating machine. I have never managed to see Kruchonykh's work except for that example. Some of Khlebnikov is interesting too in this zaumny yazyk style, but again hard to get hold of. I haven't seen the Pergamon anthology you mention; must look out for it, even though it is badly printed! I haven't seen Anselm Hollo's collected Voznesensky translations, and I must ask him if this volume has in fact appeared. I've seen a few of them in *Evergreen* and elsewhere – very vigorous though very free.

My booklet from Gomringer has just arrived, so I send you a copy – hope it may interest you!

Yours | Edwin Morgan

McCarthy, a student of Russian at Leeds University, founded *Tlaloc* (1964–70) with an emphasis on concrete and visual poetry. He wondered whether EM's typed draft of 'Spacepoem 1' (*CP*: 194) might be better served by the large-letter poster technique of John Furnival. The 'blokpoem' was a concrete experiment in the spirit of Alexander Blok (1880–1921). 'Zaumny yazyk' is the 'trans-sense language' of neologisms, odd sound combinations and morphological play in the work of futurists such as Kruchenykh and Khlebnikov (*CT*: 335–37, 423–27).

Ian Hamilton Finlay, *poet and artist*

17 March 1965

Dear Ian

Do forgive long silence but it is just sheer pressure of work. Can you use any of the enclosed b o a t s a n d p l a c e s for POTH15? (Notes: caique is pronounced ka-eek; a Van cat is a special kind that comes from Lake Van area in Turkey.) Many thanks for the two very delightful standing poems and for the poster-poems, of which I think I like best the Albert-Birot with your Circus Smack a close second – but all are a pleasure. I am thinking of putting up the Albert Birot on the wall of a little corridor that leads to my room at the university – I don't see why one shouldn't make these posters posters after all. It will be interesting to see if anyone objects – or if anyone comes to enquire how much the tock sorry tickets really cost. – I hope you will do more of these. (May I keep your *Tealeaves & Fishes* a little while longer – will have a chance to read it quite soon now, as university term draws to a close for Easter –) I will write very soon to Ernst Jandl too, and then return you his letter.

Yes it is perhaps sad in a way about the concrete divergences which you refer to, but that was inevitable, and some of the differences were there (inherent) from the beginning, e.g. as between Eugen and the Brazilians – in that case perhaps connected with the whole world of different national temperament and involvement. I always preferred the Brazilians, as you know – they were more gay, sprightly, and purposive, and I think more intelligent too; at any rate let me not defend them needlessly, the best of their work will stand, as will the best of Eugen's, I'm sure. The rifts of course became clearer in *Les Lettres* when the Noigandres poets and Henri Chopin as well as others didn't sign the Pierre Garnier manifesto. And in Brazil itself there has been wild disagreement between the Noigandres folk and the Praxis group (who see themselves as superseders). In the UK although there is some opposition to concrete as you say, it's in many cases not strong but rather tentative or suspicious or honestly probing; George Dowden's article in *Poetmeat*, for instance, was a sincere attempt to define a romanticist's suspicion that poetry was being sold over to a cold and dreaded classicism, and no one would deny this danger exists (you say, for example, that you want 'purity', and that's fine up to a point, but beyond a certain point purity is simply death, and I would run from it crying 'Ginsberg!' –), which is one reason why my humour and your boasts may be of some use, both tying concrete to certain bollards of human life and human pleasure. But in fact concrete is still spreading, diversifying, and I hope leavening…

Yes, it <u>is</u> monstrous if what you say about the <u>OBScV</u> is true. But he's still working on it and this may not be final. It's not very long since he wrote to me saying he was putting one of mine in. I don't think there would be any point in writing to the OUP; they have made him editor and an editor is perfectly free to include or exclude as he thinks fit; the mistake (as we all knew at the time) was in appointing someone so unobjective in the first place. But as we seem to be in correspondence – Dear Morgan... Dear Scott... – I might write to him direct. Let me do it in my own way.

Martin Bax tells me he has put two of my science-fiction poems in the current *Ambit* but I haven't seen a copy yet. Do you ever see the magazine?

Love from my littered desk – | Yeddie

'Boats and Places' (*CP*: 175) responded to IHF's request for 'boats, shores, tides, fish' for *Poor.Old.Tired.Horse*. Tom Scott, who wrote in Scots, co-edited *The Oxford Book of Scottish Verse* (1966) which included EM's 'The Second Life' but nothing from IHF. *Les Lettres Françaises* was edited by Louis Aragon who had been involved in Dada and Surrealism. *Poetmeat*, a counter-cultural review (1963–67), published 'The New British Poetry', Issue 8, in April 1965, featuring, among others, Roy Fisher*, Anselm Hollo*, Michael Horowitz*, Michael Shayer* and Gael Turnbull*.

Andrew Jameson, academic and translator

English Department
The University
15 April 1965

Dear Andy

It was good of you to let me know about the Flegon Press magazine – I have sent for a copy. I don't seem to have any time at the moment for translations, but I'd like at least to have some Okudzhava texts available so that I can be brooding over them even if I'm not working on them. Of the other books you mentioned in your February letter (shockingly by me not answered till now!) the only one which I haven't got and would much like to see some time is the *Vecher Poezii* 1964. I couldn't do anything to it just now but if you were able to lend it to me say about the end of May I'd be grateful: but only of course if you are not using it yourself. As I haven't ordered the Pasternak in the 'Biblioteka Poets' series I'd be glad to take your second copy as you suggest (if it comes through). And ah yes, your PS – let me know when you would like to borrow the text of my two computer talks. Both talks were to have been rebroadcast but nothing has happened so far.

I share your fondness for the verbal/musical/readoutable element in poetry and for that reason I am not wholly satisfied by or committed to concrete, or at least concrete which is purely visual in effect. I still write quite a lot of old linear type poems and can't see myself not doing so. But I think concrete was (is? – it's beginning to break up in various directions) worth investigating.

The Brazilian concretian Haroldo de Campos has been telling me about his marathon effort to persuade Ferlinghetti to open the pages of *City Lights Journal* to some South American concrete – beat suspiciousness of concrete is of course understandable – though personally I have been able to take both – after much persuasion wringing a half promise from LF that if translations could be found convincing enough he might etcetera, though "why do you down dere want to imitate dem <u>ibm</u> machines?"! So I have undertaken to try providing versions that will sell São Paulo to San Francisco...

Best greetings this cold wet | cloudy good Friday |
    Yeddie Morgan

Working in Russian Studies at Oxford, Jameson had sent EM news of a Russian magazine published by Flegon Press, and also offered to lend him poetry for translation.

Ernst Jandl, poet

30 April 1965

Dear Ernst Jandl
Forgive me for not replying more promptly to your letter. We have a new professor in the Department here, and our days are thick with discussion of new plans, courses, lectures,

etc! But I certainly hope that I shall be able to escape for long enough to see you when you come to Glasgow. I shall probably be freer on the 20th than the 19th – perhaps you could come and have lunch at the university on the 20th. But anyway, let me know when you arrive and we shall arrange something. You could telephone me at the university, and I have also given you my home phone number. Yes, Glasgow is worth exploring! I imagine it must be very different from Vienna, though I have never been there.

With all best wishes | Yours | Edwin Morgan

Jandl, a sound poet from Vienna visiting Britain in May 1965, hoped to meet EM. He wanted to explore Glasgow 'to which I feel greatly attracted as it is said to be a big and ugly industrial city' – a positive feature compared with the bourgeois boredom of Vienna.

Ian Hamilton Finlay, poet and artist

19 Whittingehame Court W2
on the last of April 1965

Dear Ian

A brief note to say it was 25 *Starryveldts*. I am glad you managed to get more from EG. I'd like to have a few myself for emergencies.

Gledfield – is it a happy field, or one where you must watch out for kites. The Wild Kite Press. I was looking you up on the map and you are almost in Sutherland. It seems terribly far. Who will ever see you? Erikr Linklatr? Kneel Kgunn? Somhairle Mac-Mac Ghill-Eathain? I know: Jane Duncan of Jemimaville; her next book will be *My Friend Ian*. And there's Kulgin Duval immured in Falkland. All this overspill? Is this a trend? And think of Biggar! There seems to be no one but me who loves 'that enchanted metropolitan twilight'. O Scott Fitzgerald! O Thomas Wolfe! 'Thrive, cities!' said Whitman. Amen to that. I can see that I shall have to stick to my post.

Is it really a farmhouse? Chickens? Pigs?

Many thanks for *Ocean Stripe* 3 which gives a quiet joy.

Why has the bow only three colours – is this a deliberate stylization to avoid a too obviously imitative effect?

Do you think you could let me have the Frances Cornford book back if you have finished with it – I'd like to look at that Blok translation.

Poetry is now halfway between trickling and pouring in for the anthology.

Back to the last – | Yours aye | Eddie

IHF had agreed to sell *Starryveldt* via Wild Hawthorn Press. Gledfield was the Sutherland farmhouse to which IHF had moved ('gled' in Scots meaning both 'glad' and the 'kite' as bird of prey). Jane Duncan was known for her My Friends series of semi-autobiographical novels and her children's stories, set in the Highlands. The anthology was the *Scottish Poetry* series that EM would co-edit with Maurice Lindsay* and George Bruce* from 1966 to 1970.

Barry Cole, poet and novelist

10 June 1965

Dear Barry Cole

It was good of you to write and enclose a copy of your rejoinder to Wiseman. I am glad to know that someone has written, as I didn't want to do it myself, though that review depressed me and made me feel isolated, as such reviews in Scotland (and how typical it was) always tend to do. It is such an uphill fight here that I can assure you an occasional mite of support comes as welcome to me as it does to IHF. I never find it easy not to be affected by reviews, and this one got me down quite a bit, especially as it was clearly a put-up job in so far as the editor had deliberately chosen someone to attack concrete poetry – which of course is common enough editorial practice to rouse controversy, but there's too much sheer malicious shooting-down in Scotland, with no attempt to understand anything new or unfamiliar, and moments of despair are always waiting to pounce when one thinks about this. I think my own views on concrete are probably quite like your own; but

to speak of anything like <u>humour</u> or <u>relief</u> is to invite blind
opposition in some quarters. Well anyhow: many thanks for
writing.

I have been much taken by the poems you submitted for
Scotch Poetry, and I hope very much that we shall be taking
two or three of these. We are still knee-deep in the last batch
of end-of-May submissions but have an editorial meeting this
Saturday to make a first leet; it shouldn't be too long before we
can let you know what we are taking.

Are you going to the Great Royal Hall Scene on Friday, I
wonder? From all accounts it should be quite an occasion!

Best regards | Sincerely yours | Edwin Morgan

Cole had sent a robust response to Christopher Wiseman's negative
review of IHF's* *Telegrams from my Windmill* and EM's *Starryveldt*
in *The Glasgow Review*. *Scotch Poetry* refers to the first volume of
Scottish Poetry, in which Cole's work appeared. EM was unable to
attend the 'International Poetry Incarnation' at the Albert Hall on 11
June 1965, but sent a poem (*CP*: 199) to be read out at an event that
featured live and taped performances from a range of avant-garde
writers, such as Ginsberg*, Ferlinghetti, Hollo*, Logue, Horowitz*,
Jandl* and Burroughs.

David Hales, editor

English Department
The University
1 July 1965

Dear David Hales
Many thanks for your letter. I was interested to hear
that your Los Angeles editor had been trying to get some
MacDiarmid material – I expect it would be the book
on MacDiarmid by Duncan Glen published last year by
Chambers at 37/6 – a useful well-documented study though
drably written and not strong on the critical side. MacDiarmid
is certainly a field to ponder, since the larger part of his work
in both poetry and prose is out of print. I think Macmillan

now hold the copyright of all the poetry, but there is a great lack of a 'Selected Essays' taken from the several volumes of literary and polemical essays which MacDiarmid has issued over the years – all of them now virtually unobtainable and commanding high prices on the secondhand market. MacDiarmid is regarded fairly generally now as a major author, and it seems absurd that so much of his writing should be unavailable.

The Faber book you mention is probably their *Modern Scottish Poetry* which came out in 1946 and is now being re-edited and brought up to date by Maurice Lindsay. As this is a book which will probably be used in schools and universities (it will be the only book on its subject), it would be worth investigating for paperback possibilities I should imagine? This anthology of course only covers the 20th century; what I had in mind was one dealing with the whole Scottish tradition. There is no hardback in this field which is entirely satisfactory, and that is why I suggested it ought to be a new book.

No, the Attila József unfortunately fell through and this is still unpublished, though a lot of poems have been in magazines. You never told me, by the way, <u>why</u> you were unable to proceed with this idea? Was there some difficulty over copyright or some other permission??

I have sent by surface mail a copy of my anthology of longer poems published here by Collins, which possibly you may not have seen.

Best regards | Eddie | Edwin Morgan

EM had written to Hales, New York manager of the University of California Press, with a proposal for an anthology of Scottish verse, from Dunbar and Henryson to the present day, with Gaelic representation.

Veronica Forrest-Thomson, poet and critic

1 July 1965

Dear Miss Forrest

Thank you for sending me your poems. The one I like best
is <u>A Propos Life</u> and the one I think would appeal most to Ian
Finlay is <u>Sea Scene from a Train</u>. <u>Antic</u> has possibilities which
I don't think have been fully exploited: its double deployment
in mirror form seems (to me) not quite interesting enough,
though I can see why you have done it. <u>Violence/Clash</u> is/
are an uneasy mixture of styles of approach and I feel the
least successful. I can see indeed from the various approaches
that you use in all these poems why you don't want a simple
label 'concrete' – you are clearly feeling your way in different
'objective' directions – but POTH as a magazine is not at all
dogmatically or narrowly conceived, and being printed there
would not commit you at all. I think you should certainly send
Ian Finlay the first two poems I mentioned, and any others
you have which are in similar modes. Mention my name
if you like. Your <u>Propos</u>-poem is very nicely and originally
done, and I think this is the vein you should encourage. –
Another magazine to try sometime is *Tlaloc*, edited by Cavan
McCarthy, 22 Brudenall Road, Leeds 6. It prints concrete as
well as 'normal' poetry.

With best wishes | Yours sincerely | Edwin Morgan

At a Glasgow poetry reading, Veronica Forrest (as she then was)
had asked about the possibility of publication by Wild Hawthorn
Press. Recognising that her own poems had more affinity with EM's
approach ('more cerebral and satirical than visual descriptive') she
had sent him some for comment.

Eugen Gomringer, poet and publisher

16 July 1965

Dear Eugen

So sorry you can't find my cheque! – I am enclosing another one for the same amount. So if the first one does turn up, will you just destroy it. It had your name on it, so I don't think anyone else would be able to cash it.

The Matterhorn: ah well, I saw the climbing party reach the top on television, and I think that will be enough for me. Very small mountains I can do, but rock-faces I leave to the dedicated! There is, however, a great beauty in snow ice sun and sky to which I am very susceptible.

I still have people asking for my booklet, but I have one or two copies left yet. I may have to ask you for some more. Are there many left now?

Every good wish – | Edwin Morgan

Gomringer had been writing, theorising and publishing concrete poetry since the mid-1950s. *Starryveldt* (1965) had already been reprinted from his press in Frauenfeld, Switzerland. A cheque for additional publications had been lost, perhaps in the complications of his planning for a mountaineering holiday in the Austrian Tyrol.

Eugen Gomringer, poet and publisher

19 Whittingehame Court
12 August 1965

Dear Eugen

Glad you got my second cheque all right: don't lose it! While you were among the mountains I was in the green valleys of Eire and walking along the Joyce-haunted Liffey. Certainly a lot of Scots go to the Continent now for holidays, but Ireland is perhaps a special favourite too, and in Dublin I heard many Glasgow voices. The overnight boat from Glasgow to Dublin has become quite an institution, with much drinking, singing, watching the stars, etc…

It's good to know that we need extra copies of the book. You should mark it 'second impression'! Would you please send me <u>30</u> copies at the moment, as I think I shall be able to dispose of these. Perhaps you would ask Ian Finlay if he wants any more?

I hope we shall have that beer sometime.

All the beset | bett | besetzt | bets | best | ∃⫪

Back from the Tyrol, Gomringer had written: 'I wanted to have a beer with you, somewhere on earth'. EM received 30 additional copies of *Starryveldt* by the end of August. Ian Hamilton Finlay* opened a bookshop/gallery in Edinburgh as an outlet for avant-garde work.

Haroldo de Campos, poet

12 August 1965

Dear Haroldo de Campos

Thanks you for your letter. I have had so many things to do that I have not yet been able to get down to translating the concrete material for you, but I hope to do it soon. I received your paraphrases of *Servitude of Passage* and *Alea I* all right and I shall get down to the translation at the earliest opportunity. May I also thank you and Augusto for so kindly sending me the Sousândrade *Inferno de Wall Street* which is a most remarkable work (though I have only looked through it quickly); you have done a good service in making this more widely known and giving it annotation. I didn't get the *Invenção* 4 which you say Augusto sent me, but I got a copy in fact from the *Times Literary Supplement* so all is well.

It was nice meeting Ernst Jandl when he was in Scotland. He sent me a sad postcard when he returned to Vienna, saying what a terrible place Vienna was! (Which I can hardly believe, though I've never been there.) My *Starryveldt* booklet has sold out, and Eugen Gomringer tells me he is having more copies printed. Jonathan Williams hasn't yet got round to doing my s i e s t a o f a h u n g a r i a n s n a k e but this slowness is not unusual – he spends so much of his time in transit across those mighty united states of his and correspondence with him is difficult! Did you know that John Sharkey in Bristol is bringing out a new magazine to be called *Lisn*, for concrete, semiotic, and allied material? I have just sent him some of my new *Newspoems* which are cutouts from newspapers, and he may be printing some of these.

With all best wishes as ever | Yours | Edwin Morgan

'Servitude of Passage' was translated as 'transient servitude' (*CT*: 286–92). The Joycean 'Alea I' would appear alongside it in the Mexican journal *El Corno Emplumado* 21, January 1967. 'Alea' is related to *aleatório*, random or indeterminate, with a possible echo of the Spanish *alear*, to alloy metals or to flutter wings or arms (see 24 September 1965). Joaquim de Sousândrade was a Brazilian contemporary of Baudelaire, whose reputation as a precursor of modernism was revived by the de Campos brothers. Edições Invenção was their publishing outlet.

Archie Turnbull, publisher

30 August 1965

Dear Mr Turnbull

Many thanks for your letter and for the photocopy of the page layout. I quite agree about the Penguin size, for handiness and I think for selling too – as people's habits seem geared much more now to the paperback format than to the older magazine size. My first impression was that perhaps the page could stand a few more lines – the right-hand page seemed a little 'thin', but this may be the poem itself. I like a fairly well-filled page, even for poetry.

As you will see, I am taking up your suggestion and sending you the typescript of my poems. Cape had asked me to submit a collection but in the event they turned it down as being 'too varied' for them (they seem to like homogeneous poets), adding lightly that they didn't 'imagine I would have much difficulty in finding a publisher'. I can understand the objection, but the use of different modes and styles is very much a part of what I am doing in poetry and I would want this to be represented to some extent. In this collection I have excluded my concrete poetry apart from one or two poems which verge on the concrete area. I have called the collection *The Second Life*, and I have added to it, though I don't think it would sit very well in the same book, the long poem 'The Whittrick', in case you might see some possibility in this. If your committee should be interested in publication, I shall of course be happy to discuss any suggested omission or rearrangement of material.

Yours sincerely | Edwin Morgan

Turnbull was Secretary to Edinburgh University Press. The discussion about design relates to the *Scottish Poetry* series. EM's rejected collection, *The Second Life*, would be published by EUP to great acclaim in 1968.

Ian Hamilton Finlay, *poet and artist*

21 September 1965

Dear Ian

c y t h e r a is lovely. I leave it lying around instead of on a shelf, and it's like having a blue cloud in the house. It reminds me of that passage near the end of *Finnegans Wake* – 'My great blue bedroom, the air so quiet, scarce a cloud. In peace & silence. I could have stayed up there for always only...' – Many thanks for this. I hope you liked the *Extra Verse* special? Robert is going to Edinburgh to do a PhD on metaphor. By the way, the EV biography mentions 2 things I haven't seen (though it also has omissions): *Canal Stripe* 8/6991 and *Origin* 6. Could you send/lend/sell me either/both of these? I like to have everything you do. I have quite a number of *Origin*s but not as far back as No.6. If you could lend me it I can have it copied and sent back quickly.

If it really is Robin Jenkins country you had better be careful that's all I can say. Love is a fervent cone-gatherer.

But I expect the west coast is far feyer than the east. Though there is always the Culbin Sands (which I have seen), and who knows what cathédrales are perhaps englouties there. Who is Dick? You must show me photographs sometime of your new outdoor concretions – Hansjörg Mayer told me about them when he revisited me on his way south.

Yes, I was sure that antisuprematist Irish postcard would appeal to your sense of – the word eludes me too. It's almost a thing you could keep outdoors. Except that then my message would soon be writ in water.

Eugen has printed another 100 of my *Starryveldt*s, so if you need any more will you write to him? Do you still receive any orders for it?

Life is very hectic here; I have never known so many things happening at once. Commonwealth Arts Festival, opening of Close Theatre Club, opening of Edinburgh's Civic Theatre, opening of university term... I shall be glad when I see November.

Yours aye | Yeddie

IHF's *Cythera*, printed by the Salamander Press (1965), was 'meant to be peaceful – a sort of concrete equiv. of some of the works of Matisse'. *Extra Verse* (c. 1959–66) published a special IHF number, issue 15. Robert (Tait)* would co-edit *Scottish International*. In Sutherland IHF and his wife Susan began their practice of reshaping landscape aesthetically, building a pond. Mayer published EM's *Emergent Poems* (*CP*: 133–36, 159). The Close, a studio theatre beside the Citizens' Theatre in Glasgow, featured experimental drama.

Haroldo de Campos, *poet*

24 September 1965

Dear Haroldo

Here are my versions of your *Servidão de Passagem* and *Alea I*, together with a few other translations I have made that you might want to pass on to Ferlinghetti. None have been published. I can't remember if I have perhaps sent some

of them before to Augusto, but anyway here they are if you
want to use them. I hope the versions of your two books are
reasonably satisfactory! I tried to reproduce as much of the
sound-effect as possible, as I think this is important in poetry
of this kind, and at times this meant I was going a little way
from the exact sense, but never I believe very far and always
in the spirit of the context as far as I understood it. I got so
interested in both books that I have translated them complete.
To save space and postage (!) I have typed out the separate
little sections continuously, with asterisks between sections.

By separate post I am sending you a copy of the
Sousândrade review, and also a copy of the magazine *Extra
Verse* which is a special Ian Hamilton Finlay number – perhaps
you have not seen it. I shall have a concrete poem in the TLS
soon and shall send you a copy when it appears.

All very best wishes | Yours | Edwin Morgan

De Campos had persuaded Lawrence Ferlinghetti to publish some
Brazilian concrete poetry in *City Lights*, with EM as translator. *Extra
Verse* had moved from Birmingham to Edinburgh to be edited by
D.M. Black (issues 12–16). EM had a review of *Invenção* 4 in *Times
Literary Supplement* 30 September 1965: 'Concrete, Theory and
Praxis'. *Servidão de Passagem*, 'Transient Servitude', is in *CT*: 286–92,
but 'Alea I' is not published there. A first version is included below,
with a second version, in response to comments from de Campos,
in the letter of 6 November 1965.

Haroldo de Campos – ALEA-I – SEMANTIC VARIATIONS
translated by
Edwin Morgan Whittingehame Court Glasgow W2 Scotland
UK

- -

THE ADMIRABLE the laudable the notable the adorable
the grandiose the fabulous the phenomenal the colossal
the formidable the astonishing the miraculous the marvellous
the generous the excelse the portentous the stunning

the spectacular the sumptuous the faerifying the faery
the supereminent the venerable the supersacred the
                                                  supercelestial
the unpolluted the uncorrupted the inviolate the intrepid

THE ADDMIREABLE the lowbabble the nauseable the
                                                  malodorable
the ganglious the flatulous the fetoranimal the cutarsadical
the fornicable the astinking the iratulous the matrocitous
the degenerous the insext the pestiferous the stomafuching
the tentacular the suppurous the faecifying the fevery
the supermuckent the veneravid the suprasacral the
                                                  supersyphilable
the pollust the upcorpsed the violoose the tumorped

PEXON
RATIC
PTICA
APTIN
NOPTA
OXTAN
TAPEX
TRICO
NEROX
OXTER
POXIC
PITON
OTPIC
AXPEN
REXON
TIARO
APRIC
NORAT
EXCON
RAPEN
CRAPT
PROXI
TRANE
EXORN

Dom Sylvester Houédard, monk and poet

19 Whittingehame Court Glasgow W2 25-10-1965

Dear Silvester: Like you I am horribusy but must seize a few minutes from the stream to answer your two letters. (Don't know even how I am going to see Jonron who are due here from Arrdgayy about the end of the week.) Glad you got my *Scotch Mist* which is not much of a 'book' is it; if any librarians order such things they must tear their hair (or haar) when they see them. I have your *KingKong* all right and will look forward to the wienerschnirkel. – You say <u>Ian</u> is souffrant! I thought it was me and you and a few others he was trying to make souffrir. He may be passing through a bad period, I don't know, but the last letter he sent to me (attacking me for not writing to *Glasgow Review*) was just impossible to answer. He could hardly be expected, I suppose, to like the polluted lake school, but it seems to me to be a genuine piece of Americana, a sort of do-it-yourself frontier concrete kit, deliberately rough and non-beautiful. Ian greatly overrates the virtues of purity. Eg his TLS letter: to put forward Webern & Satie in a period when Janáček & Britten & Shostakovich have been composing shows a weird indifference to values; Britten's *Curlew River* is a 'small' work but my goodness it could eat ten Weberns for breakfast. And as for Mondrian and Albers, what could be <u>farther</u> from poetry than these grids and squares? All this is matter for discussion, but not <u>polemical</u> discussion of the type Ian likes to engage in. I entirely agree with your wish for a serious magazine, and would support it. But who would have time to run it? Perhaps it may come out of *Tlaloc* as you suggest.

I don't see the *Lugano Review* but must try to get hold of it for Bense's article. – Haven't heard any more yet about Nan Balestrin's anthology, have you? It will be a great pity if we can't get one brought out in Britain – do you think Calder is no longer interested? He would seem a likely choice. Also have not heard for a while from John Sharkey who asked for material for a new magazine. Do you know if this is still in the offing? I sent John Furnival a poem for the o p e ni ng he is doing with me. Did you get, as expect you would,

Andy Jameson's new Colchester address? I have been sending Haroldo de Campos a fairly extensive translation of his work which he hopes will be included in *City Lights Journal* – the Brazilians had apparently a hard job convincing Ferlinghetti, I almost said the woolly-witted Ferlinghetti, having recently heard an interview he gave purporting to 'explain' his plays, as gaseous and peripheryless an explanation as one is likely to hear!.....

Sursum, etc. | Yeddie

'Jonron' were the American poets Jonathan Williams and Ronald Johnson*, visiting Ian Hamilton Finlay* in Ardgay, Sutherland. (For the *Glasgow Review* context, see 10 June 1965.) *Scotch Mist*, a booklet-length concrete poem, was published by Renegade Press, Ohio (Polluted Lake Series 7) in 1965. *King Kong* is dsh's *Kinkon* (Writers Forum, 1965). The 'wienerschnirkel' refers to 'in memoriam wienergruppe' and 'wiener kreis', written by dsh for Ernst Jandl*. The 'serious magazine' would emerge as *Scottish International*, 1968–71. *Lugano Review* had an article by the German cultural philosopher Max Bense about art theory as a branch of information theory. Nan Balestrin is Nanni Balestrini of the Neoavanguardia movement, later Gruppo 63, whose work he co-edited in *Gruppo 63, L'Antologia* (1964). John Sharkey edited *Mindplay: An Anthology of British Concrete Poetry* (1971).

Haroldo de Campos, poet

6 November 1965

Dear Haroldo de Campos

Thank you very much for your letter, and I am glad you have given detailed points of criticism. I have been working on these, and I hope the following suggestions will help to meet the points you raise. I entirely agree with you it is important to have accuracy wherever humanly possible!

ALEA I: I must apologize for missing the MUNDO LIVRE meaning; this was stupid of me. I would suggest a new aleatory column, based on FREE WORLD, as follows:

```
                    FEWERDOLR
                    FOWLREDER
                    DREERFLOW
                    LOWFEEDRR
                    FROWLEERD
                    REERFOWLD
                    FLEDERLOW
                    WEEDFLORR
                    FERROWELD
                    REDFLOWER
                    FLEERWORD
```

For the ADMIRÁVEL/ADMERDÁVEL opposition, could
we have (I offer 3 suggestions, one of which might suit) either
THE UNSURPASSABLE... THE UNSHITPASTABLE,
or THE EXEMPLABLE... THE EXCREMENTABLE, or
THE IRRESISTIBLE... THE EERIESHITTABLE?

SERVIDÃO DE PASSAGEM: Instead of my poetry fly-
by-night, which perhaps gives the wrong impression (though
I understood the meaning all right), could we have pining
poetry (a possible alternative: a lean poetry, but this misses the
alliteration)?

In him i'm hungry: Could we have:

                         i name the noun
                         i name humanity
                         in mid-naming is hunger

                         i name hunger

ferrous man: Yes, I was not really happy with this phrase myself.
I would suggest the two lines should read: bland man
                                        branded man

yakkity/rabbity: I would like to keep the yakkity, which is
meant to suggest an overbearing sort of talk (yakkity-yak, more
an American than a British usage) and I would propose for the
2 lines:
           yakkity man

yes man

<u>lonely grindinghood</u>: Yes, OK for <u>only</u>.

For the difficult last 5 lines – I have thought hard about this,
and I am not sure whether this might meet the case:

> only grindinghood
> bone-grindinghood
>
> no mirage to brood
> through savage wood
>
> transient servitude

– Or possibly 'trespass servitude' instead of 'transient
servitude'? I think 'transient' conveys better the double
meaning you describe, though 'trespass' could do this too if
it is read both as noun (implying the legal meaning) and as
verb (giving almost a command to the reader to break this
servitude).

Do let me have any further comments or points you may
want to bring up, and I shall be glad to try to meet them. I will
look forward eagerly to receiving your *Theory of Concrete Poetry*.
Have the ICA in London sent you a copy of the catalogue for
their exhibition *Between Poetry & Painting*? It contains some
quite interesting material.

> With all best wishes and greetings | Yours sincerely |
> Edwin Morgan

De Campos had sent detailed comments on EM's 'Transient Servi-
tude' and 'Alea I' (two further developed versions are attached, from
EM's files, the first possibly reworked from a French translation
from the Portugese). Edited by Jasia Reichardt, *Between Poetry and
Painting* was an 85-page catalogue of a 1965 exhibition of concrete
poetry.

Alea – I – Semantic Variations

Haroldo de Campos

(note: this is not a word-by-word translation, but an approximative structural paraphrase of the brazilian original text)

THE ADMIRABLE the notable the laudable the adorable
the grandiose the fabulous the phenomenal the colossal
the formidable the amazing the miraculous the marvellous
the generous the excellent the portentous the fantastic
the spectacular the sumptuous the fairyful the fairylike
the meritorious the venerable the sacrosanct the seraphic
the incorrupted the impolluted the ineffable the intrepid

THE ADMERDABLE the obnotchable the laughbabble
                                                        the malodorable
the gangrenose the flatulous the phlegnormenal the
                                                        cularsessadist
the fornicautious the armazing the misragruinous the
                                                        nightmarvillous
the degenerous the achecellent the poortrashtoady the
                                                        filthastic
the exploitacular the consumptuous the fearfoul the infernilike
the micturitious the venerealable the cacosham the syraphilis
the incorerrotten the impaludal the inafailure the intrap

LORDREFEW
DEERWORLF
ROWFEDERL
LOWDREFER
WELERFORD
FELOWDERR
WORDFELER
REEFWORDL ·   (note: the reader (operator)
DOLERFEWR   may go on, at pleasure,
WELFEDORR   making new semantic variations
EREFWORDL   within the given parameter)
FEWERLORD

Alea – I – Semantic Variations

THE UNSURPASSABLE the laudable the notable the
adorable
the grandiose the fabulous the phenomenal the colossal
the formidable the astonishing the miraculous the marvellous
the generous the excelse the portentous the stunning
the spectacular the sumptuous the faeryfying the faery
the supereminent the venerable the supersacred the
supercelestial
the unpolluted the uncorrupted the inviolate the intrepid

THE UNSHITPASTABLE the lowbabble the nauseable
the maloderable
the ganglious the flatulous the fetoranimal the cutarsadical
the fornicable the astinking the iratulous the matrocious
the degenerous the insext the pestiferous the stomafuching
the tentaculour the supurous the faecifying the fevery
the supermuckent the veneravid the suprasacral the
supersyphilable
the pollust the uncorpsed the violoose the tumorped

FEWERDOLR
FOWLEREDR
DREGRFLOW
LOWFEEDRR
FROWLEERD
REERFOWLD
FLEDWEROR
FREDERLOW
WEEDFLOR
FERROWELD
REDFLOWER
FLEERWORD
FREEWORLD

Anselm Hollo, poet and translator

14 November 1965

Dear Anselm:

How pleasant to get unexpected cheque! – Many thanks for that, & for including my poem. *Evergreen* gets everbluer issue by issue – is it evergoing to get back to being a literarymag again? I thought your selection & remarks good & to the point. I was delighted to have *Word From the North* & it has the good effect of making one want to learn Finnish. It has both you & them; you haven't imposed yourself on the poets, yet I can feel your touch. I liked the poems by Eeva-Liisa Manner, Pekka Piirto, Maila Pylkkönen, & Pentti Saarikoski better than the others. Speaking of shamans, do the Lapps have any poetry? And another question: how hard is it to write 'projective' verse in Finnish – do the long words not tend to fall into metrical (e.g. trochaic) patterns?

There are two of your books I've seen referred to but haven't managed to get, & I'll be happy to pay for a copy of each if you still have any available: *Lover Man*, & the *Poems by R.G. Dienst*. I don't know how much they are, or I would have sent a postal order with the letter. – Did *Horde* ever appear again? I have been wondering if you were able to do anything with these poems of mine that you had. The one about the old man will be appearing in the anthology (first of an annual series being published by Edinburgh UP) *Scottish Poetry* 1 which should be out before Christmas.

'Here we go' along the frosty pavement to the midnight letterbox with the best northern greetings, foamback carcoat, careful strides, plnk, Londonwards – redmouth grins, receives all, end of Sabbath –

Yours ever | ≡)||

Horde, a 'cross-over' magazine of experimentation in jazz, poetry and drama, was edited by Lee Harwood and others and ran for one issue in December 1964. A second issue edited by Hollo was advertised in Issue 1. The poem about the old man is 'In the Snack-bar' (*CP*: 170).

Iain Crichton Smith, poet and novelist

Dear Iain

I don't know of anything that just ideally meets the bill. In fact there's a great lack of such a book. The Pelican *Modern Age* which you mention is all right as far as it goes, but it's rather scrappy & incomplete (& prejudiced). The two other best paperbacks I can think of are: G.S. Fraser, *The Modern Writer & His World* (Pelican, 1964, 6/-) which has 100 pages dealing with poetry & gives quite a good background & has a bibliography for further readings, & Babette Deutsch, *Poetry in Our Time, 1900–1960* (Anchor Books, Doubleday, New York, 1963, $1.45) which is short on facts & dates & so on but does discuss trends & interpretations & some individual poems. Less up-to-date, and in hardback, are Geoffrey Bullough, *The Trend of Modern Poetry* (Oliver & Boyd, 1949, 10/6) & V. de S. Pinto, *Crisis in English Poetry* (Hutchinson, 1955, 10/6). Apart from these, all I can suggest is the series of pamphlets published by Longmans for the British Council at 2/6 or 3/6 each: Stephen Spender, *Poetry Since 1939* (1946), Alan Ross, *Poetry 1945–50* (1951), Geoffrey Moore, *Poetry Today* [period 1950–57] (1958), Elizabeth Jennings, *Poetry Today* [1957–60] (1961), R.N. Curry, *Poets of the 1939–45 War* (1960). Of course, Kenneth Allott's *Penguin Book of Contemporary Verse, 1918–60* (1962, 6/-) could virtually be used as a textbook, it has so much useful information in the introductory notes to each poet; and it could be supplemented by Robin Skelton's *Poetry of the Thirties* (Penguin, 1964, 5/-) and A. Alvarez's *The New Poetry* (Penguin, 1962, 3/6), & the Penguin Modern Poets series. There are some more elementary textbooks which are meant for schools, but I don't know much about these – probably you will know them in any case,

I would like very much to have a copy of your Gaelic poems when it comes out. In fact, I would be greatly obliged if you could let me have any of your other Gaelic books – you had an earlier volume of Gaelic poetry, hadn't you? – as I like to have the 'complete works' & in any case I still have hopes that I might someday learn Gaelic. What you say about the six Gaelic poems increases my desire to do so! Have you translations of these poems? They would be worth publishing.

I have been too busy so far this term to do much writing, though the TLS has taken a longish concrete poem & a translation of a longish poem by Voznesensky (he's very interesting I think, one of the most interesting poets of his generation). I suppose you would hear from EUP about the anthology *Scottish Poetry Number One*? We hope it will be out before Christmas. I believe it is quite a good collection, though inevitably with a few shall we say less than strong spots…

All the best | Eddie

Iain Crichton Smith (1928–98) and EM had been friends since the mid-1950s, and when Smith moved from Oban to Dumbarton as a secondary school teacher, they would meet to discuss poetry, politics and philosophy. Smith's brother in Southern Rhodesia had asked him to recommend a good and cheap textbook on modern poetry for a friend there.

Maurice Lindsay, poet and editor

3 February 1966

Dear Maurice

That's good news about the Faber anthology. I have put the book down on our prescribed texts list for next session. The MacDiarmid selection looks as if it will do very well for our purposes; the *Drunk Man*, good though it is, is really too long and difficult for a course that has to take in so many other things. About the address you ask for: I can't find the address of the secretary, who is not in one of our classes, but the president would I suppose do as well, & he is Angus Somerville, 2 Cecil Street, Glasgow W2.

I liked the easy, unforced style of *Kaleidoscope*, though I think you can <u>stretch</u> your audience a bit more once the thing is established. I felt especially with the cartoonist that he missed the chance to put over the serious side of his art by being <u>too</u> flippant – I think one can have a light touch and yet make real points. What about a programme on Tom Moore and his Irish Melodies? This could be wonderful, both visually and musically. I'm sure Moore is underestimated by present-day criticism. Even if he isn't, the songs are always affecting, on a level that is hard to define, partly sentimental, partly a genuine sadness.

Yours aye | Eddie

Lindsay's edited collection, *Modern Scottish Poetry*, was due to be published by Faber, and EM had asked whether it would be available by the beginning of the autumn term. The student addresses were for publicity purposes. Lindsay was Programme Controller at Border Television, based in Carlisle, and *Kaleidoscope* was a new arts programme.

Iain Crichton Smith, poet and novelist

8 May 1966

Dear Iain

Many thanks for submitting the poems, which I have now passed on to George Bruce and Maurice Lindsay. I find them all interesting and would be glad to print any of them. The Clearances one is pretty long of course and it will depend on space. By the way, you didn't give it a title – do you want it to have one? You have titles for the 5 sections but not for the whole poem. I've also a query about a word in the 'Shepherd' poem – is it <u>wing</u> or <u>wind</u>?

I'm glad you liked my poem about the old man. It was one of those poems that come out of a very intense actual experience, and I wanted to be as true to the event as possible. After I had written it I wondered if it was too 'realistic', too prosaic or almost reportorial, but quite a number of people have commented favourably on it, so it seems to work as a poem. I have also heard various people saying they found your King Lear poem very interesting. The book seems to be selling quite well. Yes, the MacDiarmid poems were good, weren't they? – even if they were 30 years old!

It was odd you should ask about whether I was bringing out a book of poems. The Edinburgh University Press phoned recently to say that they would publish a collection – I had submitted it to them about 9 months ago, and was beginning to lose hope. I am very glad this has happened, as I have poems scattered all over the place and people often ask where they can get hold of them.

The concrete poetry exhibition hangs in the balance and indeed may not come off, though I'll be sorry if it doesn't. Ian Hamilton Finlay is being at his most temperamental and difficult, refusing to exhibit, etc... and the Arts Council is rapidly losing patience, as definite decisions and arrangements have to be made now. Breakfast-ruining letters crowd the post. All this when I have plenty on my mind from the approach of the end-of-term exams and thinking about next year's syllabus. Is it only in Scotland that it is so hard to get people to agree and cooperate? I sympathize very much with your cri de coeur about teaching, though it's not easy to find a solution. In some ways the university is better, and yet even there there is a lot of hard slogging to be done, since with the big classes of say 3 or 4 hundred it is only partly true to say that you are 'teaching English literature to those who are interested'. A lot of the interest has to be created, or very carefully nurtured. This can be rewarding, but a good deal of it is hard uphill work. Life becomes a constant battle with time, to get done what you yourself want to do. The whole situation is very difficult.

I'll look forward to hearing your 'Deer on the High Hills' on the Third.

All the best as ever | Eddie

Smith had submitted work for the second volume of the *Scottish Poetry* series. EM's 'In the Snack-bar' appeared in *Scottish Poetry* 1.

Richard Coe, academic

English Department
The University
27 May 1966

Dear Dr Coe

Many thanks for returning the magazines so promptly, and also for sending me your lecture on Ionesco which I found most interesting.

Yes, do keep the copy of the translation I sent; I have others.

I suspect that your opinion of Genet's poems is the right one; and it might be argued that I have transformed rather than translated them. It is very hard to say, in a case like this, how much the translator has genuinely 'found' in the original. Yet there was certainly something which sparked me off, although I could see and deplore what was often a secondhand or blownup rhetoric in the text.

I would indeed be grateful to have a copy of the bibliography which you say you will be kind enough to send me.

Yours sincerely | Edwin Morgan

Coe was compiling a bibliography of Jean Genet, including works in translation. EM lent him magazines where his translations had appeared – in Coe's view 'not only more poetic [...] but more original than the originals'. *The Theatre of Jean Genet: A Casebook* (1973), edited by Coe, includes EM's 'Thief into Poet ... into Dramatist', together with part of his translation of 'The Condemned Man'.

Alan Riddell, poet and editor

19 Whittingehame Court
28 May 1966

Dear Alan

Thanks for your letter and for the poems.

I'm glad to know that *Lines* is in the offing and will look forward to it. I am enclosing a few things as you request: two pieces of my own, and some translations from German concrete poetry. If the German poems appeal to you and you want to print them, I could add a few notes on the poets and/or what they are doing in these particular poems. The Christmas card was printed in the ICA Bulletin but that is for members and hardly counts as publication.

I liked the poems you sent, and would want myself to have them considered for *Scottish Poetry* 2, but I am not sure whether you wish to submit them. Could you let me know soon? The difficulty (which you touch on in your letter) is simply that Maurice Lindsay finds himself unsympathetic towards concrete, and George Bruce, though a bit more open, is far from keen, so that (going on a majority vote) the amount of concrete poetry I can get in is not likely to be much. I have managed to squeeze one of my own into SP2, but I think only because it had high semantic content! Your 'Race War' might get by on semantic grounds, the other two would I think only irritate my co-editors; but if you like I shall submit them – and of course any others you want to send. Let me know as soon as you can, as we have a meeting on Saturday to discuss the latest submissions.

I was sorry I couldn't get down to see the Blackheath exhibition, but I am pleased to hear it looked good.

All the best | Eddie

Riddell, editor of *Lines Review*, had submitted some of his own experimental poetry for the *Scottish Poetry* series.

Ian Hamilton Finlay, poet and artist

Dear Ian

First, a piece of news that coincides with the question you have just asked. The Arts Council have let me know, as your sponsor, that you will be getting one of the bursaries – £350. It is not an enormous sum, but I am sure it will be useful. I can only tell you this unofficially at the moment, so you must sit tight till you hear from them, but I imagine this will not be long. Apparently they take the idea of sponsoring quite seriously, and I am to keep in touch with you and see that you <u>do</u> produce concrete poetry and <u>don't</u> spend your substance on riotous living (though riotous living in Ceres on that sum hardly seems a likely proposition)! I feel rather like a sudden godfather, and should perhaps be sending you a silver mug. Anyhow, I'm glad that you decided that you could accept an award; the money just might make all the difference in some difficult situation. I will write and give Ronald Mavor your new address. (If he will not think I am pulling his leg; it is almost incredible, a poem in itself.)

I hadn't much of a time at Oban, but these things happen. At least my room had a telephone, so I could phone down for a lightly poached egg and up it would come. But I ate practically nothing for a week. When we left, they let me off half my bill, which was nice.

Many thanks for the Vasarely, and the two little books. I take it that the Vasarely is meant to be operated by the viewer, slid about to produce shifting patterns? And therefore is not to be framed? Is the sheet of paper in the middle protective, or meant to be kept there? I liked this print very much. I also liked the combinative surprises of the 'small songs' – quiet, warm, clear, and I think a logical development from what you have been doing. I can only give a first immediate impression of the 'patch' ocean stripe poem, an interesting semi-semiotic experiment which carried me along well until a doubt arose with the last page – whether the introduction of the stars was a sudden and almost joky mutation from realism into fantasy, or whether in fact you want us to see such a 'thing' as 'star potatoes' or 'star sails' (and therefore one is tempted to imagine night scenes on land and sea)? I think Emil Antonucci's touch is just right.

I am sorry your new place is so small and unworkable-in. Maybe something else will turn up, if you can make do for a while. It must be very exasperating and frustrating. Still, you have a garden, and surely something can be done with that once you have overcome your distrust of its tendedness...? If I hear of anything else I will let you know.

Love | Yeddie

IHF had moved from Sutherland to Coaltown of Callange, Ceres, by Cupar, Fife. EM had sponsored him for a grant from the Scottish Arts Council, of which Ronald Mavor (son of playwright James Bridie) was the Director. IHF had sent a print by the Hungarian Viktor Vasarely (1906–97) who developed Op Art through his geometrical paintings. Emil Antonucci, a New York designer and publisher, worked on IHF's Ocean Stripe series.

Ian Hamilton Finlay, poet and artist

11 July 1966

Dear Ian

I haven't written to the Arts Council yet about the glass-poem, but will do so today. It seems a very nice gesture to me, and I would think they would be most pleased to have such a thing. But I will write and then let you know. I got little done last week as I had to prepare a lecture for a summer school at Jordanhill, and go to a wedding reception at Strathblane (an evening reception, dreaming groups under the garden trees, very Arnoldian), and get my TV set exchanged, and queue up for travellers' cheques and schillings for the Tirol, and meet Philip Hobsbaum (who is joining the English Department here) (not your kind of poetry, I think – except that the title of his book *The Place's Fault* will strike home ironically to you just now), and copy out poems for Arlington (which I won't be able to visit unfortunately), and fill in visa forms for Budapest in October. I am now doing some more translations of Edgard Braga for Stephen Bann, and more computer poetry for John Sharkey who has apparently got some money at last and means to go ahead with *Lisn*. – When I got your explanation of the star potatoes and star sails, and looked again at the book, everything was at once clear, and I think that given the explanation the whole poem now works perfectly to the end; but I am still worried by the fact that the explanation is something I would never have guessed, and wonder if anyone would? I think you would have to collect other opinions about this. But it is possible that notes would need to be provided – I mean for full understanding, as you would want it to be understood. (I am thinking of *Futura 7* where you have supplied notes, and these undoubtedly do help the reader – perhaps are even necessary.) There seems to be some difficulty or limitation here, in that the symbolism (of circles, triangles, squares, asterisks) is not complex enough to carry the associations you have in mind, and the actual arrangement (i.e. stars above potatoes, stars above sails) almost invariably suggests what I 'got' (wrongly) as night scenes; this is a question of the natural expectations of how things are placed in relation to one another. The earlier pictures are all naturalistic (if I can use that word) in that things are in their normal places/relations; then suddenly at the end this is no longer so, and one has to make an adjustment to a double metaphor. This is the bit where I feel most readers would trip up as I did. But I may be wrong about this. – I will indeed think about a possible POTH and would be very glad of the chance to do something. Perhaps an idea will come on the shores of the Achensee. – I wish I could help about a cottage; I have been making inquiries but without success so far.

Love | Yeddie

IHF feared that the gift of a glass sculpture in thanks for his Arts Council bursary might be disapproved of. He explained that two puzzling images ('star potatoes' and 'star sails') came from his own rural iconography of potato harvests (white against the soil) and white sails on Orkney, where he had worked as a shepherd. EM's Edgar Braga translations were published in a *Beloit Poetry Journal*, in a concrete issue edited by Stephen Bann* (*CT*: 302–305).

Alan Riddell, poet and editor

15 July 1966

Dear Alan

Thanks for an interesting *Lines*. About my computer's
carol which you mention: I'd prefer underlining to italics,
as I want it to look as mechanical and straight from the
computer as possible; and I hope your printer will watch
to get the underlining right, since it is a bit tricky, and the
ICA Bulletin made several mistakes when it printed it! This
sort of poem has to be quite exact or it loses its point. – I
think (though I haven't tried it out) that your suggestion
of obscuring your 'seek' on the second time round is a good
one, since when someone hides the seeker makes mistakes
and his search is 'obscured' by the deliberate tricks of the
hider. – I wish I could have got to the Arlington show, but
am just going off to Austria on holiday and will miss it. I sent
some MSS rather late and I don't know if Ken Cox was able
to include them. – The Scottish Arts Council <u>were</u> going to
back a concrete show at Edinburgh during the Festival but
this has fallen through. It's a long unhappy story. You know
who up in Ardgay (now in Ceres) was angry that I and not
he had been asked to put the show together, and the upshot
of a mort of violent communication (and other accidental
factors contributing to make him ill-disposed to the outside
world in general) was that he refused either to contribute
or to cooperate, and the Arts Council felt that they had had
enough and washed their hands of the matter – leaving the
idea at least open for a further attempt on some later occasion
if the climate should become mellower. Scotland, in short,
stands where it did. If Jim Haynes wants to put on a concrete
show as you suggest, you had better warn him of the hazards!
I would certainly be very wary myself about how I took part
in any such activity in future.

I expect to be back in about ten days, and then I hope catch
up with some writing. One good piece of news is that when
I come back I am to see the EUP about my own poems; they
are going to publish a collection, and we have to discuss what

is to go in and what not. I don't know whether concrete can be included, though I want it to be.

All the best | Eddie

The poem referred to is 'The Computer's Second Christmas Card' (*CP*: 142), previously published in *ICA Bulletin* 155, February 1966. Riddell did not reprint it in *Lines Review*. Despite his move from Sutherland to Fife, Ian Hamilton Finlay* seems still at a prickly remove from 'the centre'.

Ian Hamilton Finlay, poet and artist

15 August 1966

Dear Ian

I am back from Ach-on-Sea. There was so much rain that we had to fall back on such things as Tyrolean Evenings, trips to the Dolomites, rummy, bingo, and watching the world cup in German on television. (When it became evident that Germany and England were going to be the finalists it became very confusing, and I began to suffer Alienation or something.) On the last but one evening there was a great Schuhplattler competition which John (the friend I was with – he's in fact a champion dancer) won, his reward being a bottle of wine with a golden monkey embossed on it – as Austrian as all the jolly bottom-slapping and up-ending we had to go through. I was glad I at least didn't get the booby prize – a sausage – which went to a German. I think both of us should have got a golden monkey for doing the Schuhplattler in the kilt. The best thing was a chair-lift one sunny morning up into the Karwendel, each person isolated in his own little rickety chair, swinging slowly and steeply up through the huge pines and space to the summit, really a quite new experience, there are so many things you can do with your mind as you go up that you feel as if you were cast adrift, it is exhilarating and yet in a sense it is too free, almost frightening, you think you would make more of it the next time if you could collect your thoughts... And I came back with a musical cigarette-box, a Tyrolean tie, some dried edelweiss, and a broken camera. We resisted leather shorts, thinking the kilt was eccentric enough. When we got back we popped a bottle of Asti Spumante I had picked up on the Dolomites trip, and savoured the euphoria of return.

I like the idea of one-word poems for POTH and enclose a batch for you to choose from. I'll write to Jon Silkin as you suggest. It also seems Aram Saroyan's cup of tea? I'm very fond of some of his short pieves. Sorry, how ridiculous: PIECES! The other enclosure is a sort of half-way poem, half-way between a poem and a 'ready-made'. It is probably infringing a manufacturer's copyright but I don't suppose a few copies passed round will do any harm. There are only a dozen copies in the 'edition'!

Yours aye | Love | Yeddie

EM and his friend John Scott had holidayed at Achensee in the Austrian Tyrol. IHF was commissioning one-word poems, with a longer title, for *Poor.Old.Tired.Horse* (e.g. *The Boat's Blueprint*: water). EM's were republished in *Dreams and Other Nightmares: New and Uncollected Poems 1954–2009* (2010: 53). Aram Saroyan was a New Yorker, working in minimalist and concrete poetry. The enclosure was *Sealwear* (1966), a limited handmade edition based on a catalogue of waterproof clothing. (When the Edwin Morgan Archive went online at the Scottish Poetry Library in 2009, the manufacturer did enquire about the booklet's origins.)

Iain Crichton Smith, poet and novelist

19 September 1966

Dear Iain

You've been addressing your recent things to Whittingehame Road instead of Court, and they've been chasing me about marked NOT KNOWN! The J. Arthur Dixon Natural Colour Photogravure King Size Postal Print of Stob Coire Nan Lochan arrived eventually all crumpled up like an elephant's ear and had evidently been thrown away and retrieved somehow by a virtuous person or postman. However, reading between the cracks – yes, I have seen a copy of *Poesie Vivante* which was sent to me, though I don't get it regularly. It seems to be devoted to international cooperation etcetera and prints poetry in various languages and in translation. I had a translation of a French poem in one number.

John Gray was on the phone about the poetry competition and I explained how you were placed. But he has a plan – since I think he's keen to have you in the programme – to come up with me to Oban and record at least a part of it there. I've said this is all right with me (so long as he picks some day when I can get away), and I expect he'll be writing to you about it. I hope this idea will be feasible. By the way if you see the *Scotsman* this Saturday there will be an account of the school magazine competition which I was helping to judge (with Eric Linklater and James Scotland) last week. There was an announcement of the actual awards in today's issue. The poetry prize goes to Stornoway, though I myself had voted for your boy Malcolm MacAffer who gets a special mention. There were really quite a number of good poems. In fact I thought the poems were on the whole better than the stories. The main award for the best magazine overall went to Carrick Academy.

I'm enclosing three poems, from which you can perhaps get something suitable for your school magazine anthology. I chose ones that (I hope) met your (sober? though maybe not entirely sedate?) requirements, and also that might be of some interest to discuss. I would be very glad to see the magazine when it eventually appears.

No sign of Karl Marx! Though I must say it is a curious sensation to look round in the Reading Room and wonder whether perhaps <u>he</u>, or <u>she</u>, or <u>that odd one there</u>, is engaged on something that will be equally epochmaking. The man on my left was reading Irish archaeology, the woman on my right the French Symbolistes, the man opposite was frowning over Griboyedov and Gogol (in the original). I find this juxtaposition comforting and even stimulating, and never find it difficult to work or concentrate there, public though it is.

All the best as ever | Eddie

John Gray, a BBC sound engineer who had worked with film-maker

John Grierson, was later in charge of arts and features in Radio Scotland. The British Library Reading Room detail reflects EM's habit of working there during the summer vacation.

Cavan McCarthy, editor and librarian

1 November 1966

Dear Cavan

Sorry not to have answered your letter sooner, but I've been away in Hungary on a British Council tour and have just returned to a huge mail. I don't have a spare copy of that *Glasgow Review* (and the magazine is now defunct as you surmise), but here are the details of Creeley's letter which perhaps you can pass on to Lynne Cohn:

> *The Glasgow Review*, Vol.II, No.2, Summer 1965, p.36.
> A letter from Robert Creeley which itself has no heading but is part of a large correspondence under the general heading 'Concrete Verse'. It is written from Placitas, New Mexico, 14th June, 1965, and begins:
> Dear Sir,/ I should like to protest the review by Christopher Wiseman in the spring number of *The Glasgow Review*… Signed Robert Creeley. The letter defends the work of Finlay and myself from Wiseman's attacks.

There's nothing else by Creeley in TGR.

Can't help you with Sergei Biely (? Andrei), sorry. Speaking of Anselm, I read one of his poems ('Message from the Border') when I was lecturing in Budapest, and it was much approved. The Hungarians are much interested in English and American poetry now – they had heard about concrete poetry and wanted to know more – they do an enormous amount of translation and keep up pretty well, at any rate down to the Ted Hughes generation – I saw versions of Updike and Kerouac in the shops, and went to an excellent production of the Marat/Sade play – one of their poets, Sándor Weöres, is an extraordinary virtuoso who in addition to normal syntactical poems has written both visual and phonetic concrete-type

experimental poems (I tried in vain to get copies of these, his books sell out immediately and books are seldom reprinted in Hungary because of shortage of timber/paper) –
Is the enclosed version of Michaux any use for *Tlaloc?*

All best wishes | Eddie

McCarthy had enquired about the letter from Robert Creeley on behalf of Lynne Cohn, who was compiling the poet's bibliography. (See 10 June 1965.) He had also asked about a translation of Biely by Anselm Hollo*, and the original text. EM admired Weöres* and translated him extensively (*CT*: 63–101, 469–82). His Michaux translations are in *CT*: 273–79.

Iain Crichton Smith, poet and novelist

9 November 1966

Dear Iain
I am sorry to be so long in answering your letter – but I have a good alibi, as I have been in Hungary on a British Council tour and am now trying to catch up on a pile of correspondence that was waiting for me when I got back. On the Lorn M problem: entrance regulations now are so tricky and uncertain (because of the pressure on university places) that I really wouldn't like to commit myself on this particular case – I don't myself have anything to do with admissions, and would hate to give wrong advice. I would suggest the best thing to do is for Lorn M to write and present his problem to the Adviser of Studies in Arts, Norman C. Anderson, who is both knowledgeable and sympathetic. I wouldn't think, frankly, that the idea of submitting creative work in lieu of Highers would cut much ice, but if he does mention this possibility when he writes to Norman Anderson, tell him to say that I know and think well of his poetry (as perhaps you do too), and perhaps between us we could in this offer something like backing. – Another possibility that strikes me: it might be worth trying the University of Stirling which will be taking its first students next year; I don't know what their entrance

requirements are, but this would be worth inquiring about, as a new foundation might have greater flexibility.

No, I hadn't heard that Charles Senior had not been well. I didn't have his Inverness address and had rather lost touch with him. I have always liked him too. I must try to drop him a note if I can.

I <u>was</u> quite interested, in fact, about the no-bard thing. It seemed to me that (although I couldn't judge of course) this was probably a healthy astringency, and one that Eisteddfodians too might apply. Competitions like these have no doubt some value in keeping culture alive but is it really <u>poetry</u> is always the nagging question at the back of one's mind.

I have just been reviewing Hugh MacDiarmid's new whack of autobiography – unorganised but interesting as usual. He mentions you as belonging to the école Norman MacCaig is maître d'. So there ye are pigeonhol'd sir; in the catalogue for poets ye go.

Yours aye | Eddie

Lorn Macintyre had contacted ICS for advice on university entrance without the requisite Higher Grade passes in school. Smith had been one of three poetry judges at the Gaelic Mod, who had decided not to award any prize that year. MacDiarmid's* biographical *The Company I've Kept* (1966) was reviewed by EM in the *Times Literary Supplement*, 17 November 1966. On Charles Senior, see also the letter of 2 September 1968.

Ian Hamilton Finlay, *poet and artist*

24 November 1966

Dear Ian

I must write, though I am still ploughing through a backlog (can one do that?) of the things that sprang up while I was in Hungary. It was really a very good trip, though you must not think I was all the time Dallying on Balaton or enjoying the Arnoovoh. The day of pleasure at Balaton was only a brief reward at the end of the poets' conference, and even it was pretty highly organised to take in a display of folk-dancing, an evening of Hungarian poetry (without translation), and a visit to an art exhibition at which we were suddenly presented with vast sheets of drawing paper and poster pens and 'requested' (who could refuse and not lose face?) to produce an instant poem or at the least a pungent message. Apart from spending days with earphones on listening to broken French, I read a paper on translation, and I lectured on modern poetry at Budapest University and at the British Embassy. Before I went I had offered to lecture on concrete poetry (with slides) but the authorities didn't take this up; however I slipped it into the lectures I did give, and it stirred up a lot of interest. They have a very good poet, Sándor Weöres (whom I met), who has already written quite a bit of both visual and phonetic poetry though outside the concrete movement as such. I tried very hard, but without success, to bring back examples of this; all his books are out of print and he hadn't even himself a spare copy to give me. But someday and somehow I shall get hold of it and see if it is possible to translate it.

Now speaking of Hungary and the *Beloit Poetry Journal* – (a) I think your w a v e / r o c k glasspoem on the cover is terrific and would love to have such an object (b) my all-free Hungary trip not only saved me but made me some money, as I was paid for various translations, TV interviews etc. and as a result have a bit of money which instead of frittering away I would like to put to good use by purchasing or better commissioning some splendid object that would please both you and me. Can I do this? Some such object as would in size be all right for say the sideboard of an ordinary livingroom, big enough to be a distinctive item but not overpowering? Some sort of glasspoem might be ideal, as my room faces south and gets a lot of light, stands high, looks out mostly to sky and roofs, hills in the distance, and even by a stroke of luck water (the boating-pond in Great Western Road, with two swans on it). Do let me know what you think, and I'll be eager to hear if you have any suggestions.

Both the *4 Sails* and the *6 Small Pears* pleased me very much. After Paean I must call you Aean. I haven't got any inscriptions for you yet but hope to do some when I get a little freer. (Get a little what?)

> here lyes the litill freer
> rouning in goddes ear
> his habit he hath broke
> and he was boren in stoke

Enough, enough.

Write soon – | Love | Yeddie

EM had been a British Council representative in Hungary with George MacBeth. Balaton is the largest freshwater lake in Central Europe, and a tourist attraction. 'Arnoovoh' is *art nouveau*. IHF was developing concrete poems using glass, stone and steel, and had moved to Stonypath croft, Dunsyre in Lanarkshire, and begun a lifework of 'avant-gardening'.

Ernst Honigman, academic

English Department
The University
29 November 1966

Dear Ernst

Thanks for your second (urgent & anguished) letter: I have written to Sylvan Barnet saying that I cannot accept his offer at any rate during the coming year, though I asked him if it could be kept open. Peter Butter made it clear that with Nigel's prior application I couldn't get away next year. I also of course told SB quite frankly about my domestic difficulties. These were very much in my mind, and were one of the reasons why I took so long to reply. SB's letter arrived just after I had come back from my Hungarian lecture-tour and found that my mother's blood-pressure had gone up, she'd been having dizzy spells and so on, and I was very depressed and felt it was really impossible to get away for any lengthy period. The whole thing was complicated by the strange coincidence that at exactly the same time I received another American offer – or more strictly, a feeler rather than an actual offer – which as it was a 'Writer in Residence' proposal seemed to me more immediately attractive than the offer from Tufts as it would leave me more free to do what I wanted. All I could do with <u>that</u> suggestion of course was to give very much the same reply – that I couldn't pretend not to be interested but that it was impossible for me to commit myself in my present circumstances. So at the moment that is the highly unsatisfactory state in which things stand, and I'm afraid the American dream must remain a distant prospect, though it is certainly not a prospect I intend to lose or forget about.

The Hungarian tour was very interesting, if exhausting. I was lecturing mainly on modern poetry, though I also talked about translation, and read some of my own poetry and translations. Budapest is large, fascinating, often beautiful, filled with that European sense of history and involvement and violence and guilt that hits you when you penetrate deep into the continent: buildings in the main streets still with bullet-holes, fiercely restored literary cafes, monuments to revolutionary poets, monstrous monuments to the Russian army, ill-lit streets at night, yet sophisticated conversation and interest in modern literature, Kerouac and Updike in the bookshops, a remarkable performance of the Marat/Sade play – and my interpreter was a girl who had just written a thesis on 'Loneliness in Modern Drama'!

I'm delighted that you're enjoying Tufts and Boston and will look forward to hearing all about it someday. I hope Elsie is enjoying the American scene too.

Love to both | Eddie

A fellow lecturer in English Literature at Glasgow University, and subsequently professor at Newcastle, Honigman was a visiting professor at Tufts University, Massachusetts. Sylvan Barnet, Chairman of Department there, wanted EM to apply for a similar post. Nigel Alexander, son of the retired Professor Peter Alexander, also lectured in Glasgow. The writer-in-residence opportunity had been mentioned by William Pratt*, below.

William Pratt, academic

19 Whittingehame Court
29 November 1966

Dear Bill

Many thanks for your letter and for the *Sewanee Review* which has now also arrived. I haven't had time yet to compare the Rilke versions with the originals but they read very well and they seem to avoid very successfully that sense of strain (and even acrobatics) that the exigencies of rhyme and metre induced in e.g. Leishman, ingenious though he was. I haven't done any more Rilke myself so far, but will still be interested to hear if you do decide to try a Golden Book.

No, concrete poetry is not a money-spinner! Except that for an exhibition of it in London I sent some MSS which I had carefully written out in coloured inks and these were all sold; but as I had asked only about £1 for each it didn't amount to much. I shall have to raise the price the next time! I can see that you are highly sceptical of the whole movement, and I won't try to convert you in an airletter, but you will have a chance of seeing how it fits into the rest of my poetry (or doesn't) when the Edinburgh University Press bring out a fairly substantial volume of my poems which they are setting up at the moment; I'll send you a copy when it appears, perhaps early next year. It will contain both 'normal' and concrete poetry (presenting the printers with delightfully formidable problems in typesetting). Emmett Williams in New York, by the way, is preparing a large anthology of concrete, and I shall have 10 poems in that, together with explanatory notes and general statement. I think you underestimate the serious possibilities of the movement, but we'll see...

I do indeed remember our friend Nicolaisen, and read his regular articles on place-names in the *Scots Magazine*! Please give him my best wishes when you see him.

I would certainly be interested in your suggestions of Writer in Residence or the Elliston Poetry Lectures. What does the latter involve? I have some ideas about poetry which I would relish the task of putting into shape for such an

occasion. In case it will be of any help to you, I shall enclose
with this letter a curriculum vitae I prepared some time ago
for a chair I didn't get – it will give some facts if you are
required to produce these in support of an application. (One
fact it doesn't mention is that I have been reading my poems
at various places on our own unlucrative British poetry circuit
– Edinburgh, Newcastle, Durham, Nottingham, with Dundee
coming up shortly.) I had an invitation to teach modern poetry
next year at Tufts University in Boston, but had to turn it
down as one of my colleagues will be having leave of absence
and two can't be spared at once. In any case I would have
found it hard to get away, as my mother has not been too well,
and I don't like leaving her for a long period at the moment.

I never thanked you, by the way, for the Alastair Reid
article and the profile of Peter Alexander, both of which I was
very glad to see.

All the best as ever – | Eddie

Pratt, trying to interest EM in working in the US, had mentioned
that Bill Nicolaisen, formerly of the German Department at Glasgow
University and then of the School of Scottish Studies in Edinburgh,
was a visiting professor at Ohio State University, and that American
poets often took part in fairly well-paid 'lecture circuits'.

Duncan Glen, publisher and poet

24 December 1966

Dear Mr Glen

Here I am still with that article unwritten. Since I came
back from Hungary one thing after another has come up to
prevent me from getting on with it. I really am very sorry
about this and you must be fed up with me I am sure. There is,
however, another possibility that I have been thinking of in the
last few weeks. There are five or six people who are either at or
have recently left Glasgow University who are at the moment
writing promising poetry in a variety of styles. Colin Kirkwood
and Robert Tait have appeared in *Scottish Poetry 1* and will be

joined in *Scottish Poetry 2* by Stephen Mulrine. Alan Hayton was also in No.1. William Hart was the prizewinner in a BBC student poetry competition. All these five are I believe interesting and serious practitioners and although they don't strictly form a 'school' they have appeared at the same time and place and it would be very good if they could be seen together. My idea was, if you thought this was feasible, that instead of an article by me you might print a selection of poems by these young poets, with perhaps a short statement by each, and/or a brief introduction by myself. Obviously you won't want to commit yourself until you've seen the poems, but I thought I would just ask you first of all if you thought favourably of the idea. I think there is definitely something 'happening' in Scottish poetry in the Glasgow area at the moment, and it would be useful to signalize this – by examples if possible, rather than by talking about it.

One of these poets, Alan Hayton, has given me a typescript of a fair number of his poems, which he hoped you might consider for some future Akros Poets publication. I am enclosing these poems to let you see them, and perhaps you will give me a verdict in due course. Although clearly there would have to be some sifting out, I am much impressed by some of these poems.

With best wishes for the New Year – | Yours sincerely | Edwin Morgan

Glen, who taught graphic arts, published *Akros*. While championing MacDiarmid*, this key journal was also open to younger writers. The student writers mentioned appeared in *Scottish Poetry* 1 and 2 (1966, 1967). Glen agreed to use their work in *Akros* 5 or 6, and this developed into the idea of a small edited collection: *Four Glasgow University Poets* (1967), William Hart declining his place in the collection.

Ian Hamilton Finlay, poet and artist

c. 24 December 1966

(Towards Christmas, Ian Hamilton Finlay had sent EM a copy of his one-line poem 'Arcady', with the expectation of a reaction. The poem is as follows:

ARCADY

ABCDEFGHIJKLMNOPQRSTUVWXYZ

He also sent some mock-academic questions on the poem, outlined below. EM supplied answers to these and to 'A Question on the Questions, for Boxing Day', together with some poetic variations of his own.

Some questions on the poem, for Christmas Day

1) The poem is no more than an alphabet with a title. Why should an alphabet be presented as a poem and given the title 'Arcady'?

2) 'Roam' is a verb we associate with Arcady. Can one roam among the letters of the alphabet? Might it be that the letters are compared to the fields and forests, mosses and springs of an ancient pastoral landscape? If so, why?

3) Is it relevant to the effect of the poem that the letters are given caps, when they might be in lowercase? Could letters possibly have existed before words? Can you imagine their appearance?

4) The original Dada-ists of 1916 wrote a number of poems composed entirely of single letters. Do you think that 'Arcady' is, a) a non-poem; b) a neo-Dada poem; c) a poem that tries to civilise a neo-Dada cliché by turning it into a light-hearted classical conceit?

In your opinion do the questions show a classical conceit?)

19 Whitefrost Court
Glasgow W2

Dear Ian

Attempted Answers to Questions Put

1. To show how far one can go, & at the same time to show
the limitations of 'how far one can go' – i.e. one cannot do
without the title. An alphabet by itself would not work, unless
something was done with it typographically, or unless at
least one letter was omitted or displaced. I don't agree that
'the alphabet [is] presented as a poem', unless 'as' means 'as if
it was [i.e. but it isn't]', since in this case the 'poem' includes
the title inseparably. I can imagine John Gielgud reading the
alphabet aloud & trying to tell us it was a poem, but I don't
think this would be convincing. In any case, your presentation
of it does not seem to ask us to read it aloud, & certainly not to
emphasize one letter more than another.

2. One can, but your poem doesn't ask us to, because it is
printed in a straight line, the italics even emphasizing the
one-way process. My first reaction was to read the alphabet
straight through to see what had been done with it; on finding
that apparently nothing had been done with it I felt some
'anxiousness' or 'disappointment' & at once read through
again, more slowly; then I thought about the title, saw what I
thought was a reasonable explanation for the straight alphabet,
& received pleasure, the pleasure being limited a little, or
remaining shall we say cool, because the word Arcady does
not have for me quite all the delightful associations you are
perhaps assuming it will have. Some of the associations of
'roaming in Arcady' are pleasant, but others suggest artificiality,
conventions, classicism in a bad sense, faded shepherds &
feeble pipes, & perhaps above all the idea that a Golden Age

has existed in the past, which I do not believe. (I have also read Sidney's *Arcadia*, which I recommend to you as an antidote to the Arcady idea!) The word Arcady chills me, whereas the word Metropolis – even as I type it here I feel it – stirs my blood. Other people of course can have the opposite reaction. – To return to the straight alphabet, I saw this, in conjunction with the title, as an expression of the classical ideal, 'Arcady' being not so much a place to roam in (this did not occur to me at all) as a stasis, something frozen on a Grecian urn, teasing us out of thought. (The colour of the paper also suggests nicely the clear blue sky of Greece.)

3. Yes. The caps increase the classical effect; in fact the poem would not work in lc. The caps also underline the idea of 'alphabet', just as the title does too, 'Arcady' being a kind of rhyme with 'alphabet' & even suggesting the alphabet with its a-c-d-y. I don't know if <u>letters</u> in the strict sense could exist before words – the alphabet is quite a recent invention in man's history – but some kind of signs perhaps could, or at least be contemporaneous with the first words. You end up with pictures, don't you? Cave man would have some pictographs as well as pictures and would presumably also have words. One still <u>feels</u> that words must have come first, if only because talking is more necessary than writing. On the other hand, gestures & noises must have come before talking, & gestures at least could be translated into sign form at a very early stage, sticks on the ground, smoke signals, etc… Chimpanzees? Do they prove anything? I suppose painting chimpanzees aren't found in the natural state, but they do take to the brush with remarkable readiness; perhaps their image-making abilities aren't much below their vocabulary of grunts & chatter after all? – Did you ever read Golding's *The Inheritors*? – And lastly, gbmmn'r shrb'mm't 'b 'rkd'mn'r!

4 (a) No, because it either is or has an 'idea' & also makes an impact which one recognizes as being within the general area of poetry, however specialized the direction of the impact. (b) Not <u>essentially</u>; superficially, yes. (c) This shows the natural penetration of self-aware creativity (POW!).

To return to the glass-poem idea. I am still keen, and would like very much to take up your suggestion to come & see some things in glass, stone, & sheet metal once you have them. I'm determined to regard the Hungary money as a windfall, and could in fact go up to £30 or £40. I got about £80, but had to leave some of it in Hungary. Banking it was a strange incident. The man who took me to the bank in Budapest & interpreted for me told me I must open an account but I must not use my real name. 'But what will I use?' 'Any name you like.' 'You mean I can say Robert Burns?' 'Why not?' So we went into the bank, & the clerk solemnly wrote down the name of Burns without turning a hair. Burns doesn't know it, but he now has a few thousand forint which I suppose are helping to build up the Hungarian economy. Unfortunately neither he nor I can use them.

The landscaped Cythera looks most attractive – I do hope you get this realized somewhere. America, I must say, seems the best hope, unless you can interest say the Duke of Bedford or Lord Montagu of Beaulieu (have you tried any of the stately homes or statelier grounds people, I wonder?). With the cutback on spending, on that hateful word 'frills', it is probably not the best of moments to try schools & colleges, though they <u>should</u> be interested in such projects. I was down lecturing recently at the University of Warwick, which is still very largely at the sea of mud stage, with a vast long-term programme of building over a huge site near Coventry. One of their building complexes will be some kind of cultural centre where something of yours would obviously be a possibility. I mentioned your work to George Hunter who is the English professor there & an old friend of mine (from Glasgow), & although it is really only a long shot I think you should write to him & at least make some suggestions (I mean of the kind of things you do or would like to do) which he could pass on to whoever is responsible for the building programme. I don't know how open they would be to new ideas of this sort, but maybe it is worth exploring? If you do decide to write, the address is: Professor George Hunter, School of Literature, University of Warwick, Coventry, Warwickshire.

Why not try the University of Stirling too? Nearer home, & even more uncommitted architecture-and-art-wise than Warwick.

What is Christmas in Dunsyre like? Do you have mince pies? I am just about to heat one here, heat, I mean, & then eat. All round is snow, & fog gathering. As there are no chimneys in Whittingehame Court, Santa Claus has to squeeze through the window-cracks like a very faint fine mist & reembody himself inside when he thaws out. On the other hand, the flat roof is very convenient for the reindeer resting…

Love to all, & best wishes for 1967 | which is nicer to write than 1966 | Yeddie

PS I return the pretty Cytherean plan

PPS Many thanks for delightful *Tealeaves & Fishes*: a fine collection.

19 Whiterthanwhite Court
Glazegaw W2
26 Boxing December Day 1966

Dear Ian

Answer to Boxing Day Question

Fishing

Love, | Yeddie

Ancillary supplementary postscript gloss, by way of bolstering & evincing the natural viability of ARCADY:

AVERNUS

ZYXWVUTSRQPONMLKJIHGFEDCBA

BACHELOR

ACEGIKMOQSUWY

<u>SPINSTER</u>

BDFHJLNPRTVXZ

<u>FAMILIES</u>

ABaCDdEFefGHghIJjjjKLkMN.OPpQRqqrrqSTttUV.
WXxxxxxYZz

<u>AIR</u>   <u>EARTH</u>
                              BCDFGHJKLMNPQRSTVXXYZ
AEIOU

                    <u>SPACE</u>
                    987654321

IHF awarded his friend high marks for his answers: 95% +. EM's own
alphabetic play on Boxing Day reveals his creative mind at work
in concrete mode, freed by the holiday from normal term-time
discourse. A One-Word Poem issue of *Poor.Old.Tired.Horse* followed
(No. 25).

Stephen Bann, editor and academic

31 January 1967

Dear Stephen
    The Festival poem seems to be going very well and I am
glad your arrangements are all working out so far. I think
that in answer to your question about how many three-word
phrases we should have for the posters: I would suggest 18
– because even allowing as you say for the 'public need to
collect & identify' I think <u>all</u> the available elements should be
available, and that means, in effect, 18 (or of course more). The
best thing would probably be just to take one of the 5 groups I
had typed – it would scarcely matter which.

Ian Hunter's suggestion of having parts of the poem on the Festival program sounds good. Perhaps it could be treated decoratively, by e.g. something like running the words together, say as borders or stripes – goldseadiva tinglingtransistorbucket blowypoetryterrace blueboatbirds etceteraetcetera…

I have never asked you but I suppose I should – does payment come into this, and what would I be offered?

Sincerely yours | Eddie

Bann, lecturing in the history of art, explored links between his subject and contemporary visual culture. The new Brighton Festival offered the opportunity to extend concrete poetry into the wider social environment. EM had written a 'Festive Permutation Poem-Happening' that included 90 three-word phrases for posters and postcards, in different groups of combinations of adjectives and nouns evoking the seaside festive theme. In the event, its use was less widespread than he had hoped, but some did appear on posters and bus windows.

Ian Hamilton Finlay, poet and artist

23 March 1967

Dear Ian: Trawler-man: A hoy

Term has just ended and I come up for air and beg forgiveness for tardy reply to your letter. Life is really very difficult – one in the morning, two in the morning, trying to catch up but never quite making it… And even though it is the Easter vacation, I have 200 papers to mark; there is never any real respite till the summer. At least I got my Brighton environment-poem done and accepted, and Stephen is busy with the final arrangements. What is your 'something less ambitious' at Brighton to be? It is a pity about the poem/pond.

How disappointing about Warwick and Helen Crckshnk too. I really thought something might come of Warwick. Stirling is still an unknown quantity of course. If you would like me to try, I could forward your letter to someone there. I have met the Registrar and the Principal (I was interviewed for the English chair, though I didn't get it) and it might still be worth trying, if you feel like it.

Yes certainly I will propose you for a bursary. I had been thinking of suggesting it. It would help me if you would let me have (very <u>soon</u>) a wee list of all the things you have done since the last award. I know of course the POTHs and other things you have sent me, but there may be other things you could mention, to make it an imposing List of Activities. Then they will say money well spent and (I hope) consider you again.

I will look forward to seeing the Dairy Gallery when it is ready. Next weekend I have to go to Brodick to (the things one does!) judge a children's writing competition. The overall prizewinner is a boy who wrote a long remarkable bit of autobiography about his terrible time at school – a very emotional boy, not stupid, but who suffered from dyslexia and no one understood this – almost Dickensian in its misery and yet this is Arran in the 1960s. My god, Scottish education!…

I am sorry that my NEWSPOEMS (Creeley and other) are down in London at the moment with Brian Lane of Gallery Number Ten, but when they come back I will let you see them.

Will your TEAPOTh ever see the light of day, do you think? That was one I was always looking forward to.

I enclose a poem I wrote to celebrate the end of term. It always has that effect on me.

Love | Yeddie

IHF had hoped to make an installation for the Brighton Festival. EM had suggested that he try to interest the new campus universities in his poem-sculptures. Helen Cruickshank (1886–1975) was a Scottish poet, cultural activist and supporter of aspiring poets. IHF asked EM to sponsor him for a second Arts Council bursary, as he developed Stonypath as a site for poetry, turning an old dairy into a gallery.

Duncan Glen, publisher and poet

10 April 1967

Dear Mr Glen
    First, about the Glasgow poets. Many thanks for your letter and the suggested arrangement of the poems. I think the idea of a separate pamphlet is a good one, and I agree with your suggestions about title, layout, and publication. Obviously it would be an advantage if the book <u>could</u> come out before the end of this term (the biographical details, for one thing, would be out of date by October), so I hope this might be possible. I agree to the omission of Alan Hayton's last poem. With regard to Colin Kirkwood's introduction, I'd be glad if you could let this stand. I made the point to him myself, but he has strong feelings about the particular as against the general and this was the sort of comment he wanted to give, so I think we must leave it as an idiosyncrasy. In my own introduction, would you please alter the last sentence from 'All four have appeared in…' to 'All four have been represented in…' On the inside title-page of the pamphlet, I think 'Introduced by Edwin Morgan' is better than 'Edited…' Robert Tait does in fact want the subtitles 'Ghost Series: poem 1' etc. to appear as well as the main titles. I think it should make quite a good pamphlet. It will probably be best if you send proofs to me for correction.
    I am enclosing a dozen concrete poems for the 'typographical' exercise. They present a variety of printing 'problems' but I hope also quite an interesting selection of material from a reader's point of view. Two which I found difficult or impossible to type I have written out. I hope the 'Russian Formalism' piece will be feasible, by using capital Z and/or N? The point of it, I should perhaps explain, refers to the literary idea of 'ostranenie' (meaning something like displacement or alienation) which the Russian formalist critics discussed during the 1920s (the idea has been re-discussed recently, with the revival of interest in that period). 'Ostranenie' can be printed in Roman capitals with the exception of the penultimate letter which is in Russian like a capital N reversed, so my poem simply makes this its point: the word is 'displaced' or 'alienated' by having one letter knocked out, but the letter

1960s   185

in fact converges on the empty space from all directions. The only other one I should perhaps comment on is 'Gnomes'. I'd like this to be printed very much as I have it, i.e. difficult but not impossible to read. It reads diagonally upwards from left to right, and makes a series of <u>gnomic</u> statements, 'fast bets best', 'cast fits fist', 'zest jets jest,' 'west eats east', etc… it is meant to be a puzzle, but with a solution. The title is a puckish pun. In 'The Computer's Second Christmas Card' I'd like the words and letters to be underlined as typed, not in italics; the idea is to have something looking like a mechanical message coming hot from the computer. If there are any other queries or problems do let me know!

Best regards | Edwin Morgan

PS Would you add something to the acknowledgements in the Glasgow poets volume: 'Acknowledgements are due to the editor and publishers of *Nik* & *Epos* in which poems by C.K. and S.M. first appeared.'

Glen suggested that he might be able to use some of EM's concrete poetry as a student project on his graphic design course at Preston Polytechnic. This led to the pamphlet *Gnomes* (1968), which included poems such as 'Strawberry Fields Forever', 'Archives', 'Dialeck Piece' and 'The Computer's Second Christmas Card' (*CP*: 139–42).

Ian Hamilton Finlay, poet and artist

19 Whortleberry Court
11 April 1967

Dear Ian

Oh I had hoped <u>hoped</u> to get down to Dunsyre and the Wild Pentlands sometime over Easter but I have never got clear of a mass of things piling up and now I must leave it (if this is all right with you) till next month when late May brings the end of the session and I shall (touching wood all over the room) have more free time (ah freedom is a noble thing but where is it to be found). The weekend in Arran which I told

you about was agreeable enough (on the Sunday I was taken
in wellingtons to see the Standing Stones on Machrie moor
which are an impressive sight – it was a bright cloud-flying
cold brisk day and we went with a dalmatian called Zombie)
though I do wish that when people ask you to undertake
such jobs they would make it clear they are not going to
pay you – for the not exactly light task of judging a hundred
entries, the public duties of prizegiving and speechmaking in
the company of the Lord Lieutenant of Bute who decided to
grace the occasion, for the nice little fare to the happy island
and back, I received one local pottery salt-bucket filled with
heartfelt thanks, and that was all. I came back with the Lord
Lieutenant's grandniece Barbara who was hitchhiking to
Inverness, but was thinking of going to the Philippines to 'do
something with her life'. I suggested she should try Africa
instead and left her with that thought. – Dyslexia is a blockage
of the ability to recognize and reproduce words correctly and
so it holds back the whole reading/writing learning process
and shows itself for example in a characteristic backward-
spelling that might come out somginthe lkie sith or the child
might (like Leonardo) want to do mirror-writing. The dyslexia
boy (whom I met) is clearly talented and is interested in art as
well as writing but is still very mixed up and uncertain about
what he will do – school has had a horrible influence on him
which he will find hard to shake off – has left an inarticulacy
and sort of fierce withdrawnness – he wants to leave Arran and
I think he ought to. It tears my heart to see someone like this.
There is so little one can do, when so much damage has already
been done. But I hope, and think, that he has some resilience.
– John Grieve: ah yes indeed! – a wonderful sad comedian
whom I have long admired. I'm sorry I don't have his address
but if you wrote c/o White Heather Club the letter would
find him. I always wish that John Grieve, Alex McAvoy, and
Philip McCall could form a regular comedy team – it would
be the funniest thing possible. I saw the Inveraray hornpipe
you mention, it was really very nicely done. But Grieve, like
so many other Scottish comedians, is better than the material
he usually has to deal with (Rikki Fulton and Stanley Baxter
are two others) and has never made the mark he should have
made. Scotland – the Land of Blasted Buds. – And speaking of

blasted buds, I am glad you were asked by the AC to nominate
a novelist, even if you couldn't (you old meanie!!) find one.
About a dozen nominations have been received, so I shall
soon be busy poising claims. You may find you will be able to
nominate Tom Wright some other year, as I gather the idea
is to vary the prize from fiction to drama to poetry etc. As a
prize it is certainly not to be sneezed at. – It was very good of
you to send me the detailed list of your undertakings; I have
sent in the sponsoring application and made I think a good
case; but of course you will understand that there might be a
reluctance to give a bursary to the same person in consecutive
years – I don't know what the policy on this will be, and it will
probably depend on what competition there is and also on
how much money there is. – About Stirling: perhaps the best
way of doing this would be if you were to write a letter to <u>me</u>
outlining in very general terms the kind of idea(s) you have in
mind and asking me if I would pass on either the actual letter
or the ideas to some relevant person at Stirling? If you prefer,
of course, I can just send a general note of inquiry to begin
with. Let me know how you'd like to get it done. – Yes, <u>surely</u>
George Bruce will do something for POTH25 – if you can't
persuade him I can have a go – but in some ways it would be
more suitable for television where examples that can't easily
be described can be seen; would you not yourself prefer a
television discussion if this was possible? – I close my letter
to the marmalady sounds of Tony Da Costa's Electric Home
Organ seeping through from the flat above – he installed it
to soothe the long hours of retired leisure when he gave up
business, and it now takes its place beside the guitar and the
dachshund and Mrs Da Costa's clogs on the kitchen floor
which she says are good for the feet. Is Dunsyre quiet?

Love | Yeddie

EM had awarded first prize in a schools competition to an autobi-
ographical piece from a dyslexic boy. IHF could not find 'dyslexia'
in his dictionary and asked for an explanation. He wondered if EM
knew John Grieve, whom he had seen on *The White Heather Club*, a
BBC Scottish dance programme. The Arts Council had asked IHF to
nominate a novelist for a bursary, but he claimed to be unable to

think of one. Once *Poor.Old.Tired.Horse* 25 was published, he hoped
to persuade George Bruce* to review the whole series on his BBC
Arts Review.

Evelyn Morrison, secondary school pupil

Department of English,
The University
16 April 1967

Dear Miss Morrison

Thank you very much for your letter about 'Message Clear'.
I am glad you found the poem interesting. I know it is always
very tempting to think that the poet himself will be able to
give the 'answers' to the questions that rise in readers' minds,
but I think this is not necessarily the case, since writing a
poem is not a fully planned step-by-step conscious activity, and
the unknown factors that tend to enter into it may really be the
important ones. However, the poet can at least <u>suggest</u> what he
<u>thinks</u> he was doing when he was writing the poem – perhaps
one shouldn't put it any stronger than that!

Yes, the poem does have 'something to do with this modern
computer age'. The title is meant to suggest this – the idea
of a message being communicated with difficulty or in an
unexpected way but coming through clear in the end, and
the manner in which the poem is set out may suggest (it
does to me) the <u>scanning</u> of a text electronically, the scanning
mechanism picking out in different exploratory ways all the
component letters of the text in their correct order, trying to
make sense of its material and doing so up to a point (in fact,
from a poetic point of view <u>enriching</u> the simple message)
but never hitting on the exact and complete statement until
the last line when all its expectations are satisfied. One of the
ways in which I can imagine the poem being presented would
be like a neon advertising sign, of the kind that flashes on and
off in parts until the full advertisement is shown. Of course,
the poem is also (taking it more traditionally) a dramatic
monologue spoken by Christ, and in this sense the unusual
form is meant to help to give new life to the monologue idea,

and also perhaps to suggest that if Christ was alive his message would have to be given in terms that bore <u>some</u> relation to our computer age. – On the idea you mention of 'Jesus dying on the cross' I am interested that someone thought of this: yes, at the beginning when the poem talks about the wounds of Jesus the form of the first eleven lines also suggests a cross in visual typographical terms.

I hope this will give you some help, though I don't expect it will clear up all the questions – it would be surprising if it did!

All best wishes to you and your friends – | Yours sincerely | Edwin Morgan

As captain of a third-year class in Dalziel High School in Motherwell, Morrison had been chosen to write a letter to EM, expressing the variety of their responses to his poem 'Message Clear' (*CP*: 159) and seeking a comment.

Maurice Lindsay, editor and poet

19 Whittingehame Court
25 April 1967

Dear Maurice

Could I ask you one or two questions about the *Modern Scottish Poetry* anthology, which I'm using as a text at the university this term?

In MacDiarmid's 'Two Memories', p.55, second last line, should 'peels' really be 'peals'? It looks as if it should, but I haven't got any other text of the poems to check it by. Where did this poem appear?

In 'The Glass of Pure Water', p.56, line 4, *Collected Poems* has 'glass of water' and you have 'glass of pure water' – could you tell me which is correct? In the same poem, p.58. line 13, *Collected Poems* has 'every true poet's place' and you have 'every true man's place' – again, I'd like to know whether yours is perhaps a corrected text.

I'm sorry to bother you wish these little details, but for teaching purposes one has to be sure of the text!

I hope all goes well with you. George tells me you have managed to find a place in Glasgow. I shall look forward to seeing you – and no doubt we shall in any case be having a meeting for SP3 sometime in the near future – though even yet I haven't seen a copy of SP2. It really is beyond a joke.

All best wishes | Eddie

Lindsay, EM's co-editor on *Scottish Poetry* 1–5, was now director of the Scottish Civic Trust. His revised edition of *Modern Scottish Poetry* (Faber & Faber, 1966) was chosen as a set text on the first-year English Literature course in Glasgow University.

Peter Butter, academic

17 June 1967

Dear Professor Butter

Alex Scott sent me a copy of his letter to you, and there are one or two points I'd like to add.

On all the editors being poets: this may be slightly unfortunate, but I don't think it raises any daunting objections. One doesn't need to be a practising novelist or dramatist to represent fiction and drama properly in a general literary magazine. In any case, novelists are hardly likely to have time to edit literary magazines, and our only probable playwright, Stewart Conn, has already been approached and declined – for the same reason.

On Robert Tait as proposed editor: I know him a good deal better than Alex does, and have more confidence in his abilities. I can't agree that his verse is only 'zany'; this adjective seems to me to show a misunderstanding of what he is doing. Nor would I agree that his article on Scottish poetry is merely self-centred. Potential contributors who have been 'made enemies of' by the article ought to have another look at it in a calmer mood. Though at times graceless, it makes some relevant and valid points.

On David Black: I agree that he is to some extent an unknown factor, but it is scarcely true to say that we're 'completely in the dark' – apart from his poetry, and his university degree, he has edited *Extra Verse*, and he has a critical article on Robert Garioch in the current *Lines Review*. Not <u>much</u> to go on, I know; but perhaps enough to recommend him as an associate editor?

On Robert Garioch: this is no doubt true. If we want <u>critical</u> abilities, we should look elsewhere.

On my own part in the affair: I've already indicated to you my own doubts about the wisdom of my taking a central part in the magazine, though I've no objection to being on an advisory board. The point Alex makes, whatever his motives, is a valid one which has been worrying me throughout the proceedings. I have always valued a certain independence that I have had in Scotland, and I don't want at all to be too closely associated or too often associated with the Arts Council, worthy body though that is. But if I withdraw, will Tait and Black be able to work with Alex? I have my doubts. Robert Tait has told me that he felt at the meeting that Alex was in some deep sense opposed to the whole venture as at present conceived (i.e. ex *Feedback*), and he is obviously in little sympathy with Tait's ideas and interests and thinks they must be 'stood up to' – <u>perhaps</u> a good thing, perhaps a rather ominous statement in the circumstances. Personally, I'd much more confidently see someone like Jack Rillie taking my place if I don't come in: I'm sure he would disagree with Tait on many occasions, but his mind is at least working in the same world and with the same order of ideas. Do you think he might be persuaded, despite the difficulty we mentioned?

It's a pity that this editorial hurdle still remains to be crossed. I agree with Alex that we shouldn't rush into it too hastily – though there is some urgency on the Arts Council side if anything is to be done this year. It seems to have got to the stage now where there ought to be some serious discussion of the editorship by persons <u>other than</u> those proposed for the job. The facts and difficulties have now emerged (except that we have no actual knowledge of whether Tait and Black could work with Alex, or of what merits I and Alex would have as candidates from the Arts Council point of view), and something of an impasse has been reached. Perhaps you will be able to make some headway with John McQueen and Anthony Ross.

A final not entirely frivolous suggestion: why not take
a plunge and have this magazine edited <u>entirely</u> by the
younger generation, adding Alan Bold's name to make up the
triumvirate? These three would work together, though their
outlooks differ widely. Bold has edited two magazines and is a
good journalist as well as a being a poet and a man interested
in ideas. I have no doubt whatever that between them they
could produce a stimulating magazine. The advisory board
could then include Alex and myself, as background figures...

Yours ever | Eddie

Butter, recently appointed Regius Professor of English, wanted EM
to co-edit a new journal (ultimately *Scottish International*). Alex-
ander Scott, lecturer in Scottish Literature, objected to Robert Tait
who as editor of *Feedback* had been critical of the status quo in
Scottish poetry. Jack Rillie, EM's friend and departmental colleague,
was an almost exact contemporary; David Black and Alan Bold*
were younger Scottish poets.

Ronald Johnson, poet

13 August 1967

Dear Ronald

      Long-
        mans
        sent me your
        <u>Green</u>
        <u>Man</u>
        which I sit happily
        reading on my balcony
        in a deck-chair above traffic,
        book savouring no traffic
        except that of owls
        (but I hear two – here too –
        after dark, and I have two swans
        that sometimes labour

up from their pond and
flap over the roofs) and
cuckoos, so
savourable as
these are
in growing places.

Growing places –
light in August! –
cities wheel
growing too in
human seasons, as
this lobelia
blue against marigolds,
and a few crazy
nasturtiums
scarlet and yellow
in my window-boxes
go growing in the wind
over the edge, spilling
in their meagre life
richly out
from their earth to the earth.
One life!
And the Green Man
tramps rustling
at will through it all,
in Kansas, Grasmere,
Glasgow. Carry
grass to the moon,
astronauts! 'On hearing
the first cuckoo
in the Sea of Showers
I composed this song.'

And through this thanked
you for your fresh green book.

Sincerely yours | Eddie | Edwin Morgan

Johnson had sent EM a copy of his long poem, *The Book of the Green Man* (1967), the style of which is echoed in this letter of thanks. Kansas-born, he was a friend of the American avant-garde poet and publisher, Jonathan Williams.

Duncan Glen, publisher and poet

14 September 1967

Dear Duncan Glen

Here is a first suggestion for the *gnomes* circular. I don't know how it will strike you. I think it ought to be feasible typographically, so long as you can print words upside down! The idea behind it is that all the words are related by sound to the central title-word, they are generated by it as it were out into a fairly distant but still connected aura; and also by meaning they are related to or generated by two meanings of the title-word; also the reversed words are related to the words on top. (To take one of the less obvious examples: 'gyms' – acrobats – verbal acrobatics, 'olms' are underneath because they live in underground streams, long pale creatures like the lampreys of the poem, crossing and twisting like slow-motion acrobats…)

It should balance properly because although the words are of various lengths (4, 5, and 6 letters) I have arranged them so that there are 15 letters to the left and right of the central 'e' of 'stems' in the upper part, and 14 letters to the left and right of the central 'm' of 'names' in the bottom part.

I shall be interested to have your views on this effort.

Yours | Edwin Morgan

The title *gnomes* (so printed) was meant to conflate, in a riddling way, the gnomic and the supernatural, the modernist and the ancient. Words on the planned circular layout would include reversals or reflections such as 'zones/notes' 'names/games' and 'stems/seams' but also 'awns/imps' (awns being beards of barley) and 'elves/glims' (glims being Scots for glimpses or scraps).

Ian Hamilton Finlay, *poet and artist*

18 September 1967

Dear Ian

I wrote to John Furnival about the au pair girl but he has none left, so can I fall back on the one you said you were guarding for posterity in your bottom drawer? I promise to take good care of it and will not allow the moth to lay its eggs there. Tell me how much I should give you for it. Perhaps Bob could be persuaded to bring back both objects together? But this may be too troublesome.

Thank you for the information about the typesetting of wave/rock. Could you also tell me who, where, and when was (or were) responsible for the actual object? I like to have all the facts, since people are sure to ask me.

I found the Derain exhibition an odd mixture of joy and disappointment, and I am not much nearer coming to any real estimate of him. He is an extraordinarily difficult artist to see as a whole. Going round the exhibition almost resolved itself in the end to saying 'I like this' and 'I don't like that', with the second of these preponderating after the 1920s, though there was always an occasional good painting right up to the end. There was a large selection of his theatre sketches and designs, and these were delightful – they were light and quick and in total contrast to the rather laboured sad heaviness that you find in a good deal of the post-Fauve work he did. Needless to say, the room of Fauves was wonderful, and I was constantly drawn back to that period. What I felt about many of the pictures (from all periods) was that I would want to have more time to get to know them a lot better before I was sure what I thought of them. Derain doesn't 'give', he has no 'signature', and yet the detachment, if detachment it is, is felt to have its own kind of depths and is not cold.

I am sorry you have heard nothing yet from Stirling. I think probably the delay will have been due to the pressures of getting the first term launched – launched today actually. Perhaps now something will happen. I wouldn't nudge them yet – these things are almost inevitably slow, because they involve committees and not just individuals.

Can you tell me who published Libby Houston's book? I saw a reference to it but forgot to take a note. I'd like to get a copy.

My Hansjörg Futura has come out, nicely done apart from several bad and maddening misprints – letters and lines dropped out from three poems. I wish he had sent proofs. There is always something peculiarly annoying and temperature-raising about good typography allied to careless proof-reading. I felt I had to put in the corrections in the enclosed copy, whether it spoils the effect or not. (Spiking of correctoins, you may correct my spoiles yousrelf.)

Love | Yeddie

The 'Au Pair Girl' was a poem on perspex (in fact, IHF discovered the remaining example had split in transit). EM's wave/rock poem on glass was donated to the Hunterian Gallery in 2004. The Derain exhibition was at the Edinburgh Festival. Libby Houston, a young poet who had read with EM in Edinburgh in the late 1950s, had visited Stonypath and left a copy of *A Stained-Glass Raree Show* (1967). Hansjörg Mayer published *Emergent Poems*.

Donald Carne-Ross, academic and editor

English Department
University of Glasgow
19 September 1967

Dear Carne-Ross

How nice to hear from you again, remote from these islands though you are. I am glad you find the Greek versions still survive. What you say about the Homer pleases me particularly because with your insight into these matters you have hit on very much what I was aiming at – I have always felt that Homer would want a translation of his poem, in whatever language, to give a clear account of what is happening, because there is a sort of celebratory down-to-earthness which is important to him, naming names, describing movements and gestures, discussing tactics and strategy, and so on, and almost, in his easy power, letting the grandeurs take care of themselves. At any rate, I find that from most if not all existing translations there is something lacking in the way in which a man whose subject is war would want realism and clarity as well as 'poetry'.

For your Notes on Contributors: I'm Senior Lecturer in the English Department at Glasgow. Recent publications (since my Montale of 1959) include: *Sovpoems* (translations mainly from Russian), 1961; (ed.) *Collins Albatross Book of Longer Poems*, 1963; *Starryveldt* (concrete poems), 1965; (ed. with George Bruce & Maurice Lindsay) *Scottish Poetry* Nos. 1 and 2 (annual anthologies, 1966, 1967); *Emergent Poems* (concrete poems), 1967 [this pamphlet just published – will post you a copy]. Due later this year are: *The Second Life* (collection of poems, both 'ordinary' and concrete, from Edinburgh University Press; *Gnomes* (concrete poems) (from Akros Publications); *Newspoems* (collage poems, from Gallery Number Ten). I have also become most interested in Hungarian poetry after a visit to Budapest last year, and have been translating Attila József and other modern poets. I know about the National Translation Center because it is hoping to sponsor an English version of Imre Madách's *Tragedy of Man* on which I have been asked to collaborate by Thomas Mark (teaches at Colorado State U). So for various reasons I will certainly be interested in your *Delos* magazine, and I will think about what I might contribute – or you may yourself have some suggestions later.

All best wishes | ≡||| | Edwin Morgan

PS: Thank you, belatedly, for your kind remarks about my Montale in the N.Y. Review; I must say I felt really bad at being omitted from that book.

After working for the BBC Third Programme in the 1950s, Carne-Ross taught classics at several American universities. Now based in the National Translation Center at Austin, Texas, he was about to launch *Delos*, a journal of translation studies. He had admired EM's shrewd, accurate and 'pawky (in an un-pejorative sense)' translation of Homer.

19 Whittingehame Court
24 September 1967

Dear Bob

When I saw the letterhead, and also the notice in *The Scotsman*, I thought we were really in business. Your electric typewriter is a fine acquisition too, for the professional touch. I am not sure I like the box below the title on the letterhead, do you? It seems to draw rather too much attention to it at the moment.

I note your remarks on the various poems. I agree with you that if we like some of the Gael Turnbull pieces we shouldn't be held back by minimal-public appearances elsewhere. I certainly would like to have something by him in the first or an early number. I imagine that Alan Bold will have no shortage of briefer poems to replace the one you couldn't take for its length! I have sent the Robin Fulton poems to Garioch (by the way, did you discover what he likes to be called familiarly?); he will probably let you see my covering letter, where I said that I thought three of them were acceptable and perhaps could be taken as a group (on the same theme); if three is felt to be too many, I mentioned the one I liked best. I shall look forward to seeing David's article in due course. Good news about Iain Cuthbertson.

I have just received my copy of Stephan Bann's anthology of concrete poetry (London Magazine Editions): nicely produced book which I take it we ought to review since it gives a lot of space to Scottish concrete (Ian and myself), even if few hearts among Scottish reviewers will be warmed by the prospect. Would you like to review it yourself perhaps? You could always sign yourself Engelbert Humperdink. My own pamphlet in Hansjörg Mayer's *Futura* series has also just arrived and I enclose a copy for you. It has unfortunately some maddening misprints, as you will see.

Thanks for *Image*. Tom McGrath, by the way, came up with another idea for a possible article he'd like to write sometime: on certain trends in Scottish jazz, with particular reference to Andy Park, of whom he thinks very highly, as creator as well as performer. This could be a worthwhile piece I think.

My main piece of news is that I'm going to try my hand at something quite new – the libretto for an opera to be composed by Thomas Wilson (the young Scottish composer whose name I think I mentioned to you when we were talking about our advisory board). It's all at the beginning stages yet; we have had a few meetings and have almost settled on a subject. The BBC and Scottish opera are both interested and I think an actual 'commission' may emerge, but it is still egg-treading and confidential…

I'll see if I can think of non-poetry books to review. One that occurs to me is *Literature and the Delinquent* by Alexander A. Parker of the Department of Hispanic Studies at Edinburgh University, published by EUP. It's an academic study of the picaresque novel in Europe in the 17th & 18th centuries but contains a lot of interesting material of wider import (as its title suggests).

Ever | Eddie

Scottish International proceeded by the three co-editors forwarding submissions onwards with their own evaluations of them, with final editorial meetings in Edinburgh or Glasgow to agree copy. Iain Cuthbertson, an actor and later a director at Glasgow's Citizens' Theatre and London's Royal Court Theatre, had been asked for an article on contemporary theatre. 'David' was D.M. Black.

Nicholas Zurbrugg, academic and editor

25 September 1967

Dear Mr Zurbrugg
    In reply to your queries of 28 August:

(a) I don't regard concrete poetry as primarily a 'means of personal expression' – it is doing something different. I write both concrete and normal syntactical poetry, and what I imagine you mean by personal expression is generally taken care of by the latter.

(b) Through corresponding, in 1962, with the Portuguese concrete poet E.M. de Melo e Castro and later with the Brazilian group.

(c) But what is meant by 'wholly convincing'? Who is to be wholly convinced? I have certainly no doubt that work of value had been done long before 1965, and that worthwhile developments from 1965 to 1967 have taken place, though there have also been disappointments. What remains still very much an open question is whether concrete will continue to develop as an almost separate art or whether it will be absorbed by (after having an influence on) the general art of poetry.

(d) Gomringer; Jandl; Finlay; the Brazilians. The reasons are too various to go into in short space.

(e) Only a few of my poems are simulated computer poems; these reflect my interest in computers and the possibilities of computer creation in the arts. They are not 'anecdotal' except in the sense that a computer can only work step by step, by a path of accepted and rejected decisions. What interests me is the relation of such a method to other methods of what we are accustomed to call creation. But I have written many different kinds of concrete poem, and this is only one of them.

(f) It is not always as simple as it seems. But granted there are certain kinds of complexity which the genre cannot encompass (and does not want to). Of this I am sometimes impatient, because I like many examples of complexity and detail in art (e.g. the Book of Kells, Bosch, Jackson Pollock, James Joyce); on the other hand I like modern architecture, typography, advertising, industrial design, and many other cleancut, economical, or 'constructivist' features of the present century. So on this matter my feelings are divided, and I cannot give you a simple answer. I could hardly say I was 'critical of the simplicities' when one of my own poems consists of a single letter ('Phantom Beaver')! But I don't care much for the concrete poem where both eye and mind too quickly exhaust all it has to offer; there must be, in all art, a certain 'check'.

(g) (i) Yes. (ii) No. There is as much range from esoteric to popular in concrete poetry as there is in other forms of art.

(h) Again there is a great range of effects in concrete poetry from 'warm' to 'cold'. Some of it is outgoing, joyous, humorous, witty; some of it is stark, hermetic, forbidding; some is political; some is religious; some is mathematical; some is sculptural; some is two-dimensional, some three-dimensional; some abstracts concrete forms such as animals, some concretizes abstract forms such as grammatical relationships. I myself incline to the 'warm' rather than the 'cold' end, but I recognize that there are other points of view.

(i) I can't answer this in a general way. Each poem or group of poems presents its own problems and pleasures. Also one's work changes and (one hopes) develops. Humour, irony, and satire seem to be recurring features. The fact that I usually give my poems careful titles indicates – whatever you want to draw from that.

(j) Advantage – no slovenly writing. Weakness – Webern si, Beethoven no!

You will find examples of my poems and some discussion of my work in Stephen Bann's recently published *Concrete Poetry: An International Anthology* (London Magazine Editions, London, 1967). This book also refers to some magazines where I have had work published, and to my pamphlet *Starryveldt* published by Eugen Gomringer in his Konkrete Poesie series at Frauenfeld. I appeared in Hansjörg Mayer's *Concrete Poetry Britain Canada & USA*, and I have a pamphlet called *Emergent Poems* in his Futura series.

I enclose two examples of my poetry which you may want to use in your magazine.

Yours sincerely | Edwin Morgan

For an arts magazine in the University of Neuchâtel, Switzerland, Zurbrugg had sent questions on concrete poetry, some of which implied a narrow view of its potential.

Al Alvarez, editor and poet

8 October 1967

Dear Mr Alvarez

Thank you for your letter of 2 October. I think I would be interested in both of your proposals. At the moment I have about 20 poems of Attila József translated, which amount to probably around 30 pages. I would be glad to do some more versions to make up 50 pages or so, and also to write an introduction as you suggest.

The translations of Weöres which you saw in NHQ are the only ones I have so far done, but in fact I'd like very much to explore him further, as he and József are the two Hungarian poets I react to most strongly. I had heard myself from Peter Redgrove that he was not too happy about some of the translations, and I'd certainly be pleased to collaborate on this volume if this is all right with him. I take it this would be done by his Hungarian friend passing on some of the material to me? As I have a good many things on hand just now, it would take longer than the József (and Weöres is a difficult poet), but I would like to do it.

I think including József in your series is a splendid idea. He is a very remarkable poet and still far too little known in the west.

Yours sincerely | Edwin Morgan

EM's translations in *New Hungarian Quarterly* led Alvarez to propose his involvement in the new Penguin Modern European Poets series, translating Attila József and Sándor Weöres*. The latter had already been begun by Peter Redgrove*, who now felt that his versions were too far from the originals.

Peter Redgrove, poet

16 October 1967

Dear Peter Redgrove

Alvarez wrote to me recently about the Penguin Weöres, said you were a bit unhappy about some of the results so far, and asked me whether I would consider collaborating with you on the volume. I said I'd be glad to, so long as this was agreeable to you. I take it that his idea was for each of us to tackle about half of the poems (as was done in the Holub volume), and I suppose poems that proved intractable to you might be tried by me and vice versa. Anyway he suggested I should write to you and see what the position was. You could send me on anything that you'd particularly want me to have a go at, though naturally I'd also like to see all your versions if you have copies you can spare. The only ones I have done so far are the ones in NHQ which you have seen. Have you got, from your Hungarian friend, both literal versions and the original texts? I like to have the originals, even working with a dictionary. (I am trying to pick up some Hungarian as I go along.)

With best wishes | Yours sincerely | Edwin Morgan

Before working alongside Redgrove, EM was anxious to clarify boundaries. He had sent Redgrove a copy of his translations in *New Hungarian Quarterly* nine months earlier.

Betty Clark (Joan Ure), dramatist

17 October 1967

Dear Betty

Thank you for the information about Saturday at the Close: I will pass this on to as many people as possible, though I won't be able to come myself.

I am sorry you found the notice 'condescending': certainly not meant to be. But very little came across to me when I saw the play. I thought a good deal about it before I wrote my piece, and I read Chris Small's advocacy of it with care but could not agree with him – in the abstract I would have liked to, but it was not my experience in the theatre. You suggest in your letter that it was the production which was at fault. This may be so, but I am still not clear what the quality is that the production failed to bring out. It seemed to me (and to most people) to be well acted. What is it that you would have wanted to be different? The manner of speaking, the projection, the emphasis? I should tell you that the moment when the play came most alive for me was when the coffee was being poured and the talk was of sugar. It reminds me of an old Jean Gabin film of which I can't remember the title or anything in it except a beautiful sequence when Gabin sat at a table and cut himself some bread and cheese and took some wine. I suppose the oldest and only definition of drama is 'people doing things' – even Chekhov and T. Williams. If you don't have people doing things you're exposed to a tremendous hazard with language, you really come naked and your language has to be of cracking quality and immediacy. Even Beckett, who is a master with language, only just gets away with it – and even he bores quite a lot of people who are otherwise open to drama. It was the language (as I said in my review) that worried me most about your play. But if, as perhaps you are suggesting, it was not spoken as you want it to be spoken, then maybe there is something that has not yet got across but may do so on another occasion. It is a pity that – to revert to Chekhov – you cannot find 'your' producer. But I wonder if you would agree – perhaps not! – that a play should be able to stand up to various interpretations and that if there is only one ideal method of producing it this might be a criticism of the play? – Do please take these remarks in all freedom and friendliness! You have got to <u>make</u> other people 'know what you are about', as I have, or Beckett has, or anyone. Persuade, persuade! It has to be done <u>within</u> the work – Sisyphus and all, I know – you can't throw it onto Stanislavsky or the audience. It's hell, but it's art.

As ever | Edwin Morgan

Clark, a Glasgow-based dramatist and poet who wrote as Joan Ure

(1918–78), had complained that EM had broadcast a 'condescending' review of *I See Myself As This Young Girl*, recently performed in the Close Theatre, Glasgow. (Her letter had referred to a forthcoming event with poets co-operating with pop-singers.)

Ian Hamilton Finlay, *poet and artist*

17 October 1967

Dear Ian

Long delay answering new term beginning. Especially labours deputizing professor absent lecturing Canada. But how are you now anyway.

I was delighted with the two posters. Stephen's now looks very iconographical yet the little fleeces or fleecicules stand out too: more mimesis plus more icon together, very interesting. Yours is a Platonic defacement, a delinquence with waves. It says something about posters as well as about its subject. I wonder if there is anybody who never wants to change the message of a poster? My Whittingehame Court busstop with its separate framelike metal panels is a shifting art-gallery of altered posters and painted messages on unpostered parts. The painter comes periodically to restore the tabula rasa or status quo ante, but, as a recent rhyme has been scrawled up to tell us:

THE PAINTERS WORK IS ALL IN VAIN
THE BUS STOP POET HAS STRUCK AGAIN

It is a great pity about the 'au pair girl'. And you will not want to lose the one in the gallery. Ah well, if ever another copy is likely to be made… keep me on the waiting-list.

I entirely agree about Mr Rannie. I saw the TV. It was a rather fine moment when he was testing the mike for the Queen to speak and said 'They're not ready for us – we'll have to give the job to STV next time' – there seemed to be considerable merriment among the launching party and it's a pity the microphone couldn't have picked up some more. I admired the way Mr Rannie positively hit the mike, none of your genteel finger-tapping.

As Bob will probably have told you (or as you might have guessed) the new magazine is running through squalls of a well-known Scottish type. It really is extraordinarily difficult getting anything started in Scotland. At any rate we start without the grace and favour of the 'only lecturer in Scottish literature in a Scottish university' and also of the 'greatest living Scottish poet'. Well –

I was down at Birmingham on Wednesday, reading poems at the Birmingham & Midland Institute with Roy Fisher, poems interspersed with Sandy Brown's clarinet. Sandy is a splendid character. I met Stuart Mills and Gael Turnbull who had come through from Nottingham and Gloucester. Flew back Thursday morning, in sunny mist, half-empty plane.

I am glad the bursary thing was sorted out all right; ridiculous if it hadn't been.

Love | Yeddie

The posters, one by Stephen Bann*, were the latest Wild Hawthorn productions. IHF had praised the Master of Ceremonies at the launch of the Clyde-built liner *Queen Elizabeth II*. The other launch, of *Scottish International*, had provoked opposition from Alex Scott and Hugh MacDiarmid*. An Arts Council bursary had led to Social Security issues, threatening to reduce a small amount of sickness benefit that IHF already received for his nervous problems, and EM lobbied the authorities on his behalf.

Robert Tait, editor

23 November 1967

Dear Bob

I've passed on the Alan Bold article and the Tom Buchan review to RG. I like Tom Buchan's review, it's fine. I am more doubtful about Alan Bold's piece. As art criticism I find it most unconvincing; it begs questions all the way through, and tries to pass by waving the magic flag of Gombrich (he is always doing this; he doesn't seem to realize that Gombrich though an important art historian is well off the mark when he comes to modern painting and is very far from widely accepted). Also, I think from the evidence of the 3 photographs the painter is a poor one, showing the worst excesses of that particular style. Surely the heavy, laboured, muddy 'Descent into Hell' is a perfect example of a secondrate, wilful, uninspired painting. To invoke the names of Beckmann, Corinth, and Kokoschka is only to show what a descent there has been down to Sitte's level. What would be interesting <u>would</u> be a sensible illustrated article on <u>them</u> and on the German expressionist tradition, still neglected in this country. On the other hand, your point about 'information' is a relevant one, and especially if we are having (are we, by the way?) that article on Minimal Art, for here is the perfect opposite to Minimal Art and each might throw light on the other. My dislike of Sitte is only an opinion, formed on 3 reproductions, and it may well be interesting to people to show his work as an example of a trend. I wouldn't therefore vote the article out, if there's a feeling it could have a useful place artwise in No.1.

I wonder if you managed to talk to Cuthbertson. I told Professor Butter about the matter but he didn't feel there was much we could do, unless you can counterpersuade him. (I mean Cuthbertson.)

Yes, I have read *Writing Degree Zero* and find it very interesting stuff. Let's by all means have an article on it from Tom Buchan; I think he'd do a good job.

I have just finished a longish review of Mikhail Bulgakov's *The Master and Margarita*, a fascinating novel which I recommend. Due to be published next week. My review is anon., so you'll probably guess where it will appear.

All the best – | Eddie

Iain Cuthbertson had been asked to become a trustee of *Scottish International*, but EM suspected he had been put off by negative comments from some establishment literary figures. 'Diabolical Experiment', his review of Mikhail Bulgakov's novel, appeared in the *Times Literary Supplement*, 7 December 1967.

27 December 1967

Dear Mr Zurbrugg
I am sorry to have taken so long to reply to your letter of 6
October with its questionnaire, but anyway here now are some
attempts at an answer:

(a) I would not at all object to various typographers making
different versions of my poems, so long as my own particular
version of a poem was clearly known. The same would apply
to any other 'treatment' of it, such as its re-presentation as a
three-dimensional object. But naturally I would reserve the
right to be pleased or displeased by the results.

(b) Any version will certainly <u>change</u> the original values even
if only to a slight extent; but not necessarily detract from
them. Concrete poems may be said to have 'doubles' as we use
that term in ordinary life, i.e. meaning not truly doubles but
an interesting and perhaps strange resemblance. As regards
translation, I have always been a believer in getting as close
to the original as possible, and I don't entirely accept the view
that translation is 'impossible', although it is often very difficult
and demanding. Some concrete poetry needs no translation
or is easy to translate; other examples are near the edge of
impossibility. I have translated quite a lot from the Noigandres
group, and from Eugen Gomringer and some of the German
concrete poets. A solution often pops up like toast from a
toaster – perhaps not exactly the right shade of golden brown,
but surprisingly 'there'. There is considerable joy to be got from
translating concrete poetry successfully.

(c) One has to accept (or, of course, reject) a mingled
responsibility in such cases. I can accept it, though I can see
that there are limits. John Furnival and his art students are
doing a folder of my poems just now. I composed twelve
concrete poems based on proverbs, and these are being worked
on, with varying degrees of imagination and redesigning, at
the moment. I have seen first proofs of eight of the poems,

of which five or six seem well within the 'acceptable' limits, though I have doubts about one in particular and this one will be looked at again. But the doubtful one is <u>not</u> the most imaginative one – it is rather one that has not solved the problem of how to use the skeletal concept provided by me. In the final result, I shall still consider myself as largely responsible, but it will be a group creation too.

(d) I think it can be fruitful if it <u>is</u> collaboration. But at times the actual collaboration is minimal, as in Hansjörg Mayer's large folder of concrete poems from Britain, United States etc… I had no say in the printing of my 'Opening the Cage' in this collection, and the result came as a surprise. Although it was very finely printed and made a good visual impact, I did not myself think that the typographer's rearrangement of the word spacing improved the poem. I am willing in this instance, however, to accept and acknowledge the status of the typographer – so long as I can have the poem printed as I want it elsewhere. It is another matter when one may object to the actual typeface used, as I would object in the case of my 'Computer's First Christmas Card' in its version in the Something Else Press concrete anthology (1967). My own particular problem in this poem and many others is that I see these as <u>typewriter </u>poems where I am thinking in terms of typewriter space, equal width of letters, etc., and this is hard to reproduce in ordinary type when poems come to be printed. I am seldom entirely pleased by the results. – In answer to the last question, I have collaborated with the typographers in the printing of my book *The Second Life* which Edinburgh University Press are bringing out in a week or so – it will include concrete and non-concrete poems. There has also been collaboration – at a distance – with Duncan Glen the typographer who runs Akros Publications in Preston, Lancashire. He is printing a little volume of concrete poems for me, to be called *Gnomes*.

I hope these remarks will be of some help and interest to you.

With good wishes | Yours sincerely | Edwin Morgan

Pursuing his research, Zurbrugg was exploring the relative roles of poet and typographer in publication and printing. EM refers to *Proverbfolder* (1969) from John Furnival's Openings Press, and to his own translations of Haroldo de Campos* and Gomringer* (*CT*: 286–300).

Duncan Glen, *publisher and poet*

13 January 1968

Dear Duncan

Many thanks for letting me know about the gnomes and their setbacks – I can understand the frustrations and difficulties. Let's hope the final result meets the bill as far as our corrections are concerned.

Although Iain Smith has no fondness for concrete, it would be interesting to see what he would have to say about the other poems. He doesn't write much criticism but can be very acute. I think you should try him.

Akros editorial: yes, I thought it was confusing! It seemed a disguised manifesto for an all-Lallans poetry magazine, but I gather this is not to be the case? I feel it was perhaps a mistake to denigrate both concrete and oral poetry in order to push Lallans. The spoken poetry movement is one of the best things that has happened to poetry for a long time, and the first poet you print (Robert Garioch) is, ironically enough, one of the noted members of it and of what you call the 'travelling circus' (as are also Hugh MacDiarmid and myself – we have been reading all over the country in the last few years). It is spoken poetry that is keeping alive and indeed renewing regional language in poetry, and it is very strange that you should think it is opposed to Scots. In Edinburgh and Glasgow recently, large audiences heard live readings by three poets, Garioch, Alan Jackson, and Brian Patten; the first two quite distinctively Scottish in both language and/or outlook, the third just as surely non-standard-English and giving new meaning to the word 'Liverpool'; these readings were well received. I wish some of the arthritic poets you printed in that number of *Akros* would learn the difference between dead and living language!

Do hang onto the 'Itinerary' poems; I'd like them to appear in *Akros*, and there's no hurry.

Best regards as ever | Edwin Morgan

Glen had employed a traditional printer with a one-man business for *Gnomes*, with attendant setbacks. Iain Crichton Smith* was his choice as *Akros* reviewer for *The Second Life* (1968). In a compressed editorial complaining about 'performance poetry' (such as that of the Liverpool poets) Glenn had seemed to denigrate experimental writing. In fact, he published a range of writing, and the sales figures for *Gnomes* in London and the USA were high.

Robert Tait, editor

4 February 1968

Dear Bob

Herewith copy of my comments to RG – sorry this is giving you both so little time, but the material should not take terribly long to read.

And this is what Iain Smith put in his letter:

"Dear Mr Morgan, I am writing to you and your colleagues in reference to your new magazine, a copy of which I received today. What I miss in all magazines of the arts in Scotland – and please do not take this in bad part – is not only the lack of good readers' letters with good solid opinions on education and the theatre – as well as linguistic lists of the types of waves to be found off Orkney – I miss that too as well as good stories so that I know who after all was in love with which – I know that in this day and age old age pensioners like myself cannot depend on what you call kailyard but I call W.R. Crockett – but Vosnesensky, what airt does he come from, that's what I want to know – and Violence – and what's that footballer on the front page for? That isn't Vosnesensky is it? And really you're very cruel to Anne Edith Robertson who is by the way a guid freend of mine. Anyway as I started out to say where is your Crossword and your Chess Problem and your Draughts

Problem? I think a good crossword would raise the tone of
your magazine enormously."

Now isn't that, all in all, and allowing for various ironies, a
puzzling sort of criticism? What do you make of it? It doesn't
seem to me to hang together logically, however I look at it. But
it has apparently been written with some feeling.

I have just this minute been listening to Scottish Life
and Letters (and must hurry this to the post if you are to
get it tomorrow morning). I thought you came across good
and clear and made the main points well. MacDiarmid was
surprisingly subdued on the whole and his 'statement of advice'
could hardly be disagreed with in essentials. AS, I thought,
was a little too conscious of the occasion as being one of self-
defence for breadth of outlook. What struck me, from the four
speakers, was that there is some continuity, as well as change.

Till Wednesday at 7 – | Yours | Eddie

SCOTTISH INTERNATIONAL – comments on submissions
4 February 1968

Bernard Kodjo LAING: I find these among the most
interesting poems we have had submitted to us, and would
certainly vote to include some of them. Although they are
not always clear, their difficulties seem to me to be of a
kind proper to poetry (and also partly to reflect the greatly
mixed and contrasting experiences of a young Ghanaian now
domiciled in Scotland and married to a Scottish girl). The
verse has an accomplished and often subtle movement, and I
get the impression of careful craft. Could we perhaps consider
one of the long and one of the short poems? I'd suggest
BIRTHPLACE and GET RID OF SOCIAL DEATH, but
these are only marginal preferences.

John WOODS: This novella THE NOBLEST ART would
have to be good to justify so much space, and I don't think it
does. It has clearly been very devotedly and even ambitiously
done – the writing all through is asking to be noticed. But this

may be my reason for feeling dissatisfied (bored, even) with the result. It owes so much to Henry James and Meredith that it reads almost like a parody of their style, especially James's. There's plenty of irony and even a little humour but neither seems to be quite of the quality one would describe as – the style is catching – 'saving'. I couldn't get interested in the central character; more about the wicked old man would have helped to perk the tale up. I think my basic objection may be that the way the story is written seems, <u>at the present time</u>, to be intolerably forced and studied; the objection is not to psychological probing or interior monologue or anything like that in itself.

EM had reacted intemperately to a jokey letter from Iain Crichton Smith*, failing to register its ironies, and a sign perhaps of the stress experienced as *Scottish International* developed. 'AS' was Alexander Scott. Also attached are typical editorial comments. Bernard Ko[d]jo Laing* was a Glasgow University student poet.

Iain Crichton Smith, poet and novelist

(n.d. prob. Feb 1968)

**Morgan
Is
Stupid!**

–but relieved! I suppose it all goes to prove something about the use of irony. Maybe I was in a masochistic mood and was looking for trouble under every bush. Anyhow, many thanks for setting my mind at rest, and also for your kind remarks about the Voznesensky – which I certainly enjoyed writing, I think he really is a remarkable poet. We – the editors I mean – were discussing your Wittgenstein piece the other night but none of us felt it had quite come off; it seemed as if you were rather forcing yourself into a new area that you were still uneasy in, though there were some very interesting passages and ideas. It is also pretty long, so I rather doubt if we shall be able to take it. But do please send us other things, verse or prose, whenever you like. I hope the Lilies will have success, and I must look out for it. My Second Life seems to be selling quite well so far. It got a good review in *New Society*, a slightly surprising place. But I wonder what the TLS will do with it – they have had some strange reviews lately. By the way, you remember the young Afro-Scottish poet Bernard Kojo Laing whom we both liked in the BBC poetry competition? He has given me some most interesting poems which we shall be printing in the next number of the magazine. He is certainly a man to watch. – How is Oban, wet and windborne? Glasgow is. O traces of spring. O hounds of winter. Farbehind.

Best as ever | Eddie

ICS excused his letter 'in the voice of the kailyard' as post-flu gymnastics: 'My Calvinism is so pervasive that when I do joke people take me seriously.' His first novel, *Consider the Lilies*, was published in 1968.

George Bruce, producer and poet

11 February 1968

Dear George

I have enjoyed your *Nearly Always Summer* very much indeed, and I am sure it will be of great interest in the magazine. The sense of place is strong and pungent, and the tri-partite whiff of <u>fish</u>, <u>music</u>, and <u>football</u> establishes your Fraserburgh immediately in its own existence. I am glad you eschewed the formal I-was-born-in-the-upland-parish-of-High-Dudgeon-on-a-cold-January-afternoon approach. The presentation succeeds in having what is (I think) important, a tone of voice which is related to your own – a sort of syntactical eagerness which leaps like water from rock to rock. Your closing sentence is splendid, and opens up a formidable vista. Of course the purely <u>literary</u> side has still to come, but you have dropped little hints of this theme into the story. The next instalment will be, by me at any rate, enthusiastically awaited (which doesn't sound quite right but you know what

I mean). I will pass your piece on now to my two co-sowers-and-harvesters.

On another matter: thanks for your BBC letter of 5 February: date and time noted; so will see you and Robin Fulton about 4.15 on 21 February.

Yours aye | Eddie

Bruce produced *Arts Review* for BBC Radio. He had written this piece for *Scottish International* at EM's request, who had long admired his pithy anecdotes of Scottish literary figures he had encountered.

Ian Hamilton Finlay, poet and artist

10 March 1968

Dear Ian

I am so glad that you were pleased with the Home Service piece on POTH. There was so little space that I could do no more than give a factual outline which I hoped would not be misleading. It was not much, but at least something. I wish I could have said more.

Thank you for the kind remarks on my book. It is especially useful to me to have your comments on the concrete poems which as you quite rightly surmise give me a sense of <u>release</u>, or perhaps it could be called a species of joy, which cannot entirely be obtained by other means, though something similar happens (I think) when I use Scots inventively for translation purposes or when in the past I have at times used a Joycean word-inventiveness; I would <u>like</u> to think that a parallel though different joy can still emerge through 'normal' lyrical usage in 'syntactical' poems – I mean of course that I do believe it does and do therefore try to produce it – but I understand and respect your doubts before the whole mode. All I can say is that I still want to write poems such as (for example) 'In the Snack-bar' which is a kind of opposite to the concrete poem and is doing something (in so far as it comes off) that concrete cannot do. Your letter reads in an ironic light after this week's TLS; what on earth has got into Mike Weaver? I was astonished by his attack on me. I know perfectly well that some of my concrete poems could be called 'literary jokes' but it is unjust to say that that is all I have done, and anyone who really knows my work should be able to distinguish the grades and levels. My goodness, you never know your friends, do you? His whole letter was, I thought, in any case far too dogmatic and certainly far too narrow in its distinctions and definitions. It is easy to be dogmatic if you lightheartedly shovel half the evidence out of the way as he does. Movements are what they are, not what you want them to be.

By the way, you are the first person to dislike the cover. It is meant to be relevant, in that the flower is an immortelle... I didn't want to mix translations with the two kinds of poem already there, but I would like to have a volume of translations yet. Maybe I can persuade the EUP if I can catch them in the right mood. A companion volume would be nice.

May I say how much I got from your *Ocean Stripe 5* which I think is one of your most impressive things. (*Stonechats* nice of course, but not in the OS5 class.) Stephen's article on it is excellent, and I hope we shall have it in the next issue of the magazine, with at least one illustration if this is feasible; Bob will have been writing to you about this I expect.

But I have to prepare a lecture on Wallace Stevens so must pour myself a cup of milk and get on. Milk at midnight. Did you know that Stevens said (i) 'A poem is a pheasant' and (ii) 'Poetry is a pheasant disappearing in the brush'? These are endearing statements from a not too endearing fellow.

See and look after yourself. I hope Sue and the children are fine.

Love | Yeddie

The Home Service was the regional programming of present-day Radio 4. IHF's favourite poem in *The Second Life* was 'Spacepoem 1: from Laika to Gagarin' (*CP*: 194).

Peter Redgrove, poet

26 May 1968

Dear Peter

You will probably have seen Professor Gömöri's comments on the Weöres translations. He seems to think that at the moment they are a little <u>too</u> free in that they don't indicate the <u>form</u> of the originals. With some poetry this might not be of enormous importance, but Weöres is known as rather a virtuoso in form, and I suppose therefore we must make some approach towards meeting this objection (perhaps especially as the book will be reviewed in Hungary itself, and Hungarian translation theory tends to favour <u>complete</u> translation wherever possible). The best solution might be, since you and I have somewhat different ideas on the importance of trying to reproduce formal elements, to have half of the translations 'free' (taking the best of your versions, which I certainly would be sorry to see changed or given up) (and an introductory note could easily state that these were deliberately free versions) and the other half (my half) endeavouring at least to indicate or suggest the metre, rhyming, stanza-form etcetera of the originals. But to do my part of this I must somehow get hold of the <u>original texts</u> plus <u>really literal versions</u>. Is it possible for you to obtain these for me from your original supplier? Presumably he must have the Hungarian texts? And presumably he would send you literal versions which lie behind the literals in Folder B? (I say 'he' but I have just recalled you said 'Szabo and others' – I hope this doesn't make it more difficult.) If it is going to be very difficult to get hold of the actual texts, could we at least get a formal description of the poems, which would help? I am sorry that this particular problem is still plaguing us, but I think that, speaking for myself, it would be good if we can try to meet the objections Gömöri has raised.

Yours ever | Eddie | Edwin Morgan

EM had just contacted George Gömöri in Birmingham University, outlining his difficulties in getting copies of Weöres's books when in Hungary in 1966 (they sold out quickly), and asking for a loan of books. Gömöri offered one on loan, plus some photocopies, and also library and bookseller contacts.

John Caughie, academic

26 May 1968

Dear John Caughie

It is such a long time since I got your last letter that you may well have moved elsewhere by now, but I hope this will reach you eventually. You may remember that when you wrote you were applying for the fellowship in Buffalo – I wrote a recommendation for you, and I got Mr Rillie to send one too. I couldn't ask David Bank, as he is having a Scandinavian year (two years actually) at Uppsala. You mentioned that the competition would be very keen, and I take it that you were in fact not one of the lucky ones. Anyway, I heard recently from the Department of English at the University of Oulu and sent off a recommendation to Professor Reuter, so I hope you will have better luck there. It sounds as if it could be quite an interesting job, even if you wouldn't have Olson, Creeley, and Barth as fellow-vineyard-workers. I wonder if by this time you have decided to come back to Scotland as you thought you might. Various things seem to be stirring here at the moment in the current wave of nationalism which has surprised so many English observers. It might well be a good time to come back.

I am in the midst of Honours exam papers and looking forward to the end of what has been a rather gruelling term. My book of poems *The Second Life* has/had quite good reviews and has been selling fairly well. I have also had a couple of pamphlets of concrete poetry which I mean to send you copies of but I'll wait till I'm certain of your current address. I am glad you enjoyed Garioch's collection – he has his own way of doing things and although it is not an enormous oeuvre it is delightful at its best. He and I and Robert Tait are involved in a new magazine *Scottish International* which you may possibly have heard about. We have reached our second number after a particularly squally baptism. I am also in the throes of writing an opera libretto, the first draft of which I have just completed. I'm doing it with the Scottish composer Thomas Wilson, and we have a commission from the BBC, who want to play it in the autumn. Our story is a true crime passionnel from about 200 years back.

Let me hear how you get on with the Finnish post, and your news generally.

All the best | Edwin Morgan

EM had provided an academic reference for Caughie, a gifted former student, for a fellowship at the State University of New York at Buffalo, where Robert Creeley and Charles Olson were on the Faculty. Now another request had arrived from Finland. The opera *The Charcoal Burner* was based on a local tale of mother–son strife outlined by Wordsworth.

J.W. Lambert, *literary editor*

2 June 1968

Dear Jack Lambert

Thank you for your letters and for the books – the package of four, plus the Muriel Spark. I agree the Spark should come first. I have only had time to glance at it, but it begins with her usual enticing laconicism and I look forward to reading it.

As regards the next piece, I shall be going away on the morning of 22 June, so I would like to aim at having my review written by the 21st. I suppose I shall probably get the books in time for this, unless there are any very late surprises. For the piece after that (copy due on 9 July) I can probably leave the actual writing of it till after my return on 6 July but obviously I shall have to read the books while I am away. I can only hope it will be a thin fortnight for new novels! Would you send them, during this period, to me c/o Caledonian Hotel, Inverness.

I hesitate to mention this in case it puts you to any awkwardness, but you did say when you first wrote about the novel-reviewing last November that the fee would be £40.

Would it be at all possible to hold out for this figure?

Sincerely yours | Edwin Morgan

Lambert's original offer of £40 per review for *The Sunday Times* had been reduced to £35. The original fee was reinstated. Muriel Spark's *The Public Image* (1968) was shortlisted for the Booker Prize.

Robert Tait, editor

16 July 1968

Dear Bob

Thanks for the two batches of stuff, both of which I've commented on together on the attached sheets.

I enclose a cheque from Stephen Scobie which he sent to me as a subscription for SI (he says keep the change if there happens to be any). I think you have his address? He already has the first two numbers.

I suppose I would never in the ordinary course of events think of joining a dinner club, since I am not really a wining and dining sort of person (anyone can give me an inordinate amount of pleasure with a well-boiled free-range egg, a fresh slice of toast on which the butter just slightly melts though without running, and a newly-poured cup of good strong tea), but the present one sounds interesting and I would be glad to take up your invitation.

Some excitement on Sunday night – my colour TV, just back after a month in the workshops, went on fire. Fortunately I was in the room watching it, and managed to get it unplugged while it was still at the smoking stage. If I had been in another room at the time it might have been pretty serious as there is a curtain right behind it which would probably have gone up. The smell of a burning colour TV is out of this world. Quite unlike anything else; hot; acrid; intense; pervasive; frightening. It's when it smells that you feel its power for the first time. Talk about Pandora.

Yours hot and acrid | Eddie

Tait, a member of a dinner club meeting monthly to discuss topics of current cultural or political interest, had been asked to invite EM to join. Other members included Robin Fulton* and critic Douglas Gifford. The musician John Purser was also invited.

Nigel Tranter, author

2 September 1968

Dear Nigel Tranter

I understand from Mary Baxter, who was on the telephone to me today, that you are hoping to do something for Charles Senior who is in financial straits and bad health. I would certainly support any move you make in this direction.

Charles Senior has never been a very prolific poet but has worked steadily over the years, and his *Selected Poems* was published by Macdonald in Edinburgh in 1966. He is represented in various anthologies, including *Honour'd Shade*, *Borestone Mountain Poetry Awards*, and *Scottish Poetry 1*. He writes mainly in English, but also in Scots, and in a variety of modes and moods from lyricism and pathos to satire and comedy. Many poems have a fine perception of nature, and especially of plants, trees, and flowers, where he has in fact a specialized knowledge. Others deal movingly, though with no self-pity, with his personal plight. An excellent poem of this latter type, sent recently to the magazine *Scottish International* of which I am one of the co-editors, has been accepted by us for publication. It is clear that he is still, under his difficulties, continuing to write poetry, and I believe he is also engaged on a novel dealing with Scotland at the time of the General Strike, which sounds a worthwhile project. He is undoubtedly a deserving case, and I hope it will be possible to help him in some way.

Yours sincerely | Edwin Morgan

Mary Baxter of the National Book League, Scotland, alerted EM to Nigel Tranter's plan, and he provides detail to help Tranter argue a positive case.

Ian Hamilton Finlay, *poet and artist*

Dear Ian

Thank you very much for the nice postcard. Some of the names seem to be tempting providence, they are so grand. Would you not rather sail in the Maggie or the Flora? Of course it is hard at times to be sure where the names begin and end. Star Divine? Divine Morning? Divine Morning Star? A wavering, the overlaps like waves. I think only the kings of Egypt ought to risk sailing in the Divine Morning...

I have not seen the *Spectator* article you mention but have sent for a copy of that number. They seem to take ages to send back numbers.

As regards the Arts Council, I can't help you there in the immediate future as I have recently resigned. I wasn't at all happy about the setup whereby everyone who was a member of the various committees (literature, art, etc.) was also a member of the Council, taking financial and policy decisions. I don't think it is a healthy situation for people who themselves write, paint, etc. to be themselves in this position, as they are quite often involved, and stand to gain, in proposals and schemes and decisions they help to decide. (I refused, for example, to take the fee I am due as co-editor of *Scottish International*.) I want the Council to revert to their earlier way of working, with non-creative people on the Council itself (quite a small body), supported by various panels of persons in the arts who will give their information and advice. At the moment the various committees are not getting the support and advice they should, from creative persons, simply because many writers and others don't want to have to become members of the Council (it is a government appointment and each person has to be approved by the Secretary of State). – I don't think there is anything very hard-and-fast about procedure regarding local councils. You don't say exactly what it is you have in mind. Local councils can apply to the Arts Council for <u>support</u> in some proposal regarding the arts but only if they are already themselves prepared to foot part of the bill. Any proposal must come from them, so you would have to persuade them first. This is never

easy, as you can imagine. But a lot would depend on what you wanted to do. – I know you must have been disappointed over the poetry prize. I brought the matter up myself at the meeting, but apparently the judges had decided they had to stick to the rules (though your work was considered) which said 'book of poems' and they could not extend the category. I think that as you yourself suggest your recent work would tend to be generally regarded as coming under art rather than literature (the Axiom <u>Gallery</u>, etc.), though clearly it is a part of both – Nothing very much more seems to be happening about any proposed concrete exhibition, and the idea seems to be simmering very gently in the Skinner bosom – I agree with you that old shoes must be guarded against, as certainly they would be if someone responsible – say Stephen Bann or whoever – was in charge of the exhibition. A.S. doesn't at all disagree about this, I have talked to him about it; but for the purposes of an exhibition it is (to be objective about it) not so easy as you suggest to be <u>defined</u> by 'the company one keeps'…
What, for example, about John Furnival? Dom Silvester? Neither of them is doing 'your' kind of thing, yet a certain grouping there is unavoidable, and it would seem hard to say no to their representation. In your analogy with Mondrian, John F is nearly a surrealist! – yet you have worked with him and he admires what you are doing. – But nothing seems to have been at all decided yet.

The university opens its great slavering jaws again on Thursday. We have a new Library building that I think Rennie M would have found quite interesting.

I will now try out the fivepenny post to Dunsyre.

Love | Yeddie

The postcard was IHF's 'Sea Poppy 2', a circular poem of fishing-boat names. He thought arts funders in Scotland could have missed a positive review in *The Spectator* and asked EM to lobby on his behalf, particularly regarding local government purchase of public artworks. IHF had heard from Alisdair Skinner at the Arts Council about a proposed televised programme on a concrete poetry exhibition (which did not transpire). The 'old shoes' had possibly been exhibited at the Arlington Gallery in Camden, alongside work by EM

and IHF, and he did not intend any future involvement. 'Rennie M' is
Charles Rennie Mackintosh.

Robert Tait, editor

28 September 1968

Dear Bob
Thanks for the translations from SGS and RG and for
the new contents list, bisexuality disquisition, etc! I agree
we ought to keep in 'The Gift' as we have had it a good
while now. I hope we can have the Brecht intact. The SGS
Apo is workmanlike, and it will be quite interesting to have
it in conjunction with the more imaginative RGs. I do
like 'Victory', 'A Phantom of Haar', and 'Deleted Passage'.
Obviously we can't do anything about H. Arundel and it will
just have to slip past in the general flow.
    Enclosed: the Italian poems that will just have to await
another day (I have in any case had no time myself to get
down to them – and won't have from now on, as the new term
descends on Thursday); also an article on Robert Kirk and the
fairies which I thought you and especially RG might like to
see (in conjunction with the poems we had submitted) – you
can let me have it back sometime; oh yes, and also a letter I
got from David Angus (I presume it is the David Angus who
writes poetry and who has had some in *Scottish Poetry*) about
our not being international enough – now that's a change, so I
thought you should see it and if you want to follow up any of
his suggestions and/or write to him... I have already replied
myself of course. Could I have it back later?
    I can see you don't believe that Lorca really wrote that
wee poem! He did though – and perhaps that's why he was
murdered too. You know the theory that there are people who
attract murder, as there are those that attract accidents, or fires,
or cats... For a short poem, it has an extraordinary insight into
the 'ultimately perilous' moment, especially as it is not wholly
naturalistic. Lorca is one man I would like to know a great deal
about.
    Girls, etc.: a comment on the unalluringness of the mini-

skirt: the other day I was in the bus and it slowed down at
a fruiterers where a girl in the absolute mini was standing
looking in at the fruit; two Glasgow bodies behind me with
their shoppers started noticing her – 'Wid ye look at yon!'
– 'If she bends she's had it.' At that precise moment the girl
bent smartly down to prod an apple. Quite everything was
revealed. It was wholly ludicrous, like the flamingos upending
themselves in a zoo pond. One of the two women screeched 'O
Jesus Christ!' and then the two of them began cackling nonstop
like something out of William Dunbar. – Well, that really is by
the way, but it came into my mind when I read your comments.

Your 'field' remarks are most interesting and I do wish I
had more time to carry on talking about them (I have three
papers to write for the next fortnight, one on Chekhov, one
on Ibsen/Shaw/Brecht, one on Aristophanes!) (international?
– man!): I find field qualities both fascinating and uneasy-
making and there is probably a generation-gap or some such
thing at work here. I am even unhappy in an open-plan house
where 'rooms' do not have clearly defined functions, and that
is about the simplest kind of field. Multi-level roads (Los
Angeles approaches, say), large airports like Heathrow, even
the 'disappearance' of Anderston Cross under as yet ill-defined
impositions of alien function (partly industrial) – all these
arouse ambiguous feelings compounded of pleasure that things
are stirring plus the uncertainty of knowing how to relate
oneself to them. The nightmare of never getting <u>down</u> from the
flyover. Hell as a place where there is nothing <u>but</u> magnificent
flyovers, clover-leaf fields forever. But then perhaps everyone
feels these things, perhaps you do too? I don't feel any such
unease in the field pop music extends to – if I hear a bomber
coming low over the roofs in a Beatles number that's all right.
That is in the 'mind', so maybe it's only when life and action
take on field qualities that one feels a bit Kafka. Philosophical
question: What is 'Hey Jude'? Is it an EP? Is it a single song?
If it's divided in two at the middle, how come the second half,
non-melodic and 'mindlessly' repetitive, is musically more
meaningful than the rather charming first? Is it a lyric with
'real verbal words' or is it a mantra?

Yours | Eddie

SGS and RG were Sydney Goodsir Smith and Robert Garioch, whose translations of three poems by Apollinaire appeared in *Scottish International* 4. 'The Gift' was a poem by Robert Hughes. Honor Arundel, film critic and children's writer, had sent revisions to an earlier article. EM had submitted his own translation of Lorca's 'Murder' (*CT*: 262). Tait had also referred to EM's views in a previous letter on the 'bisexuality' of the Beatles' music. Tait liked the sociological concept of 'field'.

Robert Tait, editor

2 October 1968

Dear Bob

Thanks for the draft editorial. In fact there is very little that seems to me in need of altering. I find the Apollinaire/Brecht pairing a useful and pointed approach, and the MacDiarmid thoughts work in quite naturally. Two points I thought of: (a) As regards 'roles' and the role of eccentric genius being wished on MacD. (p.3), do you not think it is more the case that he just is an eccentric genius (though obviously he enjoys playing this up as if it was a role), and, if this is true, then (b) is there that much point in constantly 'challenging' him and giving 'adequate critical reaction' to the things he says? You are assuming that people listen to what he says and then don't have enough reaction; but what if people simply say, Oh, I see old MacDiarmid's at it again, like the Hungary do – meaning that it is a sort of poet's privilege to be interested in politics but nevertheless to be fairly likely to be foolish (and cf. Pound, Eliot, Yeats, Frost, Muir, Auden, and how many more one could name – all foolish or worse in political thinking)? I doubt whether there can be any very useful 'critical reaction' to the daft things that MacDiarmid and Pound have said and written about politics; I think that if we want to see a dialogue between writers and audience on socio-political matters we have our writers to educate as well as the audience! The eccentric like MacDiarmid or Pound has to be taken pretty much on his own terms as a case that perhaps doesn't prove anything. You know the critical furore that arose in America when Pound was awarded the Bollingen Prize – but in the end it all amounted to nothing, fascist schmascist, you had to fall back on the poetry and forget the broadcasts. MacDiarmid and Pound are not like Sartre and Brecht and Yevtushenko and other writers who are really concerned that their work should be an intelligent 'criticism of life' (whether in the Arnoldian or Soviet sense). I think your point is that MacDiarmid seems to claim he <u>is</u>, and that therefore, if people are likely to be taken in, it is our duty to rebut the claim from point to point. Perhaps this is so. It is maybe a question of whether indifference to <u>expected</u> extremist statements like MacD's on Czechoslovakia is worse or better than a laboured challenge which might merely restate the obvious. But these are only thoughts: I am not really arguing for changes, unless you want to make any.

Yours hastily – | Eddie

PS: Is the 'or between all three at once' (p.1, line 8) clear enough, do you think?! E

Tait had sent a draft of his editorial, 'Artists and Political Change'. When the Russians crushed the Hungarian uprising of 1956, MacDiarmid* rejoined the Communist Party (from which he had earlier been ejected for his Scottish Nationalism) to show solidarity. Now with the 1968 Warsaw Pact invasion of Czechoslovakia to suppress the reforms of the 'Prague Spring', he was again pro-Soviet in his statements.

Veronica Forrest-Thomson, poet and critic

7 November 1968

Dear Veronica

I am sorry to have taken such a time to answer your letter – I had an unusual concentration of work the first half of this term. I am enclosing one or two things you might like to consider for *Solstice*. The quotation in the Wittgenstein poem is from Richard Wollheim in a review but I don't know if this would have to be indicated. The little concrete one refers of course to Asprey's the Bond Street silversmiths – does this come under advertising?

Glad you discovered Fenellosa which is always interesting even though sinologues sniff. Has your supervisor got himself ex-jaundice yet? Cambridge from your letter sounds mixed but I suppose most places would be. It must be good for <u>talk</u> anyway. Like Oxford it contains an alarming number of people who will someday be famous, and pre-famous people often have an attractiveness they don't have later. I have been working on *Scottish Poetry 4* (selection now completed for 1969), and No.4 of *Scottish International* has just come out – not at all a bad number I think. A huge issue of *Hispanic Arts* (Indiana U) just out has interesting essays and statements on concrete plus anthology... (Can send you an extra copy if you like.)

  – Yes, I hope we shall meet at Christmas. | Yours |
  Edwin Morgan

When she began doctoral research on science and modern poetry, Veronica Forrest-Thomson's supervisor was ill, so there was a lack of tutorial support. She became involved with *Solstice* magazine, and asked for poems to help her 'propaganda campaign for concrete and general intelligence and wit in writing'. She had found some use of scientific metaphor in Ernest Fenellosa (1853–1908), the American Orientalist who influenced Ezra Pound's poetry.

A. McOustra, research student

25 November 1968

Dear Mr McOustra

Thank you for your letter. Mr Milligan had told me about your dissertation on surrealism, so I was expecting to hear from you. It is a fascinating subject which I myself have been interested in for quite a while. There are many books about surrealism, though some of them are not too easy to get hold of. But if you know the exact titles of books, your local library will obtain them for you (it is part of the service) if they are available anywhere in the country. There is also one bookseller who specializes in surrealist books, and although of course he normally only sells books, he might be able to help you in some way if he knew about your problem, for example he might be able to give you some surplus catalogues or other information about surrealism: his name is John Lyle, Peeks, Harpford, Sidmouth, Devon. Anyway, here is a list of the more important books that you would find useful, and as I say, you have only to ask for them at your public library.

David Gascoyne: *A Short Survey of Surrealism* (Cobden-Sanderson, London, 1935; reprinted 1968) (good historical introduction, manifestos, translations of poems by Breton, Char, Dali, Éluard, Tzara, etc.)
David Gascoyne: *Man's Life Is This Meat* (Parton Press, London, 1936) (poems by one of the few English surrealist poets)
Herbert Read: *Surrealism* (Faber, London, 1936) (good introduction, illustrations of surrealist art, contributions by Breton, Éluard)
J.H. Matthews: *Introduction to Surrealism* (Pennsylvania, 1965)
J.H. Matthews (ed.): *French Surrealist Poetry* (Univ. of London, 1966 – paperback 9/6) (good collection of poems with notes & introduction)
Jean-Louis Bedouin (ed.): *La Poésie Surréaliste* (Paris, 1964) (over 50 poets represented)
Wallace Fowlie: *Age of Surrealism* (Indiana Univ., 1960) (deals with people like Lautréamont, Rimbaud, Apollinaire, Breton, Éluard)
André Breton: *Manifestes du Surréalisme* (Gallimard, Paris, 1965)
A. Rodway (ed.): *Poetry of the 1930s* (Longmans English Series, London, 1967) (some discussion of surrealism in introduction; poems by David Gascoyne)
R. Skelton (ed.): *Poetry of the Thirties* (Penguin, 1964 – 5/-) (see introduction, also poems by Gascoyne, O'Connor, Davies, Thomas, etc.)
Patrick Waldberg: *Surrealism* (Thames & Hudson, London, 1965 – paperback 18/-) (more on the art side than poetry, but

has lots of interesting bits of information & illustrations)
Surrealism (Movements in Modern Art series, Methuen, 1956)
(coloured illustrations of surrealist art)

––––––––

Are you ever through in Glasgow? If you like, I could show
you some of these books and we could have a chat about the
subject.

With best wishes | Yours sincerely | Edwin Morgan

Researching French surrealism at the University of Stirling, McOustra
had been advised by his supervisor to contact EM for help in finding
books. EM's interest in Surrealism from the 1930s onwards is clear in
the scrapbooks he kept from the 1930s to the 1960s, as well as in his
enjoyment of surprising juxtapositions in poetry.

Robert Tait, editor

Edwin Morgan 19 Whittingehame Court Glasgow W2
27 March 1969

Dear Bob
    Isn't A4 all the rage – even for letters.
    The larger size is certainly attractive. The review section
looks well in 9 pt; though I don't at all mind 8 pt the larger is
probably better with A4. I don't like the alternative heading for
the article nearly so well as the other – it is too scattered and
the title of the article isn't salient enough. I have something
of a feeling that both author and title could stand to be bigger
and/or heavier, a little anyway. What do you think about this?
I have in mind someone flipping through the magazine – what
will his eye catch? On the other hand, the page as a page looks
well with the relatively light headings.
    'London' returned with a few corrections. I actually enjoyed
reading it!
    Also the editorial pages, which I think make our points
well now, being fair without losing the nip about glamorous
packages.
    I'm glad the Mailer was all right. I have not seen the new

Lines yet, so I don't know what you are saying about AKROS 9. But you are right in the 'broad canvas' supposition. The role you describe is one that I skirted round, out of various sorts of diffidence and inhibition, until perhaps some inner monitor was able to tell me that I could deal with things I couldn't deal with before. There seems to be a natural growth in these matters, at least I find I can't force it but have to wait for changes and phases to unroll themselves. I always remember one of these phases in poetry: 'Linoleum Chocolate', which is no doubt a very slight poem in itself, was of great psychological importance to me because it represented a breakthrough – and how late a breakthrough, dangerously late, aetat. 41! – into a territory I had never been able to enter. It was written on a heaving boat near St Kilda, when for no reason that I can discover the tiny incident the poem is based on came back to my mind and formed itself into a poem. Never had I been able to write about two girls running down the street till that moment. It was as if – and I recognized the change immediately – I suddenly realized that I was able to be free, that the albatross had slipped off my neck into the Atlantic, that the everyday things that I had always had sympathy with but never been able to write about were now in a new relation to me and could come into poetry as naturally as symbols of alienation had come in the past. My god, to be post-alienated! No-one had ever foretold me that such things happen. I suppose that's why I have a photograph of St Kilda on the living room wall. – How far the 'broad canvas' thing will go remains to be seen, but I am encouraged by your comments. It probably comes as a further growth out of the St Kilda experience. But what you rightly call the 'jouks and twists' are very much a part of my personal landscape too. Still, not to be a divided but a varied man, that's the hope.

Driving, carless, along the A4 – | Eddie

EM's review of Norman Mailer's *Armies of the Night* and *Miami and the Siege of Chicago* for *Scottish International* 6 ('Mailer Speaking for Himself') had ended with a question: Who is going to 'tell it like it is' in Scotland? Tait suggested that he underestimated the direction his own writing would take in 'mapping' Scotland on a broad canvas. 'Linoleum Chocolate' is in *CP*: 163.

Charles Rigg, Warden of Newbattle Abbey College

17 May 1969

Dear Mr Rigg

Mr Fraser Bolton

In answer to your inquiry about the above-named:

I know Mr Bolton as a young man who is intensely interested in literature and philosophy and in the art of writing. He left school at fifteen, has worked at a variety of jobs from cinema projectionist to laboratory assistant, and in his spare time has read voraciously and has also written a good deal in prose and verse. At the moment he is in the middle of writing a novel. From reading what he has written, and from long conversations I have had with him, I get the impression of an untrained but vigorous mind which is bursting with ideas and struggling to find suitable expression for them. He does have, I think, some sharp insights into Scottish life, and his problem is to find some form that will enable him to express these and at the same time to reflect his philosophical and psychological concerns. He is much interested in Edwin Muir and by a curious coincidence has worked at the bone factory Muir describes in his autobiography. In his home and social environment he feels desperately cut off from intellectual discussion and from any peace to study – both of which he craves and would I am sure make good use of. He seems to me to be very much the sort of person who would benefit from a year at Newbattle, and who would also contribute something himself to the other students. I would strongly recommend him.

Yours sincerely | Edwin Morgan

Rigg was Warden of Newbattle Abbey adult education college, where Edwin Muir had been Warden and George Mackay Brown a student. Bolton was a friend of the Greenock poet Thomas A. Clark, whom EM had also encouraged (and who moved to Woodchester to work near Dom Sylvester Houédard* and John Furnival). The young man died five months after this letter was written.

Robert Tait, editor

Oban 3133

Caledonian Hotel
OBAN
Argyll
21 July 1969

Dear Bob

I'm not sure how urgent this review is but I thought I'd better send it express from this place. I had intended as you know to get it done before I left, but I had another deadline for six short articles on Scottish poets for a forthcoming who's who (Garioch, Lindsay, Graham, Price Turner, IHF, D.M. Black) and this took me all last week. Then of course when I came up here Apollo 11 was doing its utmost to distract and both Saturday and Sunday I could think of nothing else. By good luck this hotel has TV in all bedrooms so on Sunday night I just switched on and sat up all night. There was one extraordinarily eerie 'happening' between 4 and 5 a.m. Oban as you can imagine is a very quiet place in the small hours and the only sounds were those coming from Houston and Apollo. But after 4 a.m., when the module had landed and the moonwalk had begun, the local seagulls began their early morning shriek (the hotel is right on the harbour) and these wild inhuman sounds against the desolate moonscape had an astonishingly strange yet apt effect, as if Vaughan Williams had specially written them in.

I enclose the poems by Paul Mills and will report on the other submissions when I get back. I agree that 'Child in a Landscape' and 'Passus' would be fine and possibly 'Steelworks' is worth considering. I am sending them to you instead of RG in case it is really urgent, and you could then get his opinion very quickly.

The review by the way is about 1260 words, but do cut if you have to.

I'll be here till 2 August and have given you the address

and phone number in case you need to get in touch. It has not
stopped raining since we arrived!

Yours | Eddie

The review was of Iain Crichton Smith's* novel *The Last Summer*. The
encyclopedia entries were published in *Contemporary Poets of the
English Language*, ed. Rosalie Murphy (1970).

Nikos Stangos, editor

19 Whittingehame Court
4 August 1969

Dear Nik

Thank you for your letter, and I am so glad that you
and Al Alvarez like the translations. I shall get on with the
introduction. I am just back from holiday and have a big
mail to get through, but apart from that I shall be able to do
the introduction right away – shall we say within the next
fortnight, or do you need it even sooner than that?

I am returning the translations with my comments on
the points raised. As regards 'The First Couple', I think I
would prefer to keep it where it is, unless there are very strong
arguments for having it later; the reason is just that the present
order is the order in which the poems occur in his various
books. But I suppose it wouldn't matter very much if it was
pushed forward, so long as it came before 'Queen Tatavane'
which is the last poem in the particular volume both poems
come from.

I have seen only a few of László Nagy's poems and would
like to see some more before I made up my mind about him.
I know he is highly thought of in Hungary (where I met him
a couple of years ago, briefly). But there is (in my opinion) a
much more interesting poet in Lajos Kassák who died recently
– I feel considerably in rapport with him and would certainly
like to translate more of him (I have done a few poems). He
was one of the avantgarde in the earlier years of the century, an
artist as well as poet, and altogether a worthwhile figure to do,

I should imagine. You can let me know what you think about
this.

All best wishes | ☰||| | Edwin Morgan

Stangos had sent some suggestions from Alvarez* for minor
changes to EM's translations of Sándor Weöres*. There was now
some urgency about the Introduction. He had asked in a p.s. what
EM thought of translating László Nagy.

Sándor Weöres, poet and translator

11 August 1969

Dear Sándor Weöres
How are you? I hope you are well!
You may know that I have been translating some of your
poems for a selection to be published later this year by Penguin
Books (London). I have finished the translations and am
writing a short introduction. I have been looking up some of
your mythical names in many books without success, and I
would be very grateful if you could tell me what countries and
myths these come from: E Daj ('A rejtett ország'), Kukszu,
Szibbabi ('Elsö emberpár'), Tatavane, Bulak-Amba, Aure-
Ange, Batan-Kenam, Aruvatene, Andede ('Tatavane királynö').
I hope very much that you will like the translations
when they appear. I have taken great care over them, trying to
reproduce them as faithfully as possible. They seem to me to be
very remarkable and rewarding poems, and I am sure they will
make an impact on English-speaking readers.

With all best wishes | Yours sincerely | Edwin Morgan

EM particularly admired the virtuosity and range of Weöres, recog-
nising a kindred spirit. This letter, written in plain style for a non-En-
glish speaker (Weöres's wife, the poet Amy Károlyi, would translate)
scarcely conveys his enthusiasm.

Elaine Hardman, artist and poet

15 August 1969

Dear Elaine

Thank you for sending me your poems. There's a nice fresh
feeling about them and I like the way they take up simple
things without trying to force some huge message. Things I
like: the 'still cup of cold smoke/ feeling leafy coloured', 'old/
Graham fast asleep/ like a hedgehog', 'bus red arm/ crook
enclosing/ a scrap of landscape'. Best poems I thought –
'Fresh Morning Love', 'Evening: Ladybank'; and possibly 'To
Jacqueline'. 'Harmony on a Hill' is a nice <u>idea</u> but I am not too
happy about 'fleeting', 'awesome', 'magic', I feel these should
be <u>in</u> the poem whereas they are standing outside it saying
fleeting, awesome, magic… Did you see in one of the colour
supplements that it's possible to buy a real Aeolian harp which
of course is made to do just what that guitar did (you set it in
an open window and wait for the wind)? I thought also of the
song 'The Fool on the Hill' which I very much like and which
seemed to be hovering about your poem somewhere. You
should send some of your poems to the magazines – like *Akros*
or *Lines* or *Scottish International*. Some might come back but
you might get one or two taken and it helps to see things in
print I think… – You ask to see some of my recent work so I'm
enclosing a few unpublished poems – three of them are part
of a series of 'songs' I'm engaged on at the moment – songs,
though I have no composer for them yet! – I am sorry that the
St Andrews reading never took place: there was a mixup in
the arrangements, another speaker was asked to talk about the
same subject, and my own evening was cancelled. However, I
will be reading my poetry during the Edinburgh Festival once
or twice, so you may have a chance of hearing that. I'm to be
in one of the Saltire readings in Gladstone's Land on Sunday
31 August at 5.30, and at the same place Tuesday 2 September
at 11 a.m. in a programme with Robert Tait. I also expect to
be reading in Tom McGrath's little scene at 24 George Square
on Monday 8 and Friday 12 September in the evening. – I
am very glad you have found a good friend in Tom Clark. Tell
him to be sure and send poems for SP5 – he didn't send any

for SP4. – Yes, beware of the Regency Press and any similar 'publishers'! You should not have to pay like that to have poems published.

All best wishes | Edwin Morgan

A young Fife-based poet, artist and enthusiast for concrete poetry, Hardman had contacted EM and through him had been put in touch with Thomas A. Clark, the Scottish minimalist poet. Five poems with 'Song' in the title appear in *From Glasgow to Saturn* (1973).

Duncan Glen, *publisher and poet*

16 September 1969

Dear Duncan

I see you are coping with the rigours of the new term. I am just getting ready for ours. I wish a time warp would descend on Gilmorehill and sweep it all away but that only seems to happen in pulp tales. I am full of writing ideas at the moment (have just finished a longish poem on Glasgow and its poets) but it is all frustrated by the gathering shadows of October.

Of the titles you suggest, my own preference is for *The Horseman's Word: Concrete Poems*. I'd certainly like to retain the specific title in this case, since it is an actual sequence, though I appreciate that it breaks the continuity of having 'poems' throughout the series. Still, you would probably find that sooner or later that continuity would be broken. Perhaps the actual title should just be *The Horseman's Word* (I mean on the outside of the book), with the subtitle inside saying 'A Sequence of Concrete Poems'? I think I'd like some mention of 'sequence' somewhere. I hope not to have any 'second thoughts' about the text of either that or the other book! You won't mind, by the way, putting the date of composition of *The Whittrick* somewhere in the book (perhaps at the end of the poem)?

Actually I am determined SI is <u>not</u> going to become involved in the IHF/Fulcrum campaign beyond that one little factual note, though we are under strong pressure from IHF (hour-long telephone calls to Bob Tait etc) to do so. I think the note was justified in so far as Fulcrum's non-mention of the Migrant edition amounted to sharp practice, it really was dishonest and couldn't be defended. Stuart Montgomery has now virtually admitted this, as the dust-jacket now contains a reference to the Migrant edition, and I understand he is going to have slips inserted into future copies of the book. I have no sympathy whatsoever for the anonymous letter part of IHF's campaign (I got one the other day asking me to send a donation to put SM on a plane back to Africa), and in any case as you suggest there is undoubtedly another side to the story. SM has done a great deal for poetry and I have a lot of admiration for his publishing list – I have all his books. IHF, though he doesn't seem to realize it because he sees everything so personally, is simply playing into the hands of a part of the London Establishment which would dearly love to send Stuart Montgomery back to Africa and let English poetry revert to neo-Georgian biscuit tins.

I have a copy of your fascinating interview with MacDiarmid – it really should have wider circulation. I couldn't help wishing once or twice that you had pressed home rather harder as some of the replies were shaky in the extreme! But maybe the occasion was too intimate and friendly to break lances on.

All the best as ever | Eddie

The long poem on Glasgow poets was 'Rider i–iv', published in *From Glasgow to Saturn* (1973) (*CP*: 278–81). *The Horseman's Word* (1970) appeared in Glen's Parklands Poets series. He also agreed to publish EM's *The Whittrick: A Poem in Eight Dialogues 1955–1961* (1973). *Scottish International* published a note on the intense literary and legal quarrel between Ian Hamilton Finlay* and Stuart Montgomery's Fulcrum Press.

Garig Basmadjian, poet and editor

24 October 1969

Dear Garig Basmadjian

You are right, I know nothing about Armenian poetry!
But it would be interesting to learn something about it, and
therefore I would be glad to take up your suggestion. I couldn't
at the moment give you very much in the way of promises as
far as collaboration in translating it is concerned, both because
it is still an unknown quantity (and some kind of 'sympathy' is
needed for good translation) and because my time is very fully
taken up with teaching at Glasgow University as well as the
range of writing and editing (I co-edit a quarterly magazine
'Scottish International' and an annual anthology 'Scottish
Poetry') I have let myself in for. But I would hope that with
luck something might be done. The overlapping of East and
West which you mention – perhaps it is similar to what one
finds in Georgian poetry? – sounds as if it would present
problems of great interest. Anyhow, I shall be very pleased to
hear from you and to explore the matter further.

With best wishes | Yours sincerely | Edwin Morgan

An Armenian poet, translator and editor based in Paris, Basmadjian
was interested in co-operating with EM on translations of Armenian
poetry, which he described as a 'highly original [...] fusion of East
and West'. EM did translate some poems by the Armenian poet
Avetik Isahakyan (1875–1957) in May 1977.

W.S. Graham, poet

26 December 1969

Dear Sydney

How good it was to have your letter again after all that
time and from that far off Cornwall – Madron is only a
couple of days less than the Moon away. I should have written
immediately but wanted to have something definite before

I replied, so risked waiting. I had my own plans for writing about your work, but they were forestalled, or rather met, when Robin Fulton (Edinburgh poet, creative-writer-in-residence at Edinburgh University this year, also editor of *Lines Review*, 149 Warrender Park Road, Edinburgh 9) asked me to do a substantial 3000/4000-word article on you for his June number. I think it is good because it shows that people in Scotland still remember and respect your work, and it pleased me that Fulton should think of me as the person to do the job.

I could not, if I wanted to, say much about your book in a few phrases, beyond that there is much in it I like a lot, much that drives me back into past years too imperiously for me to sort out any sensible reactions yet, and I would rather you could have the patience – sitting on a stone in Cornwall – to wait till you can read what I have to say of the collection in the context of your whole poetry. I hope the book has good success. That it is to be the Spring Choice of the Poetry Book Society, however trusted or distrusted the sieves of that organization may be, will certainly mean publicity and sales. George MacBeth will I am sure get the Third (assuming it still exists by then) to discuss it, and George Bruce (or his successor – he retires soon) will do the same on BBC Scotland.

You ask about magazines up here. Apart from *Lines* already mentioned, there is *Scottish International* (current copy enclosed); there is AKROS (editor Duncan Glen, 14 Parklands Avenue, Penwortham, Preston, Lancashire – a Scottish magazine, despite its address); and then you may (not?) have seen the annual collections called *Scottish Poetry* (four have now appeared) published by Edinburgh University Press (22 George Square, Edinburgh). I'm one of the editors of the *Scottish Poetry* anthologies and we are finishing our selection for No.5 (1970) fairly soon, so if you have any newish poems not in *Malcolm Mooney's Land*, though it doesn't matter if they have been printed in magazines, please do send them to me for consideration. Now we're both really businesslike...

I often think of you. The years are nothing when it comes to that. Do write.

Love | Edwin

Graham had sent a proof copy of *Malcolm Mooney's Land*, due from Faber & Faber in 1970, and wondered about current Scottish outlets: 'I seem to be able now to write more easily. [...] I am now able to speak about things I always wanted to speak about but hadn't the equipment'. He usually addressed him as 'Edwin'. Graham's original is in 'W.S Graham: A Poet's Letters', *Crossing the Border: Essays on Scottish Literature* (1990: 271–72).

1970s

(aged 50–59)

At the beginning of the 1970s we find Morgan confidently asserting a poetics which is advancing on three fronts. He spells these out in a letter to Veronica Forrest-Thomson as 'a poetry of fact, or a poetry of the emotional impact of scientific theory [...] or a poetry of structural exploration like concrete, in the hope that these are severally but perhaps mystically jointly leading in the right direction'. There remained, however, the problem of getting his poetry published. Edinburgh University Press, which had brought out *The Second Life* to great acclaim in 1968, now seemed to be dragging its feet over a second volume. When it announced in 1972 that it was withdrawing from poetry publication altogether, it seemed as though his work might be stalled in its prime. This was, in any case, a conflicted time in Britain, with national strikes in coal mining and other key industries creating widespread difficulties. In the letters, these are exemplified by the image of the poet typing in the semi-dark of candlelight during an electricity cut.

Disappointed by Edinburgh and still wary of London, Morgan found sanctuary in Michael Schmidt's Carcanet Press. Carcanet would publish five volumes in all during this decade, starting with *Wi the Haill Voice: 25 Poems by Vladimir Mayakovsky* (1972) and continuing with the celebrated *From Glasgow to Saturn* (1973), *Rites of Passage: Selected Translations* (1976) and the still neglected *The New Divan* of 1977, as well as a selection of his essays. In itself this would be a phenomenal output for the decade, but Morgan also continued to work with smaller presses, bringing out slim volumes such as *Glasgow Sonnets* of 1972, 'written fairly swiftly, under strong pressure of feeling, in about a week', and the early fantasia *The Whittrick*, as well as further translations. Meanwhile his work was beginning to attract new audiences through inclusion in two significant anthologies: *Worlds: Seven Modern Poets* and *Twelve Modern Scottish Poets*. His critical and academic work continued unabated, and he was made a Professor in 1975.

The erudite and playful letters to Schmidt which predominate in this period are witness to a renewal of energies on various levels. There were disagreements too – Morgan was reluctant to publish in Schmidt's *Poetry Nation Review*, being 'unhappy with the whole trend and motive' of *PNR*, especially because of the involvement of Schmidt's co-editor Brian Cox in the conservative 'Black Paper' polemics against comprehensive education. Nevertheless, the dialogue of poet and publisher continued to be a healthy one, and theirs was to be a lasting collaboration. In 1976 Morgan began a correspondence with Laura (Riding) Jackson which led eventually to his persuading Carcanet to bring out a collected edition of her poems. In the decades that followed, he would continue to be a positive advocate for new or neglected poets.

For all that Morgan's 1960s creative emergence was continued and confirmed in this decade ('like being shot from a gun' was how he described his earlier breakthrough to poet and translator Robin Fulton in the early 1970s, and that positive trajectory continued well into the new decade), there is also a subdued tone to much of the correspondence. The frequency of letters even to favourite correspondents peters out. Partly this may be put down to Morgan's increasing load of commitments and occupations, but there were also more serious burdens to be borne. These years were marked by a number of deaths which struck hard: of his mother, suddenly, in 1970, of Veronica Forrest-Thomson in 1975 at the age of 27 and, within a single week in 1978, of John Scott and Hugh MacDiarmid. Morgan had been estranged from Scott since the previous summer, following what he describes to Schmidt as 'a sudden flare-up [...] one of those tiny almost accidental things which are nevertheless very hard to undo once certain words have been said'. The next year brought more public disappointments – the failed referendum in a devolution campaign for a Scottish Assembly, and the election of Margaret Thatcher that followed. But for Morgan, who was by accident of birth tied more than most to a narrative of life by history's decades, the tension between grand events and tiny, almost accidental things would have to continue to be written out in poetry.

Book and Pamphlet Publications

The Horseman's Word: A Sequence of Concrete Poems. Preston: Akros Publications, 1970.

Twelve Songs. West Linton: Castlelaw Press, 1970.

Glasgow Sonnets. West Linton: Castlelaw Press, 1972.

Instamatic Poems. London: Ian McKelvie, 1972.

Wi the Haill Voice: 25 Poems by Vladimir Mayakovsky. Translated into Scots with a glossary by Edwin Morgan. South Hinksey, Oxford: Carcanet Press, 1972.

From Glasgow to Saturn. Cheadle: Carcanet Press, 1973 (2nd impression 1974); Chester Springs, Pennsylvania: Dufour, 1973.

The Whittrick: A Poem in Eight Dialogues 1955–1961. Preston: Akros Publications, 1973.

Essays. Cheadle Hulme: Carcanet New Press, 1974.

Fifty Renascence Love Poems. Translated by Edwin Morgan. Reading: Whiteknights Press, 1975.

Rites of Passage: Translations. Manchester: Carcanet New Press, 1976.

Hugh MacDiarmid. Edited by Ian Scott-Kilvert. London: Longman for the British Council, 1976) (Writers and their Work series).

The New Divan. Manchester: Carcanet New Press, 1977.

Colour Poems. Glasgow: Third Eye Centre, 1978.

Platen: Selected Poems. Translated by Edwin Morgan. West Linton: Castlelaw Press, 1978.

Provenance and Problematics of 'Sublime and Alarming Images' in Poetry. London: The British Academy, 1979. (Warton Lecture).

Star Gate: Science Fiction Poems. Glasgow: Third Eye Centre, 1979.

Robert Tait, editor

19 Whittingehame Court
Glasgow W2
7 January 1970

Dear Bob

Here is Hugh Murray's review of the Hernton book. It's
all right I think, though I haven't read the Hernton so can't
say how relevant it is – I get the impression it doesn't tell
me enough about the book (which I always tend to regard
as a fault in a review). The points you make about its style,
repetitions, obviousness, etc. – yes, these still show a bit, and
at times I felt I was being written down to, as if I had never
thought about the subject of black man and white woman
or vice versa. There would also, on the contrary, seem to be
some omissions, e.g. nothing about the 'purity' ideas of black
Muslims such as Cassius Clay – see his reported remarks about
wife and women, which are quite at variance with Murray's
general line, or so it would seem to an outsider. (One passing
thought: poor James Baldwin! – what a rapid transition from
adulation to contemptuous dismissal! I do think now people
are very unfair to him, though I understand why the change
has taken place.) – I've put in a few corrections.

I hope Jack Rillie's review reached you all right; he posted
it direct to you on Sunday. Marshall is a wee thing worried
about getting proofs – will you make sure he does? He has this
strong personal-responsibility thing as regards Warren and is
anxious not to let him down in any way…

I can, a little, feel for the Nye point about glossiness: there's
something in me which would really prefer to see SI printed
on toilet paper or palm-leaves or human skin, in blood or
soot or serum, and with ten mistakes to the line, as if in the
belief that sincerity and A4 don't go together – I've always
loved Baudelaire and Rimbaud and have a distinct nostalgie
de la boue. I wonder if you dig this at all? Put it another way:
I treasure all my copies of MacDiarmid's weird ill-printed
Voice of Scotland but would never dream of keeping the bland
and elegant *London Magazine* unless it had an article that
interested me. Maybe this is just lame dogs syndrome.

How are you enjoying the Great Frosty Decade? I was forced to get myself a pair of crinkly-soled boots to avoid doing a daily Gaderene swine down Hillhead Street. Flat soles are murder.

Happy dekko! | Eddie

Hugh Murray, a Black American student arrested in a lunch-counter sit-in protest in 1960, now taught on the 'Negro Campus' of the State University of New Orleans. Jack Rillie and Marshall Walker* were EM's university colleagues. Walker specialised in the poetry of Robert Penn Warren. Nye is Robert Nye. 'Happy dekko': New Year wishes for a new decade.

Veronica Forrest-Thomson, poet and critic

17 March 1970

Dear Veronica

I was greatly interested in your *Twelve Academic Questions*, especially as coming as it were to fulfil the laws and prophets of the essay on a poetry of intellect which I now belatedly and apologetically return. (I shall pass on the *TAQ* to Dr Hobsbaum as you ask, but could you please send me another copy first – I enclose postal order.) The essay tries to tease out a situation which I have myself often thought about, though any way forward except on the level of wit and irony (and this is what inevitably results from quotation and footnotes) is as hard to see as ever – hence one falls back on a poetry of fact, or a poetry of the emotional impact of scientific theory/ 'fact'/ hypothesis/ 'discovery', or a poetry of structural exploration like concrete, in the hope that these are severally but perhaps mystically jointly leading in the right direction. You are sceptical, I think, of the value of these three approaches, and plump rather for a witt(genstein)y glancing thickly allusive and deliberately uncommunicative poetry ('something of which those who try a poetry of intellect will certainly not have to be over-solicitous') for the sake of showing the play of mental activity itself, though you obviously feel that concrete or kinetic forms may be relevant since they do force the mind to readjust, through new modes of perception, to (perhaps) new modes of thinking. The question is how far the language-games can really go, when (as you admit) one is bound sooner or later to come up against the maths-barrier (or even the logic-barrier, which overlaps on maths), where from the scientist's point of view the non-numerate would be crucially crippled by not understanding and therefore not being able to use the non-verbal languages available. In other words, can one be anything like fundamental without mathematics? Are non-mathematical language-games, however 'rigorous', necessarily an indulgence and therefore a trivialisation? I tried to say something about this in my poem 'Not Playing the Game' which you may know (it's in the Penguin Modern Poets 15 – page 155); yet even trying hard to focus on the actual problem, while at the same time writing a poem, began to produce an infinite regression of ironies which might end by pleasing nobody, neither scientist, philosopher nor poet. Do you ever suspect that you are on the horns of a chimera rather than a dilemma?

Anyhow, I am sure you were absolutely right to 'make public' your explorations. They are not so 'environmental' as Prynne's, unless mental-environmental, and I found myself a little regretting the degree of abstraction from the physical (from 'that sudden warmth which took / birch trees up into Scotland' etc); on the other hand, by doing this you gain an intellectual stir-up quality, refusing any lingering by the Mill Race at Granta Place or smoky light along the Backs, walking off with Gabriel Harvey and leaving Spenser to brood. Spenser I imagine could be called the exact opposite of Wittgenstein, and yet his slow large-scale cumulative effects, vast language-games using not words but stanzas, cantos and books, remain remarkably unexplained (despite the numerologists). – The poems of yours which (neither Harvey nor Spenser but you) mean most to me, give me the most satisfaction (satisfaction as the good supervener – I mean stir-up has to be completed), are the 'Zettel', 'Acrostic', 'Alka-Seltzer Poem', and 'Three Proper'. In these I think you have got the thing going. Especially 'Acrostic'! With a poem like 'The Brown Book' you are up against the simple problem of 'how to read' it. There is no comfortable way. Does this matter? Should the notes not be incorporated somehow? Or the poem re-structured even, as a dialogue (though I know there are objections to dialogue poems)? Maybe all I am retailing is an anti-note prejudice, but if so – . I still feel the method is not working. Some of the other poems seem to have moved on from there and perhaps you have yourself had second thoughts about note-poems.

Will you be in Glasgow over Easter? I hope you will look me up and give me all your news. Do ring or write. I shall be here most of the time except 3–10 April.

Sincerely | Edwin Morgan

In January 1970, VF-T had sent a draft essay arguing for the place of intellect in the making of poetry, and including a Wittgensteinian poem with footnotes to register mocking dissent from its main statements. In February she had sent *Twelve Academic Questions*, encouraged by Philip Hobsbaum to work through her reactions to Cambridge in verse. She admired J.H. Prynne, a focus for current Cambridge poetry as Edmund Spenser and Gabriel Harvey had been in Elizabethan times.

Bobbie Hinson, American high school student

24 June 1970

Dear Bobbie

Thank you very much for your letter about my poem 'Orgy'. I am sorry I have taken so long to answer it.

The poem is about an anteater eating ants – and he finds so many that it becomes an absolute feast or orgy of ant-eating. The anteater (line 2) comes cantering along (line 1) and has an 'ant encounter' (line 3); it's as if his antenna begins to react (line 4) at the sight of such an army of ants (lines 5–8), so many he can't count them (line 9), he'd need an accountant (line 10); so the anteater (line 11) sets to eating and eating pure nectar (line 15), and he falls into a trance (line 16)....... He can't eat an ant more (line 17), the anteater can't (line 18), not an ant (line 19)......... He lies in a trance and thinks to himself 'O content!' (lines 20–21); he's at peace after his orgy, there's no more cantering today (22).

It's an example of what is called Concrete Poetry, where the typography is used as an internal part of the poem. Here, I wanted the look of the poem on the page to bristle like a mass of ants, like an ant-heap if you like, and it's only when you look closer and work it out that you see it all has order and meaning, just as there is order and meaning in an ant-heap too. Of course it's meant also to be amusing. I used only a restricted number of letters of the alphabet in order to increase word-play, as well as to help the whole poem to appear more like a swirling mass of recurring particles. I hope these remarks will help you to find your way into the poem – and I hope you will still like it after having gone through this letter!

All best wishes | Sincerely yours | Edwin Morgan

PS This poem is in a book of mine called *The Second Life* (Edinburgh University Press, 1968; obtainable in America through Aldine Publishing Company, Chicago). I am also sending you a Penguin paperback which has some of my poetry in it.

Hinson was a high school senior from Montrose, North Carolina, whose teacher had given the class copies of EM's 'Orgy' (*CP*: 162) but claimed not to know what it meant.

Alex Frizzell, publisher and bookseller

14 July 1970

Dear Alex

Many thanks for your letter. I wonder if the enclosed is the poem you were trying to remember? If so, I am thinking that perhaps you have not seen *Penguin Modern Poets 15*, where I included it – in fact I put it at the beginning, as it is a poem I rather like. (But maybe it's another one altogether you have in mind!)

You needn't in the least fear 'presuming' – I would be glad

to have you do other things of mine, whether a limited-edition or special selection, or some translations, or concrete/visual/ poster poems as and when you manage. Tell me, what are 'interchange colours'? I always prick up my ears when I see 'colour', because a number of the things I have been doing recently have been handwritten visual poems in polychrome – these have been shown in various exhibitions but so far I have found no way of getting them published. I mention it to you in case the possibility ever arises! But to return to black and white. And this may not be relevant, as it is not a typesetting job at all. I have over 100 'Newspoems' which are in a sort of collage or found-poem category, cut from newspapers and other ephemeral material; a few have appeared in magazines but I would like to have them in a collection, choosing the most successful ones, perhaps about 50 or 80 or so. I am enclosing some examples with this letter, and you can see what you think. The main problem is just how to reproduce them.

Your Austrian-illustrated Yesenin sounds interesting. Very little of Yesenin has appeared in English. I have tried him myself, with no great success. The chief difficulty is his strict metre and rhyme which tends to come out naïve (in the wrong way) in English. Though I like his poetry, I don't feel it is quite my cup of tea. In the translation line, would you have any interest in August von Platen (I have about 18 pages- worth) or Leopardi (about 18 pages) or Voznesensky (about 15 pages)? Of course these selections might seem too thin, though they would give a flavour. I could boost them up if you were interested. Cavafy I like very much, but I have never translated him.

I am just back from Oxford, New College, where I was reading my poetry to 200 American schoolteachers on summer school tour – cameras flashing, tape-recorder and microphone, these people really know what they want! (Talk about Mahomedans – I must have lost quite a bit of me on that occasion.)

Best regards | Eddie

Frizzell, a bookseller, had published *Twelve Songs* (1970) from his Castlelaw Press in West Lothian. His misremembered poem was probably 'After the Party' (*CP*: 239). He now mentioned large-type poster poems, and 'interchange colours' (designed to prevent colours merging in print). Translation was another possibility: either of Sergei Yesenin (he had met a young Austrian illustrator of his poems) or Constantine Cavafy. Contacts from the teachers' conference led to EM's 1971 reading tour of East Coast US high schools. The 'Mahomedan' refers to Frizzell's remark about the belief that being photographed diminishes identity.

Alex Frizzell, publisher and bookseller

11 August 1970

Dear Alex

Back from blue Killarney I have just typed out the Platen translations as you requested; I have copies so don't bother to return them. As you will see, there are 23 poems, which if you did like the idea would make not a bad little book. But obviously some are better than others, and you could easily drop any that you felt were not up to standard. The best, I think, are the 9 'Venetian Sonnets' (these are taken from a larger series and I have still to check the numbers of most of the sonnets in the sequence, which I will do soon). I have stuck to the strict-translation method of keeping close as far as possible to form as well as content – no doubt with some signs of strain here and there, but I felt any freer treatment would be unfair to a poet who took such pains over (often unusual) form. If you used all the poems and had one to a page, it would make a book about twice the length of *Twelve Songs*. Do let me know what you think, but of course you will probably want to wait in any case until I can type out for you the Leopardi and the Voznesensky. Would you in fact prefer something modern? Platen belongs very much to a past period, and you might feel that he is too much of a historical curiosity (or a psychological one) to be worth resurrecting. On the other hand, he does give a remarkable (pre *Death in Venice*) account of the impact of Italy on the Teutonic soul. And he is an odd forerunner of Cavafy in his interest in the clashes of histories and cultures, noble barbarians versus effete sophisticates and so on. By the way, many of these versions (some in slightly different forms) were printed in an American anthology which has not been seen over here – *An Anthology of German Poetry from Hölderlin to Rilke* (Doubleday & Company Inc, Garden City, New York, 1960) – and I suppose you would have to get their permission to reprint, not that there should be any objection. The Leopardi and the Voznesensky have only been printed in magazines. This may be a factor that will influence you if you'd rather have material that has never been in any sort of book form…

All best regards | Eddie

Frizzell finally published *Platen: Selected Poems* in 1978, after *Glasgow Sonnets* in 1972. The Doubleday Anthology was edited by Angél Flores*.

Robert Tait, editor

14 December 1970

Dear Bob

It's good to see Robert Hughes writing again. I'd certainly vote for 'The Happy Man'. It's perceptive and evocative and well-written, and the theme is interesting– 'Don't put me in one of your stories' / but of course he must / but of course if he does then that is the end of it because one may use strangers and friends and lovers in one's stories but not wives and husbands (which is why there is something almost obscene about the Brownings' love-poems) nicht wahr? My only criticism is that the story, with its really fresh opening, promises rather more than it eventually delivers, at least I found a slight growing disappointment when I saw the way it was going – it seemed more like a nice fragment of unwritten Bildungsroman than a true shirt story. Short story, how absurd, sorry. But even if this is true – and you may not agree with it – I'm sure the piece is well worth publishing.

Thanks for the work questionnaires. This I think is an excellent idea, especially if we can get a good range of jobs covered. I've given one to my friend John Scott who I believe

I once mentioned to you works as a storeman in a factory; although he has a proper workingclass caution about all such enquiries I think he may do it. I've two other pals I'd like to give questionnaires to, but they're somewhat elusive and I may not get hold of them in time: one is a truck-driver and the other is a young Irish faith-healer and cooker-repairer who is quite a character (he lays on hands and it seems to work).

Are we due for a meeting this month before or after the Yuile?

Yours | Eddie

The questionnaire was Tait's attempt to turn this issue of *Scottish International* into an open forum where people could reflect on work and workplaces in a 'snapshot survey' of an ordinary day (Tuesday 15 December, 11am–3pm). John Scott did complete the form, which was then typed up by EM, an edited selection appearing in a report in *Scottish International*, 13 February 1971.

Alex Frizzell, publisher and bookseller

17 December 1970

Dear Alex

Delighted to receive the blue toboggans – it is really very good of you to do this and it will make a fine change from UNICEF pigtails and Dutch snowscapes. I suppose it counts as a first edition too (though you have too modestly put no Castlelaw on it). And speaking of editions – to answer your query, I don't have a checklist in the strict sense though I think I have most items noted somewhere. The Baudelaire book is <u>not</u> mine, though many people, I know, think it is; by a curious coincidence I too have long been interested in Baudelaire and know his work well, and have several times been asked to review books on Baudelaire, so it is natural that many people will tend to assume I wrote that book – but no, I cannot claim it as mine. Do you know that reference book *Contemporary Poets of the English Language* (St James Press, 1970)? It lists most of my books, and all you would have to add to its bibliography would be your own *Twelve Songs* and the Akros *The Horseman's Word*, plus the following: (ed.) *Poems by Alan Hayton, Stephen Mulrine, Colin Kirkwood, Robert Tait* (Akros, 1967); (ed.) *Penguin New English Dramatists 14* (1970); (trans.) *Sandor Weöres & Ferenc Juhász: Selected Poems* trans. by Edwin Morgan & David Wevill (Penguin Modern European Poets, 1970). That fine folk-singer Archie Fisher has set two of my Glasgow poems as songs in his latest LP, *Orfeo* (Decca, 1970). I have sent him a copy of *Twelve Songs* in the hope that he may be moved to try some more! I recently sent a new collection of poems to Edinburgh University Press but I haven't heard from them yet.

We may have been in Jerusalem at the same time, isn't it curious? I was in the Middle East from 1941 to 1945, in the Egyptian desert, Sidon, and Haifa, with periods of leave in Cairo, Alexandria, Jerusalem, Tel Aviv, Beirut, and the Cedars. I wasn't writing, though; found it impossible. I'm left with a series of strong impressions and experiences which have little to do with the war – persons, places, atmosphere, things that have since filtered at times into my poetry and will likely do so yet.

Many thanks for the Robin Fulton – nice production and a nice sequence of poems.

Yours | Eddie

Frizzell had printed a personal Christmas card for EM, based on 'Blue Toboggans' (*CP*: 243). *Flower of Evil: Life of Charles Baudelaire* by the other Edwin Morgan (see also p. 368) was published in 1943, when EM was on National Service in the Middle East, where Frizzell served too, as a wireless operator. He had just published *Quarters* (1970) by Robin Fulton*.

Daniel Weissbort, editor and translator

14 April 1971

Dear Mr Weissbort,

I had just been about to write to you about Mayakovsky
when your letter arrived! I am delighted to know that you
want to go ahead with a volume, and the series as you outline
it seems an excellent idea which deserves success – personally,
I am more in favour of the larger edition and wider public.
Obviously, as you say, it will need careful costing, but I think
there is a lot of interest in European poetry just now, and
certainly Pilinszky, Hikmet and Mayakovsky (whatever the
fourth turns out to be) makes a fascinatingly varied opening
offer. I know the Carcanet publications and I'm sure they
will do a good job. My translations of Mayakovsky are of
course still available, and I shall now get down to the task of
glossary and introduction. About what length do you think
the introduction should be? One doesn't want to overload the
book with prose, yet on the other hand there is a dearth of
good critical writing in English on Mayakovsky and it would
be a chance to do something about this. And tell me, will you
have access to Russian type or do you want me to transliterate
everything into English characters? (I am thinking of the
quotations, etc.)

Here is some information about the translations which
perhaps you can make use of for promotion:

I took up the translation of Mayakovsky primarily because
I was strongly taken by his poetry and felt impelled to try
to convey the quality and pleasure and power of his work
to others. I felt I was sufficiently near his wavelength to
understand him sympathetically, and in translation that is half
the battle. But I soon discovered that the problems of making
straight English versions of Mayakovsky are formidable, and it
was almost as if the spirit of the language was against me. The
Mayakovskian exclamatoriness, the abrupt changes of tone,
the unusual mixture of fantasy, lyricism, and direct civic and
moral concern – all seemed recalcitrant to the English medium
and to English models. But with the use of Scots, I found that
many of the problems quickly dissolved. It is possible to tap a

Scottish tradition of both grotesque exaggeration and fantasy and of linguistic extraversion and dash that goes back through MacDiarmid, Burns, and Dunbar. And at the same time, it may be that the linking of the fantastic/wild/grotesque with the moral/political/social comes more easily to the Scottish than to the English poet. Sydney Goodsir Smith's Scottish version of Blok's 'The Twelve' seems to show that Scots as a language can get closer than English to the 'barbarian lyre' of the revolutionary spirit.

– I hope you can use some of this.

All best wishes | Edwin Morgan

Weissbort was co-editor with Ted Hughes* of the new *Modern Poetry in Translation* series, published with Carcanet Press. The first four books were planned: Pilinszky (Hughes), Hikmet (Taner Baybars), Vinikurov (Weissbort) and Mayakovsky (EM). He had written asking for an introduction and glossary for the latter.

Robert Tait, editor

8 August 1971

Dear Bob

I am back from Toffee Town, where the reading went quite well. I left on Saturday morning, so I don't know how Sorley Maclean coped with his reading on Saturday afternoon when he had to hold the whole fort in the absence of Hugh MacDiarmid (non-appearance due to illness, whether diplomatic or real no one seemed sure). I came back in the train with Iain and left him in Edinburgh, where he was determined to see 'Cromwell' before going on to Oban. His fixation on power-figures remains unabated. I suppose there would be about fifty people at the reading, which was perhaps not bad. We were given supper thereafter in the Festival Club, which may lack Edinburgh's chandeliers but is not unswinging. After the meal we sat around on the floor while various shades of rock were hammered out for the dancers. Big uncurtained windows looked out onto a full moon night, highly splendid.

There was a girl in black crochet and red wig, a man in a gorilla suit. I love men dressed as animals, don't you? No need to answer that kinky question! By an odd coincidence, a girl called Linda who was an ex-pupil of Iain's at Oban was there putting us on to her sketch-pad for the Illustrated London News – she has a commission to go round all the festivals. She had a short sort of Mohawk haircut and was very protective towards Iain and kept giving him advice and encouragement. Then she was swept into the dancers. We left about 2 am and wandered back to our hotel with Sorley and his wife. There was more talk in the hotel's corridors and bedrooms which would probably have gone on till cockcrow if we had not been loudly complained about by an insomniac female guest at 4 am (she was still complaining about us to the manageress at breakfast-time) (it must have made her day) and allowed ourselves to be broken up just as I was saying 'Man is God'.

I return the Lorn Macintyre interview. I think the most interesting parts for us might be: pages 1–8 (the poet's actual highland heritage, his mother, his relation to Calvinism), pages 22–35 (the 'second phase', the theme of contemporary Scotland, 'bourgeois land', and the place of ideologies), and pages 49–51 (new departures, death and loneliness, heart versus intellect). Whatever we take, there is quite a bit of repetition, and I suppose you would have to do some editing. But there is a lot of interesting and valuable material.

Iain, by the way, much approved of our first monthly number.

Yours | Eddie

EM had been to Harrogate (home of Farrah's Original Harrogate Toffee) for a literary festival. Lorn Mcintyre had sent *Scottish International* for consideration an interview with Iain Crichton Smith*, part of his undergraduate English project at the University of Stirling.

Michael Schmidt, publisher, poet and critic

11 September 1971

Dear Mr Schmidt

Thank you for the contract forms. I am returning one duly signed and initialled. All seems in order. I can't quite decide on the title of the volume yet, though I suppose it had better be kept straight and simple since it is one of a series, and your suggested *Poems of Mayakovsky* really meets the bill well enough.

Your book of essays on *British Poetry Since 1960* sounds interesting. I would certainly like to write something for you on Scottish poetry during that period, especially as the sixties have been quite a lively scene here. How would I avoid overlapping with Bill Parkinson? Do you know if he has undertaken any particular angle? There is also the problem that I have published a good deal myself in this period and I couldn't with propriety discuss that! But if we can find a way round this I'd like to write an essay for you.

I shall look forward to the books and your own poems – though I don't know if I can promise to keep my itching fingers off an unopened book till March 1972, difficult...

Best wishes | Edwin Morgan

Schmidt had asked EM to write a chapter on the Scottish poetry revival for his *British Poetry Since 1960: A Critical Survey* (1972), co-edited with Grevel Lindop. He eventually wrote 'Scottish Poetry in the 1960s' offering 'pointers across and through the scene' without mentioning his own work (but listing anthologies where it would be found). The 'straight and simple' title became *Wi the Haill Voice: 25 Poems of Vladimir Mayakovsky* (1972).

Iain Crichton Smith, *poet and novelist*

17 October 1971

Dear Iain

Sorry to be so long in answering your letter – the usual new-term busyness held me up. I think what you want to find out is very difficult. I am not at all sure that I know what happens when I am creating a poem, and whatever it is basically, it varies a good deal from poem to poem (since my poems are of many different kinds). At one extreme perhaps is the commissioned poem, like 'Hyena', 'Heron', and 'Goal!' which Penguin Books asked me to do for school anthologies: in each case they sent me a photograph of the subject, and my poem was to be an accompaniment to the photograph (a sort of reversal of the more usual habit of finding an illustration to go with an existing poem). It worked reasonably well; I was able to react strongly enough to the photographs to be roused into verbal activity, though not immediately, since I let them lie around for a while and sink into my subconscious, and then eventually had a more intense go at them and tried writing 'with my eye on the subject' as in this case it had to be. Having gone through this process I feel it has something to be said for it. Maybe more poems should be commissioned. At the other extreme is the poem which comes completely unannounced and almost writes itself: my short poem 'The Sheaf' was like that; I was on a train going south, somewhere near the Borders if I remember correctly, I was for some reason in a low state of mind, staring out at the dull fields, but then for no reason that I can now remember I suddenly felt a stab of intense emotion which I linked with myself, the journey, and the fields going past. At that moment the first lines of the poem came into my mind. They weren't worked on, they were just there. I hurriedly scribbled them down on a bit of paper, and the rest of the poem began to fill itself in, though this involved a more conscious activity of choice and rejection. The whole process didn't take long, but the feelings involved were very powerful, intense, and anxious, and not quite like any of the feelings of ordinary social life.

In between these extremes there is such a changing mixture

of planned and unplanned material coming together that I
don't think I could generalize about it. But if you can think
of anything specific to ask, I could have a shot at giving a
reply. I am enclosing a poem I wrote once called 'Making a
Poem' which might be of some interest, though you will have
to remember that the person in the poem is not strictly me (I
don't wear a scarf, and I don't have a cat or a patch cushion) but
the poem does partly reflect my own experience. I also enclose
the Hughes poem you asked for, and a Wallace Stevens you
may know. The two books may give you some further ideas and
topics for discussion. There's also things like Dylan Thomas's
interesting remarks in his letter to Treece about image-making;
Hopkins on how he came to write the 'Deutschland'; Poe (if
you can believe him) in his 'Rationale of Verse Composition';
Burns's verse epistles to Davie, Simpson, Lapraik; Hopkins's
sonnet 'The fine delight that fathers thought'…

Best of luck, | E

ICS was in a local discussion group whose members had asked him
to tell them what actually happens when someone creates a poem,
so he cross-checked his own experience with EM, who refers to his
own 'The Sheaf' and 'Making a Poem' (CP: 181, 550). Edgar Allan
Poe's essay of 1848 is usually known as 'The Rationale of Verse'.

Michael Schmidt, publisher, poet and critic

20 November 1971

Dear Michael
    Needless to say I am enormously relieved and pleased that
the article was on time and acceptable. Even not being last
after all – well now. I shall look forward to reading the pieces
you mention. Bunting is also not one of my absolute favourites,
though I can see he has gluey music all his own – but I like a
verse that <u>moves</u>. It is not enough to have images, fine though
many of his certainly are. On the other hand, his quirky
crabbitness is also a 'northernness' and in some moods this
attracts just because at least it is not smooth.

How nice of Robert Garioch to order a Mayakovsky already. I would undoubtedly value his opinion on it eventually. But if you were to try to ask him to review it this might be taken as backscratching since we are both editorial advisers on *Scottish International*. If he reviews it somewhere unasked, fine. The *Scotsman* idea is worth pursuing. Probably you should write to Robert Nye who is the literary editor. He is not himself Scotch, but is well disposed to Scottish poetry (and I believe to Carcanet) and might well be interested in a feature of some kind.

I have a promise of a review in *Soviet Studies* (a quarterly edited from Glasgow University) if you will send a copy when the time comes to Dr Alan Ross, Department of International Economic Studies, University of Glasgow.

Could you please make two small changes in my typescript of the Scottish Poetry essay: Page 7 line 20 – for <u>vehement</u> read <u>forceful</u>, and page 9 line 13 for <u>period</u> read <u>decade</u>.

From my window I am watching the snow flittering down past the orange streetlamps like – like – come on Bunting – like

> doom-grated
> orange-peel
> puffed through
> fine fans

etc.

Yours ever | Edwin | (do please drop the Mr!)

PS I nearly forgot: yes, thanks, I did review your fine catalogue!

Schmidt had praised EM's chapter for *British Poetry Since 1960*, mentioning other enjoyable chapters but demurring on the negative pages on Basil Bunting by W.E. Parkinson, while noting that he himself was not keen on Bunting's work. EM had earlier mentioned Garioch as a possible reviewer for *The Scotsman* newspaper.

Geoffrey Summerfield, editor and academic

22 January 1972

Dear Geoffrey,

'Strawberry Fields Forever' was suggested by, and bears some relation to, the Beatles song of the same title, and I suppose if you were able to play the record over first, this might get the students into the right mood. However, apart from the mood, the poem is really independent of the song, except maybe for the world 'unreal'. I imagine two lovers drifting through dewy fields of long grass – walking apart, coming together again, as the fall of the words down the page is meant to indicate – nature is mysterious but vivid all round them as in Hardy or Lawrence – the dewdrops, the slight 'smirr' of rain, the suggestion of foxes, the hazel-tree, the blackbird ('blackie' the usual Scots term for it) whistling – and I think from this you'll be able to get on to the words 'losing' and 'patter' which have more than one meaning/reference and which I'd rather not try to make too specific myself… I believe Strawberry Fields is a district of Liverpool (or something like that), but I use it as if it referred to actual fields. – I hope this helps. It's a poem which is probably asking too much of the reader, though I believe that when it's explained it can be meaningful. It is, of course, associated in my mind with the Lennon/McCartney song, which has always haunted me and seemed to be very distinctive (1967 I think it came out).

All the best as ever | Eddie

Summerfield worked in teacher education at the University of York, but was currently on sabbatical in the University of California at Berkeley. American students were responding enthusiastically to EM's poems, but confused by 'Strawberry Fields Forever' (*CP*: 139).

Alex Frizzell, publisher and bookseller

20 February 1972

Dear Alex

Thanks very much for your letter and the Songs. I am glad
to send you a copy of the Carcanet Mayakovsky in exchange –
it costs £3 so the difference in price is trifling and you mustn't
think of making it up! I have sent a copy to Christopher
Grieve and it's possible that it might appeal to him. Valda's
remark which you quote is certainly encouraging – and a
bit unexpected too I must say. I remember an earlier remark
of hers, made to me in a rude moment: 'Edwin Muir wasn't
much of a poet but at least he was better than Edwin Morgan!'
Hardly endearing! (The two names do get mixed up: I have
on more than one occasion been introduced by a forgetful
chairman as Edwin Muir, and at a poetry-reading I gave a few
years ago I was billed on a large poster as Edwin Muir even
though the poor man had been in his grave for quite some
time.) (Perhaps scholars a thousand years hence will think it
is one poet who was born in Orkney and then came to live in
Glasgow for the rest of his rather long life?)

Thank you for the nice Alex McCrindle broadsheet – and
it is good to hear that you think you can go ahead with the
Platen now. You ask whether I'd prefer anything other than the
Platen to be done first, and in fact this tempts me to consider
the Glasgow Sonnets. They are about the Glasgow of the
present time, and some of them have a deliberate topicality,
so that it would be excellent if they could be brought out as a
group reasonably soon. My only hesitation is that so far I have
only ten sonnets and I'd like to have more for a book. (Say
possibly twenty.) Could you leave me to simmer this over for a
week and see whether I can expand the sequence? – Of course
you may feel that ten is enough in any case. But I'll write again
about this very soon, and also send you the sonnets to look at.

I am just beginning to thaw out at the end of an electricity
cut. My flat is all-electric so I get the full treatment. Typing
by candlelight is quite difficult because of the shadows. I was
typing some lectures on Dylan Thomas and couldn't get that
'candle in the thighs' of his out of my mind. Where no wax is

(though in fact I was almost floating in it), the candle shows its hairs. And you can say that again Dylan.

Yours | Eddie

Frizzell had visited MacDiarmid* and reported Valda Grieve's praise of EM as 'a real poet [...] more than some of these other bastards'. He accepted payment in kind for additional copies of *Twelve Songs*. Widespread industrial disruption in the early 1970s affected his bookselling and delayed his printing projects. No further Glasgow Sonnets were completed.

Archibald Turnbull, publisher

31 March 1972

Dear Archie

It is sixteen months since I sent you my collection of poems, and I feel that I must ask you now to give me a decision one way or the other. I know the Press has had its difficulties, and I have tried not to nag you about this book, but I can't go on indefinitely like this, with no communication from you and no prospect in sight. Would you at least write and tell me what the position is. I would very much like the collection to be published by Edinburgh University Press, but if you can see no present likelihood of taking it, I would like to submit it elsewhere. It is over four years now since *The Second Life* appeared, and I think it is time I got another volume out.

Yours ever | Eddie | Edwin Morgan

Uncertainty over university funding had led to caution at Edinburgh University Press, which was dependent on the overall financial position of the institution. EM was impatient with the delay in committing to a second volume, given the success of his first.

Michael Schmidt, publisher, poet and critic

2 April 1972

Dear Michael

You nearly got another hotel letter – I have been reading my poetry in the Crown and Greyhound, Dulwich Village. But this time I did not have time to sit down and reply to your missive. Heathrow was purring to bear me back. Do you like hotels? I remember reading Eugene O'Neill's supposed last words – 'Born in a hotel room, and by God died in a hotel room!' What about a hotel in Budapest now? I've just been invited by Hungarian P.E.N. to spend ten days as their guest sometime this year, but I haven't made up my mind about it yet. Do you collect Magyar stamps? I've been in Budapest once before and wouldn't mind going back. I am really a very Glasgow-loving root-clutching person, and the mechanics of travel fill me with angst, yet I seem to be meant or doomed or prodded to go to place after place, city after city (but cities I love in any case, all cities) – Paris, Amsterdam, Cologne, Innsbruck, Stockholm, Bergen, Helsinki, Leningrad, Moscow, Kiev, Tripoli, Beirut, Cairo, Alexandria, Haifa, Jerusalem, Tel Aviv, Durban, Washington, New York… but not Mexico yet. I've been round the Cape of Good Hope and down the Odessa Steps. I've seen the Book of Kells and the Isenheim Altarpiece and Beethoven's ear-trumpet and Khalil Gibran's birthplace and Lenin's tomb. I have placed my piastres on the belly-dancer's belly-button, and skied beneath the cedars of Lebanon. I have seen the Red Sea and the Black Sea – both blue. What is it all for? Can you tell me that? Next Sunday I read at Dunfermline, where as you will recall the king sat drinking blood-red wine…

I hope you don't have frayed hands after all that book-parcelling. To take your mind off it, the resident house-surgeon at the Dove's Tail Press encloses two more treated secretions which he trusts may assuage slightly, even if they are still perhaps a little angular. Your third extract, which you described as 'sort of finished', he finds he can do nothing with, regretfully, so maybe it is in fact finished. He also encloses a copy of the earlier calcification 'The lights went out' as requested. May the pain lessen, the organism bloom. It is Easter day. Khristos voskres!

I promised to let you have epistolary comments on WTVH. Hugh MacDiarmid wrote: '... I was saying on T.V. apropos my new version of Brecht's Threepenny Opera that there are elements in Brecht with which modern English can't deal – for which it is far too refined. These elements are nearer elements in Scots, e.g. in Dunbar and Burns. This is the same claim you make with regard to Mayakovsky, but you not only make the claim but prove it in your translations. One has only to compare them with the translations into English by Marshall Reav[e]y, and others. Congratulations, and additional thanks for your brilliant introduction...' And Robert Garioch wrote: 'I read selections from your Mayakovsky translations to my seminar [at Edinburgh University], and first invited Mr Falchnikov, a lecturer in the Russian Department, to come and hear; I took him the book so that he could look up the poems in the original... He brought some of his students with him also, and his wife. They thought the translations were miraculous... Also the other people there who didn't know Russian enjoyed them as poems, and the Scots went over quite easily...' He also enclosed a letter from Falchnikov which enthused over one point (my reference to the firm Wylie & Lochhead in 'Wi the Haill Voice' as catching the right bourgeois atmosphere of the late NEP period). All this is very nice but of course we must wait till we see some published reviews, when perhaps the 'furrowed brows and confusion' you mention will be more dominant.

I do agree with you that ten sonnets is not enough, and so I told Castlelaw, but Castlelaw wanted to go ahead with a pamphlet and I wasn't able to produce ten or twenty more, though I may add some yet, as I still feel some twinges and minatory stirrings that suggest the vein has not yet been worked out – and eventually there might be a larger collection. The TLS has taken the other six, by the way.

The gulls weren't <u>flying</u> backwards, they were <u>swimming</u> backwards! I can't have been compliffeyly clear.

I think you could put me down for £100worth of Carcashares. Let a hundred flowers bloom. Khristos voskres.

Classes have not begun yet but I have 200 essays to mark

on 'Would an unbiased spectator take <u>Hamlet</u> to be a play about irresolution and delay?' Show me an unbiased spectator, as Eureka said, and I will move the world.

Shoulder on, Epaulette!

Fata Morgana viam inveniet, as the mirage told the meteorologist.

Eddie

EM's previous letter was from a Dublin hotel. The Dovetails were EM's smooth completions of abandoned poems by Schmidt (also referred to as 'gallstones'). WTHV is *Wi the Haill Voice*. Schmidt had wondered whether EM might produce further 'Glasgow Sonnets'. 'Khristos voskres' means 'Christ is risen'. Schmidt was raising capital for Carcanet Press by issuing shares. 'Epaulette' was how he had signed off his previous letter with a pun – a younger brother of Apollo.

Graham Martin, *academic*

Department of English
The University
7 April 1972

Dear Graham Martin

Thank you for your letter of 5 April. It seems to me an excellent idea that the Open University should try to bring in some modern European poetry, and I think the old hoary university objection to it can be met along the line you suggest (opening up the theme of literature & language & translation, with the added factor that nowadays very reasonable versions do exist of a fair number of poets – e.g. the German translations of Hamburger & Middleton, Neruda by Reid, Czech poets by Milner, to mention some that spring to mind; I have versions from Italian (Montale, Quasimodo), Russian (Pasternak, Yevtushenko, Voznesensky & others), Hungarian (József, Weöres, Kassák & others). It would also be possible to find decent versions of Apollinaire, Lorca, Cavafy. I think myself it's important and could be made very interesting to

see the UK/USA poets against this background. Certainly
I'd be glad to discuss it with you sometime and see what the
possibilities are. I'm afraid the first chance I'll have to be
in London will be mid-May; I've a meeting there to go to
on Friday 19 May and will stay over till Saturday. Would a
lunchtime meeting on Saturday 20th be possible for you?

Yours sincerely | Edwin Morgan

Developing literature teaching at the Open University, Martin had
invited EM to be a consultant for a new course on twentieth-century
poetry, with an international perspective.

Michael Schmidt, publisher, poet and critic

19 Whittingehame Court
14 April 1972

Dear Mustafa

How strange that we should both be feluccaphils. Or
Middle Easters. Of all these countries Lebanon is my
favourite. During the war I was stationed for a year at Sidon.
I also had a year in Haifa in what was then Palestine (long
pre-Dayan of course – I agree with you that 'Israel' [it's still
Palestine to me] is altogether another thing and I have no time
for it), and two years in the Egyptian desert. Such was my war,
sand and sun, camels, crusader castles, and conjunctivitis.

I do think you are right about 'The Clouds…' I could feel
that one beginning to take off. I now, in the absence of further
fragments, begin to feel the gap, as if an oysterish grit-cavity
had taken it into its head to throb.

Dunfermline was all right. The bus lost a wheel half way,
and we all had to change buses. Since then I have been to
Stirling to show my concrete poetry slides. On this occasion
the engine of the train broke down completely and had to be
replaced. Things fall apart, etc. It must be the spring.

How silly that was of the *Scotsman* to send my book to
Elizabeth Jennings, they really might have made an effort to
think of someone suitable. I don't at all blame her for passing

it up. But as you say, what can we do now? Could you write to them and ask if they wouldn't try another reviewer, saying you'll send another copy if they do? The *Glasgow Herald* has been silent too. Possibly it's a general problem of finding a reviewer who is qualified or willing or both. This hadn't quite struck me before, but it probably is a real difficulty. By the way, did you send review copies to the various Scottish journals I suggested – *Lines*, *Akros*, *Soviet Studies*. *Scottish International*, so Robert Tait tells me, hasn't had a copy yet. Do send one, as we'll certainly get it reviewed. No sign yet of that Guardian profile either – maybe held up for the same reason! Oh – you will be saying – that Morgan had written in good plain well of English undefiled!

I think it is nice to like novels even if one does not wholly believe in them. I hope you make progress with your own. Is 'What is it about?' too crude a question to ask?

Another epistolary comment I pass on to you, in the absence of public ones: Brian Scobie, once a student here at Glasgow and now in the English Department at Leeds, says 'It really is the best thing I've read in a while. Certainly the best thing in Scots since MacDiarmid – maybe the only thing in Scots since MacD! I have nothing to compare the translations with but it seems to work beautifully. Know anyone that needs it reviewed?!' Do you think we can take up that last offer in any way? Could you perhaps put the *Scotsman* onto him? Forgive me for quoting the praises – purely for informative/practical purposes.

I do look forward to my Pin Farm letters.

Creak out the mower. The smog is lofting.

Yours | Eos von Morgen | (Dr) Eos von Morgen

Schmidt had described his enthusiasm for the Middle East, especially Egypt. 'The clouds are in their arms…' was the first line of their joint poem 'Beginnings', later published in *Grafts/Takes* (1983: 18). Elizabeth Jennings, one of the English 1950s Movement poets, was an unlikely choice to review EM's experimental work. Schmidt was writing a novel, while running Carcanet Press from Pin Farm in South Hinksey near Oxford. Brian Scobie* was working on a volume of critical essays on East European poets. Eos, goddess of the dawn and genetrix of the stars and planets, signals both EM's interest in space and the lifting of mood that contact with Schmidt had brought.

Michael Horowitz, poet and editor

18 April 1972

Dear Michael

Glad you liked the Glasgow Sonnet in *Stand*. I'm enclosing a correct copy – the magazine had one mistake, a dash instead of a hyphen at the end of line 3. It's one of a group of (so far) ten Glasgow Sonnets, so I've put the number of it and that can be its title. Other six will be in *Times Literary Supplement* very soon, maybe this week. Certainly take it, or if you like any of the others, for the revised *Albion*.

I'll get onto Bob Tait right away about your things. I'm sorry about this – I don't know what's happened. He looks after all that side of the magazine. I'll prod him strongly.

Have a copy of my Mayakovsky which you can read in the bath in your most hairy Caledonian accent –

Best as ever | Edwin Morgan

Poet and editor of *New Departure* and *Children of Albion*, Horowitz was trying to recover poems and pictures sent to *Scottish International*, of which EM was now a consulting editor.

Michael Schmidt, publisher, poet and critic

18 May 1972

Dear Michael

How good of you to write with the slipstream scarcely out of your nostrils, and with that White Horse (which I read first as White House until a little flashbulb went off saying That's not New York you fool) brandy after-feeling still hanging around. I am glad you had a good time even if hectic. I have no doubt my last letter did sound as you say 'doleful' – I really felt bad and let-down after that long wait. I have done nothing yet as regards another publisher, for the purely practical reason (and it is another nail in EUP's coffin) that I cannot even get my MS back from them, despite telephone and even personal calls during the last month. Although of course I have copies of the poems, in some cases these are my own only copies and in other cases they are carbons of varying legibility, so it means that if EUP still fail to disgorge (but why, have they lost it?) I shall have to retype the whole collection and this will take a little time. However, enough of these boring details of how Timon took to the woods. I think that I might very well take you up on your suggestion. You will understand that I would still have preferred to be brought out by a Scottish publisher if this was at all possible, but in the absence of EUP there is virtually no poetry-publishing now in Scotland (which is a thoroughly bad situation, but that's another subject –), and Scottish poets will have to look to the big London publishers (as most of them in fact do already, Norman MacCaig with Chatto, Iain Crichton Smith with Gollancz, though Alan Jackson is with the smaller but still London Fulcrum) unless they can find something outside London (Oxford!) or in the States. It will take me a week or so to get my poems retyped, so this will give me a breathingspace to mull over your suggestion – but I do take favourably to it and am grateful to you for thinking of it. On the point you bring up about liking to edit, I am sure we can remain amicable over that.

This like yours is a business letter which I must get off to you with promises of other things to follow.

I am enclosing carcacheque as requested. Carcacheques and candlelight, and Christ receive thy saule!

Yours reviving | Mack the Phoenix

Edinburgh University Press's inability to publish a second collection led directly to EM becoming a Carcanet author. Schmidt had just returned from Mexico via New York. EM had bought ten shares in Carcanet.

Michael Schmidt, publisher, poet and critic

3 June 1972

Dear Michael

It was a great pleasure to know that you are favourably disposed towards opening up the new Glasgow-Saturn line and I agree with your proposals, i.e. to include Glasgow Sonnets and to omit Instamatics and Newspoems, keeping the Newspoems for possible later publication. Swimming adumbrations of that 1974 (?) volume – now what would go with Instamatics and Newspoems, I begin to think – come nosing up already from the silt of forebeing. I think with you that for the present (1973) volume it should be hardback plus paperback, and I would only hope that you could keep the paperback price down as much as possible, as I'm always conscious of the fact that the very people who might most want to buy (students, say) are put off by paperback prices over about 60p/70p. If it could be kept down to £1 it would help. But of course these things are a matter of calculations and economics and I know there is a limit to what you can do. I shall look forward to those 'painfully dense details' later on when you get down to sorting it all out. I am also keen to fall in with your suggestion of (sometime) a collection of critical essays. The last time I saw Norman MacCaig he said When are you going to get a book of your critical essays out? So there is one person who would buy it. Let me know when this idea begins to mature and I shall look out the relevant material for you to consider.

Thank you for Robert ('Lull') Pring-Mill's letter about the Mayakovsky. I am told that MacDiarmid is reviewing it for the *Cambridge Review*, and Tom Crawford of Aberdeen University will be doing a 'substantial' review in *Lines Review*.

Now that leetle plot I gave you was not 'fancy', my friend, no no, it is all real, there really is such a mexicyclops, it is all made for the literalist imagination, he lives and breathes and what then, my quotation marks meant to indicate it was a true account, true at least if you can believe Kenneth Anger the American underground filmmaker who wrote about him. So go, go, said the bird, Human kind can bear a hell of a lot of reality. Our Doves still languish unfed, but out of the corner of my eye I see them. Out of the other corner, unfortunately, I see a pile of B.Ed. scripts from the University of Dundee where I am external examiner.

Weirdly cold and grey here for June, but this afternoon I planted French marigolds and petunias in my windowboxes, so the sun had better turn over a new leaf soon.

Best as ever | Eddie

Schmidt proposed cutting 'Instamatic Poems' and 'Newspoems' from the *From Glasgow to Saturn* typescript. The former would be published by Ian McKelvie in 1972, and a selection of the latter in *Themes on a Variation* (1988: 61–112). Schmidt had asked for a novel plot to work on and had been sent the following in a letter of 29 May:

> I know of the existence of a beautiful Mexican child who is being held captive by scientists in Los Angeles. This child is now two years old. It is very intelligent. It has one beautiful perfect eye in the middle of its forehead and that is all. And the scientists – the doctors – they've got this child in an isolated clinic room and there are no mirrors and it has never seen another child. And the mother, of course, when she learned she had some kind of freak, looked at it for maybe a split second and screamed for the saints. They took the baby away and she's never seen it since. It's like the child has just been born out of a seashell. This cyclops child could lead the world.

Graham Martin, *academic*

17 June 1972

Dear Graham

I'm sorry not to have replied to your letter before – have been absolutely immersed in degree exams and marking! I very much enjoyed our meeting and I'm most grateful to you and your wife for such splendid hospitality.

Do you know Day Lewis's translation of *Le Cimetière Marin*? It's in his *Collected Poems* and is not at all bad, if you are still thinking of using Valéry. Steiner's Penguin I'm rather divided about. Of course I like the idea of the book, and it contains many good things, but on the whole I find myself anti-Steiner as regards his view on the very free versions that descend from Pound through Robert Lowell, George MacBeth, etc. These may be good poems but they have an arrogance about them in 'taking over' and remaking the foreign poet which is not my method of working. Of course what Pound did was very important historically – but there is still something to be said on the other side, about what the translated poets are <u>really</u> like.

Mayakovsky enclosed for your interest: these versions are close, though you might not think so!

All best wishes | Eddie

This relates to the Open University course on twentieth-century poetry being developed by Martin. The text by George Steiner is presumably *Poem into Poem: World Poetry in Modern Verse Translation* (Penguin, 1970).

Michael Schmidt, publisher, poet and critic

23 July 1972

Dear Michael
    It was good to hear from you again. Several times the image of a carcanet had swum into my brain during recent peripatetics in Aberdeen, St Andrews, and Edinburgh giving summer-school lectures and readings – and now it stops swimming and comes into focus and there is really something tangible and beckoning dated March 1973. To which let us press on. I enclose two poems which should have been in the batch I sent you (perhaps they weren't returned from EUP), and if you like them they could be added; if not, never mind. 'The Loch Ness Monster's Song' could go after 'Hyena', and 'The Computer's First Code Poem' after 'The Computer's First Dialect Poems'. I would rather like them to go in, for different reasons. The code poem is another in a series of 'The Computer's First…' poems and I would like it to accompany

the two dialect ones to show another extension of the idea of computer/human collaboration/competition. The monster's song is one that I often do at poetry-readings and a lot of interest has been expressed in it, so it would be good if it could be given a more permanent lodging that people could look up if they wanted to.

I like your suggested order of poems very much and would not make any changes. 'The Barrow' is probably best where you have it, as it is more sinister than the 'Boxers' group and wouldn't quite fit there. As for the five rejected poems, rising above inward bridlings and stifled cries of anguosh (I'll leave that mistake, it seems truer somehow!) and claims of infanticide I think I would probably agree that that you have a point in each case. It's easier to agree with you about 'Friendly Village' and 'Heron' than about the other three because these three are closely personal and hard to see objectively. The one that I am not entirely persuaded against is 'By the Fire'; but I admit I may be mistaken, as it was written at the beginning of a very strong love-affair and may have come too near the coup de foudre to be sufficiently objectifiable. If you feel sure it's going to weaken its context, then it must go.

I would share the slight misgivings you express about one or two others – the Lonelyhearts, Soho, Stobhill misgivings. When you send back the poems for my final 'licking over' I shall have another look at the Soho section and possibly it could be cut. I shall now await your 'small comments on the text' (though I must warn you I never find it easy to make alterations, even when I think something is wrong, once a poem has gone cold).

It is an amazing grace that Mayakovsky without benefit of DJ should be climbing the charts to the 400 mark. I have now almost completely sold the remaining 12 of the 22 you sent me, and so I am enclosing a cheque for £12 with this letter to bring us up to date. Would you please send me another dozen of the paperbacks, as I shall likely be able to sell these during readings at the Edinburgh Festival next month, and could you also send half a dozen hardbacks at trade rates for giving to people; if you put both lots on the same bill I can let you have a cheque right away.

You have no idea how fine it is to think of things actually

going forward! – I mean after my couple of communicationless
murky brooding years of the eup. 'The years of the eup/ May
thou ne'er sup!' (old proverb).

Are gallstones quiescent and calm these days? No gravelly
chips and orts to niggle the woodpile? No ossi di seppia for the
calcium press (or Calcium Press?)? Lurk, lurk.

All best regards | Saturn Glasgow

Schmidt had reordered EM's *From Glasgow to Saturn* typescript,
cutting some poems he found sentimental or whimsical. All made
their way back through the 'Uncollected Poems' section of *Collected
Poems* (1990) except 'Phoning' which was in *Penguin Modern Poets
15* (1969) and returned in *New Selected Poems* (2000: 47). The poem
about Soho was slightly cut. DJ, or disc jockey, is a quip about
the lack of reviewers for *Wi the Haill Voice*. Carcanet's energy is
contrasted with the tardiness of Edinburgh University Press ('eup').

Alasdair Gray, artist and writer

19 August 1972

Dear Alasdair Gray,

Thank you for your letter, and I value your remarks on the
sonnets. I think you are right about the 'very Scottish biting
of my own tale' in IX, though after I had written it and was
reading and rereading it I began to wonder if those lines
were ambiguous in their implications – but I let them stand.
Your mention of Turner is very interesting, a painter I like a
great deal. I often also think of Atkinson Grimshaw (what a
name!) whose pictures of wet gaslit city streets and wharves,
including especially those of Glasgow and Liverpool, have long
fascinated me.

Probably your quickest way to buy copies would be to write
to the publisher: Alex Frizzell, Castlelaw Press, West Linton,
Peeblesshire. The special signed edition costs £1.50 but there
will be an ordinary edition at about 50p which should be ready
very soon.

Best wishes | Edwin Morgan

EM had sent a copy of *Glasgow Sonnets*, and Gray had commented on the 'courageous Calvinism' of line 11 of Sonnet IX ('and barricaded windows be the best'), as well as comparing its tone to a Turner painting of an industrial landscape under a storm.

Alexander Porteous, academic

15 October 1972

Dear Alexander Porteous

My apologies for taking so long to write – the new term has been a busy one, and it's always a rather hectic time. I have been thinking about the MacDiarmid 'problem', and it's not easy to know just how to persuade. All I can do is suggest a list of poems that appeal to <u>me</u> and hope that some quality will rub off when others read them. He does often write badly, and so some picking and choosing is necessary; on the other hand, in some of the long poems there is such a mixture of good and bad that it would be unfair to write the whole thing off (though some do, e.g. Iain Crichton Smith in his *Golden Lyric* booklet). Anyhow, here is a list for you to try:

> Au Claire de la Lune, The Eemis-stane, Somersault, Empty Vessel, Gairmscoile, A Drunk Man Looks at the Thistle, The Skeleton of the Future, Stony Limits, On a Raised Beach, Water Music, The Seamless Garment, Second Hymn to Lenin, Lo! A Child is Born, Direadh III, Bagpipe Music, Reflections in a Slum, Crystals like Blood, The Glass of Pure Water, Old Wife in High Spirits. And <u>parts</u> of In Memoriam James Joyce and The Kind of Poetry I Want are clearly very good even when you may have doubts about the whole operation (though I don't think myself it is quite the right way to look at it to pick out the plums of aesthetic bloom).

I like many poems <u>other</u> than these, but these are ones I frequently find myself coming back to. I like the strangeness of perspective and analogy in the early lyrics, the range and power of the *Drunk Man*, the use of politics and science as difficult

subjects or properties which at times do have real success in a
striking way, the very original sort of discursive meditation you
get in *Raised Beach* and *Direadh*. I see what you mean by the
'idiosyncratic nationalism' stumblingblock but I don't find it
worrisome in the best poems – indeed it's more worrisome in
his prose. The better poems seem to have a manner of scooping
it up and giving it an imaginative bounce and this works.

I'll be interested to hear if you have any success with
(shades of Wordsworth in the Tropics) MacDiarmid in the
Antipodes. If the Caledonian Antisyzygy exists it ought to
provide a perfect stepping-off-point for Tasmania!

Yours sincerely | Edwin Morgan

An expatriate Scot lecturing in English literature in the University of
Tasmania, Porteous was keen to find convincing critical arguments
for Hugh MacDiarmid's* greatness as a poet.

W.F. Carmichael, academic

15 October 1972

Dear Mr Carmichael

Thank you for your letter. To generalise is to be an idiot, as
Blake said, so perhaps you have caught me saying something
I really ought not to defend wholeheartedly. Also, the remark
came in the conversation of an interview, in the context of
the idea that enjoyment and entertainment may sometimes
be looked at suspiciously by those who demand an obvious
seriousness from anyone claiming to be a serious artist. The
interview is a few years back now, and I don't recall exactly
what my line of argument was (everything was compressed in
the printed interview), but I think I was taking up the point
of the incidence of comedy in my poems, and also the fact
that I had worked in concrete poetry which clearly involves
word-play as well as mental play. In recent developments
like concrete poetry and sound-poetry, language (including
words, letters, sounds, typography, and space) becomes an
area of (seriously-intentioned) play, as the Swiss poet Eugen

Gomringer has described it: '[The new poem] becomes an object to be both seen and used: an object containing thought but made concrete through play-activity, its concern is with brevity and conciseness.' This of course is only one development in one art, but I believe that it is only a highly specialized form of something that is fairly widespread if not universal: one might define an artist as someone who understands that 'playing' with his chosen material (words, stone, paint, sounds, or whatever) is not a waste of time but on the contrary allows him to be brought into mysterious collaborative contact with the element of chance and the unexpected which is necessary, even in a carefully planned work. Some works (Joyce's *Finnegans Wake*) may involve an unusually large amount of play, others (the clearcut almost naked poems of Brecht – I mean his free verse ones, not the rhyming ones or ballads) may show very little. But there does seem to me to be something about the ambiguous, almost paradoxical nature of play that links it to the creative process – in that play suggests both (on the one hand) freedom and enjoyment and experiment and yet (on the other hand) an activity that has rules and involves opposition and tension and an end-result. (I have a poem about this called 'Not Playing the Game' in *Penguin Modern Poets 15*; it might interest you.) A work of art is very free in the sense that nothing just like it has ever appeared before, but it is also a battleground of forces that has to have its own logic of working-out. The play of light on water, yet also the play of Fischer on Spassky!

I don't know if this is of any kelp to you –

Yours sincerely | Edwin Morgan

A senior lecturer in architecture in the Edinburgh College of Art, Carmichael was researching architectural technology and its relation to creativity. He had seen EM quoted in the *Scottish Field* as saying that 'all arts contain an element of play' (as in the final sentence).

Douglas Dunn, poet and editor

23 October 1972

Dear Douglas Dunn

Thank you for your letter and for taking three of the Instamatics for *Antaeus*. Yes, you are right: there were some from this series in *Scottish International* – also some in the first number of *Decal*. Some appearing in *Glasgow Review*, *Akros*, and *Lines*. The poems are all based on news items as seen in newspapers (or in one or two instances television), and they attempt to fix in terms of art things that would otherwise be lost in the flux of ephemera. Each is presented in visual terms, as if a camera had been present. The 'recording' or 'objective' aspect was important to me in the writing of the poems, but of course this doesn't rule out the other less conscious motivations which other people might discover, once they see the whole group. A collection of them is being published in November (apart from printing delays, etc.) – 52 altogether – as *Instamatic Poems* (Ian McKelvie, 65 Lakenheath, London N14 4RR, 90p). (I'm afraid it may be too late to include *Antaeus* among the acknowledgements.)

My next general collection of poems (it won't include the Instamatics) is due from Carcanet Press about April 1973 – to be called *From Glasgow to Saturn*. This will be a fairly substantial book, containing poems (non-concrete) written since *The Second Life*.

Best wishes | Yours sincerely | Edwin Morgan

Accepting the Instamatic poems for *Antaeus*, Dunn asked for comment on the extent and purpose of the series.

Archibald Turnbull, publisher

10 December 1972

Dear Archie

Thank you for your letter. I'm glad the sales of SP6 have been reasonable and I'm sure the Christmas season will provide a fillip.

It is certainly good news that you will be contemplating a second printing of *The Second Life*. Do you think there is any possibility that this might be in paperback? Publishers seem to be bringing out more and more poetry in paperback now (even for first printings). I think *The Second Life* is still good value in hardback at the present price, but presumably that price would be raised quite a bit by the time the second printing appeared, and I am sure there are many people who would be attracted by a cheaper paperback edition. The practical question, of course, is <u>how</u> many, and that I don't know. But perhaps it is worth considering? – About the possibility of an enlarged edition, although I realise this would be a selling point, I am not too keen. I think the book has a certain form and unity that (with its title) belongs to a period in my writing, and I would not be happy about unfocussing all that by bringing in later poems. Also, I don't think Carcanet Press who hope to bring out my next collection in the spring would take kindly to the idea. I would really much prefer the book to be reprinted as it stands.

I'm very glad you still hope the Press will go on publishing poetry. It would be a great pity if it didn't.

Yours | Eddie

SP6 is the sixth volume of the *Scottish Poetry* series. Turnbull had contritely explained EUP's delay in coming to a decision on a second volume, noting that the Press had 'earned distinction through your work'.

Geoffrey Summerfield, editor and academic

1 January 1973

Dear Geoffrey

My first letter of the year – greetings!

I am honoured and delighted that you want to include me in your eight poets, and will cooperate in every way I can. Will you be sending me a possible list of poems you'd like to include? About how much space will there be? I shall take up the various points as you have enumerated them:

1. You can let me know the specific points you'd like to have expanded. Other points may depend on the choice of poems.

2. My own favourites would probably include 'Trio', 'Glasgow Green', 'Afterwards', 'One Cigarette', 'Message Clear', 'The First Men on Mercury'. But obviously you will have to think of the purposes of the book and balance this against my personal preference. What you suggest about 'reservations and second thoughts' is interesting and I am sure I could make some sort of comment on those lines (e.g. if 'King Billy' was included I might make the point that it was written before the present troubles in Northern Ireland and I would now very likely feel inhibited about writing it if the man had died recently). I might also make some comment on reactions I have myself had during readings in schools under the Scottish Arts Council's 'Writers in Schools' scheme, if you think this would be useful.

3. Juvenilia – ah, oh, well… yes, there certainly are some, and possibly the best thing to do would be for me to look out a few possible and send them to you to pick out anything that might fit. At least almost everything I have is dated and so can be 'placed'. Surviving texts go back to 1936.

4. I am excited by the possibility of photographs, and what immediately strikes me is Glasgow, as my continuing environment, and fortunately extremely photogenic both in old squalor and present transformation. But there's also the stars, rockets, computers, the 'last horizon', if this side of things can be illustrated.

5. You shall have new poems as suggested.

I look forward to the operation.

Best as ever | Eddie

Summerfield had begun to commission for the influential Penguin schools anthology, *Voices: Seven Modern Poets* (1974). With photographs, poets' commentary, and a mix of their own favourite poems and the editor's, the intention was 'to help lively-minded 16–17 year olds into contemporary poetry'. The juvenilia feature was finally dropped, but EM offered poems written at high school: 'The Pond', 'The Opium-Smoker', 'Rain', 'Doubt' and 'Nocturne'.

Michael Schmidt, *publisher, poet and critic*

27 February 1973

Dear Wynkyn de Worde

Thank you for the congratulations. It really was a nice thing to happen, and as I see from your letter it probably does have quite a string of consequences (though as for those 'polite drawing-rooms' I shall keep away from <u>them</u> as long as possible). (Actually I'm on the board of management of the Poetry Book Society, but this has nothing to do with the choices, which are made by independent Selectors.) But to wait till June! I shall be scrabbling with impatience, especially if the book is actually in my hands quite soon. Still, as you point out, the wait has its advantages too. John Smith's will now have to postpone their signing-session. Will you be telling them about the change of plan? They had been thinking up what would have been a very decent display, to include some of my handwritten visual poems (you haven't seen these, done in fibrepens) plus ancillary buikies like Instamatics, Glasgow Sonnets, Haill Voices. By June it's just possible there might be another to add to them – a volume of translations which is coming out from the Poni Press of Portobello (does Wynkyn know Poni?). (Or does Wynkyn know Portobello?)

But enough of me. I really am most pleased and glad if it will help the Carcanet. Perhaps it will also boost the sales of the Mayakovsky, as a side-effect?

I do wish I had more time to rejoice. At the moment I am trying to collect some thoughts for a two-hour seminar on Pluralism in Recently Literary Theory ('The Plura lists, goes down with all her hands') and am uneasily aware that I have two fat PhD theses to examine for Cambridge and Edinburgh in the near future. Sorry, this is back to me again. Print on, Wynkyn! Print out! Print off! The prints of time are on winter's traces! If Wynkyn comes, can print be far behind?

Best as ever | Piers Plowmorgan

From *Glasgow to Saturn* was a Poetry Book Society Summer Choice, with a delay in publication affecting a planned event in John Smith's bookshop in Glasgow. Schmidt had signed his last letter as Caxton, a hard-pressed printer. Wynkyn de Worde, who worked with Caxton and improved his printing process, is sometimes seen as the first typographer in English. The Poni Press was run by Tom Buchan, who had replaced Bob Tait* as editor of *Scottish International* before it ceased publication.

Morag Morris, academic

English Department
University of Glasgow
25 March 1973

Dear Miss Morris

I am sorry not to have answered your letter before now, but I had to wait till the end of a somewhat gruelling term to get time to think about it.

I find myself very favourably disposed towards your outlined proposals, but you might have to discount a degree of bias in this, since I myself write poetry and am naturally much interested in modern literature in general. Oddly enough, however, I have a lot of sympathy for the other proposal, in that I have always been a bit more of a science addict and in the 'two cultures' debate found myself more on Snow's side than Leavis's (despite the fact that <u>both</u> of them write badly and are a poor advertisement for their ideas). But there is no necessarily complete split between the two proposals, and I could envisage quite a lot of fruitful overlapping. In a science-based university, after all, it would seem perfectly natural to investigate the scientific aspects of 'English', whether language or literature, but perhaps doing something of an M.I.T. with such affairs as linguistics, translation, computer analysis of texts, and so on. Whether that would properly come under a School of English I don't know, but it could certainly be allied to such a school. I have always thought it disappointing that Strathclyde, which began by being in Surrey's position and then developed an English department, and which has a professor who has made a special study of science fiction, should have grown up in complete isolation from the science side of the university, and into a very normal historical English course – though to be fair, it should be said that they have a 'campus writer' in attendance and have a lively practice of inviting writers to take occasional seminars with their Honours students.

I think the arguments you adduce for a study of modern poetry are good ones and their truth would be brought out in practice. At Glasgow we have now an entirely 20th-century (or almost entirely – we do go back a bit into the 19th) course for our large first-year class of 450+ students, and this is generally found to hold their interest (though there will of course be grumbles about this or that writer or text). For us it represents a complete reversal of the old system: when I was myself a student the course was Chaucer, Shakespeare, and Wordsworth, with neither Victorians nor moderns. This year our prescribed reading for the first-year class includes, for example, Joyce's *Dubliners*, Lawrence's *Rainbow*, Forster's *Passage to India*, Orwell's *1984*, Shaw's *Mrs Warren's Profession*, Beckett's *Endgame*, Peter Nichols's *National Health*, and selected poetry by Yeats, Hardy, Eliot, the First World War poets, the Thirties poets, and Sylvia Plath. As a somewhat massive gesture towards older things, the poor souls have also to do *Little Dorrit*! Philip Hobsbaum and myself both lecture on modern poetry, so the students are in touch with the creative aspect of the subject and probably find this useful. In addition, there is a quite separate Scottish Literature department, of which the head is another poet, Alexander

Scott. And we also have a campus writer who has no academic stirrings at all, his sole duty being to help students with their writing and to get on with writing of his own. This year it is a poet, George Bruce (ex-BBC), who has had great success in attracting students from other faculties than arts and who has been astonished at the interest shown – which would be an argument in favour of your proposals.

It might be relevant to mention the fact that since the autumn I have been involved in the Scottish Arts Council's scheme called Writers in Schools (I believe there's a similar scheme in England) by which writers visit schools, read and talk about their work and answer questions. I have been to about 15 schools and have been greatly struck by the lively response, sometimes from small groups of sixth-formers, sometimes from an audience of several hundred. If one can still use that awful word viability, it seems that modern poetry certainly has it, in the sense that one cannot fail to communicate through it with young people to whom it has become a much more <u>natural</u> means of expression (i.e. not effete or straw-in-the-hairish or namby-pamby) than it used to be. I have no doubt that dramatists and novelists would also get across, but poetry at present seems to have special communicatory potential.

Argument still rages, of course, as to how far one should now go back, since the more modern work we do the more difficult it becomes to deal with the earlier material in any depth. At Glasgow, our second year plunges the students rudely back to medieval and renascence literature, the scope being roughly Chaucer to Milton. And we often feel that there must be something very odd about the fact that the great majority of those who take English (i.e. those not going on to the 4-year Honours course) never hear a word on either Augustans or Romantics – which is quite a swatch of silence. But we find that the 20th and 19th centuries (late 19th I mean, mainly) are so rich in themselves that it would be hopelessly superficial to try to keep up the old myth of doing continuous literary history. If you want a precedent for doing intermittent or partial literary history… here it is! (Though of course our Honours people will have done, in some sense at least, the works, from *Beowulf* to Peter Nichols.)

I am myself convinced that modern literature, and
particularly modern poetry, has much to offer science students
as well as arts students, and I think the reasons you list on your
third page are very sound and defensible.

If there are any particular points you'd like to take up with
me, don't hesitate to let me know. Best of luck with your
efforts!

Yours sincerely | Edwin Morgan

PS The enclosed poem may amuse (or confuse) you –

A graduate of Glasgow University, now teaching a poetry option
part-time in the then mainly technological University of Surrey,
Morris wanted to argue for the establishment of a Department
of English there and asked EM for his opinion on various options.
The poem enclosed is unknown, but possibly one of his computer
poems.

Bernard Kojo Laing, poet

19 Whittingehame Court
5 July 1973

Dear Bernard
I was very glad to get your letter and poems and to know
that the books reached you all right. I am enclosing a new
book of mine with all my best wishes: I hope it contains some
things you will like (some of the 'songs' you will know already).
As you will see, I have been lucky in being made the 'choice' of
the Poetry Book Society, which helps sales, and the publishers
have taken the risk of putting out the book in hardback and
paperback together, which is becoming quite a common
practice. For your own collection, which I personally find
extremely interesting, possibly the best publishers to try would
be Routledge & Kegan Paul (68–74 Carter Lane, London
EC4V 5EL), Chatto & Windus (40–42 King William Street,
London WC2N 4DF), Cape (30 Bedford Square, London
WC1B 3EL), Macmillan (4 Little Essex Street, London
WC2R 3LF), or Hutchinson (3 Fitzroy Square, London W1P

6JD). In view of the fact that your poems are difficult, it might not be a bad idea to have a covering note or preface saying something about your life and background... anything that you think would help publishers' readers with that old intercultural hyperdrive! I'm sure that the three very long poems would benefit from a word in the reader's ear. I found 'Christcrowd' packed with running impacts but very hard to disentangle as a whole, and the impression remained that there was some key which perhaps existed but had not been supplied, and this worried me and made me long for more clarity. I preferred the shorter 'Godsdoor' and especially some of the sequences of shorter poems like 'Hospital Poems', 'Eleven Bit-Worlds', and 'Three Songs', which is a form I think you should continue to explore. I like the wild humour, too, which now and again swirls up and is probably a useful corrective to the omnivorousness that in the longer poems has a tendency to swallow up the reader as he leaps from image to image on the poem's tongue. Do you want me to send back the poems or do you have another copy?

I'm sorry I don't have Stanley Downing's address – have long lost touch with him. *Scottish International* and *Lines* both have a slightly uncertain future at the moment. *SI*'s financial position is far from healthy, and the new editor, Tom Buchan, is about to take over from Bob Tait who wants more time to do some writing of his own. Robin Fulton may still try to edit *Lines* from his new teaching job in Stavanger (Norway) but this may prove difficult to say the least. Duncan Glen's *Akros* is still going strong, however; why not send him some poems sometime? It's still a Scottish magazine, though he lives in England (14 Parklands Avenue, Preston, Lancashire).

I have had an American couple staying with me for a few days and have been showing them the glories of Loch Lomond, Oban, and Glasgow. This is the couple who put me up for a while when I was in New Jersey on my poetry tour. They couldn't get over the number of sheep we have in Scotland, and were also fascinated by the masses of lupins and rhododendrons. I wonder what would have caught their eye in Ashanti? In about a week's time I am going with a friend to Dublin for a week, and after that I hope to get some writing done.

I hope the family are well – all my best wishes. |
Edwin Morgan

Laing took an MA degree at Glasgow University in the late 1960s
and also discussed his poetry with EM, who subsequently wrote
him academic references for administrative posts in Ghana. He
would win literary awards there for both poetry and fiction. Stanley
Downing was another student writer. Bill and Mary Todt provided
hospitality during EM's reading tour of American East Coast high
schools in May 1971. They met Iain Crichton Smith* in Oban.

Iain Crichton Smith, poet and novelist

4 August 1973

Dear Iain
Here's the *New Saltire* which has my article on Scottish
publishing, plus the following number which contained the
publishers' replies. Perhaps it will give you some sort of lead.
Although it's a while back, the situation hasn't changed much.
The big publishers are still London-based and London-
oriented. EUP was going to do great things but has practically
ceased its literary activity. It's at least good that there are more
small presses here than there were in 1961 – Reprographia,
Caithness Books, Scottish Academic Press, Club Leabhar, etc.
– and it's probably easier for poets, if not for prose-writers, to
get started off in print in Scotland. Novelists and dramatists
come off worst. *Scottish Theatre* did print some Scottish plays
but seems to have stopped doing so. A novelist will almost
inevitably be published in London. John Herdman's short
novel came out with Akros, true, but will it get reviewed, will it
get known, will it sell?

Best of luck with the forum – | Eddie

ICS was taking part in a forum in Oban on Scottish literary culture
and had asked to borrow *New Saltire* 2 (November 1961) where
EM's 'Who will Publish Scottish Poetry?' appeared. EM included *New
Saltire* 3 (Spring 1962) where his 'The Beatnik in the Kailyard' was
first published (reprinted in *Essays* 1974: 166–76).

Nicholas Zurbrugg, academic and editor

21 October 1973

Dear Nicholas

Many thanks for your comments of the 18th. Here are some re-comments flying southwards, flying finding, foundings, foundlings.

On the <u>newspoems</u>: I agree that these could come under the category 'treated', but I wouldn't agree with your defining it as 'placing pre-existent material in the new context suggested by the isolation of the exhibited material from its old content' or 'choosing the old image to be reorientated by the new caption' since this seems to miss the main part of the 'treatment', which implies the destruction or cancellation of the original context: there's a complete disjunction of the found message from the original news text, and this is what makes the process interesting. Possible objections to the triviality or ephemerality of the original material are undercut by the transformation effect, which is presumably where anything creative could be claimed to come in – in other words, as I read the paper and take in its ordinary journalistic message my eye (eye plus brain no doubt) also sees another unintended message which physical scissors then proceed to isolate until the original has gone <u>and is not meant to be even remembered</u>. (I.e. I'm not aiming at ironies between untreated and treated in the newspoems.) You call it 'simply a verbal collage' but really it is the opposite of collage if collage (e.g. Schwitters) implies juxtaposition and overlay; the intention in the newspoems is to <u>pare away</u> and thus to reveal, not <u>place together</u>. I see it as being more like sculpture than collage – finding a form that is hidden in a larger mass. I had hoped that you might print some of the more complex ones, like the 'Creeleys': could you not put in one of these, since it would show the 'stretching' of the method into quite a difficult area? Could you not also put in one that is more <u>visually</u> interesting than the four you have chosen? (Some, for instance, are near-concrete poems in appearance.) I am anxious that if the newspoems are to appear at all they should be chosen to show the <u>range</u> of the method. So please do have second thoughts about your choice!

The found-in-prose poems are <u>untreated</u>, except that one would probably have to regard things like line-division as 'treatment', since line-division in itself can have a large effect on how the reader takes the text. (The only exception in the poems I sent you is 'Deer Hunt', where I had introduced a few small changes that I now feel must go, as the point of the exercise is that the words should be the same; I enclose a revised version, and would you please use this if you print it.)   Your doubts about the method sound very massive! But don't you think the area has to be explored? In the abstract, it's easy to think up arguments against it, but always one must come back to the pragmatic point: what sort of things does it produce? The three little pieces I 'found' in Cowper's letters, for example, are not in the result <u>like</u> either Cowper's letters or his own poetry, they are something else, have been made something else, first by the eye which jumped on them and isolated them and then through typographical redeployment. You use the phrase 'crippling of poetic potential', and this would probably be true if one was doing nothing else! – poets as remora, suck, suck. But I see it as only one (and perhaps tangential) aspect of general creative activity which is nevertheless worth pursuing (and from different angles) because we still have a great deal to learn about how creation works, and found art throws us back on a number of basic questions. As a further contribution to the débat, I am enclosing a still different sort of untreated found-in-prose poem – seven poems I have extracted from a book of travel sketches published about fifty years ago. As the note on the last page of the extractions will explain, these are merely unaltered extracts of phrases that were printed in italics in the original (for emphasis), yet I think you will agree that they produce a strangely beautiful modern poetry.

The reassembled poem! – well, I see the objection to Boileau et Narcejac (or Frankenstein as you say), and as you observe, this is moving nearer to normal creative activity and may not fit your purposes in the magazine. Still, as the difficulty of doing it made clear to me (you should try it sometime!), the limitations in using exactly the same words are interestingly severe – interestingly, since they raise the whole problem of how far the reassembler <u>can</u> escape from the original, how far he can only 're-do' it from a different point of view, or how far the very struggle to 'make it new' may in such instances be productive because provoking. I think all this is at least relevant to the 'found' discussion. I would plead with you not to decide too narrowly beforehand what the found area comprises, but rather use the issue to open into public view the whole potential of the idea. My view is that it's not at the stage for judgment yet, except in an interim sense. It's only one among many things I'm doing, but the <u>doing</u> seems to be more to the point at the moment than the doubting. If the sun and moon should doubt, they'd immediately go out! (Now that's a found – what's the word for piece of prose?)

I enclose the best copy I have of 'Notice in Hell' – is this any clearer than the one you have?

All best wishes till 5 December – | Eddie

Zurbrugg was editing a 'found poem' number of *Stereo Headphones* 6 ('The Treated Text'), Summer 1974. EM discriminates his own techniques in the 'Newspoems' ('Notice in Hell' is in *CP*: 119) and in 'found poems' (*CP*: 588–93), based on Cowper's letters and *Tramps across Watersheds* by A.S. Alexander (Glasgow, 1925). Boileau-Narcejac was the *nom de plume* of French crime-writers Pierre Boileau and Pierre Ayraud when they co-wrote. EM was also working on a 'reassembled poem' for a festschrift for Basil Bunting, edited by Jonathan Williams (Jargon 66, *Madeira & Toasts for Basil Bunting's 75th Birthday*, [1975] 1977). This was 'An Ode Recoded', using the words of Bunting's 'Empty vast days…' from his 'First Book of Odes'.

Harry Chambers, editor and poet

27 October 1973

Dear Harry Chambers

Thank you for your letter. I'll look forward to the Larkin Phoenix at the end of next month.

The poets' worksheets number sounds an interesting idea. I am enclosing the manuscripts of the four *Glasgow Sonnets* you mention (i, iv, v, x); as they are in pencil I thought I had better let you do the photographing rather than do it more inexpertly myself. I always work in pencil, which is admittedly not the best thing for the immortality of one's MSS! What I have sent you is not strictly speaking a worksheet, since it is the <u>only</u> manuscript; each page, with its corrections, shows the whole working I had on the poem. Although I sometimes write out and rework corrected versions, I dislike doing this, and most of my manuscripts are single-page, like the enclosed. The *Glasgow Sonnets* were written fairly swiftly, under strong pressure of feeling, in about a week.

With best wishes | Yours sincerely | Edwin Morgan

Editor of *Phoenix*, Chambers had written to ask for material for a forthcoming double issue on poets' worksheets, to include drafts by Heaney, Longley, Thwaite, Porter, Dunn, Harrison, Conn and others. He particularly admired the 'Glasgow Sonnets' selected.

Michael Schmidt, publisher, poet and critic

8 January 1974

Dear Michael

And a Happy (Harry? Hairy?) New Year to you too!

I am most glad you think a decent book can be made out of the essays and I admire your arrangement. The section headings seem reasonable if we are having sections. My only query is what about the 'James Bridie' essay which isn't on your list and isn't mentioned as a possible omission? I'd like it to go in if you don't object to it; I suppose in section 3.

The three omissions I accept. The Laxness piece was written on request for a festschrift and is slight. I agree that the *Beowulf* introduction would tend to overload the book. The one I am more reluctant to give up is 'The Fold-In Conference', but I had another look at it in relation to the rest of the book and I think it probably would stand out too much by itself. You don't say whether you reject it for <u>that</u> reason, or because it is dedicated to William Burroughs, or because it is an example of Experimental Writing (which I gather you cannot be doing with in your present but I trust temporary Neo-Reactionary Poetry-Nation phase!)? (I am, as I'm sure you must have suspected, deeply suspicious of the aims of *Poetry Nation*.) But the 'experiment' of 'The Fold-In Conference' was deliberate and thought-out. I attended all the sessions, and at the end I had no hesitation in making my account of the affair a tribute to Burroughs, since it was he who made the most strong and convincing impact – you could have heard a pin drop when he was speaking. My use of cut-up and fold-in technique enabled me to combine the tribute with an ironical (but in detail very close) account of the conference. This is a piece of writing which I would defend (as you see!) and would like to see reprinted (since it is quite lost where it is), but nevertheless, I think you are right in not wanting it in the present book. So cut Cranford mike, over and out. It will go into my next Carcanet book which will be called *Experimental Writings, Agrapha, Apocrypha, Apocalyptica, and Arctica.*

I spent Christmas with a friend in Amsterdam and wrote twenty poems when I came back. (Short, admittedly – between ten and sixteen lines each.)

I shall look over the essays for any necessary corrections or alterations as soon as you can send them back. (You will have to send them back, as there are some I don't have copies of.) What about the visual poems referred to in 'Into the Constellation'? Can we reproduce these as they were done in *Akros*? I think they are necessary as part of the article, since readers will not normally have any access to them, unless they are shown.

How goes the reprinting of FGTS?

All best 1974s | ≡)ll

Schmidt's editing of *Essays* (1974) had begun. The essay on Haldór Laxness (Icelandic poet, dramatist, novelist and Nobel Prize winner) was 'The Atom Station and the Degrees of Realism', published in Reykjavik in 1962. 'The Fold-In Conference' was written in the 'cut-up and fold-in' style of William Burroughs to describe the International Writers' Conference at the 1962 Edinburgh Festival, including a stormy debate between Hugh MacDiarmid* and Alexander Trocchi. The poems begun after Amsterdam would become the 100 sections of 'The New Divan' (1977). EM calls *Poetry Nation* 'neo-reactionary' since from a Scottish perspective the idea of 'nation' was open to challenge.

Robin Fulton, poet and translator

31 January 1974

Dear Robin

We are rivals for Victoria! Not really though. Robin Skelton asked me if I would apply for the post but I have told him I cannot get away next session as one of our professors will be on sabbatical and I have to deputize. I will drop him a line however to try to boost your chances. He wants to put me in a queue too for possible future engagement but I made polite noises without committing myself, as I'm not really too keen in any case. I didn't fancy the job as he described it, and I'd much rather go to America than Canada if any transatlantic possibility should emerge. Stavanger and Tromsö both sound bleakish, and I can understand your feelings. Perhaps the Victoria door will swing open, I hope so.

Glad to know *Lines* will still be feasible by remote-control. I have unfortunately not long sent off a sequence of 20 short poems to Eric Mottram for the *Poetry Review* – about a month ago – I haven't had any reply yet, so he may not be taking them. But I'll let you know. And if anything steams up in the meantime...

Scottish International is still gritting its teeth and looking for money. Tom Buchan is full of ideas, but the creditors will soon be knocking at the door. It's a most unhappy phase. We think we can pull through; touch and go. Did you know that Glasgow University Press (what? yes, it now exists as an official entity) is to take over the annual *Scottish Poetry* anthologies? I am no longer involved, but I gather the aim is to continue the series much as before – though it will probably be more 'Scottish' as Alex Scott is to be one of the editors. There has been no public announcement about it yet.

I have a reading in Stone tomorrow. That probably sounds faintly enigmatic, if not runic. It's the Stone that's near Stoke. At the moment I wish very much I was there and back, these Aslef-haunted days when long train journeys are about as uncertain as they were in the early days of steam. Mr Bleaney wouldn't find it so easy now to spend Christmas at his sister's house in Stoke. It is a curious feeling to be living in a country which is markedly and visibly running down – ill-lit or unlit shops with many empty shelves and large areas cordoned off to prevent pilfering, terrible public transport, longer and longer delays in repairs and services (I've been waiting seven months for a thermostat for my central heating), the bland face of Lord Carrington on TV saying industry might have to think of a <u>two</u>-day week (and a no-day week, what then? like Beckett's people we shall all be in the cylinder, where there is neither central heating nor peripheral heating, and the bus and the train do not come): doesn't unhumorous Norway have its points?

Best regards | Eddie

Fulton edited *Lines Review* from Stavanger in Norway, where he was now teaching. Robin Skelton's Creative Writing courses at the University of Victoria, British Columbia, featured various visiting writers from the UK. 'Mr Bleaney' is a poem by Philip Larkin. Strike action in mines and transport in the 1970s (Aslef was a railway workers' union) had a serious impact on UK society.

Ian Hamilton, poet and editor

4 May 1974

Dear Ian

Thank you for taking the poems. I am glad you like them. I sent the first twenty in the sequence to the *Poetry Review* four months ago but have heard nothing about them. I have written again to Eric Mottram today to jog his memory, and if he returns them or still doesn't reply I can let you see a further batch. I am also working on others in the sequence, and will perhaps be able to send you some of these soon. I don't know if I can say very much about the shape of the sequence, since it is still in process, and indeed it is only a sequence in a loose sense. 'Divan' in Persian just means a collection of poems, the *Divan* of Hafiz, a great lyric poet contemporary with Chaucer, being one of the most famous of such books, a collection of mostly short poems on love, time, death, riches and poverty...

I got very excited reading and thinking about Hafiz, though the poems I have written only refer to him occasionally and obliquely. His work was only something that stimulated me to find a means of writing not a long poem but a group or series of short poems that might be fairly substantial if considered as a whole (which is why I want if possible to publish them in batches rather than singly). There are hints of 'story' here and there, there are some recurrent themes, and the Middle East (where I lived for a few years) is a fairly pervasive background. But how far such things help to bring organization or unity, I find it hard to say at this stage.

If you want to have a short note about the poems, could you select what you like from the above? But I don't want to overload ten short poems with commentary!

All best wishes – | and I thought your first number
    excellent – | Eddie

For *The New Review*, Hamilton had accepted 10 stanzas from 'The New Divan', but asked for detail on the context of the whole sequence. Other stanzas were published in the same year in *Ambit* 60, *Aquarius* 7, *The Honest Ulsterman* 44/45, *Weighbauk* 2, *Lines Review* 50, and *Poetry Book Society Poetry Supplement*.

Michael Schmidt, publisher, poet and critic

23 June 1974

Dear Michael

To be more full about what we briefly said on the phone today. I would be perfectly happy if your proposed timetable for essays/translations/next poems can materialize. So, to answer your specific questions: (a) yes, (b) at a very rough estimate, 225–250 pages, (c) I shall ask Tom Buchan to let you know, since he has been doing all the negotiations, (d) yes yes! – or, to be serious, I shall get TB to send you the material and then you will see. Trying to look at it objectively, I do think it would be an interesting and unusual book.

[Parenthesis about *PN*. I am still unhappy about *PN*, and

I am unhappy about being unhappy about it too, though that
doesn't help very much. As you suggest, it isn't just the title,
which is a small thing. It is the whole trend and motive of
the magazine, which I cannot but associate with the ideas
of your co-editor, and these ideas – I am thinking of course
of the Black Papers – are deeply repugnant to me. As I have
expressed my opposition to this movement fairly clearly, my
friends would think it strange if I started contributing to a
magazine edited by, as it were, the enemy. I enjoyed meeting
and talking to Brian Cox, and I have absolutely nothing
against him personally, but he is working to bring about
something which I am working to prevent. If I am wrong
about this, you must prove it to me by printing things very
different from anything that has appeared so far. At the
moment *PN* seems to be part of a campaign that I just can't go
along with. Perhaps I will get out of these feelings or perhaps
PN will change. Let's forget this paragraph. Put a square
bracket round it all and hope for better days.]
 I look forward eagerly to that new catalogue…
 And I shall get onto Tom Buchan right away.

Best as ever | Eddie

Carcanet took over the volume of translations, *Rites of Passage*
(1976), from Tom Buchan's Poni Press which had liquidity problems.
EM's reservations about the bi-annual *PN* (*Poetry Nation*, then from
1976 the quarterly *PN Review*) stemmed from its perceived right-
wing bias. Brian Cox of Manchester University not only co-edited *PN*
but was co-author of the conservative 'Black Papers' on education,
arguing against comprehensive schooling.

Michael Schmidt, publisher, poet and critic

29 June 1974

Dear Michael
 <u>Our</u> dialogue will continue anyway! I would like to get
your worrisome square bracket question out of the way, and I
am truly sorry if being published in *TNR* really does pain or

puzzle you as you say it does, but I do think you are making too much of it. You mentioned Tomlinson as another apparent renegade, but you had no mention of the more glaring case of Douglas Dunn who was one of the sandwichmen for *TNR* and was evidently regarded as a catch for the first number (I at least waited till I saw what the magazine looked like before I submitted anything!): so do you interrogate DD as you do EM? And what about Colin Falck – it seems to be quite possible to be Carcanet and *TNR*, or do you regard him with the same sorrow? Dunn and Tomlinson – to say nothing of Christopher Ricks, John Carey, and Seamus Heaney – evidently share my view that there is no disgrace in sending things to *TNR*, and you surely can't be against all these, or regard them as in some way meretricious? You call *TNR* a ragbag, but that is just a noisy term for a general literary-cultural review which is not of the other (i.e. missionary) type. I can think of good magazines of the past which belong to both ragbag and missionary categories and I don't believe one is superior to the other as a type. Juxtaposition v. consistency – an old argument, but I must say I prefer juxtaposition, and it's more likely to come in the rague-bague. Unfortunately – to curve your argument back – I doubt if *TNR* will be ragbag-bold <u>enough</u>: I can think of a number of subjects and authors that I would be happily surprised to find in its pages: but at least it has not slammed its gates, manifesto-wise, as *PN* has (but not Carcanet), against such subjects and authors. (See Cox, *CQ*, Summer 1973.) But – a but again! – we shall no doubt both go on with internal mullings and communings – nothing is final – <u>Là</u>, tout n'est qu'ordre et beauté, but not here yet, said the man.

Yes, I think your 'essays' salient is a good territory to push out; I shall look forward to the Christopher Middleton you mention. Prose is to be encouraged, isn't it? Praise prose and keep your powder dry. Do you know that John Davidson has some very interesting little-known prose (in novels, essays, sketches, etc.)?

Congratulations on reaching the A-level! One of our professors, John Bryce, is an admirer of your poetry, and it's just possible he was the instigator, if he has been concerned with the papers.

I hope you will be hearing soon from Tom Buchan about the translations. At the moment the collection has the provisional title *Rites of Passage*. Do you like this, or should I think again? (One objection might be that there are several books already with this title – including a book of poems by Edward Brathwaite...)

Best as ever | Eddie

Schmidt challenged EM's unwillingness to appear in *Poetry Nation*, while being willing (inconsistently?) to contribute to *The New Review*, edited by Ian Hamilton*. Brian Cox co-edited *Critical Quarterly* [CQ] as well as *Poetry Nation*. One of Schmidt's poems had been set as a practical criticism exercise in the Scottish equivalent of A-Level, the Certificate of Sixth Year Studies.

Robin Fulton, poet and translator

5 August 1974

Dear Robin
    It was good of you to send me a copy of *Tree-Lines*: many thanks. I shall certainly recommend it for the university library. I must say I think you have been badly served by your illustrators, in this volume and before. Harley Elliott's rough sketchy drawings don't go with the poems, whereas by a classic contrast the precise and beautiful cover photograph does; or at least so I feel. There are many things I like in the book, sections 1 & 6 particularly, and of the individual poems 'Survival', 'Passing the Somme', 'Beginnings', 'Open and Closed Spaces', 'MacDiarmid Symposium' (a splendid comment!), 'No Answer', and 'Remembering Trains'. The section I find hardest to get into (except in the obvious incantatory/choric sense) is 5. 'In Memoriam A.B.' is a strong sequence – I admired it before and it seems to stand up well in the context of the book.
    Can you use the enclosed for *Lines*? It's from a sequence in progress. You may recall I mentioned in an earlier letter I had sent another part of the sequence to Eric Mottram: I have now heard he is to print it. Some of the poems have also been

in *The New Review*. As regards the title, I use the word as in the 'Divan' of Hafiz, meaning a collection of poems (though in individual poems I also take up the word's other meanings of 'assembly' and 'couch').

How is Stavanger standing up, or rather, how are you standing up in Stavanger? I have been with a friend for a week in Holland, and I have a week in Ireland coming up. The September holiday weekend will find me (if I can get there) giving a reading at the Theatre in the Forest, Grizedale. Poets in the fells! Wordsworth lives! At every beck a call.

All the best | Eddie

Tree-Lines (1974) was published by New Rivers Press, Berkeley, California.

Edwin Morgan, *poet*
(handwritten)

To: Edwin Morgan Esq
19 Whittingehame Court
GLASGOW G12 0BG
Gross-Britannien   21 August 1974

What can I say except einen schönen Gruss aus Deutschland? Even "schön" invites a note: we would not say we would not call a public fountain "Der Schöne Brunnen". There is much of interest to the linguist, e.g. a village called Unteroberndorf. But I think my main impression, & what makes it such a holiday for me trying to keep up with Literaturegeschichte is the TIMELESSNESS – obvious with the vineyards & other crops, enhanced by the relatively little war damage and the fantastic skill in restoration, & the fact that they seem still to build with visible timber framing, like English lath & plaster. But as every village (almost) has medieval fortified walls round it, & a baroque church, medieval and baroque cease to seem relied names. And even in the deepest recesses of art, when one finds mannerism and baroque in German 14–15CC painting & sculpture, one is pleased that art history too is nonsense.

EM sent this postcard message home to himself, on the back of a card with a view from the vineyard slopes towards Regensburg: 'Blick auf Regensburg von den Winzerhöhen'.

Roy Fisher, poet and academic

19 Whittingehame Court
28 October 1974

Dear Roy
Many thanks for the illuminating cutting. It certainly helps to prove, if proof were needled ifprof war addld ifoff cmppneededtha really are there and are keeping a watchful eyasson aliasson onoffman macuripot farohossop even though it's only telescopes so far.

Till Nottinghame – | Edwin

Fellow poet and academic based at the University of Keele, Fisher had sent EM an item with misprint from the *Staffordshire Sentinel*, suggesting that the language confusion in EM's poem 'The First Men on Mercury' (*CP*: 267) had been close to reality.

Gael Turnbull, poet and doctor

4 January 1975

Dear Gael
Many thanks for the *Sapling*. I particularly liked the title-poem and the Virgil variation on Aeneas and Dido.
I would've enjoyed the chance of accompanying you at the Cambridge Poetry Festival Forum, but I've already had to refuse. (I was to have taken part in the Scottish forum.) The festival comes in the first week of our third term and I am so tied up with lectures and seminars (and the Glasgow-Cambridge round trip takes up so much time) that it's impossible to get away. If it had been during the Easter vacation I might have made it. Though like you I am not

exactly a luster after forums, and much prefer just to read and if necessary answer individual questions about my work. I am sorry not to be able to give you moral support. I hope you can still find some congenial co-forumer. When I am lecturing on *The Cherry Orchard* I shall listen hard for the 'distant sound like the sound of a string snapping' which will tell me that Cambridge has broken into poetry, or perhaps that your sapling has pushed up another flagstone.

All the best as ever | Eddie

Turnbull's *A Random Sapling* (Pig Press, 1974) includes the Virgilian variation 'Went to Hell' (*There are Words: Collected Poems*, 2006: 220).

Andy McKillop, teacher of English

12 February 1975

Dear Andy

Thank you for your letter. I am glad you are doing such interesting things at Cambridge! I enclose a copy of 'Spacepoem 2'. This was not included in a book because in essence it's only a basic text for performance and scarcely stands by itself as a poem; it was written specifically for radiophonic treatment. The three Spacepoems were broadcast with radiophonic effects on the BBC Scottish Home Service (as it then was) on 19 June 1966 in the 'University Notebook' programme. The producer was John Gray, and I had Robert Trotter as reader/collaborator. I don't myself have a tape of the programme, so you would have to try the BBC in Glasgow, though I believe they are notably loath to part with recordings. The programme probably would be of interest to schools, if you can get hold of it.

'The First Men on Mercury': no, there was no first draft in English – I switched my galactic decoder direct to Mercurian and out it came. I tried to create the impression of a meaningful language which could be pronounced but which was different from languages we know. It is on the verge of being translatable into English all the way through, and I think it is possible to follow the Mercurian's thought-processes fairly accurately, but I did not have a specific English equivalent from word to word at the back of my mind. George MacBeth claims to find a Scotch pawkiness in my Mercurian speaker, but I don't know about that. After he told me this I began to look at it again, and it is true that I allow some satire to attach to the English/pukka quality of the earthman (he is definitely English and not American – perhaps an unlikely situation); maybe it should be called 'The First Englishmen in Scotland', after all.

Did you see the long science-fiction poem 'Memories of Earth' I had in *Akros* a few issues back? It might be of some interest, as having an attempt at a more extended treatment.

All the best from the Department and myself – |
    Edwin Morgan

A recent graduate from Glasgow University, now training as a teacher in Cambridge, McKillop asked for information on EM's space poetry for a school science fiction topic.

Michael Schmidt, publisher, poet and critic

11 January 1976

Dear Michael

Many thanks for the congratulations. Trevor Royle had told me before Christmas but sworn me to secrecy till the awards were announced (late January he said). It <u>should</u> help sales.

How goes *Rites*? And *Divan*? Gareth Reeves recently sent me publicity forms to fill in and send to Dufour, for both books, which I shall do as soon as I can. I have just finished a 6000-word piece for the Open University on Three East European Poets (Herbert, Holub, Popa), and will now have to switch very rapidly to the Pre-Raphaelites and Swinburne for a new set of lectures at GU. Switch to Swinburne, ha.

The other night I was idly scanning our joint gallstones, and I must say they seemed to stand up pretty well. If we could strain to produce say three or four times as many, we could have a wee buik of them that might really prove of some interest. I think we toyed with the idea once before. Do you have any stones, shards, ossi di seppia, etc., which you could again start to send out up northwards? *Biodes*, we might call the book.

I'm glad Alan Young and Peter Jones enjoyed the tape. Desmond sent me a copy. It was an intensive five days working on it at the Radiophonic Temple but I think the results are worth it. I hope it will make a kind of case for sound-poetry in that each of the experiments was an experiment with a point.

And so he adjusted the gasjet, poured himself a stiff absinthe, and pulled down his Lesbia Brandon…

Happy new year | Eddie

Essays had won a book award from the Scottish Arts Council, where Trevor Royle* was Literature Director. BBC Radiophonic Workshop made recordings of EM's sound-poems. *Lesbia Brandon* is an unfinished novel by Algernon Charles Swinburne (1837–1909).

Tom Leonard, *poet*

15 June 1976

Dear Tom

Your letter came all right this morning. As I said on the phone, I almost wrote to you myself to make much the same point. I had no idea there would be such a gap between the English and Scottish marks – a First on one side, a Third on the other. As you can imagine, it was a not unpainful examiners meeting, to use two negatives. Even the submitted creative work cut no ice with the opposers, though Philip and I both brought it up as strongly as we could. I really thought it was going to be a 2.ii. Interestingly, in the end it was our three external examiners who turned the scale and melted the adamant. I hope very much it will still be possible for you to do the Thomson, as he's always been an interest of mine too.

I liked the conceptual poem, and after brooding over it found myself writing

Unfinished Poems – 1

I am wearing fibre.
    Fibre vibrates.
Why are you not wearing fibre?
    Fibre vibrates.
Yon one was wont warily to want to wear a fibre.
    Fibre vibrates.
We went on whistling under fire.
    Fire vibrates.
Then they gave me this shirt.

It is probably very unwise to write '1' after the title, but you never know; I have been thinking of the idea of 'unfinished poems' for a little while, and this may jog the thing out of its burrow. It may turn out to be merely a catalyst piece.

You must come out sometime and show me those photographs. How about Monday evening (21st)? I shall be away on 18th and/19th giving readings at Durham and York. Then I have examining to do at Newcastle 24th/25th. If the 21st suits – say about 8 pm?

Yours | Eddie

English Literature and Scottish Literature staff disagreed over Leonard's grading in his Joint Honours degree. His intellectual and creative approach to Glaswegian Scots language contradicted the traditionalism of Alex Scott. The possibility of postgraduate research on James ('B.V.') Thomson (1834–82), author of *The City of Dreadful Night* (his application is referred to in the opening sentence) depended upon achieving an Upper Second Class (2.i) degree. EM and Philip Hobsbaum were both supportive. Leonard's *Places of the Mind: The Life and Work of James Thomson ('B.V.')* was published in 1993. The poem became one of ten 'Unfinished Poems' dedicated to Veronica Forrest-Thomson, who died in 1975.

Michael Schmidt, *publisher, poet and critic*

14 November 1976

Dear Mikhail

Thank you for yours of the 5th. I look forward to the proof fruits of the IBM loom and promise to keep a tight rein on corrections. I enclose a list of acknowledgements for *Divan*.

Alex Scott tells me the Scottish Arts Council has promised £200 for reproduction fees for *ScotSatVerse* and says it is now safe to go ahead sending out letters to contributors/publishers of copyright material. I am about to concoct such a missive.

Regarding copyright payments and copies of *Rites*: I have searched my files but have no trace of the furrin correspondence – I'm fairly sure I returned these letters to you. Didn't I give them to you when I visited the Corn Exchange on one occasion?

On *PNR*: yes, I do promise to think about it, on my midnight couch or even on the pavements grey. I know it must seem absurd to you to have these hesitations, but I find the main drive of *PNR*, if one can judge from the first number, extremely alien (the two essays by Sisson in particular). I am sure you will want to persuade me that that is a poor reason for not contributing, and no doubt you are right. I don't want to be stupid about it. But just give me a little time?

Best as ever | Eddie

Schmidt's proofs of *The New Divan* were painstakingly done on his new IBM machine: 'Your blasted computer-ish Wittgenstein and so on poems gave me acute dyspepsia' (see 'Wittgenstein on Egdon Heath' and 'Lévi-Strauss at the Lie-Detector', *CP*: 354–55). He worried about lack of news of a grant towards EM's anthology, *Scottish Satirical Verse*. He also wondered whether, as Brian Cox had resigned from *PN Review*, EM might reconsider his refusal to send poems: 'I shall begin to feel you have a racial animosity against Mexicans and Englishmen [...] How amusing that people should have to consult their consciences before sending my magazine work.'

George Newson, composer

Dear George

Many thanks for your two letters. I'm glad you like the Shakespeare poem. It isn't going to be read in Southwark Cathedral after all, unfortunately; the organisers have changed the venue to Stratford at the end of July, and I won't be able to be there, so an actor will read the piece. (Perhaps I should give him 'instructions'!)

As regards the *Winter's Tale* opera idea: well, I would like to have a go at the libretto, despite the obvious difficulties, so do mention my name if you are negotiating.

I am enthusiastic about your new proposal for treatment of the Divan poems, and I have no objections at all to their being used in this way. Taking up your suggestion that there ought to be nine rather than seven, to meet the number of the muses, I am enclosing three more from the sequence, and I would suggest adding these and dropping 72, with possibly a slight redistribution, as follows:

Calliope – epic poetry, theme of war – 50.
Clio – history – 29.
Euterpe – Dionysiac music/joy/pleasure – 38.
Thalia – comedy/pastoral – 27.
Melpomene – tragedy – 19.
Terpsichore – dance – 70.
Erato – love poetry – 20.
Polyhymnia – lyric poetry/harmony – 69.
Urania – astronomy – 80.

As regards the middle-eastern milieu of the sequence, it might well prove possible and interesting to give a slightly oriental flavour to the music – I don't know how you feel about this. For some reason which I can't quite define, the viola seems to be a peculiarly suitable instrument to have involved with these poems. I can almost begin to hear the possibilities.

Let's meet as you suggest on Thursday at four in the club, and see what we can make of this.

Yours musingly | Eddie

The Shakespeare poem is 'Instructions to an Actor' (*CP*: 402), relating to *The Winter's Tale*. Newson was trying to secure a commission for a work based on the play from Peter Hemmings of Scottish Opera and Alexander Gibson of the SNO. The nine poems from 'The New Divan' were a mooted commission from James Durrant, a viola player.

Michael Schmidt, publisher, poet and critic

13 March 1977

Dear Mikhail

Sleeping in my suit from Leicester (no sleepers on the overnight train), jolted awake at every imaginable station from Loughborough to Kirkconnel, I brought back a crumpled and stubbly carcass to Glasgow yesterday morning and read your letter over a pot of pretty strong tea and hot buttered toast.

I am sorry that I am committed to review Maurice Lindsay's big history for Q – I have just received it but have not yet had more than a glance through. I am relieved that the little MacDiarmid storm seems to have blown itself out.

Will get working on *ScotSatVerse* introduction etcetera as soon as I can. Term breaks for Easter at the end of next week, which will give me a chance to make progress.

Laura Riding got through. Or rather Mark Jacobs did. It was a fairly intense three-hour oral. Doctor-elect Jacobs will now be trying to get the thesis published as a book, and although most theses don't make good books unless with some rewriting his own dissertation reads well because he is so absolutely committed to his subject; it's difficult, but not dull. I have been rereading the last paragraph of your letter and wondering if Carcanet should perhaps become (pioneeringly) interested in Laura? She is one of the most difficult of modern writers in both verse and prose, but there is undeniably something impressive there, and it ought to be better known.

Most of her work is out of print (some of it has been done recently in extremely expensive photographic reprints which are in any case not easy to obtain from America); her *Collected Poems* of 1938 (when she stopped writing poetry and turned to other things) ought to be reprinted; there should be a selection of her prose; and there should be a book about her (critics have held off, I suppose, because she has appeared such a formidable nut to crack). If you would like to mull this over in the watches of a few nights and days – (O nights and days, O queen of the night, O graves, O mores!), maybe you could let me know whether I might suggest to Mark Jacobs that he should get in touch with you? The current number of *Chelsea* (New York), by the way, is entirely devoted to LR. It would seem a good moment to do something about her.

I shall be in Manchester on 28 March, at the Didsbury Faculty of the Polytechnic where I have to give a reading in the early afternoon. Michael Freeman of the English Department there may have mentioned it to you. As my train back to Glasgow will be 6pm, it would be nice if I could see you sometime, perhaps around 4? I'm not sure when the reading will finish, but certainly by 3.30.

I am out of *From Glasgow*s and *Rites*es. Could you let me have 10 paperbacks of each and five hardbacks of each, when you have a moment? Please send to university address.

Ever | Gottschalk Jackson

EM was External Examiner at the University of Leicester for a doctoral dissertation on Laura Riding, or Laura (Riding) Jackson* as she now preferred. Schmidt also admired her work, and Carcanet would become her UK publisher. He wondered whether EM would review *History of Scottish Literature* by Maurice Lindsay* for *PN Review*, but he was already committed to the journal *Q*. The name 'Gottschalk' means 'servant of God'.

Lord Harewood, arts administrator

23 July 1977

Dear Lord Harewood

I had a letter from George Newson recently in which he said that he had been discussing with you a number of possible subjects for a new opera which he is hoping to compose and for which he would like me to write the libretto. He mentioned that you had said you wished to see a copy of my 'Columba' libretto, and I now enclose this. The text is for an opera which Kenneth Leighton is working on in Edinburgh; I believe he has finished the first two acts. He wants me to add a couple of scenes in Act 3, and this I have still to do. There are also one or two minor changes not incorporated in the text I am sending – it is of course an organic process all the time! I always write librettos with staging very much in mind, and try to have a clear exposition and good dramatic development. Previous texts include *The Charcoal-Burner* (with Thomas Wilson), *Valentine* (with George Newson), and an as yet untitled piece for Martin Dalby.

I hope you will find some interest in *Columba*.

Yours sincerely | Edwin Morgan

Harewood was Musical Director of the English National Opera and Artistic Director of the Edinburgh Festival. He had met with George Newson* to discuss various proposals. EM had also recently written for Newson a libretto synopsis based on *Sir Gawain and the Green Knight*. *The Charcoal-Burner* was recorded by BBC Radio in 1969, and the work with Martin Dalby was *Coll for the Hazel: A Spell for Four Voices* (1979).

Michael Schmidt, publisher, poet and critic

29 August 1977

Dear Mixtec

I was glad to hear from you – glad also to have the extension for Scottish Satirical Verse! I had not been writing as I was painfully aware that I was making slow progress and had little to report. It has been a distracting and depressing summer, in both the inner and the outer worlds. I won't bore with all the details, but for example the flat had to have two walls replastered after discovery of bulges and cracks, and this has meant a major mess, white dust everywhere, books piled up in rooms during the 2–3 months before drying-out allows repapering, etc. And what was really quite a pleasant break in Tenerife this month turned bitter at the end – a sudden flare-up with the old friend I was with, one of those tiny almost accidental things which are nevertheless very hard to undo once certain words have been said (we were both edgy after a 24-hour plane delay). Other things too seem to have conspired to make these last few months a right bad patch. Oh well, I addressed an Edinburgh summer school on James Thomson and *The City of Dreadful Night* – that was well received!

The glossary – to go back to our book – proved to be a big job, especially as regards the earlier poems, and I chipped away at it all the time the plasterers were on top of me. It is now virtually finished, though not typed out. I did it first, rather than the introduction, because the distractions suited its mechanical nature. I would now hope to march into the introduction during September, before term starts.

Will next year be better, I wonder? The British Council want me to lecture and poetry-read in Czechoslovakia at Easter. They want me to go in a missionary spirit, and to bear with frustrations. Ah, Europe!

It might be a good moment to try my hand at some more of the Schmidt-Morgan nodules.

Anyhow – I must shake out of all this. Tell me to write something. Give me a commission. Stay me with flagons. (I know, Scottish Satirical Verse first!)

All best wishes | Eddie

Schmidt worried about lack of contact from EM regarding *Scottish Satirical Verse,* and offered to delay publication. EM's holiday quarrel with John Scott led to an estrangement that lasted until his friend's death from cancer in the following year, with an abiding sense of guilt thereafter.

Melville Hardiment, poet and editor

9 September 1977

Dear Melville Hardiment

Thank you for your letter and for *Albab.* I look forward to reading the magazine and I certainly like the idea of the Arab/ Anglic meeting-place. (I wonder if you saw my last book *The New Divan* which has a long Middle East sequence?)

As regards the publishing of *A Migrant Four* – that's fine by me. I have kept in touch with Gael, Roy and Mike over the years as far as distance and accident have allowed and I have always enjoyed our meetings when they took place. I think the book could prove an interesting collection, perhaps especially in the light of what we have gone on to do since Migrant days. When I was being interviewed recently, the interviewer (a knowledgeable chap) asked me about the Migrant period and what it meant, and this brought it all back to me in a curiously unexpected way. My only problem is that my own connection with the magazine was mainly through translations rather than original work, and this period (1959–60) came just before my most productive time (1962 onwards); it was a kind of breaking of the ice, but I was still not fully through. However, if I can include some post-Migrant poems, as you suggest, this will help to put things in focus. I shall go ahead and think what to send you. About how much material do you want?

(By the way, you have me down as <u>Edward</u> Morgan in the review!)

I enclose subscription | Best wishes – | Yours sincerely | Edwin Morgan

Hardiment was co-editor of *Antiphon* (Glasgow then London) and developing a short-lived arts review, *Albab*, with accompanying pamphlets: here, *A Migrant Four*. He had earlier connections with Beat writers such as Ginsberg*, Burroughs, Gysin and Corso, and with Gael Turnbull*, Roy Fisher* and Michael Shayer* as a Migrant poet.

Trevor Royle, arts administrator

2 November 1977

Dear Trevor

Tom Leonard has asked me if I would drop you a note in his behalf, in connection with his application to the Scottish Arts Council for recording equipment to help him with his projects in sound poetry.

I would strongly support his application. Although the cost of the equipment is considerable, this is because he needs high quality hi-fi for the sophisticated collage-type sound-effects he wants in the work he has in mind; it would either be impossible, or not worth doing, on inferior machines. He has been working for a number of years now in a makeshift way, using inferior equipment or having brief and inconvenient access to others' machines. He has now reached the point where the seriousness of what he is doing is simply being blocked by these facts. I have heard much of what he has already done and can vouch for its serious intent and genuine originality – to say nothing of qualities that are often highly entertaining. In a wider sense, I know him well enough to say that he is a man of complete integrity who is only asking for what he needs to use and who is not out to collect some high-grade toys for himself or his friends. In addition, the area he is working in – sound poetry – is at the present time in a ferment of development and exploration in many countries, and it would in my view be a great pity if one of its most interesting practitioners, here in Scotland, was to be held back by difficulty of access to the necessary hardware. I very much hope that his request will be given favourable consideration.

Yours ever | Eddie

Now better known as a military historian, Royle was in the 1970s an innovative Literature Director of the Scottish Arts Council. With Joan Hughson, Leonard* was organising *Sound and Syntax*, an International Sound Poetry Festival in Glasgow for May 1978.

Sebastian Barker, poet and editor

18 June 1978

Dear Sebastian Barker

I am sorry to learn, from your letter in *Gay News*, that Eddie Linden had died – I did not know. I have very little to contribute to your memoir, but such as it is, it is perhaps worth passing on, and you can use it if you like. Because Eddie liked keeping in contact with Glaswegian acquaintances he used to phone me from London, far from sober, often on Saturday nights around midnight. I remember particularly one such phone call, when in the course of talking about his magazine and other things he suddenly said apropos of nothing, 'Eddie, you know I'm gay!' (As we are both 'Eddie' there was always a certain bizarre touch in these conversations.) I said, 'I know, I know you are, Eddie.' He went on in a loud voice, 'And I'm bloody proud of it!' Me: 'Okay Eddie, right, I know, I know you are.' Then we went back to talking about poems and articles for the magazine. I met him relatively infrequently, usually at poetry-readings and similar occasions, but we had many a long talk at such times and I have vivid recollections of him from that. I was not personally a part of his gay life but he talked frankly about it and found me a sympathetic listener; it was clearly an essential aspect of the man.

When your memoir is eventually published, perhaps you could drop me a note, as I would like to buy a copy, and it might never appear in the Glasgow bookshops.

Yours sincerely | Edwin Morgan

Barker had advertised in *Gay News* for personal recollections for a 'memoir' of Scottish poet and magazine editor Eddie Linden. This was published as *Who is Eddie Linden?* (1979). Along with several others, EM assumed that Linden had died.

Crispin Elsted, printer and publisher

17 July 1978

Dear Crispin Elsted

The last few months seem to have been inordinately filled with business of all kinds and I am still trying to catch up with some unjustly neglected correspondence, including your two letters. I am sorry of course that in your Scottish trip you found it impossible to fit Glasgow in, as I am sure we could have an interesting talk on a range of subjects, but it is good that you were able to visit Ian Hamilton Finlay – his 'environment' really has to be seen and walked through, even though there are some excellent photographs of it now in various places. (No garden here in my block of flats; balcony window-boxes with tagetes and lobelia are all I rise to!) After an extremely busy June, with university examining to do at Newcastle and Edinburgh as well as on home ground, I gave myself a week up at Loch Rannoch and was blessed with sunny days throughout. I shall possibly have another week somewhere in August but have nothing arranged yet, and this year I don't expect it will be anywhere exotic. I take it you will be making your plans to return to Canada fairly soon?

I was very much interested in your remarks on technology, and on the 'terminology' technology in poetry. I am sure you are right in seeing the habit of quotation in Moore and Olson (and I suppose in Williams and MacDiarmid) as not only or merely or perhaps even referential but as 'a direction of thought rather than a thought per se'. Coincidentally I was giving some thought to these matters recently, when I had to write a paper on MacDiarmid's late poetry for a conference at Falkirk. I examined some of his borrowings, acknowledged and unacknowledged, and tried to put them in an international context of the time, from Pound to Enzenberger. The more one looks at it the more extraordinary the amount of borrowing and encapsulation and/or re-creation or simply 'pointing' begins to seem. No doubt it can be related to clichés of 'knowledge explosion' and 'museé imaginaire', but there is more to it than that, as you yourself surmise. There must be, if one could find them, strange links between the deliberative and aleatory use of quotation – Lowell versus Mac Low (even the names are in some weird collusion –)…

One very curious effect in MacDiarmid is obtained when many successive lines of a poem will have a flurry of unusual or technical words with the same initial letter, obviously drawn from a reading of the dictionary, perhaps stored in a list, and then linked together in a large context (or at least an extensible context) in such a way that purely chance alliteration, the alliteration of dictionary context, is converted into some strained yet fascinating meditation, as if there was some world in which these words actually could belong together, though drawn from a dozen different disciplines (my d is catching).

I have been writing a sequence of poems about stone/rock under the general title Vestiges of Creation – tipping my hat to Chambers's own ripple-rousing stone of the nineteenth century. I do not at all know whether a sequence is any true answer to the question or problem of the long poem, but it seems at the moment to be what I find most fruitful; it, itself, as a method, possibly raises as many questions as it solves, but these questions – questions of connection, of ripple, of field, of scatter – have a way of stimulating the imagination and even of pleasing it. Comments I have collected on <u>The New Divan</u> (the sequence, not the book) range from 'utterly baffling' to 'just what poetry was needing'. Ah well, we have been told that man is a pattern-seeking animal and also a lateral-thinking animal, so…

I look forward to hearing from you again when you have the time.

Best wishes to both | Eddie

Elsted and his wife were Canadian fine press publishers engaged in doctoral research in Kent. He asked whether EM saw technical terminology (e.g. of space exploration) as a kind of technology within poetry, exemplified in Jackson Mac Low's *Light Poems*. Robert Chambers (1802–71), Scottish publisher and editor, published his speculative *Vestiges of the Natural History of Creation* in 1844. 'Foundation' (*CP*: 387) was part of the stone/rock series, and possibly 'Ore' and 'Mt Caucasus' (*CP*: 412, 415).

Michael Schmidt, publisher, poet and critic

1 October 1978

Dear Michael

As regards the Burns: no, I don't think the line numbers will be different, it is just a question of a few variant readings.

I would have liked to take a little jaunt to Manchester as you suggested, but the tentacles of the new term have been all around, even though we don't 'start' until Thursday, and I couldn't find a feasible day. So December perhaps! And in the meantime, and once I get myself properly energized again, I hope I can think of future projects...

I hear sometimes from Laura Riding who is clearly very pleased that you are doing her book. I agree that it is hard not to fall into her extraordinary prose style when writing to her: her letters seem almost to demand that the recipient swing (should swing) towards her on the same (at best a similar) kind of (and one uses the word advisedly) trapeze.

Best as ever | Eddie

Schmidt had asked whether EM's intention to alter some Robert Burns texts in *Scottish Satirical Verse* would alter the line numbers already set.

Laura (Riding) Jackson, poet and critic

28 November 1978

Dear Mrs Jackson

Your letter, and the charming photograph-postcard it enclosed, arrived today, and I am replying at once in order to enable you to send in your application for a Fellowship in early December as you wished. I need hardly say that I shall be perfectly willing to act as a referee on this occasion, and shall promptly provide the USA National Endowment for the Arts disbursers (if that is the word) with whatever assurances they may ask for. You may rely on me to say and do whatever I can in the matter, and I hope very much that the award will indeed come your way and make your 'life-experience' book a material possibility (I mean material in the first, necessary sense – it will obviously be metamaterial too!). It would be a book to look forward to.

I have not seen George Fraser for a little while, but we keep in touch, and I have involved him recently (willingly on his side!) in co-examining a Ph.D. thesis one of my students has finished on Basil Bunting.

No Spanish bayonets in bloom here; we have severe frost at the moment, icy roads, promises of snow to come. A good many lingering forlorn roses, doused in hoarfrost, present perhaps the right kind of heavy beauty, ominous, for late November. Yet ominous turns out to be not right after all – there is the whole potential of cheer, of renewal, in December and January. I hope you find this, this time around, in spite of difficulties and trials, as I hope to also.

Best wishes as ever | Edwin Morgan

L(R)J had written on 22 November 1978 requesting a reference for a year's Fellowship from the USA National Endowment for the Arts, to help her complete a planned intellectual and literary memoir. Poet and critic George Fraser of Leicester University had supervised Mark Jacobs' recent thesis on her work.

Gregory Cunningham, *teacher of English*

8 December 1978

Dear Mr Cunningham

Thank you for your letter of 19 November. I am glad to hear of your interest in sound poetry. The festival of sound poetry in Glasgow in May was quite a success, and Tom Leonard who was the chief organizer and also of course one of the performers managed to gather together most of the noted sound poets from Europe and America. We had Bob Cobbing, bpNichol, Lily Greenham, Jerome Rothenberg, Jackson Mac Low, Henri Chopin, Bernard Heidsieck, Gerhard Rühm,

Ernst Jandl, Franz Mon and others on our list. Although
they have all, in their different countries, published books, the
nature of their work is such that the printed page gives a very
poor idea of it (and in many cases there could be no printed
text), so that a list of a few records and cassettes might be of
more use to you than a bibliography. (I can give you names
of books if you wish.) One problem unfortunately is that
because the material is so scattered and international, the discs
and tapes may be hard to get hold of (I find the Welsh Arts
Council's Oriel Bookshop in Cardiff is the best supplier of this
kind of thing – strange as it might seem!). Anyhow, for what
it is worth, here are a few records, which among them contain
work by nearly all the participants in the festival:

Henri Chopin: *Audiopoems* (Tangent TGS 106).
Experiments in Disintegrating Language (Arts Council of Great
Britain AC 1971).
Lily Greenham: *International Language Experiments of the
50s/60s* (Edition Hoffmann, Frankfurt, S-1).
Text-Sound-Compositions / Stockholm Festival 1968 (2 records,
Fylkingen Records, Sveriges Radio, Stockholm, RELP 1049 &
1054).
Sound Texts / Concrete Poetry / Visual Texts (Stedelijk Museum,
Amsterdam, 1970, RSC 246).
Phonetische Poesie (edited by Franz Mon, Luchterhand
Schallplatte, F 60 379).

And one or two cassettes:
Henri Chopin: *Le Voyage Labiovelaire* (S Press, Düsseldorf,
Cassette No.9).
Jackson Mac Low: *The Black Tarantula*, etc. (S Press, Cassette
No.33).
Jerome Rothenberg: *Horse-Songs*, etc. (S Press, Cassette
No.25/26).

I hope this will be of some help, but let me know if I can
give you any further information.

Yours sincerely | Edwin Morgan

A secondary teacher of English in Alloa, Cunningham had written to EM after the *Sound and Syntax* festival in Glasgow to enquire about availability of tapes of the performances.

Michael Schmidt, publisher, poet and critic

3 February 1979

Dear Michael

It was good to hear from you, and since good and bad are mingled in this yarn of things, I feel bad about *Scottish Satirical Verse*. Ever since I took it on I seem to have been doing about twelve things at the same time, and there has never been a free stretch when I could properly break the back of it. At the moment a bibliography promised for the British Council is equally clamouring for attention (and <u>nearly</u> finished), as also is an anthology of longer Scottish poems I am co-editing with Alex Scott (due, notes and all, glossed and all, by end of March) (and <u>at</u> the end of March I am committed to a tour of Turkey for a fortnight giving readings and lectures). All these matters and projects and demands would be manageable if I did not have a full university job which makes it very hard to do much at all during term-time. However, I am as anxious as you are to complete the book and get it out and fulfil those nice eager orders. The glossary is only in need of final checking and you shall have it very soon. The introduction should not take long if I can just find myself a few clear days to get into it. The notes on the poets/poems will admittedly take more time, but possibly they do not (in what is after all to <u>some</u> extent a popular rather than specialist book) require to be particularly long or elaborate?

Last week I spent three days reading/lecturing in Paris at the Musée d'Art Moderne and Institut Britannique; another reader was Andrew Motion, whom I hadn't met before – a most agreeable and intelligent fellow.

Peter Robinson at Cambridge, who is like myself an admirer of Veronica Forrest-Thomson, suggested recently that I might ask whether Carcanet would be interested in bringing out a posthumous 'collected poems' from her scattered and unpublished poems and pamphlets? MUP, as you will know, has just published her critical book *Poetic Artifice*.

I had been thinking myself (what you mention) that it is time for a collected poems of my own, and if this seems practicable for 1981 (not 1980 – 60th birthday?!) I would greatly look forward to it. I think collected rather than selected – though clearly a selected would have its uses. Let us think about it. As a collected it could have a fair number of additions since the *Divan*.

Best as ever | Eddie

PS: Please would you send (university address) 12 Glasgow/ Saturns.

The British Council task was on nineteenth-century literature, for a bibliography of English literature, 1500–1980. The Longer Modern Scottish poems anthology, which EM worked on with Alexander Scott from 1979 to 1984 as part of a three-volume project, never appeared (possibly because of funding for copyright). *Longer Scottish Poems* from earlier centuries appeared in two volumes (1987). EM's 'Unfinished Poems' commemorating Veronica Forrest-Thomson* are in *The New Divan* (1977) and *CP*: 373–80.

1980s

(aged 60–69)

The 1980s seem a to-and-fro decade, opening with a retiral and closing with a 'coming out'. Between these points there is a restlessness. Taking early release at 60 from professorial teaching and administration, Morgan moved into 'the third life', as a full-time writer at last. His letters convey a sense of freedom, whether on foreign reading tours or engaging with new audiences in schools, theatres and concert halls. There is also the freedom to say no to particular projects, although more frequently the answer is affirmative.

Is there a sense perhaps of packing the emptier days of retirement with new commitments to add to those he did not want to give up? He continued to act as external examiner to several universities, and to supervise doctoral research, while also judging several major competitions in poetry and translation. Invitations to read his poetry across the UK could be fitted around international work in Israel, Ireland, the Netherlands, Austria, Italy and Germany.

Such busy-ness perhaps could never quite assuage the sense of guilt Morgan felt about a year's deliberate estrangement from John Scott before his death from cancer, aged 60, in 1978. He dedicated his first Collected Poems, *Poems of Thirty Years* (1982), to his lost friend. Its final section of Uncollected Poems 1976–1981 contains some sobering examination of his own character, as when in 'The Coals' he reflects on the self-reliance and discipline learned from his mother, 'which is both good and bad':

You get things done,
you feel you keep the waste and darkness back
by acts and acts and acts and acts,
bridling if someone tells you this is vain,
learning at last in pain.

Within this mindset, the hardest thing 'is to forgive yourself for things undone'.

He had scope now, at least, to devote his energies to Scotland's political and cultural life. A final bitter event of the late 1970s had been the failure of the Scots to vote in sufficient numbers for devolution of political power from London to a Scottish Assembly. Morgan felt it was important not to dwell pessimistically on that result, but instead to view it as a spur to creative effort that might build a more confident sense of Scottish identity. In the 1980s, younger Glaswegian writers such as Alasdair Gray, James Kelman, Tom Leonard and Liz Lochhead all published important new work. Morgan's *Sonnets from Scotland* (1984) formed part of that creative climate.

This visionary sequence ranges through past, present and future Scotlands, meshing historical detail with science fiction and political critique. That it was published by the new Mariscat Press in Glasgow was all to the good. That its co-founder, Hamish Whyte, was a Senior Librarian in the city's Mitchell Library, a poet and astute young editor with great knowledge and love of Glasgow, was even better. He became Morgan's bibliographer and Scottish small-press publisher, whose regular output of pamphlets and larger volumes kept the poet in touch with his Scottish readership, as well as providing the building blocks for future Carcanet collections.

Drama offered new forms of connection. Morgan's work of translation for the Medieval Players discovered ways to make older European plays speak to contemporary audiences. His poetry of these years develops a focus on the dramatic monologue and narrative forms, trying on, as it were, various possible selves: the playwright Shakespeare, the monster Grendel, the storyteller Jack London, the acrobat Cinquevalli – each of these in his own way an outsider. This was something Morgan recognised in himself. Laws against homosexuality were repealed in Scotland in 1980, much later than in England, but it was only as he approached 70 at the end of the decade that Morgan overcame the caution of a lifetime and undertook a series of interviews dwelling explicitly on his own orientation and gay experience.

These were years too of political drama, a period of bitter ideological conflict between Right and Left in Britain culminating in the national miners' strike. Internationally, communist rule was shaken across Eastern Europe, and collapsed with astonishing speed. Morgan had travelled more widely there than many poets, with correspondents in Czechoslovakia, Hungary and Poland. He had even taken a trip to Albania as soon as flights began to operate to Tirana, and claimed to like what he saw there, on a weekend's acquaintance.

He viewed what was now happening not only through his own sense of history and socialism but through the eyes and ears of younger poets to whom he was, in various ways, a mentor. Peter McCarey, whose Russian-based research he supervised, for instance; or Iain Bamforth working and travelling as a doctor in Europe and beyond; or Tom Leonard, more local and more radical, with whom he performed in support of the striking miners – these and others provided news of the present and thoughts for the future in cards and letters as varied as the stamps they bore. For the ageing poet, variety was the spice and grace of life, and variation his freshest source of forms and themes.

Book and Pamphlet Publications
Scottish Satirical Verse: An Anthology. Edited by Edwin Morgan. Manchester: Carcanet New Press, 1980.
The Apple-Tree: A Medieval Dutch Play in a version by Edwin Morgan. Glasgow: Third Eye Centre, 1982.
Poems of Thirty Years. Manchester: Carcanet New Press, 1982.
Grafts/Takes. Glasgow: Mariscat Press, 1983.
Master Peter Pathelin. Translated by Edwin Morgan. Glasgow: Third Eye Centre, 1983.
Sonnets from Scotland. Glasgow: Mariscat Press, 1984; 2nd impression 1986.
Selected Poems. Manchester: Carcanet Press, 1985.
From the Video Box. Glasgow: Mariscat Press, 1986.

Newspoems. London: wacy!, 1987.
Themes on a Variation. Manchester: Carcanet Press, 1988.
Tales from Limerick Zoo. Illustrations by David Neilson. Glasgow: Mariscat Press, 1988.

Nicholas Zurbrugg, academic and editor

19 Whittingehame Court
Glasgow G12 0BG
8 April 1980

Dear Nick

Trying my mightiest to answer your questionnaire as reprompted by Griffithmissive of 28 March I found it altogether too huge to deal with in any succinctish way (beyond making the too obvious points that you can't do Dada twice and that Neodada must be more ludic than shocking, that after the liberation of the 60s [on the wave of which *Stereo Headphones* was founded, even though at the end of the decade] poetry almost everywhere became more conservative as the 70s wore on, and that as visual poetry weakened sound-poetry strengthened and became more and more <u>sonore</u> Chopinly speaking) and therefore I fell back on the poetic and oblique way out of composing a little permutative piece which if thought about will give some answers to some questions. If it's unsuitable, don't hesitate to say so! I enclose it anyway, with my best wishes, computations, congratulations, commemorations, hopes and huzzas for the 80s-type stereos heads and phones now emerging from the womb of Brisbane.

More coincidence: just after I read your letter with its scenario of Aschenbach in Surfer's Paradise I watched Tony Palmer's TV film on Britten (good film, nicely done) with many shots of the *Death in Venice* opera and Aschenbach dying in his deck-chair to the pitiless arabesque and cartwheels of Tadzio. Actually the whole surfer mystique, though now somewhat mocked, I find powerful.

I may not be able to afford a surfboard, as I am taking an early retirement at the end of this academic year (at sixty – a stick, not a surfboard!), and hoping to live quietly in Glasgow and keep writing.

Best as ever | Eddie

A *mot* and its range

'I threw the bottle-rack and the urinal into their faces as a challenge
and now they admire them for their aesthetic beauty' –
  Marcel Duchamp to Hans Richter

I threw their faces and the bottle-rack into the urinal as a
  challenge and now they admire them for their aesthetic
  beauty.

I threw their beauty and their faces into the urinal as a
  challenge and now they admire them for their aesthetic
  rack-bottle.

I threw the urinal and the challenge into their bottle-rack
  as a beauty and now they admire them for their aesthetic
  faces.

I threw the bottle-rack and the aesthetic beauty into their
  faces as a urinal and now they admire them for their
  challenge.

I threw their bottle-faces and the challenge into the rack
  as a beauty and now they admire them for their urinal
  aesthetic.

I threw their urinal-bottle and their faces into the challenge
  as a beauty and now they rack them for their 'admire'
  aesthetic.

Teaching in Griffith University, Brisbane, Australia, and editing the
final issues of *Stereo Headphones* (1982), Zurbrugg had sent two
questions: Q1. Have there been any advances in poetry since Dada?
Q2. How do you think that experiments in art and poetry have most
significantly advanced in the last ten years? EM refers to the sound
poetry developments of Henri Chopin, using tape recording to
manipulate the human voice, then answers obliquely with 'A *mot*
and its range', published in the journal in 1982.

George Newson, composer

23 May 1980

Dear George

I did get your lost postcard as well as your letter, so there are evidently good public-spirited citizens about! I would have replied sooner but have had a busy patch. The idea of doing something with *The Winter's Tale* does appeal to me, as it is a play I have always liked. It would have to compete with another libretto I have agreed to undertake, with Kenneth Leighton, for a commissioned opera to be performed at Ampleforth in Yorkshire by the English National Opera in 1983 (nothing like looking ahead!) to mark a centenary. The subject we have decided on is St Francis of Assisi – the drama of the life, with its changes of direction and interesting range of characters, attracted us as being theatrically and musically challenging as well as being acceptable to the pious patrons. This will obviously take quite a bit of work and time; but since I will be (hope to be, expect to be!) more free from the autumn onwards, I don't see why I shouldn't also take up your suggestion. (One problem I foresee is the instant one of competing with Shakespeare's existing text – but the necessary simplification of opera may in itself help a different language to emerge.) So I shall think about this in the intervals of marking exam-papers during June.

Thank you for the birthday wishes. The day was celebrated at the Third Eye Centre with a poetry-reading, a buffet supper, the cutting of a cake, and the unscheduled falling of the main guest backwards off the platform after he had scraped his chair too near the edge. An alarming moment, though not without its comic side. No bones broken, but I was exceedingly sore the next day, I can tell you. I enclose a couple of recent poems for your interest.

All best wishes | Eddie

In 1976 Newson and EM had co-written *Valentine*, based on various events sharing the 14 February date (such as the St Valentine's Day Massacre). First performed at Glasgow University, another performance was now to be recorded by Radio 3 at Queen's University, Belfast. EM wrote the libretto for Kenneth Leighton's *Columba*, performed at the Royal Scottish Academy of Music and Drama in 1981, and in Glasgow Cathedral in 1986. The St Francis opera for the Benedictine school at Ampleforth did not materialise.

Charlie Gormley, film producer

3 July 1980

Dear Charlie

'Clearing my desk', or rather pre-clearing it – it isn't cleared yet – must be my excuse for not replying sooner to your letter. It has been a hectic month with much making of speeches, sifting of documents into disposable/nondisposable, sifting of books ditto, plus all the usual exam-marking trauchle of the period. It has all been very distracting and I have really had no chance to think about the film. I agree with you that the Arts Council letter is not on the face of it an open-arms welcome, but they do seem to want to keep the idea going. I am going up to Loch Rannoch tomorrow for a week, and maybe I can mull it over a bit in the intervals of bird-watching. When I come back, let's meet as you suggest. Perhaps you can give me a ring that weekend and we can fix some place and time.

The desk will still be there if you want to use it, with your real telephone, scrap paper, rubber bands, mug of pens… and the books will still be on the walls though not for long. All that will be left eventually will be a model of a ship's ventilating system, which is one of the Department's sacred objects and is passed on from generation to generation.

Best wishes | Eddie

Gormley had sought Scottish Arts Council funding for a film on 'the age of literacy', which he planned to open with EM clearing his desk in the University, ending one life and beginning another. EM had a timeshare lodge in a Loch Rannoch holiday village.

Vivian Bone, editor

5 October 1980

Dear Vivian

Thank you for your letter of 29 September. Your correspondent is right that Eminescu's importance is generally agreed, and it would be good to have a book of English translations. (There was a *Poems*, trans. P. Grimm, in 1938, doubtless long out of print.) I would think the best publishers to try are: Carcanet Press, Anvil Press, Calder & Boyars, Elek, Cape, O.U.P., and Secker & Warburg, especially the first three, since they publish a lot of translation, often from the less-known languages. I don't know of any prizes (there are translation prizes, but they seem to refer only to French, German, and Italian), but of course there are Arts Council grants for translations, which publishers can apply for, and that might be relevant. If your correspondent is looking for a person to recommend the book, perhaps he could get in touch with someone like Dennis Deletant who lectures in Romanian at the University of London.

Your final paragraph was a bit of a bombshell; I had no idea *The Second Life* was appearing in paperback. This had been discussed a long time back but I had heard nothing and thought the idea had lapsed. I do wish someone had told me, as it may affect the *Collected Poems* which Carcanet aim to bring out in 1981, and which they mean to include all of *The Second Life*. I am of course very pleased that the paperback is appearing, but it may complicate matters with Carcanet. We shall have to see.

With all good wishes | Eddie

Vivian Bone was then Assistant Secretary (Editorial) at EUP, and asked for advice to give to the unsuccessful proposer of a book of Romanian translations. A paperback reprint of *The Second Life* had been under consideration by EUP since December 1972.

Archibald Turnbull, publisher

18 March 1981

Dear Archie

I don't know whether you have noticed – I have only recently seen it myself – that a line has slipped out of the reprinted *The Second Life*. On p.60 ('Strawberries') at the bottom, after a space, there should be the last line of the poem

let the storm wash the plates

as in the first edition. As it's such a crucial line in the poem, it's a most unfortunate omission. Do you think an erratum slip would be possible, or is there any other way of getting the line back in? I had not bothered to check the text when I first saw the reprint, as I thought it had been reproduced photographically, and I discovered the mistake the hard way, when someone asked me for 'Strawberries' at a reading and I came to the end of it and stumbled to a bemused stop!

Yours ever | Eddie

Reprinting *The Second Life*, the printers had masked off the final line of 'Strawberries'. A speedy repair was managed.

Peter McCarey, poet and translator

29 March 1981

Dear Peter

The two references have now winged their way, so I hope one of them comes home to roost and lays the golden egg. Thanks very much for the Ossian and Blok books. The Ossian is most interesting: I knew in general terms of the Macpherson impact but had no idea of how extensive it was. The author seems to have done his homework, referring to Derick Thomson's book and to *Scottish Literary News*! The Blok study, which I have only glanced at, appears to be fairly straightforward on life-and-works lines – though it is interesting that it should quote Akhmatova at the beginning and Remizov at the end. Is Remizov back in the fold? I look forward to a closer dip. The translations of Georgian poets which you mention sounds as if it might be worth having. I can't think of anything else, unless (unlikely!) Aigi is publishing; I haven't seen anything since his Munich *Stikhi* of 1975.

So it is really Shéstov? I have a *Dictionary of Russian Names* which clearly says Shestóv! Still, I suppose the Russian man on the ground must know. My commiserations on the Gogolian library system. Libraries, far from being calm retreats, seem to collect angst like railway stations. The B.L. can take days, not hours, to get a book for you. And what, if not to make you feel like a guilty intruder, is the purpose of the very large very black very armed guards in the lobby of the Library of Congress (though I must admit they were quite civil if you dared to speak to them). The splendid new Mitchell extension, by the way, is still an unopened sleeping beauty (mm, rather dubious metaphor).

Lanark has caused quite a stir; got a long review in TLS; is selling well in America; and yes, to answer your question, really is good! I have an extra review copy which if you like I can keep for you and give you when you return, if you don't mind a copy lacking dust-wrapper. The book had a launching during the 'Glasgow Bookfest' which has recently finished its three weeks' run. Apart from Alasdair the bookfest brought such talking, beaming, signing, performing luminaries as Anthony Burgess, Melvyn Bragg, Ivor Cutler, and Spike Milligan. I ran some public seminars on poetry, fiction, and criticism, in which among others Philip Hobsbaum, Anne Smith, Allan Massie, Tom Leonard and Archie Hind took part. I also wrote a poem – well, verses – for the opening of the bookfest, which I read at the Third Eye.

I liked the Nerl and Novodevichi poems. It is curious to think of Solovyov and Allegra in the Novodevichi. I am glad you have managed to get about a bit and see Suzdal and Vladimir. Your frescoes and Tartars brought to mind *Andrei Rublyov*, the film of Tarkovsky's about the ikon-painter which I saw a few years ago. I don't know whether you saw it – a remarkable picture, but then all his pictures are remarkable. I wonder how he is regarded in Russia? Is there any material about or by him? He seems to be (grudgingly?) accepted? He visited London and Glasgow recently in connection with his latest film, *Stalker*. I missed his talk in Glasgow (I was giving readings in Wales) but I saw *Stalker* and found it very gripping and powerful. I also found myself writing about Tarkovsky, in the poem enclosed!

I don't know whether you have heard there is to be a Mayakovsky exhibition at the Museum of Modern Art in Oxford in the autumn, later in Edinburgh at the Fruit Market Gallery – plus various ancillary events such as readings, films, etc. I'll let you know when I hear more about it; I gather they're going to consult me about the literary side of it. Maggie Moore will probably be interested?

The papers tell me that even Russia is to have Summer Time. 'Give us back our hour!' Don't say they're about to join the EEC...

Wisdom, Hope, Love, Faith go with you – | Eddie

Pursuing doctoral research on MacDiarmid and Russian poetry, McCarey encountered bureaucratic delays. He had asked EM as his supervisor for a grant application reference, and reported on visits to the grave of the philosopher Vladimir Solovyov (influential on MacDiarmid) and his sister Allegra in Novodevichy Cemetery, and to various churches and icons. 'Tarkovsky in Glasgow' is in *CP*: 428–29. EM contributed an essay on Mayakovsky's language for the exhibition catalogue and read translations in Glasgow (see 23 March 1982).

Jiří Marek, academic

4 June 1981

Dear Dr Marek

This is a very belated reply to your last letter. I have been in Canada; but also I was waiting to see if I could get hold of a copy of William McIlvanney's novel *Docherty* which is out of print but which would have been a good example of the sort of book you were in search of in your letter. Unfortunately even a secondhand copy of *Docherty* has proved elusive. It is an excellent straightforward realistic novel set in a mining community in south-west Scotland at the beginning of the century (it was published in 1975, but never got into paperback). I am, however, sending you separately two paperbacks which you may find helpful: Lewis Grassic Gibbon's *A Scots Quair: Sunset Song* (the first novel in a trilogy), dealing with historical and social changes in an agricultural part of north-east Scotland early in the century, and Gordon Williams's *From Scenes Like These*, written thirty years later and presenting a clash between town and country values in Ayrshire during the 1950s. The two books make quite an interesting comparison, as Williams in fact refers to Gibbon and is aware of both continuing and broken traditions. In another package I am sending an outstanding novel which just appeared in hardback, *Lanark*, by a Glasgow author, Alasdair Gray. This book, which is partly naturalistic and partly makes use of science-fiction and allegorical techniques, has received a chorus of praise from reviewers, and I recommend it to you myself. Perhaps it could be translated into Czech! (It is worth considering.) You mention Alan Sharp; I liked his first novel very much; the second part of the proposed trilogy, *The Wind Shifts*, was still interesting but less good; since then, he has been swallowed by Hollywood and has faded from the literary scene. He was brought up in Greenock and Glasgow and I thought his talent showed great promise when *A Green Tree in Gedde* came out in 1965. But it has not been followed up.

I hope you are keeping well and are looking forward to the summer.

With best wishes | Eddie

Marek lectured at Palacký University, Olomouc, Czechoslovakia, which EM had visited on a reading tour in 1978. He wanted to develop their modern English literature courses through Welsh, Irish and Scottish writing, and EM gave advice, supplied texts (repaid by LPs of Czech composers), and paid for a subscription to the quarterly *Books from Scotland*.

Kulgin Duval, book dealer and friend

23 June 1981

Dear Kulgin

Many thanks for your letter and its progeny of cards – a pity we missed meeting in Toronto (sounds like a popular song), but let's not miss meeting in the Tummel/Rannoch environs. I arrive at my lodge on Friday 3 July when you are still making your way southwards from Harris, so I shall have to forgo Colin's kind offer and fall back on Glen's Taxi Service. But I'll be delighted to have dinner with you (and Irene Worth – of Kinkanja, as you remind me – if she is there at that time) on a night that suits you – perhaps Saturday or Sunday? And I hope you could both (or all, as the case may be) come and have dinner at the hotel some other evening – Monday or Tuesday? If I seem to be squeezing the dates it's because I shall have only four days instead of a week this time – I leave on the morning of Wednesday 8th to go down to Loughborough University and receive an honorary D.Litt. on the 10th. I don't know whether in this reduced time schedule your suggestion of a visit to the new Pitlochry theatre for a soufflé will be feasible, but I'd certainly love to go if it can be arranged, since I haven't seen it yet (the theatre I mean), and even if it is only Home's grouse soufflé I wouldn't at all mind a bite. What am I saying – at the moment I wouldn't dare to take my shirt off, being black & blue with bites from a friend who got slightly carried away on Friday – ants in Kinkanja are nothing to it. – A hundred tons of topsoil sounds as if it would do for the Hanging Gardens of Babylon. Do you know Bacon's essay on gardens? He had some bright, if imperial, ideas, that one.

'My' (i.e. Kenneth Leighton's, with libretto by me) opera *Columba* has come and gone at the Theatre Royal and got some decentish reviews. The production toned down some of Columba's physical strength and roughness, and missed some other dramatic points, but sets and lighting were highly effective, and there was a splendid chorus. Whether it will be taken up, and done elsewhere, we shall have to wait and see. It's a full-scale work, so the expense and risk are somewhat daunting. Kenneth's (new) wife tells me she was sitting in front

of us at *The Light-House* last year and was fascinated by the
conversation!

Best as ever | Eddie

EM had been reading at the International Poetry Conference in
Toronto in May 1981. He usually visited Duval and his partner Colin
Hamilton* at Frenich, their Perthshire home and landscaped garden
(hence the tons of topsoil), when at Loch Rannoch. Irene Worth, a
friend of Duval, was an American actress who appeared in the first
production of T.S. Eliot's *The Cocktail Party* as Celia, who dies near an
anthill. Duval had uncharitably compared Douglas Home's play at
the new Pitlochry Theatre, *The Grouse Moor*, to a soufflé.

Michael Schmidt, publisher, poet and critic

15 July 1981

Dear Michael

That was excellent news from you, on my return from
Loughborough. No magic practices, truly. I did mention the
matter to a couple of people, but I can't imagine that was what
caused the coffers to ope. I am delighted that we can go ahead.
I am sorry about the illness at home and I hope things get
better for you soon.

We never quite settled contents, did we? I have looked
out my letter to you of 2 July 1980. Would you agree with
the selections I suggested from *Gnomes* and *Instamatic Poems*?
If so, that leaves *The Vision of Cathkin Braes* as the main area
of doubt. The more I think about it, the more unsatisfactory
my suggested excerption seems, and I'm inclined to think the
book should either be in as a whole or omitted – what do you
think yourself? Before you decide, I want to complicate the
matter further! – During 1951–52, when *Cathkin* was being
prepared for publication, the idea was that it should be one
of a complementary pair of books – like the smiling mask of
drama it was to be mainly comedic, and the other book was to
be the frowning mask and to have mainly dark/heavy/'tragic'
poems. This other collection, *Dies Irae*, was accepted and

announced for publication in 1951 by Lotus Press, in their Acadine Poets series, but funds failed them towards the end of 1951, the series was discontinued, and *Dies Irae* was never published (except that many of the individual poems were in magazines). If we put in *Cathkin* as a whole, then probably *D.I.* ought to be in too, to give a fair overall picture of what I was writing around 1946–50. Alternatively we can omit both books and start with *The Cape of Good Hope* (1955). I am enclosing a typescript of the *Dies Irae* collection, which like *Cathkin* had translation as well as original verse, for you to look at.

I believe I gave you, last year, copies of poems written since *The New Divan*? I am enclosing a further selection of such poems. I have the feeling that 'Cinquevalli' and 'Jack London in Heaven' would make a strong conclusion to the book, and the others could be worked in before that.

I shall look out any corrections to the texts already published and let you have them; some I know you have already, but I think there are others.

By the way, if we do put in *Cathkin* and *D.I.*, I can mention briefly in my prefatory note the matter of their publication and non-publication.

Bulbs were flashing in Loughborough but I haven't seen any results of this activity yet. I safely delivered my speech (on poetry and science, what could be more proper?) and received my scroll and a rather handsome dark blue tie with the Loughborough emblem of peacock and key picked out on it; there was, thereafter, a splendid lunch, and conversation with Sir Maurice Hodgson, chairman of ICI, who was getting an honorary D.Sc. and who revealed that he has a Sony refrigerator ('the best kind') in his car.

Best as ever | D. Litt

The Scottish Arts Council had agreed to subsidise the production of *Poems of Thirty Years* (1982). EM had gone to Loughborough University, which had an emphasis on science and technology, to be awarded an honorary D.Litt., the first of nine such academic honours.

Poetry and the Golan heights may seem an incongruous
combination, but that is one of the places where I found myself
recently, on a poetry-reading tour of Israel, in company with
three poets from England – Patricia Beer, Michael Schmidt,
and Robert Wells.

The aim of the week's visit, under the auspices of the British
Council, the Arts Council of Great Britain, and the Friends
of Israel Educational Trust, was to give readings in Tel Aviv,
Jerusalem, Haifa, and on a kibbutz, to meet Israeli poets, and
to give a seminar at the Hebrew University in Jerusalem. We
had excellent and large audiences at the Tsavta Theatre in
Tel Aviv, and the Khan Theatre in Jerusalem, but Haifa was
a disaster: the reading in the Municipal Theatre had been
scheduled for the unsocial hour of 10.45 p.m.; and eight
people stayed out of their beds to listen to us.

"Haifa is dull," we had been warned by wagging tongues
in the other two cities. Not so our hotel, high on Mount
Carmel, with huge picture-window views over the whole
city and bay. The hotel in Haifa was the optimum point of
our accommodation; at the other end were the Presbyterian
austerities of St. Andrew's Hospice in Jerusalem, where I,
as the only Presbyterian had to defend our Spartan heritage
against the ribbings of my Anglican companions.

We saw a good deal of the country, from Masada in the
south right up to the barbed wire of the Lebanese border. We
were driven along the Golan Heights to appreciate its strategic
value; we spent a dark wet stormy morning at the Sea of
Galilee, and an exceptionally hot and brilliantly clear morning
at the Dead Sea; we scampered like troglodytes through the
dripping half-restored Crusader cellars of Acre; we took the
cable-car up to the spectacular fortress plateau of Masada,
where Herod's triple-terraced northern palace, clutching sheer
rock, is a wonder even today.

As a country for lovers of contrast, it is hard to beat.
Halfway along the Via Dolorosa, in the old city of Jerusalem,
we heard a sudden fierce chant of "Allah akbar! Allah akbar!"
from a group of youths who threw a few desultory stones in

our direction. God is great, indeed; but which God?

Perhaps the most telling contrasts are between old and new. We were shown round the Museum of the Jewish Diaspora in Tel Aviv University, where on three levels devoted to Family, Community, and Faith, the whole story of the Jews from prehistoric times is set out in a series of visual and verbal displays.

But suddenly the intense atmosphere of the past is broken: a computer room, where visitors can feed in the name of any town or city in the world, and be presented, when they have completed their tour of the building, with a printout giving detailed documentation of the Jewish history and composition of their chosen place.

We tried Glasgow, Exeter, Leicester and Mexico City (Michael Schmidt has a Mexican passport) and duly received our printouts, efficient and alarmingly informative.

I wonder if my friend and colleague Michael Samuels, of the chair of English Language at Glasgow University, knows that his essence nestles in a computer in Tel Aviv, from which he can be recompounded at the prod of a button, as one "notable in the university as well as in the community" of contemporary Glasgow? Ah well, nobody's perfect; the computer spelt his name wrong.

Edwin Morgan

EM kept notebook records of his travels for future reference or writing. The Presbyterian allegiance here may well be for journalistic purposes. Michael Samuels wrote to say that he had never been at all prominent in the Jewish community but that his wife's family, whose name was Samuel, had certainly been, 'so perhaps the Tel Aviv computer can be excused...'

R.D.S. Jack, academic

15 December 1981

Dear Ronnie

I have just managed to steal out from under being one of the judges in the mammoth National Poetry Competition and reading 20,000 poems, and am trying to catch up with put-aside letters, including yours of 20 November. So with that apology, here are some thoughts:

Robert Garioch: translations of Belli; also war memoirs *Two Men and a Blanket*.

Hamish Henderson: translations of Gramsci; some war poems and songs.

Joseph Macleod ('Adam Drinan'): poems (e.g. in *An Old Olive Tree*); book on Italy, *People of Florence*.

Rachel Annand Taylor: *Aspects of the Italian Renaissance*; *Leonardo the Florentine*; also poems show general Italian/Renaissance/Rossetti influence.

George Campbell Hay: translations (Scots) of Italian poems in *Wind on Loch Fyne*.

Douglas Young: translations (Scots) from Dante in *Auntran Blads*.

Robin Fulton: translations (English) from Saba, Ungaretti, Montale & Quasimodo in *An Italian Quartet*.

G.S. Fraser: translations from Cavalcanti in Lind's *Lyric Poetry of the Italian Renaissance*.

Edwin Muir's autobiography (& also Willa Muir's).

Edwin Morgan: translations of Montale in *Poems from Eugenio Montale*; translations of Quasimodo, Leopardi, Balestrini in *Rites of Passage*; translations of Tuscan folk-songs (Scots – printed with many mistakes!), Ariosto, Michelangelo in Lind's book as above.

Norman Douglas: novel *South Wind*; other books like *Old Calabria* and *Siren Land*.

Compton Mackenzie: novel *Extraordinary Women*.

Eric Linklater: novel *Private Angelo*; history-book *The Campaign in Italy*.

Muriel Spark: many novels set in Italy where of course she has long lived.

Allan Massie: novel *The Death of Men* (based on Aldo Moro murder).

I can't think of much in the drama line. A Scots Galdoni, *The Servant o Twa Maisters*, which I haven't seen.

Oh, I forgot my own *Fifty Renascence Love-Poems*, which has versions from Petrarch, Tasso & Marino.

This is a right disordered list, but perhaps you can sort out what you need from it. It's surprising what there is, really, when one starts to think about the matter. Garioch's Belli sonnets are among the very best things he did. Hamish Henderson's interpreting and championing of Gramsci is also notable. And I know that speaking for myself I regard Montale as one of the greatest modern poets (you may have seen my semi-obituary review of his last collection in TLS recently). One could write a book on Spark the italianizzata (yet not entirely italianizzata). If Muir's stay in Rome had come earlier, how different his poetry would have been! But I must leave all trends and speculations to you –

With all best wishes of the season – | Eddie

Jack had been asked for a survey article on the Italian influences on Scottish literature. Since his knowledge of twentieth-century sources did not match his expertise in earlier periods, he had requested directions to pursue.

Tony Lopez, poet and academic

16 December 1981

Dear Antony Lopez

Thank you for your letter of 22 November. I don't know of anyone who has collected reviews of Graham's books, but it's possible that Alan Hancox, the bookseller in Cheltenham, might be able to help you. Some of his catalogues have had masses of Grahamiana. Another Cheltenham link is the special issue of the magazine *Promenade* (No.65, 1955) which was published there and which Graham was asked to put together by himself. It is full of little clues which you could probably follow up. William MacLellan, the Glasgow publisher of the 'Poetry Scotland' series, might have recollections of Graham. So would J.F. Hendry, sometime of the New Apocalypse. Vivienne Koch (if she is still alive – I don't know anything about her) must have known him well, and you may have seen her pieces about him in *Briarcliff Quarterly* (April 1946), *Sewanee Review* (Autumn 1948), *Poetry Quarterly* (Winter 1947–48). The late Burns Singer was of course a close friend and disciple. You might track down some of his ideas through New York University, where Graham gave an Adult Lecture Course on 'Forces in Contemporary British Literature' in 1948. I knew him before the war, when I was in my late teens. We were not close friends in the ordinary sense, in that we did not meet all that frequently (I was in Glasgow, he in Greenock), but we had a close involvement with one another – conducted largely through letters – as young poets, and each influenced the other. I went into the army in 1940, and he left Scotland shortly after. Since then, we have had bursts of correspondence, but only very occasional meetings, in London, Glasgow, and Edinburgh.

I hope perhaps these remarks will be of some help to you in your thesis.

Yours sincerely | Edwin Morgan

Researching the background context at the start of his doctoral studies on W.S. Graham* at Cambridge University, Lopez had enquired about reviews of the poet's early volumes. EM would later be the external examiner for Lopez's thesis, and provide academic references thereafter, as well as admiring his avant-garde poetry.

23 March 1982

Dear Michael

Possibly this will reach you before you phone on Thursday: it's a poem I'd like to add to the list. At readings people often ask for it, and at the moment it's not available in any of the books. It would come in the list of contents between *The Second Life* (1968) and *The Horseman's Word* (1970).

I will try to produce some sort of address-list for you (though not by Thursday!). Mind you, it really is a task – I should get a secretary. Time seems to be a vanishing commodity. Next week: Monday, reading at school in Edinburgh; Tuesday, Mayakovsky rehearsal at Tron Theatre in afternoon, reading in Edinburgh in evening; Wednesday, final rehearsal at Tron in afternoon, performance of dramatized reading of Mayakovsky's Futurist period with two co-readers in evening (complete with black rollneck and large yellow tie); Thursday, partly free to look up old address-books etc., but cleaner comes in morning and old friend comes in evening; Friday to Sunday, Joyce conference at Leeds University (reading paper on Joyce and MacDiarmid, imbibling Guinness reception, hobnobbing with Seamus Heaney, etc.)...

Yes, on the whole I agree with you about copyright; I read your editorial with great interest. It's complex being a fairly prolific producer of copyright material (copyright good) and at the same time a prolific consumer (copyright bad). Now that I have to get my photocopying done commercially – and I do a lot of it – I have discovered that the relatively restrictive but readily pirated university regulations were an Azdakian golden age; Rank Xerox have a palatial Copying Chamber equipped with every machine known to Alphaville in the centre of Glasgow, but they will not copy a single page of any book, far less 10% of the volume, and it is no use quoting the law at them. 'It is a house rule that we do not copy books.' Rather like one searching for an abortion, I had to find, by trial and error, a 'little place' that does not ask questions and has no inhibitions about copying 30 or 50 pages of a book. But I can't help feeling that at any time this facility might put up the shutters. And portable home copiers (I have one) are no solution: too slow, and poor with books. It is a bad situation.

Hillhead I am indeed in. I cannot hear the Bingham's Pond gulls for the travelling loudspeakers of (in alphabetical order) Jenkins, Leslie, Malone, and Wiseman. I suppose you are right that Jenkins is 'a man of some substance' (considering his past activities, you mean?), but I cannot say that he has shown such substance in Glasgow, and even in Hillhead he seems an unusually alien body. He is staying at the Pond Hotel, almost opposite my front windows, and I occasionally see him and his cohorts disporting themselves on the brink of the swan's way (yes, there are actually swans in the pond). He appears to be drifting to the top of the polls, though only just, and may well get in. Malone is po-faced, and Wiseman is no-faced (I agree with you entirely about the beard). Either of these two could be used in an illustrated dictionary at 'uncharismatic'. Leslie I shall vote for, though everyone is sure his party has no chance of winning; he is an honest square-shouldered dependable watchdog of a vet, who because he is not a 'wild man' may steal quite a few Tory and Labour votes. Never at any election has my letterbox disgorged such a blizzard of 'literature' (what a word!), most of it from the official parties but some of it very nasty indeed, as all the little fringe groups try to whip up their pet specialities, whether anti-Pope or anti-gay or anti-feminist or anti-union or anti-Ann-Summers – they never seem to be pro anything except capital punishment, it's a great thing to fall back on. There's something ominous about the Eighties, so much hatred boiling and swilling about near the surface of society – do you feel this?

Jusqu'à jeudi – l'aprés-midi d'un téléphone – | Eddie

The late addition to *Poems of Thirty Years* was 'The Flowers of Scotland' (originally in *Penguin Modern Poets* 15, 1969). The address list was to aid pre-publication sales. The reading was linked with a touring reconstruction of an exhibition organised in Moscow in 1930 by Mayakovsky. The two co-readers were Alan Riach* and Margaret Moore. Azdak is the rascally judge in Brecht's *The Caucasian Chalk Circle* and *Alphaville* the 1965 dystopian science-fiction film of Jean-Luc Godard. In EM's parliamentary constituency of

Hillhead, Roy Jenkins was standing for the new Social Democratic Party.

Jiří Marek, academic

17 May 1982

Dear Dr Marek

This is a belated but none the less grateful reply to your letter of 8 January. I was waiting to hear something definite about a paperback edition of Alasdair Gray's *Lanark*, and I have recently learned that this is due to appear in September; so I shall send you a copy then, if you do not mind waiting all this time! I mentioned the possibility of a Czech translation to Alasdair Gray (I didn't put it more strongly, since one mustn't count one's chickens before they are hatched, and there's many a slip 'twixt the cup and the lip, and there's no doubt a Czech proverb about that too) and he was most pleased and excited at the prospect. It is very good of you to go to so much trouble in the matter; I think the book is worth it. I shall be most interested to hear how things progress.

My own 'collected poems' – the actual title is *Poems of Thirty Years* – should be out about August or September, and I shall send you a copy. I am busy correcting proofs of it at the moment. Various projects have been rather hanging fire during the last month, since I had a burglary here with a number of unpleasant complications (one of the burglars had hepatitis, and also cut himself badly on a broken window) which are just gradually sorting themselves out. The thieves did not take my records, but they took my record-player, so I cannot solace myself with Dvořák at the moment!

With all best wishes | Yours sincerely | Edwin Morgan

Marek had approached Odeon publishers regarding a Czech translation of *Lanark*, and another copy of the novel was needed for a second reviewer. EM had cut himself clearing up broken glass after his flat was burgled, as described in 'The Break-In' (*CP*: 463–64).

Michael Schmidt, publisher, poet and critic

9 August 1982

Dear Michael

Handsome book, sir! The individual copy and the batch of
six have both arrived. Does the colour represent both the sea
and the depths of space? Anyhow, it's an eye-catching design
which will be noticed in bookshops. And the pages are well
set out and clear, and I think the smaller type for some of the
awkward concrete poems was probably the best solution. On
a first run-through I have noticed a sprinkling of misprints
which I have noted on the attached errata list; do you think it
would be possible to have these printed as an insert?

Helen Lefroy has sent me, as from Laura Riding, her
Progress of Stories. I shall write to her, but would you please
reciprocate by sending L(R)J a copy of my book?

Trevor Royle will be interviewing me about the book on
Radio Scotland's 'Prospect' arts programme, and *The Scotsman*
have interviewed me for some sort of 'Profile' to appear on
their Saturday supplement pages.

By the way, I never got back my copy of the contract! Could
you please send this on sometime?

Are your new premises more splendid than the old? I
imagine the Corn Exchange as having a mysterious hierarchy
of rooms, topped off with the residence of the Corn King (or
Corn Queen) him/herself.

I have treated myself to Vol. 3 of the OED Supplement.
It is organogenous, panmictic, quanking, retrodictable, and
saucerian.

All the best | Eddie

Poems of Thirty Years (1982) had a striking cover of midnight blue
and aquamarine. Carcanet had recently moved from Salford to
Manchester's Corn Exchange, into smaller but considerably more
salubrious accommodation, according to Schmidt.

Dick McCaw, producer

Dear Dick

Many thanks for the contract forms, two of which I duly
return. I hope the tour of farces goes well (Goswell), cracks
sides, fills purses. I am about halfway through the things that
prevented me pathelinizing in December/January – 6000
words on Glasgow writing, 2000 on 'Scotland in 2083' (sic) (a
commissioned piece for the *Glasgow Herald* which celebrates
its bicentenary on 27 January – whaur's yir *Times* noo eh?),
and a talk on 'Patronage of Literature' (ho ho); I am about to
plunge into my Byron essay, or rather plunge into the actual
writing of it, and then Sorley Maclean waits. After that, plus
the examining of a large Ph.D. thesis, I confidently expect to
be in the mood for French farce.

I know hardly any more about Hans Sachs than my books
tell me, or Wagner in his *Meistersinger*. Apart from his pro-
Luther poem 'The Wittenberg Nightingale' he seems to have
written masses of Shrovetide-plays (Fastnachtsspiele) which
are said to be humorous, well-observed, and good theatre.
And written in wrough and wready verse, which strikes a
familiar note. Some have been translated, and I could see if
the university library has any versions. I doubt if I could get
very far with the medieval German by itself, but with existing
translations as a guide I might manage something, though
obviously that would not guard against error. It does look as
if he would be very much the Meds' cup of tea. I can't think
of much else that is of Lutheran import. There are references
to Luther in Lyndsay's *Satyre of the Thrie Estaits*, which is a
reformist play though not fully Protestant; but it's in fairly
thick Scots. A medieval version of John Osborne's *Luther*?
An Evening of Collage, Sachs/Lyndsay/Wagner/Osborne?
'What are the Medieval Players up to?' – Michael Billington.
I shall let you know if anything comes to mind. – There's a
good Sachs entry, by the way, in the Penguin *Companion to
Literature: 2: European*, p. 685.

I hope you are well, defying January, etc.

All the best – | Eddie

Working on a documentary about Martin Luther, McCaw had found references to Hans Sachs (1494–1576), and asked for guidance. He was the producer for the Medieval Players, based in Goswell Road, London, for whom EM translated *The Apple-Tree* (1982), a medieval Dutch play, and *Master Peter Pathelin* (1983), a fifteenth-century French farce. The Arts Council sent contract forms for the latter. The *Glasgow Herald* article was 'The Dancing Dervish revolution in Scottish way of life' (24 January 1983). 'Voice, Tone, and Transition in *Don Juan*' is reprinted in *Crossing the Border: Essays on Scottish Literature* (1990, 109–29).

Michael Schmidt, publisher, poet and critic

27 February 1983

Dear Michael

Belated thanks for your letter of 10 January clearing the copyright position. I wrote to EUP as you suggested and not having heard from them I take it that the position must be agreed. I shall pass things on to you in future.

I have been correcting proofs of my/our 'grafts' for Hamish Whyte's Mariscat production (cover design by Alasdair Gray), which should not be too long in appearing. My four Glasgow subway posters, rejected by the Strathclyde Transport Executive but now being published by the National Book League (i.e. they won't actually be seen underground unless I take them there some dark night with flypostering-paste), should also be ready soon – will send you copies. As for our next book, which you enquire about, yes indeed there must be something! What about a small book: my *Alphabet of Goddesses*? This is a sequence of 26 poems on classical goddesses (ostensibly, but really on women, men, life, death, love, and all that) which was set off by seeing an exhibition of drawings by Pat Douthwaite during the last Edinburgh Festival, and would require a preface explaining this fact, plus possibly one of the drawings as a frontispiece. I always regretted that *The New Divan* did not appear separately as a sequence; the *Alphabet* is shorter, but would I think make a worthwhile book. Let me know if you'd like to see a copy of the sequence. – There are also a dozen or so uncollected essays from 1976 to date, possibly too ragbaggy to make a book? – 'The Translation of Poetry', 'Gavin Douglas and William Drummond as Translators', 'MacDiarmid's Later Poetry against an International Background', 'Joyce and MacDiarmid', 'The Poetry of W.S. Graham', 'Mayakovsky: The Poet and his Language', 'The Future of the Antisyzygy', 'Voice, Tone, and Translation in *Don Juan*', 'Glasgow Dialect in Recent Scottish Literature', 'Poets in Schools', 'MSS in a Bottle' [report on the National Poetry Competition], 'Scotland 2183', [and one to be written shortly on Sorley MacLean].

All best wishes | Eddie

Hamish Whyte* published *Grafts/Takes*, a double book with the 'Grafts' (the dovetailed joint poems) running one way and the 'Takes' (previously uncollected Instamatic poems) running the other. The subway poems included the Subway Piranha, Giraffe, Cat and Budgie. Originally commissioned for the Glasgow Underground, they were considered unsuitable by officials ('there are no piranhas in the Underground'). EM's free use of phrasing from the catalogue of Pat Douthwaite's exhibition in 'Alphabet of Goddesses' (*CP*: 464–77) led to a threat of legal action. The essays listed were included in *Crossing the Border: Essays on Scottish Literature* (1990).

Joy Hendry and Raymond Ross, editors

21 June 1983

Dear Joy and Ray

I am very sorry to have to admit defeat over the Sorley MacLean essay, but I have tried various approaches without reaching anything really satisfactory. The doubts I had when you first broached the subject have simply been reinforced. Time and again I found that the points I wanted to make were too specific not to be made in the actual language of the poetry, and it did not take me long to see the various inadequacies of existing translations. I simply could not quote with confidence. What I wanted to do was to start off from his own reference to Blok, and make a comparison between the two poets; there are many interesting points of similarity and contrast to be brought out. But I felt the whole exercise, quoting from both writers in translation, was becoming more and more unreal, and I have had to give up. Sincere apologies – but when you don't have confidence in what you're writing, the results don't satisfy.

Best wishes | Eddie

Hendry*, editor of *Chapman* magazine, and Ross, advisory editor of *Cencrastus*, were planning a volume of critical essays on Sorley MacLean and recruited EM to consider his work in relation to European (later redefined as Eastern European) traditions.

Carl Heap, director

4 August 1983

Dear Carl

Here is the Famous and Affecting Farce. I hope it won't present you with too many problems! I enjoyed translating it, and I must say I think it is a very funny play and ought to do well in performance. (I laughed aloud two or three times when I was finally typing it yesterday, which I trust is a good sign.) I have a lot of admiration for the original, which is wonderfully compressed and economic in its effects, if a shade delphic at times in comparison with the more spelt-out modern French prose version. The English version sits very loosely to the text, has continuous omissions, dilutes the luxurious religious oaths, and bowdlerizes the whole vocabulary, especially that of bodily functions. I have restored the outspokenness and I hope the pungency. (It might be that you would want to make a cut or two if you happened to be playing to a children's audience – though I'm not sure!) After our talk on the phone, I decided in fact to cut very little – a line or two of proverbs/fables which are merely decorative and would mean little to us here today, and one course of the 'feast of languages' which in its totality seemed to be a shade indigestible. I have made a different choice of languages, and used languages rather than dialects, to help the communicability (!) of this splendid section for a modern audience; I took some care with it, and as you will see there is a smattering of sense (the themes of sickness, doctors, death, and money) with impertinency mixed. I am dying to hear it! – There are, here and there, some deliberate anachronisms; I felt it was the sort of play that permits this and indeed encourages it. I don't know whether there may be problems of tone; the Judge, for example, switching from a straight or brusque official courtroom voice to various degrees of raillery – but these changes seem to be in the original, and I hope they are manageable. (In this, as in more obvious ways, the play reminds me of Jonson's *Volpone* – to which I have smuggled a reference!) – An interesting technical feature of the original is the way the rhyme straddles (usually) the end of one speech and the beginning of the next; it's a fine linking effect, though it may not always be necessary or possible to do very much with it in the actual production.

Do feel perfectly free to make your own cuts as required – and changes too if a phrase or line turns out to be unstageworthy. Let me know of any queries. Flexibility is all! I very much hope you will find it a speakable text.

Sometime, could you or Dick give me details of the three Xeroxes you sent up (original, modern French, English version), as there was no indication of what books they were taken from, and I'd like to have this as part of the background information.

With best wishes, | Eddie

Heap was director of the Medieval Players, planning to tour with EM's translation of the fifteenth-century French farce *Master Peter Pathelin* (1983).

Daniel Weissbort, editor and translator

4 April 1984

Dear Mr Weissbort

Thank you for your letter of 23 March, which has been forwarded to me from Glasgow University (I left in 1980).

I have written a number of articles on translation, but they have tended to be general rather than particular and detailed in the way you are looking for. I find in myself a great reluctance to write <u>about</u> translations I have made, partly because I don't usually keep notes and drafts, and partly because I don't want to go over <u>again</u> the ground which has been covered so intently and thoroughly during the process of making the translation. After the initial hard work of getting into the foreign poem and understanding it, the translation itself (if it goes well) begins at some point to take off, just as original poetry does, and the lightning and unplanned solutions one finds (often the best ones) are not really amenable to later 'explanation' as part of a conscious strategy of translation. I'm sure there are interesting things to be said about my Mayakovsky versions, but I would rather leave it to others to say them!

I am sorry that I don't feel attracted towards writing the kind of piece you have in mind. I would rather get on with more translation (Aigi, at the moment)! But thank you very much for the suggestion, and all best wishes for the book.

Yours sincerely | Edwin Morgan

Weissbort*, a founder with Hughes* of *Modern Poetry in Translation*, was co-editing a book on the practicalities of translation, including a section on working drafts. He had praised EM's translations of Mayakovsky as 'the only ones that gave any real sense of his brilliance'.

James McGonigal, academic and poet
(handwritten)

Rannoch
11–7–1984

Dear Jim

I'm writing to you from my 'lodge [with mod. cons] in the wilderness'. You'll be glad to know that I did, after humming and hawing with myself, send off the chain letter to four people. I really don't like chain letters, but as you say, the cause… One of my chosen targets, George Mackay Brown, wrote back with a delightful <u>sancta simplicitas</u>, saying he didn't think he understood the instructions, and would probably break the chain! (However, peace is in his <u>prayers</u>, and he hoped that would forgive him.) I await the flood of postcards.

Thanks for the Writers' Workshop card with its splendid catcher's mitt cover (do I get the prize for guessing correctly?) – most of the names already known to me, and it's good to see the continuity of what was always one of the best of the workshops. I like your poems, especially the 'Dawn Chorus', with their sense of the interweaving of human and natural life. 'November the mad axeman' is good! I wonder if the 'Particular tempos of heartbeat' are a shade abstract or artificial in the context? (My dawn chorus here, by the way, is a real awakener – gulls!)

Like you, I've been 'talking about poetry' – to a British Council international summer school in Aberdeen – teachers of English from Senegal to Bulgaria to Thailand, a high-powered and articulate lot. If Britain 'lost its empire', the English language seems to have gained a new one. Whaur's yer <u>civis Romanus sum</u> noo, eh? I left the students struggling manfully with Aberdonian dialect. That should shake them in Sofia! Fortunately my brief, unlike yours, didn't quite regress to Simonides: it was 'contemporary poetry', i.e. what happened after Larkin and Hughes? I also gave a reading, and signed copies of the Glasgow Subway posters which the British Council must have bought up and were distributing to the students.

I was much interested to hear about your ferification of

one third of the garden – a sort of anti-Stonypath? Let me know if you attract new fauna. I suppose the time to worry would be if you discovered you were yourself sprouting leaves like a green man, the wodwo of Hightae. (They are, I see, hoping to implant artificial gills in divers, so that they can stay underwater for several days.)

Your remarks about the local police prompt me to recount: a short time ago, at home, my buzzer buzzed; I lifted the receiver: 'Police here, can I have a word with you?' I pressed the button for him to enter the building, my mind racing, trying to think what it was that might have caught up with me – an awful moment, with a strange kind of passive inevitability about it as I heard the lift purr up. However, it was only to return a watch that had been stolen in the burglary two years ago, and which I had almost forgotten about. It still goes, but I doubt if I'll ever wear it. The burglar, or more likely the person he sold it to, has had names illiterately inscribed on the case, to disguise the watch or simply to claim its new ownership. It was horrible to be reminded of the break-in, so long after the event, and for a few days it was all churning around in my mind again. I wonder if a case is ever described as 'closed'? (Unlike a watch-case.)

Hamish Whyte (Mariscat Press) aims to publish my 51 *Sonnets from Scotland* on 30 November. I gather he has booked a 'launch' in the Mitchell – I'll let you know more about it later. It would be nice if you were free to come along and imbibe a sherry or whatever. Next year Carcanet plan to bring out a *Selected Poems* which would also include recent uncollected work like the *Alphabet of Goddesses* (but not the Sonnets). A paperback of *Poems of Thirty Years* is apparently still on the cards, possibly for late 1985, but nothing definite yet. At the moment I'm busy with a modern version of the *Second Shepherds' Play* for the Medieval Players, scheduled for production in Glasgow Cathedral in October. Maybe you'll get to that too! (Always presuming lightning sticks to the York area and doesn't cross the border seeking whom – or whose transept – it might devour.)

I hope Andrew's toothache was successfully dispersed, and that all are well.

Best wishes as ever – | Eddie

Back home on the 13th.

The chain letter arose from a peace initiative. McGonigal was a member of Dumfries Writers Workshop, run by Glasgow University's Department of Adult Education. York Minster was struck by lightning in July 1984 and damaged by fire.

Marshall Walker, academic and friend

19 Whittingehame Court
28 October 1984

Dear Marshall
　　Many thanks for PC of 4 October and letter of a week later. I am enclosing the latest Medieval Players programme, plus a badge which will doubtless make Elsie the only Medieval Player in Hamilton (unless the Dean wants to wear it as a new way of asserting his authority); the Players adopted the apple as their emblem after the success of *The Apple Tree* in 1982. My version of *The Second Shepherds' Play* had its première in Glasgow Cathedral on 9 October and is now touring around Scotland, England, and (spring 1985) Australia (how about adding NZ to the trip? any chance of support from Arts Councils, Universities??). I'm hoping the Third Eye will print the play, as they did the other two plays, and of course I'll send you a copy if and when. The Cathedral performance went off well, though I was hardly in a state of natural enjoyment as it was thought proper for me to sit in the front row between the Lord Provost and the Minister of the Cathedral, and worse still, some wit suggested just as I sat down that I would have to say a few words at the end, which fortunately didn't happen. Afterwards a select band of guests repaired (there's no other word for it) across the maidan to Provand's Lordship for a low-raftered supper of wine and avocado dip.
　　It's good to have an idea of what is in the Japanese magazine, and I'm grateful to you and your Japanese colleagues. Please pass on to them the enclosed 75-year-old

card as a tangible memento of thanks, if not quite as tangible as a bottle of Tansan would have been! Other translations of my poems have been appearing in Poland and Italy. An Italian woman poet whom I met at a summer school has made excellent versions of the 4 subway animals and these are apparently causing merriment in Milan, where she lives.

I go to Manchester in a week's time to see Michael Schmidt and agree a contents-list for the 'Selected Poems' he aims to bring out next April. I won't include the 'Sonnets from Scotland', to give the Mariscat book a chance to sell, but I want if possible to squeeze the Goddesses in as a group. Michael also wants me to 'think about prose' – whether essays or a longer work I shall find out when I see him.

I had four days in New York and three in Washington at the end of last month with an ex-student of mine, Andrew McCallum, who is writing a book on the cinema (especially American); we had booked for a quick film-buffs-orientated package tour of Hollywood ('you will meet at least one director and one star') but this was cancelled when not enough people booked to make a viable party, and I went to Cooks to arrange the week in NY and Washington to fill the gap. Memorable view on a hot sunny day from the top of the World Trade Centre; awful chaos of hotel (Omni Park Central) which had just been taken over and had painters and electricians everywhere; pilgrimage to Oscar Wilde bookshop in Christopher Street; Greyhound bus to Washington with a boisterous cluster of blacks in the back seat sending a haze of marijuana forrad (though the driver did his best – 'Ladies and gentlemen, may I remind you that you may smoke only regular cigarettes; no pipes, no cigars, no marijuana'); second pilgrimage to Kennedy eternal flame at Arlington and then to that strangely powerful Iwo Jima monument with the bronze men and the real flag; high-camp-charm waiter service at the Capital Hilton ('My name is Clyde, and I shall be serving you throughout this meal').

No great news here. My aunt keeps pretty well. I've booked Christmas dinner for us and my next-door neighbours the Hamiltons at the Grosvenor Hotel where we were last year. Whittingehame has been having more visitations: another attempt at the front entrance, and the security buzzer put out of action; two cars broken into, and one driven away; a graffito inside the lift which had been painted out has just been carefully reinscribed as before (this has a really sinister effect). Marcella Evaristi is writer-in-residence at Glasgow University this year; I talked to her the other night at the Mitchell Theatre where her play *Commedia* has been getting good notice and good houses. I keep my ears open for news of jobs for returning professors but there's nothing you won't have seen in the public prints. There is much dissatisfaction with Norton-Smith at Dundee but whether that will lead to anything I don't know.

I hold myself in readiness for your 'questions about poems', any time. In schools, I'm told, 'Glasgow Green' is creeping up the popularity stakes, though it hasn't replaced 'In the Snack-bar'.

What else? Oh, I gave a reading, unpaid, in London in support of the miners. In a fortnight's time I have a four-day reading tour of the Netherlands with George MacBeth and Elaine Feinstein; will report on that in due course.

Love to Varvara and Elsie and all – | Eddie

After teaching at Glasgow University, Walker became Professor of English at the University of Waikato, New Zealand. He remained EM's literary executor, keeping a timeline of events towards a biography. Elsie is his New Zealand-born daughter. Walker's Japanese colleagues had translated two of 'Ten Theatre Poems' (*CP*: 360–62). Myra Parrot, EM's mother's sister, lived at 16 Whittingehame Court. Scots-Italian dramatist and screen-writer Marcella Evaristi had a distinguished career in Scotland before becoming mainly London-based.

Alasdair Gray, artist and novelist

13 January 1985

Dear Alasdair
    Happy new year and all that!
    I believe you know Ian Rolfe of the Hunterian Museum

(the Bearsden shark probably links the three of us)? He has asked me to ask you if you would be interested in a project that is coming up. He is arranging a big travelling exhibition of Scotland's paleontological digs and discoveries of recent years which is meant to make the general public aware of the interest and importance of such matters. It will include fossils, photographs of sites, reconstructions, drawings and paintings, as well as material relating to Stan Wood the 'fossil man' and his struggles for recognition and money, and material on the wider question of conservancy v. despoliation, cowboy specimen-hunters, etc. Ian wants someone who will write, from the facts and material supplied by him, one hundred captions/labels for the exhibition, each of maximum of 50 words, in a style which will be clear and attractive for the general public and at the same time if possible literately interesting, not po-faced as per museum glass-case practice but pointed and not without wit.

All this was on the phone to me, and he mentioned your name and asked if I thought you might be interested – I said I would find out. He also would need to know what sort of fee (aha) would be appropriate, if you did take up the suggestion.

If you didn't want to take it up yourself, do you think Donald Saunders would be interested (I am thinking of *The Glasgow Diary*)?

He needs to find someone fairly soon, so perhaps you could give me a ring once you've had a chance to think about it (and maybe ask Donald Saunders).

Fine cover that for the *Sonnets*! I liked it right away, as I'm sure Hamish would tell you. The idea of variation within a pattern was just right. Many thanks!

All the best | Eddie

Ian Rolfe*, Deputy Director of the Hunterian Museum in Glasgow University, was organising an exhibition of discoveries made in Bearsden near Glasgow by the gifted amateur paleontologist, Stan Wood. The exhibition included the Bearsden Shark fossil, which featured in 'Carboniferous' in *Sonnets from Scotland* (*CP*: 437), dedicated to Rolfe, and in EM's final collection, *Dreams and Other Nightmares* (2010: 46).

Ian Rolfe, museum administrator

Dear Ian

Many thanks for the design brief. I'm glad Donald
Saunders is going to take part in the operation. I don't know if
there's very much in the way of comments and suggestions that
I can make – it all seems an excellent scheme – but here are
one or two.

Among the Objectives, perhaps one could add a greater
public knowledge or awareness of the whole geological time-
scale and of the changes that have affected 'Scotland'. What
was Scotland physically like at the time of the Bearsden
sharks? Why Bearsden, Cowdenbeath, Bathgate? It's the sort
of thing that would lend itself to visual treatment. Under
Resources, I think video is very important in attracting public
interest, and (depending on finances obviously!) the more
imaginatively the 'educational' aspect of audiovisual aids can
be presented the better. (Cf. the Smithsonian in Washington.)
(Not that you have that sort of funding, I know!) In the
Outline Detail section you mention Hugh Miller (p.9); he is
such an interesting figure that possibly something more could
be made of him, even just starting from the *Crassigyrinus* skull?
Miller and Wood as non-academic but not anti-academic
finders?

The only other point I wondered about: any case for the
odd literary quotation being interspersed, if relevant? E.g. the
passage near the end of Shelley's *Prometheus Unbound*, rather
remarkable I suppose for its date (1819), where he imagines
the earth's paleontological secrets being revealed:

The anatomies of unknown wingèd things,
And fishes which were isles of living scale,
And serpents, bony chains, twisted around
The iron crags, or within heaps of dust
To which the tortuous strength of their last pangs
Had crushed the iron crags; and over these
The jaggèd alligator, and the might
Of earth-convulsing behemoth, which once

Were monarch beasts, and on the slimy shores,
And weed-overgrown continents of earth,
Increased and multiplied like summer worms
On an abandoned corpse, till the blue globe
Wrapped deluge round it like a cloak, and they
Yelled, gasped, and were abolished; or some god
Whose throne was in a comet, passed, and cried,
'Be not!'. And like my words they were no more.

(P.U. IV.303–318)

(Interesting that Shelley had a cometary as well as an
inundatory theory to account for the extinction of the species.)
    I'll be interested to hear how things go.

Best wishes | Eddie

Rolfe had sent the preliminary design brief for the travelling exhibition, *Mr Wood's Fossils*, asking for comment.

Emma Richardson, creative writing teacher, North Carolina

24 February 1985

Dear Mrs Richardson
    I enclose the results of the Poetry Contest, together with
the original poems. I found it a pleasant task to do the judging,
and I think the school is to be congratulated on the general
standard of writing achieved. The 'Honorable Mention' list
could probably been extended by one or two more. However,
I stuck to the rules! I thought 'A Caged Dove' stood out in its
recreation of the atmosphere of turn-of-the-century Dublin
and the state of mind of the young man; quite a difficult theme
to take up, and well presented despite a few roughnesses here
and there. 'November Graves' has a nice mixture of images
and folk wisdom (in Scotland, I've heard a similar belief,
except that it involves January, often our worst month, rather
than November). And the sharp pictures and sensations of
'Harvesters' are neatly generalized out into something broader
in the last two lines, which I thought was good.

I send my best wishes and encouragement to you and your creative writing class.

Yours sincerely | Edwin Morgan

Emma Richardson taught in Lee County Senior High School, on a faculty link with Campbell University in North Carolina. Her husband Tom Richardson was a visiting academic in the Department of Scottish Literature at Glasgow University and asked EM to judge the entries. North Carolina has cultural heritage connections with the Scottish Highlands.

Charles King, editor and educational advisor

1 March 1985

Dear Charlie
    Here are some names that occur to me – it's a fairly full list, simply to cover the field: obviously there's a better case for some rather than for others, and in fact I set the names down as they occurred most readily and strongly to me.

W.S. Graham, Liz Lochhead, Tom Leonard, Alastair Mackie, Burns Singer (if dead as well as living are included), Ian Hamilton Finlay, Alasdair Maclean, Alan Jackson, Douglas Dunn, D.M. Black, Stewart Conn, George MacBeth (if 'Scottish'), W. Price Turner (if 'Scottish'), Maurice Lindsay, Walter Perrie, Alan Bold, Andrew Greig, Kenneth White (if 'Scottish'), Iain Bamforth (if you want someone under thirty)

and of course the Gaels: Sorley MacLean, Derick Thomson, Angus Nicolson, Donald MacAuley; and George Campbell Hay (if dead as well as living included).

I would have loved to go up to Orkney with you in the car, but the festival organizers have already started making travel and accommodation arrangements, and I think that to be fair to them I should stick with that. But it would be good if you could make the visit there in any case, and I would look forward to seeing you. I expect to be there 21–24 June.

Do give me a ring if you are to be in Glasgow, and we can have a meal or a coffee or whatever suits. I was pleased to see Tom Leonard's dedication to you in his recent little book. Now you have your character, spelled out, no escape! Tom has a great loyalty and directness in these matters – admirable man. We are both involved next week in some readings in Glasgow in support of the miners – and in the present crumbling debacle of the strike they need all the support they can get.

Best regards to Vera and yourself | Eddie

King was Advisor in English for Grampian Regional Council. He edited an influential schools anthology, *Twelve Modern Scottish Poets* (1971), and now intended to extend that with *Twelve More Modern Scottish Poets* (1986). EM's trip to Orkney's St Magnus Festival is recalled in his letter of 22 June 2001. Tom Leonard's* dedication to King as 'music lover, socialist, optimist', and supporter of writers, appeared in his political pamphlet *Satires & Profanities* (1984), sponsored by the STUC with proceeds to the NUM.

Robert Crawford, *academic and poet*

4 March 1985

Dear Robert

I am delighted that the viva went well, and I hope you manage to place the thesis. I enjoyed the Eliot/MacDiarmid essay, which put a number of points of comparison that had not struck me before; I am a little surprised *Edinburgh Review* demurred, but I imagine some other magazine will certainly take it: *Essays in Criticism* sounds very possible, and *Agenda* seems to retain an interest in MacDiarmid, or there's *Cencrastus*.

The British Council have just informed me that the Struga festival dates have been put back to 4–10 August, and this leaves me free for Edinburgh Festival happenings (unless the dates are changed again – once bitten, etc.!); so if I can fit with any of your plans for readings, I'll be glad to.

Many thanks for the TS of S&S, which I have much enjoyed. It 'poaps and fizzes' indeed throughout. And it was an excellent touch to include the Flyting of C & H. Apiary assistants both, I think! I hope you will not be too disappointed if I say that I do, as you surmised I might have, have reservations about writing a blurb to appear on the book itself, but short of that, I'll be glad to recommend, buy, review, etc., and generally help the book along as well as I can. (It's a purely personal problem: Maurice Lindsay is an old acquaintance, and a blurb would make it seem I had gone out of my way to underwrite the attack on him – it would seem a bit below the belt. Impersonally, I can accept the attack, and I daresay he can too, but the blurb would personalize the issue, and I think it's best left between you and him. I'm sorry about this perhaps unnecessary solicitude.)

I look forward to seeing you during the first fortnight of April when you are in Glasgow. Give me a ring.

All best wishes | Eddie

Crawford's thesis was published as *The Savage and the City in the Work of T.S. Eliot* (1987). A previous reading arrangement had hit last-minute problems. The transcript of S&S was *Sterts and Stobies* (Obog, 1985), jointly authored with W.N. Herbert and including a 'flyting' between both poets in energetic Scots language. They rejected the 'establishment' of Scottish letters, represented by Maurice Lindsay*.

Peter Levi, poet and translator

22 March 1985

Dear Peter Levi

Here are my thoughts on the books of translation, which I have now been through.

One initial point: I notice that the rules of the competition state quite clearly that each book submitted must be 'by a single translator'. This, I'm afraid, makes it impossible for us to accept the Pasternak, the Bobrowski, and the Sabais. (I read them, of course, and I doubt if any of the three would in fact be on my short leet; the Pasternak lacks strength and bite, the Sabais is, as you remarked on the phone, rather slight despite one or two good poems, and the Bobrowski poems I found shadowy like the book's title, reclusive, downbeat, and lacking in structure and memorability.)

Of the two Romanians, Sorescu seems to me agreeable enough, but slight, sometimes trying to do what Holub does with much greater assurance and flair; and although I gave Ivanescu every chance, I found him monotonous and repetitive, almost unreadable at length, even if sprinkled with rather nice tantalizing Jamesian interiors here and there. The Leopold Staff is altogether too thin and weak to be a candidate. Great claims are made for the Södergran, and the translation is certainly a labour of love, but there is far too much 'I scatter the violets of memory on the golden pavements of dreams' and 'all flowers wait for the moon's kiss / in endless longing' – she has on this evidence no command of the abrupt creative strangeness of Emily to whom McDuff compares her; there are only a handful of really striking and convincing pieces, in my opinion. The Du Bellay, as you rightly said, is not Du Bellay. It was an enterprising idea to have a collection of 'The Regrets', and it reads easily enough, but Sisson's trouble is that he has no ear, and these stumbling lines with their bizarrely careless rhymes don't begin to meet Du Bellay's precise sense of sonnet structure; Sisson doesn't seem to understand that one can be conversational and lively <u>within</u> regular structure, as Du Bellay and his contemporaries showed. And Goethe, what are we to do with Goethe? I admire Hamburger greatly – he is one of our best translators – but I cannot see the little Goethe book as one of his best performances; the poems he has chosen are mostly those that need a light and sprightly touch, and sprightliness is not one of Hamburger's many virtues. The 'Roman Elegies' are a valiant attempt, but perhaps only Clough could do justice to them. In other poems, exigencies of metre and rhyme lead Hamburger into unwonted awkwardnesses. The La Ceppède is in some ways a remarkable feat, and one must give high marks to Bosley for dedication and determination; what I wonder is whether, despite the general rehabilitation of the French baroque poets, La Ceppède is quite worth it? He seems to me to be more doggedly dogmatic than truly imaginative. Still, worth considering. I think the Holub must be considered too, for the great interest of the poems, even if Osers lacks that final crispness one would like to see. The Quasimodo is highly useful and worthy in a general sort of way, but it is true (I have translated quite a bit of him myself and know his work fairly well) that Bevan is very cavalier as regards form, especially line-length, rhythm, metre. And he has some bad unnecessary inversions like 'where hovers / the image of the world', 'where rises / the gentle Ardenno hill'. My favourite for the prize, at the moment, is Hamburger's Huchel; here, the translator is perfectly on the wavelength of his chosen poet, he sticks well to the form, and Huchel's strong, dark, pungent, and to me very impressive poetry is well worth presenting and recommending to the English-speaking world.

It looks as if my short leet would be Huchel, La Ceppède, Quasimodo, Holub, and possibly Du Bellay and Södergran (the last two for their curiosity value?). I wonder how you feel about this?

Best wishes | Edwin Morgan

The European Poetry Translation Prize, in memory of the Romanian poet and translator Corneliu Popescu, was won by Michael Hamburger. His translation of Peter Huchel's *The Garden of Theophrastus and Other Poems* was co-published by Carcanet and the Raven Arts Press, Dublin.

Arthur Uphill, bibliographer

10 April 1985

Dear Mr Uphill
Thank you for your letter of the 9th. Ah the Insect Trust Gazette: those were the days when magazines really had titles! It was good of you to point out my Genet to Richard Coe.
Your query is one that has often come up, as you can

imagine. The brief answer is No, the Baudelaire book is by a namesake, a minor poet in America, older than myself and now deceased, around 1960 if I recall. Perhaps the most authoritative way of putting it is to quote to you from the introduction to Hamish Whyte's *Edwin Morgan: A Selected Bibliography 1950–1980* (Mitchell Library, Glasgow, 1980):

> It might be worth noting here that a book often attributed to Edwin Morgan, *Flowers [sic] of Evil: a life of Charles Baudelaire*, Sheed and Ward, 1944, is in fact by another Edwin Morgan. It was recently listed in a bookseller's catalogue thus: "Author's first book… Sheds an interesting light on his early religious development." Edwin Morgan himself said of it, "it has been attributed to me so often that I have almost come to believe I did write it."

On the last remark, it is curious that I could have written it, in the sense that I was fascinated by Baudelaire as a student taking French at Glasgow University before the war, and came to know his work well; though I would have been hard put to get the book written as I was in the army from 1940 to 1946. The fact that I am fairly knowledgeable about Baudelaire, and have reviewed books on him, no doubt helps to perpetuate the myth!

Since I once had a copy of my namesake's book but have now lost it, I would very much like to buy your copy, if you would let me know the price and if this is agreeable to you.

Yours sincerely | Edwin Morgan

Cataloguing for Bertram Rota Booksellers, London, Uphill had queried a confusion of initials in an old British Library catalogue (Edwin D. and Edwin G.). The firm sold EM the book for a nominal £5.

T.C. Swartz, space travel promoter

16 February 1986

Dear Mr Swartz

Thank you for your letter and enclosures of 29 January.

May I first of all express the sense of shock, and sympathy for the bereaved families, which I felt after the recent Challenger disaster. I am glad nevertheless that the Shuttle programme is to continue despite this setback; I am sure that was the right decision. I have certainly no desire to withdraw from your own Project Space Voyage, and although it is obviously too early for you to make any forecasts about postponed expedition dates, I have no doubt you will send out information as and when it becomes available.

I enclose signed copy of the Conditions form as requested.

Yours sincerely | Edwin Morgan

Swartz was President of Society Expeditions Space Travel Company, organising the first public access programme to space. He had written in the wake of the Space Shuttle *Challenger* disaster of 28 January 1986.

Michael Schmidt, publisher, poet and critic

8 August 1986

Dear Michael

Catching up with correspondence (having been in Brighton, Aberdeen, etc.), I must thank you very much for the novel which I look forward to reading and which I see has an admirable conciseness, unlike some blowzy South American fictions one could name!

I am pleased that my monster will swim in the London Underground. As you say, £25 is not exactly a monstrous reward, but it's good publicity. I look forward to receiving my copies of the poster, and if I could have 20, that would be good, and allow me to send some to interested parties.

As far as I know I shall be free next August/September for the Waterloo poetry-burst and would certainly be glad to take part in subsequent peregrinations, All The Way/With Poetray. I must keep myself in training.

Yes, let us indeed think about the next book. It should probably include the poems in *Sonnets from Scotland* and *From the Video Box*, Mariscat permitting, which I'm sure they will, plus uncollected poems since the *Selected*. If there were two sonnets to the page, this at the moment would I reckon amount to around 75 pages altogether. It might of course be more – one hopes, with hands firmly on the wooden table – by the time you started to print. When would you think the contents ought to be finalized?

All best wishes to Claire and the family | and to yourself – |
    Eddie

Schmidt had sent EM a copy of his novel, *The Colonist* (1983), together with news that Poems on the Underground wanted to use 'The Loch Ness Monster's Song'. A poetry jamboree was being organised by Faber, beginning with a reading in Waterloo Station then extended across the UK. The next collection would become *Themes on a Variation* (1988).

Stephen Fox, academic

24 December 1986

Dear Dr Fox

Edinburgh University Press passed on your letter of 12 December. You are very welcome to use my poem 'Message Clear' in your article.

The poem was written on 16 August 1965 and was printed in the *Times Literary Supplement* on 13 January 1966 (followed by a curious correspondence, which you might like to look up – it is reprinted in Geoffrey Summerfield's anthology *Worlds* (Penguin, 1974)). It is one of a group of six similarly structured poems which were published as *Emergent Poems* in a pamphlet in 1967 (in each, the text of the poem 'emerged' from or was generated by the letters in the words of a famous quotation). Although I was interested in the potential of computers at the time, and wrote some simulated computer poems, 'Message Clear' had no computer aid and was written as an ordinary poem. In fact, it was written with a great deal of emotion, very quickly, after I had been visiting my father in hospital. He had terminal cancer, and I had been much distressed by what I saw of him. He died in November. I would not describe myself as a believer, but I had a traditional Scottish Presbyterian upbringing (both church and Sunday School every Sunday, much learning of the Bible by heart, etc.) and my feelings about an imminent death quite simply and surprisingly took the form of a monologue spoken by Christ on the cross. There is of course a tension between the title and the text. I did not want the 'message' to be 'clear', except that perhaps eventually it may become so. The whole statement of the poem is conditional, 'if...' And the reader must struggle towards the final line.

I hope these brief comments may be of some help to you.

With best wishes | Yours sincerely | Edwin Morgan

Writing an article on methods of teaching poetry at university level, Fox wanted to use the presentational difficulties of 'Message Clear' (*CP*: 159) as an example, and asked for additional information on its creation. The *TLS* correspondence is in *Worlds*: 275–77.

Charlotte Ronn, advertising executive

23 January 1987

Dear Ms Ronn
    Thank you for your letter and enclosed information about the Scottish edition of Trivial Pursuit. It was all quite helpful and stimulating. I thought it would be useful to take up the Burns idea, and I enclose a 10-verse poem which starts off as a parody of Burns's 'To a Haggis' – a haggis being part of your own proceedings at the launch. It is written in the 'Burns stanza', and the Scots is not, I hope, too difficult. I have tried to

cover the six categories. The local references would all, I think, be generally known in Scotland (even the Cardinal Folly, a large and impressive disco in a listed church in Glasgow, is reasonably famous). (The punk piper really exists; he played in the streets – and played well too – during the last Edinburgh Festival; he was much photographed.) I shall be interested to hear what you think of the piece.

Yours sincerely | Edwin Morgan

Ronn was an advertising executive, organising the launch of a Scottish version of the board game Trivial Pursuit. The punk piper, Angus McNiven, was tracked down and appeared at the launch alongside EM.

TRIVIAL PURSUIT CROSSES THE BORDER

Fair faw your honest sonsy dice,
Chieftain o board games, slee and wyce,
For noo auld Scotia in a trice
    Has fund ye oot,
And thinks baith Hell and Paradise
    Trivial Pursuit.

His broo is furrowed like the sea,
He grins, he fidgets, rows his ee,
Cracks his knuckles, scarts his knee
    And cries: 'Nae doot
I'm mad, but thon's my cup o tea,
    Trivial Pursuit!

Is it ferry or brig tae the Black Isle?
And hoo lang is the lang Scots mile?
Kin ye gae tae Freuchie? It's no my style.
    I'll sail fae Bute,
Wi Cleopatra on the Nile
    In Trivial Pursuit.

I'll hae a jog wi Gregory's girl,
I'll busk a punk piper's skirl,

I'll gie the Cardinal Folly a whirl
    And, what a hoot,
Watch Connolly play Havergal
    At Trivial Pursuit.

I'll dauner up then tae Loch Ness, it
Seems the monsters no depressit.
Nemo me impune lacessit
    Said Wallace to't.
Hunting the English, ye maun confess it
    's nae Trivial Pursuit.

I'll skelp auld Tam o Shanter's mare,
I'll gie a bridie tae Burke and Hare,
I'll kick Peter Pan richt doon the stair
    Wi my left foot,
And wi my richt gie *The Kingis Quair*
    Trivial Pursuit.

I'll steam a stamp wi James Watt's kettle,
See mouldy Fleming beat the Dettol,
Watch Tar McAdam shaw his mettle
    For wheel and boot,
Whaur thistles gie the Hielan nettle
    Trivial Pursuit.

And think o aw the caber-tossers
In the land o Lobey Dossers,
The moothie-men and squeeze-boax jossers,
    Fiddle and flute,
Wi Irn-Bru biled doon fae hawsers –
    Trivial Pursuit.

Sae welcome aw my merry freens,
The haggis is burstin at the seams,
Whisky skinkles its gowden streams;
    Enjoy the fruit
O' frenzy and the teasin o the teams:
    Trivial Pursuit.

Rattle your dice and read your caird;
They've got new questions by the yaird
Wad whummle baith John Logie Baird
    And Tammy Troot.
Mak for the hub and dinna be scared
    O' Trivial Pursuit.'

Peter Day, student

21 March 1987

Dear Mr Day
    Many thanks for your letter and for the effective
permutations of your poem, which I enjoyed. Let's see if I can
give at least a brief sort of answer to some of the questions
you raise. (And yes, your digression on mothers was true
in my case too, a long time ago mind you!) I still feel well
disposed towards the Christmas Card and the Pomander,
both of which (especially the first) have been reprinted a
good deal in anthologies, and both of which I include in my
poetry-readings, so there has really been no loss of continuity,
and they are still 'present' to me, even if they belong to a
certain period of my writing. On Peter Finch's point about
recollection of emotion versus simple material: this is also
very much Finlay's view, the idea that concrete ought to be
anti-expressionist and non-confessional, but I'm not at all sure
that this is the whole story, in fact my own 'Message Clear',
though structurally controlled, was written under a strongly
emotional impulse (after a visit to my father, terminally ill
with cancer, in hospital). In any case, as I'm sure you'll have
discovered there is no universally agreed definition of concrete,
and battles have been fought over the different manifestations
of it. I like Houédard's typed designs (I devised the word
typestracts for them, which Dom Silvester accepted and tried
to make current) and I wouldn't agree with the view that
there's nothing in them but technique and ingenuity; some of
them, admittedly, do go nearer 'art' than 'poetry'. I think he is
exploring space, and dimensions, and is far from being stuck at
the 'pretty picture' phase. On your last point, it is sometimes a

matter of using concrete technique at a particular moment for an effect which could not be gained any other way, as in 'The New Divan' No.92; but I think also it shows in a liking for clearcut linguistic and visual effects (in the imagery, say) and possibly too in certain numerological dispositions of lines or stanzas where the desire is to let the structuring be visible (as, in a more specialized sense, it has to be in concrete proper).

That's a real block of a paragraph up there – I hope you can find your way in it! Do feel free to write whenever you want. And best of luck with the maggie's opium, mariner's oakum, what I mean is, magnum opus.

Best wishes | Edwin Morgan

A final-year student at Crewe and Alsager College, Day's dissertation was on 'Concrete Poetry: Its History and its Present'. The reference to mothers was that 'every artist seems to have a mother, who tells them to stop wasting their time and settle down to something more serious'. Peter Finch's visual poetry focused on language as material rather than expression.

T.C. Swartz, space travel promoter

9 April 1987

Dear Mr Swartz
               PROJECT SPACE VOYAGE

I am sorry that because of changed circumstances I have to cancel my confirmed reservation (Priority No.102) for Project Space voyage. Would you please therefore return my fully refundable $5000 escrowed deposit. I enclose the documents and certificates as required by the cancellation conditions.

Yours sincerely | Edwin Morgan

EM was booked as passenger 102 on flight 6, planned for 22 November 1992. He would have been 72 on that date. What caused him to cancel his reservation is unclear.

Alan Riach, academic and poet

20 April 1987

Dear Alan

Well I finished that extraordinary Symmes book and have now passed it on to Dr McCarey from whom you will doubtless receive a 'second opinion'. I must admit I skipped here and there, finding the ubiquitous triple dotting… extremely irritating… and the disconnectedness that might be a virtue in poetry… somewhat worrying in a prose story. I think I was also a mite disappointed that the title promised more than ever appeared; perhaps I was misled by Verne/Poe/ERBurroughs expectations; the hole, in fact, seemed to be fairly peripheral as holes go. Like your father, I enjoyed the 'sea' part of it best, especially such longish passages as escaped the plague of dots. The great virtue of the book is in <u>what</u> it brings together; you're forced to think and to rethink. Its weakness, no it's not exactly a weakness, its problem for most readers I imagine is simply its density, and the difficulty of perceiving a goal. Anyhow I'm very grateful to you for shooting it across my bows.

I've been giving readings in Bolton, Wigan, and Leigh. Yes, Wigan Pier yet, now done up for tourists. In Bolton I saw Whitman's canary (whaur's yer Flaubert's parrot noo?) in its little glass dome in the public library, a touching object. Towards the end of Whitman's life a group of mainly working-class admirers in Bolton sent emissaries to talk to him in America, and he was greatly taken by the 'staunch tender fellows' and kept writing to them to the end. When his canary died it was stuffed and sent to them as a mark of gratitude. There's something wonderful about this – almost absurd – yet moving and strange. But I do wish the toon cooncillors would give it a new dome, after a century the glass is badly cracked.

I liked your Berlin story. As election fever, a cloud no bigger than Grendel's hand, begins to fizz, not that there is any date yet, though people seem to think June likely, Alan Brownjohn of the Poetry Society in London is collecting poets' voting intentions, plus reasons for choice; I said SNP since I saw

Scotland as 'a frustrated republic and would like to help it to
become a real one.' It is a nice question whether, once we all
have EEC passports instead of British ones, it will be easier or
harder to write the 'Scottish' of your story?

Do you have some prospects of staying on down there,
or shall we expect to see you in June or July? In May I have
a couple of readings in Manchester and will also take the
opportunity to discuss my next Carcanet book with Michael
Schmidt, which he projects for 1988. I think the only other
bit of immediate news is that one Dan Sweigert, of Batavia
(Illinois, not Indonesia) is busy setting my 'Message Clear'
to piano roll music (for player pianos). Letters become holes
in rolls. Symmes Roll, and a vicus of recirculation from the
northern periphery –

All the best to you | Eddie

Having completed a PhD on Hugh MacDiarmid* at Glasgow Univer-
sity, Riach was now a research fellow in the University of Waikato. He
had reviewed *Symmes Hole* by Ian Wedde (1986) in the New Zealand
journal *Landfall* 160. In Germany, Riach's nationality ('Scottish') was
punctiliously rewritten as 'English' by a customs officer.

Kenilworth School pupils
(handwritten)

18–11–1987

Dear Tanya, Jenny, and Sarah
     Thank you for your questions!
     In the Instamatic Poems, I was writing from newspaper
stories, not photographs. I found it interesting to recreate these
events <u>as if</u> someone had been there taking quick shots with an
Instamatic camera. I wanted to choose some moment where I
could 'freeze' the story, for dramatic effect, without giving any
buildup or explanations.
     'Newmarket' is what people would call a 'sound-poem',
where the subject is shown very directly and immediately
through the sounds: here, a mixture of horse plus the jockey's

encouraging sounds to his mount – and of course he wins the race at the end, 'That's it!' Newmarket in a nutshell!

With best wishes | Edwin Morgan

Dear Kirsty, Adam and Andrew
Well, I shall try to deal with some of your problems, if I can!
(1) Yes, the man in the German poem is already dead. It was taken from a newspaper report. The idea was to make the test more realistic and convincing.
(2) What inspired me to write poetry is very hard to say. I started when I was 11 or 12, wrote quite a lot at school. I loved writing, words, language, rhythm. It seemed natural to me to want to put experiences, feelings, stories, into rhythmical form. So there must be something that is inborn or at least shows itself very early. But the actual craft of writing is a slower and more gradual process which takes patience and hard work.
(3) I have always felt that poetry, in common with the other arts, should be willing to experiment, to try new means of expression. The 20th century has seen many experiments with language and form, and I react sympathetically to innovation, while not giving up more traditional methods.

I hope you have plenty of time for your hobbies as well as for the dread exams!

Yours sincerely | Edwin Morgan

These are just two examples of more than half a dozen handwritten responses to the same class. The Fifth Form pupils had written group letters asking questions about poems they had studied from Geoffrey Summerfield's* *Worlds* anthology.

Hamish Whyte, publisher and poet

28-11-1987

Hamish

Here's another Kassák poem, untitled, 1921, for your interest. It's a sort of early concrete; he called this kind of poem a képköltemény, a picture-poem, and it has some links with his work as an artist (Constructivist avant-garde, 1920s especially). Handwritten – how do you translate hand-writing? I've kept (kép-d) very close. Kassák's early years were poor and often starving, like József's. I find this poem, avant-garde or not, a moving document. Translation unpublished so far.

I was checking the dates of the other poem, which you asked about. It was published 1922, and one critic I've read says it was written during his Vienna exile, around 1919–1922; but I imagine he must have been working on it before that, sometime nearer the epic trek to Paris in 1909 which is its subject.

Eddie

Whyte, EM's Scottish publisher, was also his bibliographer. EM admired Lajos Kassák (1887–1967), a radical avant-garde Hungarian poet, painter, designer and editor, and worked intensively on his poetry in the summer of 1975. The handwritten poem is in *CT*: 419–22. The other poem is probably 'The Horse Dies the Birds Fly Away', his translation being published in *New Hungarian Quarterly* Vol. 28, No. 106.

Colin Hamilton, book dealer and friend

10 January 1988

Dear Colin

It's quite difficult to know just what would be right for Bill Gibb's memorial service. The enclosed photocopies are the first suggestions that come to mind – I don't know whether Irene Worth will find any of them suitable. The two Muir poems are lyrical and positive, and I like 'The Bird' especially, but they may be felt to be not very relevant. Volpone's wooing of Celia is also lyrical in its way but is a sort of bizarre extravaganza of how they would keep dressing and re-dressing as they act out Volpone's imaginative fantasies. The description of how Anna Livia Plurabelle was dressed in *Finnegans Wake* is marvellous to read aloud; it is certainly comic, but it is so lyrical and inventive that I don't think the comedy need be a bar, within the memorial occasion. Ben Jonson, though born in London, was of Scottish descent; and Joyce was at least an Irishman! I can see I have given you problems. If I come up with any other ideas I shall be in touch.

Marble floors sound very cool and pleasant; one thinks of courtyards, fountains, arches… but perhaps I am wrong! Talking of houses; you'll be interested to know I have sold my timeshare week for £2500, which is not at all bad. I remember you said I should just come down to £2000 to be shot of it, and I would have done so if a buyer in Essex hadn't come up with the higher figure. Having waited so long to sell, I shall probably now have withdrawal symptoms, and dream about that helicopter pad.

Do thank Kulgin for the Stromness photographs. I love these camera gatherings. You must send some from Kerala.

All best wishes as ever | Eddie

Hamilton had asked EM to suggest texts suitable for a memorial reading for the Scottish fashion designer, Bill Gibb, prominent in the late 1960s and 1970s. The American actress Irene Worth was to read, a friend of Hamilton and Kulgin Duval*. The building materials relate to the house that Hamilton and Duval were having built in Kerala.

Robyn Marsack, editor

9 February 1988

Dear Robyn Marsack
Thank you for your letter of the 3rd. In answer to your queries: I think it was decided to have no title for the first

section of uncollected poems, but to have the year date of each poem in brackets after its title in the list of contents.

'A Celebration' and 'The Grey Man' were to be omitted, but 'Apple Girl' is still in.

I enclose copies of the *Newspoems* for you to cannibalize. We didn't in fact discuss how these were to be reproduced, but I agree that your typesetter should set the titles, and the printer find the best way of reproducing the actual text – which has to be reproduced as it is, with its variations and imperfections, since that was the point of the exercise, as my explanatory note (I hope you have that?) describes. I'm unsure about the dating, but I think the best method might be to remove the dates from the poems and have them in the list of contents after each title, as in the first section. What do you think? NB the two 'New English Riddles' will still require the 'answer' to be printed upside-down at the bottom of the poem.

The *Video Box* poems could well be run on, with a four-line space between each numbered poem as you suggest. I think Michael envisaged the Sonnets as two to the page, but if there is enough space available I would certainly prefer one a page.

I phoned Mary Lockhart and confirmed the new date of Friday 13 May with her.

It would be good if we could meet sometime to discuss some of the points about the book and have the actual material in front of us. I shall phone you tonight and see if we can arrange something.

Best wishes | Edwin Morgan

Marsack had joined Carcanet after postgraduate work in Oxford and the United States. She would become Director of the Scottish Poetry Library in 2000. Based in Glasgow, she worked closely with EM on *Collected Poems* (1990), referred to here, and *Collected Translations* (1996). Mary Lockhart was organising readings at Glasgow's Mayfest, where *Themes on a Variation* (1998) would be launched in the People's Palace on Glasgow Green.

Anna Ortolani, British Council, Naples

24 May 1988

Dear Anna

I arrived back safely with no problems en route. I am now busy sorting out the mail that has piled up even after four days! My best thanks to you for that horribly early start on Sunday morning, and for our most enjoyable visit to the National Museum – a really impressive collection which I wouldn't have wanted to miss.

You will remember that we talked in the car about the possibility of another visitor, and I mentioned the name of Liz Lochhead. I think she would be an excellent choice, as she is a good poet and playwright and a warm and outgoing person who would enjoy talking to people concerned with any kind of public performance – poetry, cabaret, theatre. Her address is 11 Kersland Street, Glasgow G12. Her main books are *Dreaming Frankenstein and Collected Poems*; *True Confessions and New Clichés*; and *Tartuffe: A Translation into Scots from Molière*. (All published by Polygon, Edinburgh.)

I shall wait with interest to see how Cinquevalli sounds in Italian!

With all good wishes | Edwin Morgan

25 May 1988

Dear Anna

I meant to ask, when I wrote to you yesterday, whether by any chance you had discovered in your car the Naples guidebook and postcards which you'll remember I bought at the National Museum on Saturday? They were not in my luggage, and I have a feeling that I left them either in your car or (on Saturday afternoon) in Luciana Gilli's car. Please do not give yourself a lot of trouble, but if you could check I would be obliged. If there is no trace of the Naples guidebook (the postcards don't matter) I wonder if sometime you could

send me another copy, and I could send you a book in return.
I tried without success to get a guidebook here before I left,
and I would like very much to have one. Sorry about all
this!

Best regards | Edwin Morgan

The British Council in Naples invited EM to take part in their 'Living
Writers' series, coinciding with a major exhibition on Giacomo
Leopardi (1798–1837), whose poems he had translated into English
and Scots (*CT*: 229–44, 326–30). Anna Ortolani had organised a
lively two-day visit there, with opportunities for trips to Pompeii
and the National Museum.

Michael Schmidt, publisher, poet and critic

15 December 1988

Dear Michael
    I caught my train and got back home pretty well on time.
Thanks for very agreeable meeting, talk, lasagne, and projection
of prospects. As soon as I can disentangle myself from seasonal
disruptions I shall get the essays together and let you see
what the collection looks like. In the meantime I enclose nine
double-page spreads from the Scrapbooks – all I was able to
photograph before the books went into Glasgow University
Library – in order to give you an idea of the publishing
possibilities/problems. As you will see, colour would really be
required; black and white would miss many of the effects. The
books are a mixture of autobiography, documentary, and art.
I do not think there is anything quite like them, and I regard
them as very much part of my 'works' (which you are going
to publish some day in several volumes, are you not!). I even
managed to keep them going, though on a reduced scale, when
I was in the army during the war, so that there is no break
from 1931 to 1966. There are 16 scrapbooks, totalling just over
3600 pages. They contain, inter alia, abstract paintings made in
my early teens, wartime photographs taken in the Middle East,
and the two halves of a pound note I split to show that it could

be done. Have I whetted your appetite? Is the proposition, as they say, viable?

Best as ever | Eddie

EM had tried since the 1950s to interest publishers in his voluminous scrapbooks. Their scope, and mixture of surrealistic collage and reportage, and implications for copyright and production costs, had made this an unappealing proposition. Schmidt suggested working on the wartime materials, which are more limited, but nothing came of this. The other 'collection' mentioned became *Crossing the Border: Essays on Scottish Literature* (1990).

Christopher Whyte, poet, novelist and academic

17 June 1989

Dear Christopher

Thank you very much for the tape and transcript. I think you have done a tremendous job. The only mistake I have come across is 'bar room' for 'barrack-room' on the second p.1, two lines from the bottom. My first thought is that it reads well and that there's nothing I specifically at the moment want to take out (unless the rather feeble reference to Shakespeare's sonnets at the very end). Of course there are things that ought to be conflated with it from the second interview (like the whereabouts of the Oak and the Good Companions, etc.), and I agree with you that we should work on the first two interviews rather than the third. I am not sure that a huge amount of editing will be required, apart from the little bits of conflation, and unless for reasons of space. The point of the operation was that it should be spontaneous and truthful, and we don't want to lose that flow if we can help it. I owe it to you that I found it so easy to talk about things I hadn't talked about in that way before. It was strangely liberating, once I had made the decision to do it. I shall be seeing Hamish Whyte on the 21st and shall give him a copy before then so that we can discuss it. I've no doubt he will let you know his ideas about the editing.

I'm glad you felt the Glasgow interview went well – let's hope something emerges.

I enclose a recent poem that might interest you.

Another Italian meal one of these days? – I hope so!

All good wishes | Eddie

Whyte, a young academic and poet in English and Gaelic, interviewed EM for Hamish Whyte's* *Nothing Not Giving Messages* (1990), marking the poet's seventieth birthday. The interviews focused on his life as a gay person and the edited transcripts would mark his 'coming out'. The Oak and the Good Companions were 1950s gay bars in Glasgow. Whyte, who had been lecturing in Rome and Edinburgh, had applied for a post in Glasgow University's Department of Scottish Literature.

1990s

(aged 70–79)

Morgan's 1990s were a very public decade. The poet was much in demand, much in the public eye, writing for the stage and appearing on it, finding new creative partnerships and revisiting former ones. The decade began with publication of his *Collected Poems*, and there was also a critical study, *About Edwin Morgan*, edited by Robert Crawford and Hamish Whyte with chapters by Iain Crichton Smith and Douglas Dunn from the older generation, and by Crawford, W.N. Herbert and Peter McCarey from the new generation of poets. An accompanying volume, *Nothing Not Giving Messages: Reflections on Work and Life*, was Hamish Whyte's own selection from interviews, lectures, broadcasts and statements given by Morgan over the previous thirty years.

This last featured the interview with Christopher Whyte mentioned in the letter of June 1989, in which the poet came out at the age of 70. Today, such an act would seem belated in the extreme, but is understandable for one of his time and background – homosexuality was not decriminalised in Scotland until 1980. Readings of his love poems by a generation of teachers and pupils were hastily revised in view of this new identity, and Morgan showed his solidarity as a gay poet by engaging in readings, conferences and publications themed around sexual identity. At the same time he became even more chameleon-like in the poetic personae he adopted, voicing demons, spermatozoa and various other forms of wildlife.

The *Collected Translations* of 1996 stands among his finest achievements and, as he later argued, is really a *Selected* from a much wider body of work. He continued to publish new poems and translations with Carcanet and Mariscat throughout the decade as well as fulfilling a schedule of public commitments which would exhaust a much younger man. Translating Rostand's *Cyrano de Bergerac*, that ventriloquial classic, into Glaswegian Scots created an immediate and perhaps also a longer-lasting impact. In one sense it enabled him to clinch the case he had been making since the 1950s for the vitality, flexibility and relevance of urban Scots as a creative medium. In another, it encouraged him to try an even more radical approach in his version of Racine's classical tragedy, *Phèdre*, where Morgan without irony has the ruling classes speak not in English but in the previously despised Scots language of the margins. This was not only an artistic statement but a political one.

His combination of local and international interests continued the innovations begun in the 1960s. In a sense, he could revisit that decade by proxy with a fresh sense of confidence in a sympathetic audience led by a new generation of artists. These included Ian Hamilton Finlay's son Alec (or Eck), a poet and publisher of the avant-garde, musicians such as Tommy Smith, and theatre practitioners from companies large and small. Letters of this period show a flourishing interest in performance and a continuing generosity towards younger poets, alongside an increased combativeness towards more conservative voices in society.

Always looking to the future but with an undiminished curiosity about the past, Morgan was a fitting figurehead for Scotland's cultural rebirth, and these years show a renewed energy for social engagement. He was made the inaugural Poet Laureate of Glasgow in 1998. The last letter in this selection, to Alec Finlay, begins with a list of his garlanded achievements, continues with an invocation of love and its 'passionate abandon' (to which, as some letters show, Morgan was still prone), and ends with the admission that he has been diagnosed with cancer – with the defiant insistence that 'at least I can still write!'.

Book and Pamphlet Publications

Collected Poems. Manchester: Carcanet Press, 1990; paperback edition 1996.

Crossing the Border: Essays on Scottish Literature. Manchester: Carcanet Press, 1990.

Hold Hands Among the Atoms. Glasgow: Mariscat Press, 1991.

Edmond Rostand's Cyrano de Bergerac. A new verse translation by Edwin Morgan. Manchester: Carcanet Press, 1992.

PALABRARmas / WURDWAPPINschaw by Cecilia Vicuña. Translated by Edwin Morgan. Edinburgh: Morning Star Publications, 1994.

Sweeping out the Dark. Manchester: Carcanet Press, 1994.

Dragon Train: An Escap(ad)e, by Velimir Khlebnikov. Translated by Edwin Morgan. Edinburgh: Morning Star Publications, 1995.

Collected Translations. Manchester: Carcanet Press, 1996.

The Maker on High by St Columba. Translated by Edwin Morgan. Glasgow: Mariscat Press, 1997.

Virtual and Other Realities. Manchester: Carcanet Press, 1997.

Christopher Marlowe's Doctor Faustus in a new version by Edwin Morgan. Edinburgh: Canongate, 1999.

Demon. Glasgow: Mariscat Press, 1999.

Iain Bamforth, poet, doctor and critic

19 Whittingehame Court
1 October 1990

Dear Iain

I was really pleased – though you might not think so
since it has taken me five months to reply! – to receive your
letter of birthday wishes and to have your news. The main
celebration was a very agreeable though very hot afternoon on
the Renfrew Ferry which has been glassed over and moored
at the Jamaica Bridge to be used as a venue for all sorts of
functions. Buffet, bar, Scottish poets reading, plus Roy Fisher
from England. But what with interviews and other sorts of
media exposure, the 'birthday' seemed to go on for weeks, and
I was glad during the summer to retreat into a spate of writing,
finishing a collection of seventy poems which will probably be
published next year, not by Carcanet who have plenty on their
hands with the *Collected Poems* due to appear shortly, but with
Mariscat here in Glasgow.

Your April letter was of course from Germany (from 'West'
Germany, an entity that has only one more day to live) but you
mentioned the possibility of a move to the Australian outback
for a year (certainly a year's <u>experience</u>, I would imagine,
though maybe my image of planes, radio-telephones and wild
dingo bites is out of date). I got your address from Robert
Crawford, who I gather is keen to keep open the links his
magazine *Verse* already has with Les Murray and the down-
under. I've seen your name at various times above perceptive
reviews, but I always wondered whether your medical labours
would leave you time and energy to develop poetry (Williams,
I know, and there are other examples, but still…). I was
interested by what you said in your letter about moving into
a 'more accessible, less neo-Calvinistic' poetic writing and
away from (I agree) a too tight and restricting Hillism. I
look forward to seeing the results of what you evidently feel
to be some kind of liberation. The matter of Scotland too,
even from New South Wales, will be hard to avoid. It is a
very strange moment, when almost everyone believes some
constitutional and/or other change is standing at the door,

and necessarily so, yet a combination of nervous and nerveless hands seems unable to grasp the knob and open up. It is as if it was Frankenstein's monster on the other side. Still. 1991 or 1992 will surely force hands. By that time you may be back among us! I was moved by your letter, and am extremely glad that we have not lost touch. It would be good to hear from you sometime about life in Broken Hill.

With all best wishes to your wife and son and to yourself | Eddie

After a period as a GP in South West Scotland, Bamforth worked in the American Hospital in Paris, met his German wife there, lived in Germany and now had a year's post as Medical Officer in Broken Hill, New South Wales. The seventy poems were published as *Hold Hands Among the Atoms* (1991). 'Hillism' refers to the style of Geoffrey Hill.

Donny O'Rourke, poet and editor
(handwritten)

4–10–1990

Dear Donny

You may be interested to know that I've had a lot of reaction to our programme, all of it favourable, though one or two thought my life 'fairly whizzed past' and would have liked a longer programme. On the phone to my milkman, I got his wife instead, and she said 'Are you the Morgan that was on TV?' – she thought it was great. A number of, shall we say, figures from the past phoned up – TV in the role of re-establisher of severed connections. I thought it worked very well. The Charing Cross flyover poem was a bit strained, but that was inevitable. It's a pity there was no time to comment on some of the still photographs (e.g. the kilt/USSR), and in the scrapbook scene we rather lost the point about the gay 'pin-ups' (I remember you used the word). I was particularly pleased with the desert war scenes, and it was a brilliant shot to move from my Cosgrove poem to the soldier with the cigarette – oddly enough he was not unlike Cosgrove, with that gallus quality which has always attracted me. The darkened room/'Dear man...' scene is the one that sticks in my mind for atmosphere. The Botanic Gardens, as a setting, seemed lacking in point. Perhaps we could have had more of the city – and the stars!

My best thanks for your devotion in the filming. Let us have a meal sometime (and it's my turn). Give me a ring when you have a moment.

All the best | Eddie

O'Rourke was Head of Arts and Documentaries at Scottish Television. Cosgrove, a fellow soldier during EM's time in Lebanon, is recalled in 'The New Divan' (*CP*: 295–330), and appears in EM's scrapbooks (see 15 December 1988) used in the film. 'Dear man, my love goes out in waves' (*CP*: 512–13) was published in *Themes on a Variation* (1988).

Sam Gilliland, poet and translator

13 September 1991

Dear Sam
You are quite right about Cernuda and his Glasgow poem. I am enclosing a version of it I had in my *Rites of Passage* book, for your interest. It certainly suggests he found the city a fairly grim northern place after Seville, though the poem is wonderfully atmospheric. The translation was included in a play about Cernuda which was put on by Strathclyde students in 1988 and which I saw; the play suggested that although unhappy in Glasgow he was not devoid of solace (like Lorca he was homosexual). I did not meet him at Glasgow University – he arrived not long before I was called up and he had gone when I came back after the end of the war. I was much interested by your account of Sá-Carneiro, and it would be very good if you could manage to bring out a collection of translations, as he is simply not known here but by all accounts ought to be – especially as Pessoa's name has gradually made its way, through translations, in recent years.

You should certainly try the SAC again, particularly as they are (with 1992 looming up) about to be more concerned to encourage European translation by and of Scottish writers. Do give my name as a referee if you think it would help, and if you can let me see the portfolio you mention, this would give me a better overall picture of what you have been doing. I sympathize with what you say about isolation: a degree of it is necessary if we are to write at all, or with any depth of thinking and feeling that really is our own, yet it can become as you say a 'ligature' – feelers and lifelines and messages have to be sent out – even Hopkins had Bridges! To go back to the SAC; I don't know when the next batch of applications for bursaries is due, but I think it might be a propitious time to have another go, especially if you can claim interest from a publisher in what you propose to work on.

Yours aye | Eddie

Gilliland was working on a collection, *After Lorca*. EM had commented on Lorca, and on Luis Cernuda (1902–63) who, after Lorca's assassination, went into exile, working briefly at Glasgow University. His 'Cementerio de la ciudad' became 'A Glasgow Cemetery' (*CT*: 268). Gilliland also translated Mário de Sá-Carneiro, who in 1916 committed suicide aged 26, while planning with Pessoa a third issue of *Orpheu*, a journal of Portugese modernism.

Gael Turnbull, poet and doctor

To Gael Turnbull   27 January 1992

Even as we remember how Salomon August Andrée
Ascended with two companions in a hot-air balloon
From the frozen fastnesses of north-west Sweden
And hovered for three days over the crumbling floes
In his search for the North Pole,
Until the gas gave out, and he crashed to the ice,
Lingering to write his log
In unimaginable cold and hunger,
All three bodies being found well preserved in 1930

By a Norwegian skipper, and the diaries recovered
To plot that *folie de grandeur*,
Or too as we recall the Scotsman Alexander Mackenzie
Canougrie [*sic*]
Who essaying a similar adventure in 1929
Rose in his hot-air envelope from Spitzbergen
(Where he had obtained compacted peat
Sufficient to fuel him to the polar *Schlusspunkt*)
But overpowered by fumes he lost consciousness
And was rescued clinging to a bubble of wretched wreckage
Not many miles from the great desolate island
Of his taking off, asserting to the disbelief of many
He had hazardously been to the Pole and back,
So it is we know
Every emission of hot air is a flatulent *hubris*
Like the pervasive but vapid guff of a Ramsay MacDonald
Trying in vain to mount above his own mediocrity,
Or like the 'baseless fabric' of a Neil Gunn vision which

    (transcribed from a single handwritten sheet
    which is thought to be a rejected passage
    from either *In Memoriam James Joyce* or
    The Kind of Poetry I Want; Nat. Lib. of
    Scotland Acc.50687/2)

Daw Gzböddi | (Research Assistant to | Prof. E.G. Morgan)

Turnbull was writing about the Edinburgh eccentric and pioneer, Alexander Mackenzie Carnougie (1898–1980), who claimed to have undertaken a single-handed journey by dirigible balloon to the North Pole in 1929, to be rescued from an ice-floe near his starting point of Spitzbergen. He thought MacDiarmid* might have mentioned Carnougie in *In Memoriam James Joyce*, and asked EM's help in tracking the reference. Hence this pastiche.

Alan Riach, academic and poet
(handwritten)

11–5–1992

Dear Alan

Thanks for your West Plaza letter which came with nice celerity today, and also for your month-back one which crossed with mine. Good too to have a copy of the SPLA notice – gospel-spreading stuff! The Glasgow Poets talk is not promised anywhere, but I hesitated to send it because it wasn't really intended for print, I have a different style when I'm writing a talk (different typing too – use of ampersands, use of capitals for all titles so as to catch my eye) and there are often little bits of syntax which would look inelegant in print but are taken care of by the speaking voice. However, your second time of asking has prodded me into sending it, if you'd like to put it in *Avizandum* – as long as you indicate it's just the text of the lecture as given. You can normalize the conventions or print it warts and all, as you think best.

Isn't John Purser's book splendid? He should get a medal from the Scottish Parliament inscribed PRO BONO CALEDONIAE PUBLICO. I have booked the series of concerts based on his researches to be given at the Edinburgh Festival. His book is only one among many things that run counter to the election results, and I share his underlying belief that really there's no going back, yet we are up against a government that not only means to preserve the Union but is searching for ways to <u>strengthen</u> it, and one can only hope it overreaches itself in this, and thereby precipitates a broader discontent than manifests itself at the moment. The demonstrations in George Square (which I've attended) are all right as far as they go, but a crowd of five or six thousand is not enough to impress those who don't want to be impressed. If it was a hundred thousand now…

I am off on Wednesday to Aberystwyth for my annual poet/lecturer stint. Whitman is my main departure this year – a lecture for his centenary. I'm talking about his prose as well as his poetry; I think it's been neglected. I shall also have a centenary lecture on MacDiarmid, though what the Welsh will

make of him I don't know. Sandwiches of Crewe! Cartons of
Shrewsbury tea! It takes a day to get there.
  I trust your Nietzsche and Mahler lecture went off well.
Deep waters these. I've been listening to R. Strauss's settings of
three J.H. Mackay lyrics, sung by Siegfried Jerusalem – there's
a name for you. Striking songs too.
  Good short stories recently from James Meek (*Last Orders*,
Polygon) and (more especially) Duncan McLean (*Bucket of
Tongues*, Secker & Warburg).
  Bucket of rains out there as I write. Wellington weather!

All the best | Eddie

Riach had written on West Plaza Hotel notepaper, with a copy of
the Scottish Poetry Library Association newsletter, advertising a
talk on his Selected Poetry and Prose volumes in the Carcanet Mac-
Diarmid* series. The 'Glasgow Poets' talk was delivered on EM's trip
to New Zealand, and Riach wanted it for *Avizandum*, the annual
review of the NZ Scottish Studies Association. John Purser had sent
a copy of his *Scotland's Music: A History of the Traditional and Classical
Music of Scotland from the Earliest Times to the Present Day* (1992). EM
was Visiting Professor at the University of Aberystwyth.

Richard Price, poet, editor and librarian
(handwritten)

16–7–1992

Dear Richard
  I should have written ages ago, when I got your welcome
and juicy Hilton National letter, but I've been inordinately
tied up the last two months – last three months actually –
after accepting a commission to make a version of Rostand's
Cyrano de Bergerac for Communicado Theatre Company.
They're putting it on as a Festival Fringe production, in the
newly-opened Traverse Theatre Mark II/III – an interesting
drum beside the Usher Hall, and a perfect illustration of The
Times We Live In, with a financial centre <u>above</u> and the
theatre <u>underground</u>. As my version is in what is basically
a Glaswegian Scots, with one or two characters speaking

English, I was reminded of what you said in your letter about that unhappy ASLS lecture and your 'objector' – he was wrong, and I thought we had got beyond that crude way of arguing and that one can not only use English but write things like concrete poetry and still be committed to Scotland, while keeping various kinds of Scots as an option we may want to use on this or that occasion. Whether *Cyrano* was a good choice remains to be seen! (Now in early rehearsal stage.)

My visit to Aberystwyth was somewhat briefer this year, because of the pressure of *Cyrano*, but I duly gave my readings and the two centenary lectures. The audience for Whitman was a good deal bigger than the one for MacDiarmid, which was probably to be expected (though still disappointing). I think the Welsh, like the English, will take a lot of persuading before there's any general acceptance of HM as a major figure – and this despite the Celtic connection (of course these are P-Celts, to whom Q-Celts are something of an aberration in any case). I'm not sure, to answer your question, if Wales has a figure of similar stature, though if he wrote in Welsh I could not judge. The Welsh themselves would probably say Saunders Lewis, an almost exact contemporary of HM, and like him a nationalist, but unlike him a fervent Catholic influenced by right-wing French Catholic writers. He wrote mostly in Welsh; anything I've seen in translation has not appealed. So you see I am prejudiced just like my Welsh counterparts!

I see Derek Jarman is to make a science-fiction film set in the future, *The Ruins of Canary Wharf*, script by Iain Sinclair. Only joking – but wouldn't it be a stunner? Since I made *Downriver* one of my 'Books of the Year' I'm glad to see it has been picking up awards. (On the *Herald* they hadn't even heard of him.) Very gritty and not very lisible. But for all that, etc. I haven't read your 'Vanished Library' book about Alexandria, though what you say about it is interesting – Alex seems to have been a focus for Informationists!

Did you take your 'Tie-breaker' any further, I wonder? I really like it, especially question 3. 'Without water we would wilt, wither, waste, whistleless, wetless, witless.' Space may be the last frontier (well, it isn't really, it's time), but the sea too is as full of mysteries as it was in Captain Nemo's day. I was reading recently that observations and measurements of the suction marks on dead whales show conclusively that squids far larger than those known to science are still lurking playing and propelling themselves through the depths. Think about it! The sea, which is most of the earth, is very frightening, but that is probably a good thing, since if we all came from it originally it would be wrong to want to return to it, like returning to the womb: we have to shake the drips off and go out, onto land, into the air, into space, eventually into time. Mind you, I expect pressure of population will make us try to colonize the sea (the Japanese are already onto this). Ah, Poe! (as MacDiarmid would cry), we have seen your cities in the sea which make the Hanging Gardens of Babylon look like parsley!

I seem to have returned to MacDiarmid, and can only add that this new *Selected Poetry* edited by Alan Riach (Carcanet) seems to be a very fair and useful collection (still lots of unglossed <u>English</u> words, however). I must hasten to my next task, which is to compile a cassette for ASLS – poems with linking commentary, educational uses in mind.

I was touched by what you wrote about your father and the employee with AIDS. That human reaction was so good and so real and so many light-years away from the moralizings of the tabloids which really make you sick. The Methodist overseer seems a poor Christian too. How can people <u>be</u> like that?

The Glasgow Fair is almost upon us. Archbishop Winning has been publicly lambasting Glasgow Airport for issuing free condoms to holidaymakers bound for the hot and sexy Costas.

I trust the new BL is steadily slotting into place. Will you and Jackie have a break during the summer?

All best wishes | Eddie

Price had written on hotel stationery. Referring to EM's Scots version of Rostand's *Cyrano de Bergerac* (1992), Price recalled having his views on MacDiarmid* denigrated by an audience member at an Association for Scottish Literary Studies conference, because of his 'English' accent. His 'Tiebreaker' poem included the challenge: 'In a phrase of not more than ten words / justify water'. Price's father had visited one of his charity shop employees in hospital, whereas the minister overseeing the project had refused to visit on 'moral grounds'.

Michael Schmidt, publisher, poet and critic

8 September 1993

Dear Michael

I pass on a thought or two. I gave a series of daily readings during the Edinburgh Festival (with Gavin Ewart, at Old St Pauls Church), signed books, talked to people about the books that were available. Usually they bought the *Selected* and cast longing but unmoneyed eyes on the *Collected*. I came away with a strong impression that what is really wanted is something in between – a more substantial *New Selected Poems* which would bring the little red book up to date (after all it is nearly a decade old now) with 'Sonnets from Scotland', 'From the Video Box', and part of *Hold Hands Among the Atoms*. I don't know what stage our present forthcoming book is at, but is it possible to have second thoughts about it? I also learned in Edinburgh that Polygon are interested in doing a new *Selected Translations*, and if this proved acceptable to you (of course it may not!) it could release the translations from our at-present-projected book and strengthen the case for a *New Selected*. Would all this still depend on Penguin, or have they gone off the boil entirely do you think with their own selection?

I would be very glad to hear what you think about these matters. The summer (which lasted here for about six days) has been swept off the map by customary sheets of rain. I hope you had something better!

All best wishes | Eddie

8 September 1993

Dear Michael

After you phoned this evening – how about this as a scenario:

Scrap our present proposed volume.
Scrap thoughts of Polygon.

Bring out nice fat juicy *New Selected Poems* in 1994 which could include some recent uncollected poems as well as those I mentioned in my letter – possibly removing some items from the present *Selected*.

Bring out in 1995 (let us mark my 75th birthday!) a *Collected Translations* (paperback?) plus a paperback *Collected Poems*. There might even be a *Collected Plays and Librettos* (*The Apple-Tree, Master Peter Pathelin, The Charcoal-Burner, Columba,* [*Cyrano de Bergerac?*])??

Let me know your mulled thoughts!

Best | Eddie

The New Selected Poems would need to wait until 2000, but a paperback *Collected Poems* and *Collected Translations* both appeared in 1996. Poems from *Hold Hands Among the Atoms* (Mariscat Press, 1991) and a broad selection of uncollected translations appeared in *Sweeping Out the Dark* (1994).

Dorothy McMillan, academic

14 October 1993

Dear Dorothy

Thank you for your letter of the 8th and list of poets. I had been making up my own list which was very similar, and I've been thinking about it and having another look at some of the poetry, but really don't feel at all confident about finding a 'story' to tell, since there are no 'schools' or groups, there is no older generation to add perspective, and the most interesting poets are the youngest (Jamie and Kay) who have inevitably a limited amount of material for discussion. The middle generation is – Liz Lochhead. (If Veronica Forrest-Thomson had survived, what a marvellous foil she would have been to Liz and vice versa.) I like CarolAnn Duffy and her poetry both, but it cannot be easy fitting her (and some of the others) into the Scottish story. My feeling is that whoever does write the essay will find problems, but that probably a woman contributor would be the most likely to sympathetically trace a 'story' from the material. I am sorry to be such a stick-in-the-mud about this.

All best wishes | Eddie

Co-editing *A History of Scottish Women's Writing* (1997), McMillan of Glasgow University had asked for a chapter on contemporary women poets. She finally wrote the chapter herself.

Richard Price, poet, editor and librarian
(handwritten)

30–3–1994

Dear Richard

I'm enthusiastic about the Four Snaps – many thanks for the batch safely received. The colour has turned out amazingly well. I hope this will prove a bit of bait for *Southfields* (for which I enclose subscription). Thanks also for *Gairfish* (I enjoyed the Finlayesque 'Davydeep'), Turkish poems (yes, like other Turkish poetry I've seen, very engaging and often moving), and your own poems (I like especially the Lifer's Kick, and the dramatic carpet dialogue – and many so-well-observed details like the Venetians skewed to a fan – and the mood, oh yes recognizable, of 'I never meet / a man but fear him'). I can well understand your worries about the small flat and environs and can only hope you will light on something suitable and affordable. If Richmond did become possible – I've been there and agree it would be fine. Any chance of a promotion and more purchasing-power?

What news have I? Well, a composer (Martin Dalby, lives in Drymen) is busy setting 'The Loch Ness Monster's Song' for mezzo-soprano and small orchestra, to be played during Mayfest in Glasgow. I hope the soprano is really mezzo, otherwise the gruffer moments will be difficult. You may have seen in the papers that a submarine crew is up there at the moment, ready to scour the bottom line (as commentators say) and also to combine science and tourism by offering short jaunts to five passengers who will gaze through a porthole and see – and see – 'We are now,' said Captain Nemo with a slight frown, 'at 100 feet, and if the pressure is not too great, I shall insert a probe into the silt, which must be rich in micro-organisms. Good gracious – !'

I find myself in a strange mood at the moment. A new stage in a relationship – totally unexpected – exciting – but very unsettling – I'm neglecting the things I ought to be doing ('ought' in the businessy, non-creative sense) and spending much time looking out at the rain and writing poems – quite a lot in the last few weeks (sample enclosed) – and oddly enough not about the relationship but on other subjects, yet somehow the feeling that comes from a single source is busy channelling itself somewhere, magnetizing and vivifying – so the mind is one and all things are connected – Anyhow, don't think, dear Richard, that when you are safely into your seventies it is going to be slippers and Coronation Street, you can be shaken to your core, yea, even in Richmond or Anniesland, the trembling of the veil, I assure you.

Happy Easter! | Eddie

EM had been experimenting with distorting Polaroid images through his photocopier; to these he attached enigmatic titles. Price had made copies of four 'photocopioids', partly as flyers for *Southfields*, his new magazine, and also sent poems for comment. EM's renewed relationship was with Malcolm Thomson, a care worker from Glasgow's East End, to whom he dedicated *Themes on a Variation* (1988).

David Kinloch, poet and academic

Vatmansmorn 1994

Dear David

I have been reading my meter and await with trepidation for the estimated but not estimable bill to come through. 'Estimated' bills are another form of disempowerment, down with them! Anyhow, to your letter, for which many thanks. I am sorry to see the demise of *Verse*, but on reflection I think I agree with you that such things have their time and place and probably ought not to be stretched out unnecessarily. *Verse* was always a rather odd hybrid, but that was part of its interest, and it broke down some good mulchy new ground. I am enclosing six poems from the series I am still working on. Two of them – Nos. 4 and 6 – you should already have, as Richard Price took them for the magazine in June last year, though they haven't yet appeared; I've retyped them and given No.4 a title, which it didn't have before.

I am not long back from my annual reading/lecture/ seminar stint at Aberystwyth. The college is on a hill, and this year it was weirdly perched above thick rolling sea-mist from Cardigan Bay. The isolation seemed well suited to a seminar I was asked to sit in on, by a German postgraduate student, on deconstructive architecture (exemplified by a 'Holocaust' extension to a museum in Berlin), where deliberate hiatuses in building are introduced in order to force thinking about the so-called unthinkable. I was not persuaded, though I gather the building is going ahead. Another trip to Berlin is called for!

I look forward to your Polygon collection. Actually *Paris-Forfar* appeals as a title (shades of that film *Paris, Texas?*) – it is unusual, and the English will not be able to pronounce it.

Best as ever | Eddie

Kinloch co-edited *Verse* with Robert Crawford* and Richard Price*. As a self-employed writer, EM could offset VAT (Value Added Tax) against literary earnings. The due date was always the end of a month, and his diary notes the electricity reading for 1 April 1994. The series mentioned was 'Virtual and Other Realities', providing the title for his next Carcanet collection (1997).

Stella Halkyard, archivist

Dear Stella Halkyard

Thank you for your letter of the 14th. You are very welcome to use my poems for the concrete exhibition. All four of them are in my Carcanet *Collected*, as you probably know. I am particularly pleased you have netted the warning poem, which never seems to get mentioned or anthologized but which I rather like.

Only last week I was asked at a student poetry society to read my 'dsh: recollections of a vortex' and say something about the man, both of which I duly did. I mentioned the fact that there must be a considerable dsh archive, including a mass of unpublished work, and said I hoped it would gravitate towards some institution and not be dispersed (though he would probably prefer the latter!), so it is good news that it all nestles and rustles in Rylands. I'm sure it <u>will</u> be researched, as he was a pretty remarkable dom. By the way, for your interest, all the letters he sent to me are signed Silvester, not Sylvester, and I always took it that that was the correct spelling; the y seemed to creep in more and more as he got published. I treasure his letters (and cards, etc.) and also the various typestracts he gave me, one of which I have framed on a dressing-table. (I offered the word typestract, which I invented and which dsh liked and used, to the editors of the new OED, but they declined to take it, citing not enough printed evidence...) My dsh file will eventually find its way into <u>my</u> archive at Glasgow University Library – though doubtless <u>everything</u> will end up in the Internet!

I enclose for your interest a recent publication which could be said to enter concrete territory.

Yours sincerely | Edwin Morgan

As archivist at the John Rylands Library in Manchester, housing Dom Sylvester Houédard's papers and other concrete poetry, Halkyard was organising *'From Line to Constellation': Concrete Poetry at the Rylands*, an exhibition that contained EM's 'Archives', 'Pomander',

'Dogs Round a Tree' and 'Warning Poem' (*CP*: 140, 173, 551, 554). The recent publication was Ian Hamilton Finlay's* 'Evening will come they will sew the blue sail' (Graeme Murray/Fruitmarket) which includes an essay by EM.

Christianne Ritchie dos Anjos, teacher

17 January 1995

Dear Ms Ritchie

Thank you for your letter. It is good to hear from you again and to know that you are still interested in Scottish poetry! So let me try to answer your question about William Carlos Williams.

When I began to write poetry, and to read a lot of modern poetry, I was scarcely aware of Williams at all, largely because his work was little known and little published in Britain. He didn't appear, for example, in either the *Faber Book of Modern Verse* or the *Oxford Book of Modern Verse* (both 1936), and the first of these was a very influential anthology which I remember being greatly excited by. I really only came to Williams much later, after the war, and at first he didn't appeal to me – I thought him prosaic and flat. But this changed! After the Beats appeared on the American scene in the late 1950s, there was a general shakeup of the American tradition, signalled most notably in Donald Allen's anthology *The New American Poetry 1945–1960*, and I could see that there was a new respect for Williams (e.g. in Allen Ginsberg), for his speech rhythms, for his down-to-earth detail, for his anti-academic stance. I read him again, and found a new admiration for him, which I still have, especially for poems like 'Tract', 'Burning the Christmas Greens', 'January Morning', 'The Great Figure', 'The Locust Tree in Flower', 'The Drunk and the Sailor', and of course *Paterson* (in parts!). I think what I learned was that could you write about <u>anything</u>, including the most ordinary things in your own environment (my Glasgow, his Paterson).

I hope these few remarks will be of some use to you, and I wish you best of luck with your course. I am of course most pleased that you have been enjoying my poetry.

With best wishes | Edwin Morgan

A Brazilian teacher and postgraduate student with Scottish family connections, Ritchie had visited EM in the summer of 1994. Now completing a dissertation on modern Scottish poetry at the University of São Paulo, she needed to link EM's work to North American writing.

Alec Finlay, poet and publisher

31 January 1995

Dear Eck

Having routed your dragon train through to Edinburgh, I can now give some sort of answer to your HH queries in your letter of the 12th. As I said in my previous letter, I don't have the correspondence to check by, so my remarks will have to be somewhat general and subject to the quirks or quarks of a thirty-odd-year gap. However, I think there is some truth in what you say about an 'unusual alliance between the folk revival and the progressive forces in Scottish poetry'. MacDiarmid, who had become distinctly reactionary by that time, circa 1960, went out of his way to attack both; the attacks were usually separate, but inevitably the attacked felt something of a common cause. Although I was never in any real sense a folkie, I was an old friend of the late Norman Buchan and was well aware of what was going on in the folk world. I also admired HH and the work he was doing as a collector, though in fact I came to my admiration of him not along the folk path but through his *Elegies for the Dead in Cyrenaica*, which I thought a strong, stylistically adventurous (avant-garde?) book of a kind that MacDiarmid could never have written even though he too had been in a war, and which of course I felt a special kinship with because Hamish and I had both been in the North African desert campaign. We also shared an interest in language and translation, and I remember he showed me a letter of Gramsci's which made a plea for

Sardinian against Italian, like similar pleas for Scots against English but based on unMacDiarmidesque arguments about the actual spoken language. I joined Hamish in admiration for Jeannie Robertson, whose way of singing was something I had not heard before, and in fact I introduced Jeannie when she gave a recital at Glasgow University, doing my homework both on the particular ballads she was to perform and on the requisite of whisky she would need to sustain her. Having heard, on records, many famous singers of opera or lieder straining every nerve to be <u>expressive</u>, I was fascinated by the fact that JR's singing was anti-expressive, classical, often emphasising the wrong word or making a pause or link that ran counter to the sense, because that was how it had always been done; an Easter Island statue instead of a Callas. Hamish and I also had a mutual friend in the late Alan Riddell, who founded *Lines*, appeared in *Poor.Old.Tired.Horse*, and wrote both traditional and concrete poetry. The three of us knew, admired, and defended Alexander Trocchi, which MacDiarmid and your Dad did not! – interesting cross-current there, which could well be followed up if you feel like it! You'll probably have seen Hamish's reminiscences on some of these points in *Cencrastus* last year. There are many other things that would be relevant – I think especially of links between the folk revival and the spread of poetry-readings, a link of performance, of a sense of the public – but I shall stop now and get this off to you and if you have any further queries do let me have them and assuming that the <u>dragon</u> has not <u>devoured</u> all my memories I shall do my best to reply.

All the best | Eddie

EM's translation of *Dragon Train: An Escap(ad)e*, by Velimir Khlebnikov, is in *CT*: 423–26. HH was Hamish Henderson, the Scottish folklorist and song-writer whose letters Finlay was editing. He viewed both Henderson and EM as using the folk music revival in 1960s Scotland to counter the proprietorial approach of Hugh Mac-Diarmid* to the poetic use of Scots language. EM had little correspondence with Henderson, but they shared a radical politics and attended some of the same political and cultural gatherings.

24–2–1995

To: Lesley Baxter, Artworks Press
From: Edwin Morgan, 19 Whittingehame Court, Glasgow
G12 0BG.

Dear Lesley Baxter

Thank you for your fax of the 23rd. I'm sure I shall be able
to talk to Ross sometime during the week of 6 March (not the
Friday).

As regards the 'story' of the poem, it is really very tenuous.
The idea you mention – that the monster is looking for his
friends and not finding them – is one that has got about –
but it was not my main intention. It is true that there are
suggestions of the word 'diplodocus', and my monster is
doubtless looking for any such prehistoric survivals, but the
main thrust of the poem was to have the monster surveying
the whole contemporary scene after he comes to the surface
in the first line, expressing his (uncomplimentary) reactions to
the world, getting quite angry in fact, and sinking under the
surface with a blip at the end.

I must say I am not too keen on the idea of explanatory
notes, unless perhaps a factual background note on the Loch
Ness Monster itself, which is quite interesting as it goes back
to the 6th century, when St Columba is said to have seen the
beast. If the poem is being split up page by page, however,
it would be good to have the whole poem shown at the
beginning. I am very doubtful about having a 'dictionary', since
I don't see it as a poem in code, as it were; it's not something
you can 'work out' in that way. The monster expresses moods
and feelings rather than ideas. My job was to find sounds that
would suggest (i) a bubbling, gurgling watery environment and
(ii) the guttural speech of a large and strange aquatic creature.
Words like splash, gabble, snuffle, bob, and gruff are meant to
be evoked, but there is no one-to-one correspondence. And of
course, as I'm sure you will have noticed, the monster swears
several times (unless he thinks he sees a French seal – phoque).
Can you explain that to the young persons? Or do we leave

that in a decent silence!

I would much rather have the poem appeal to the child's imagination than have too many things spelt out.

I look forward to hearing from Ross in due course, and discussing the visual side with him.

With best wishes | Edwin Morgan

Baxter's proposal for a children's picture book based on 'The Loch Ness Monster's Song', illustrated by Ross Collins, a recent graduate of the Glasgow School of Art, had been enthusiastically received at the Bologna Children's Book Fair. EM eventually provided an endnote on the monster's history.

Louise Dalziel, radio producer

23 June 1995

Dear Louise

Just to let you know that the box of books arrived safely, for which many thanks. I look forward to scanning the contents. I agree with you, from what I have seen so far, that there seems to be a strange gap in information, and even in interest, between ejaculation and zygote. Once we get to zygote everything perks up, page by page, but the actual journey of getting there appears to be largely uncharted. At least it leaves scope for the imagination; no one can tell me I got it wrong! My eye was caught by a sentence in one of the books (Klein et al): 'Direct observations of fertilization in human beings have never been made; thus, all in vivo estimates are retrospective.' This is a striking admission, and I must say it surprised me. It looks as if poets will have to beat medical technology to it. Anyhow, we shall have a go. I shall let you know how things – still at an inchoate stage, though I have ideas of a first-person narrative – progress.

Best wishes | Eddie

Developing a programme about conception for Radio Scotland, Dalziel commissioned a poem of between 15 and 20 minutes in length. This became 'A Voyage' (*Virtual and Other Realities*: 13–20). She sent books from the BBC Research Library for background. As 'Arrows of Desire', broadcast on Radio 4, it gained Silver in the Sony Radio Awards, 1997.

David Shuttleton, academic

13 July 1995

Dear David

It is good to hear from you, and I must say I am delighted to learn of the developments that have happened in the wake of my seminar. It was a splendid turnout for what I thought might have attracted only a small (if select!) circle. Your 'Queer at the Edges' book proposal sounds excellent (by the way, there was no 'whimsical flyer' enclosed – could you still send this?), and I'd be glad to contribute something if I can. I'm afraid it couldn't be in the near future, as I'm totally caught up in two commitments at the moment, for a play and a long poem. Regarding a subject or title, I have a problem that I recently published an article on Scottish gay or possibly gay writing from historical periods into the early twentieth century; it's called 'A Scottish Trawl' and is in Christopher Whyte's *Gendering the Nation* (Edinburgh University Press, 1995). This is probably just what you wanted for your book, but obviously I can't repeat the material. All I can suggest is that I might be able to write something on say half a dozen contemporary Scottish novelists and poets who have published gay work. Whether there would be any umbrella theme I really don't know yet. Can I think about this? But at any rate put my name down on your list.

On a visit to Dublin recently, I was pleased to see the clearly gay couples strolling in the sunshine in St Stephen's Green or (with two carrier bags each) turning the key in the door of their tiny flat after the week's shopping. There was even a Dublin Pride festival, with the approval of the city fathers. It is all happening.

With all best wishes | Eddie

One of EM's best attended seminars at Aberystwyth was 'In your face and high time too: how do we discuss gay literature, and who are "we"?'. Shuttleton and his colleague Dianne Watt then set up a series of staff–postgraduate interdisciplinary research seminars on gay issues, out of which came *De-centering Sexualities: Politics and Representations Beyond the Metropolis* (Routledge, 2000). EM contributed 'Transgression in Glasgow: A Poet Coming to Terms'.

Alec Finlay, poet and publisher

24 August 1995

Dear Eck

It's good that Polygon are to publish *GB* and *Dancers* again. Many people today will never have seen these poems. In answer to your <u>horse</u> question: I have been looking up dates, and my Mayakovsky translation, 'A Richt Respeck fur Cuddies', was first published in the magazine *Migrant* No.5, March 1960. I imagine your dad must have seen this, because of the Migrant connection, though whether it had any influence I don't know. The splendid Tolstoy horse may indeed, as you suggest, be whinnying somewhere in the background of the three of us; I had certainly read and admired the story. I had other Mayakovsky translations, as well as a variety of poems and translations, in the early numbers of P.O.T.H., e.g. 'Forcryinoutloud' and 'Hymn to a Jeddart-Justicer' in No.2, May 1962.

I think I would have some problems about your linking of your dad's early work and 'folk'. The irony and sophistication and literary reference take the poems a long way from folk. One of the *Dancers* poems is called 'Folk Song', but it is self-evidently not that! I am also not so sure about the 'voices'. Most of the *Dancers* poems are autobiographical IHF poems, and the book gives a fairly marked impression of <u>a</u> voice; indeed that was what most people noticed when the book came out, it was a 'new voice' in Scottish poetry. In *GB* too, it is one voice all the way through. One time I was this, another time I was that, etc. Can you really call this 'dramatic'? Isn't it rather a storyteller's voice, a voice which you hear even in his actual plays, which could be called 'undramatic'? There are lots of questions lurking about here! You are perfectly right, of course, about the 'spokenness', and how that disappeared when concrete came in. The question of whose voice it actually is is always a tricky one. In the late 1950s I was writing the dialogue poems of my *Whittrick* sequence, where I give dramatic voices to a variety of people from Joyce and MacDiarmid to the Brontës and Marilyn Monroe. All these poems are linked by the idea of the 'whittrick', which is no doubt 'my' idea, but at the same time I did want to dramatize my sixteen separate characters. Really only someone other than the author himself can say whether these are 'Morgan poems'. In poems like 'Glasgow Green' and 'Good Friday', from the early 1960s, I used Glasgow voices as dramatic inserts in poems which were otherwise in English, but I did not write, as Tom Leonard was to do, poems entirely in Glaswegian. I found the beginning of the 1960s a very liberating time, and I was able to switch without effort from directly personal poems ('One Cigarette') to dramatic characterizations ('Je Ne Regrette Rien'). Actually speaking as or through a character goes a long way back in my work. One of my poems written at school was set in the Far East and called 'The Opium-Smoker'. Was that 'me'? I shall leave that for biographers.

Thanks for the D.T. I look forward to the whole train of them in due course.

Rain today. Hosepipes away.

All the best | Yeddie

Polygon republished *The Dancers Inherit the Party* by Ian Hamilton Finlay*, edited by Ken Cockburn* with other early work including *GB, Glasgow beasts, an a burd, haw, an inseks, an aw, a fush.* Alec Finlay wondered whether the title of *Poor.Old.Tired.Horse* was influenced by EM's translation of a Mayakovsky poem (*CT*: 120). EM returned to the idea of a folk music influence on his father's work (see 31 January 1995). The DT was a first proof of *Dragon Train.*

Louise Dalziel, radio producer

4 November 1995

Dear Louise

I am delighted to have your positive reaction to the poem.
Regarding the question you raise about the two voices, I
suppose the first difference I tried to indicate lay in the metre
itself: the egg has a shorter four-beat line with careful rhyme,
to suggest her tight, static, self-contained status, whereas the
sperm has a longer blank verse line with very varying rhythms
to suggest his active darting probing nature, the absence of
rhyme giving him the freedom the egg lacks. I thought of
the sperm's voice as having at least a Scottish timbre (he does
use one or two Scottish words like 'breenge' and 'blash'), and
in the main as having a range of tone (and pitch and speed)
in accordance with the agility of his body: he's a gallus and
(forgive the pun) spunky character, a Gulliver on his travels
but not naive like Gulliver, quite sophisticated and quirky, a
quick learner in new situations, an engaging self-questioner,
and perhaps above all someone who is aware of us and our
reactions, a would-be communicator, even of impossible
things! Yet his moments of awe and wonder are just as real as
his jokiness. I liked your 'spider' comparison for the egg, and I
daresay her voice could well have at times an undercurrent of
the sinister, although we clearly also feel sympathy with her
half-fulfilled longings. But I am sure you will have your own
ideas about the voices, and I shall be interested to hear how
things go, once you get your teeth into the programme.

With best wishes | Eddie

For 'Arrows of Desire', Dalziel originally thought of intercutting the
sperm's journey with a surrealist collage of sounds. This ultimately
became inserts of five imaginary monologues from literature, based
around births, written by Patricia Hannah. The actors chosen for the
voices described here were Bill Paterson and Sian Phillips.

Joy Hendry, editor and poet

11 November 1995

Dear Joy

I enclose a poem for Norman's commemorative booklet.
I thought *sortes Virgilianae* would appeal to Norman the
classicist. The *sortes* are quite genuine, by the way – eyes closed
and a finger stabbing the page – and it is strange how much
sense they make. There must be something in the old idea!

Best wishes | Eddie

SORTES VIRGILIANAE

Hear guns go off in the shrivelling air –
they sprint eight feet and –
the fox has gone. But the gean tree's still working away,
the inelegant way they land.
A shunting engine butts them
with a mind narrower than this pen,
a million things today,
and gave him a bad time of it –
and God trembled
in the sexual flame.
If only I could wrap up
and sit up straight, following their ears
as though evoking brilliances could show
you bringing me messages.

(from Norman MacCaig, *Collected Poems*)

Joy Hendry*, editor of *Chapman*, had asked for a poem for MacCaig's
85th birthday. EM used the classical technique of the Virgilian fates,
a divination by random selection of passages from the *Aeneid*, or, in
this case, from MacCaig's *Collected Poems*.

Richard Price, poet, editor and librarian
(handwritten)

4–12–1995

Dear Richard – Do forgive the gap since my last. I have had
my head down in many writings. Halloween saw me finishing
a long (well, 300 lines) poem for the BBC on 'conception',
a mini-epic voyage of the central character from ejaculation
to fertilization – and I do give the little smout a character –
which was due to be broadcast on Radio Scotland this month
but has now been taken over by Radio 4 for broadcast next
April. Although it's highly imaginative – <u>had</u> to be! – I did
quite a bit of reading to make sure I had the facts right – facts
such as they are – much of the detail is still obscure, isn't that
amazing? Anyhow I enjoyed this test of my nothing-not-
giving-messages belief. I'm afraid it's all very pro-life, so it
won't please <u>every</u> feminist on the block (but some, I'm sure).
While this was going on, I was also finishing *Gilgamaster*, and
the five acts are now with Communicado and have had an
initial run-through reading by the actors. It seems to go well,
though obviously some changes will be required. No decision
yet about music and songs, but the cast like the songs, so I
just wait to see what can be done with them. We may still go
Turkish! As if these two projects were not enough to keep me
from idleness (and writing letters to long-suffering friends),
I have been composing some 'Glasgow' poems to be carved
on granite pavement slabs in the Candleriggs, at the entrance
to the City Hall. How long will they last, do you think? (I
gather it is a <u>very</u> hard granite, resistant to beer, urine, vomit,
fish suppers, etc.) (but skateboards, tackety boots?) My next
immediate job is also a commission, from Tommy Smith the
jazz saxophonist, to write a sequence of poems for him to set
to music at the 1996 Glasgow International Jazz Festival. I
have <u>started</u> that. A January deadline looms!

I was most pleased to have your *Marks & Sparks*, usual nice
cleancut production from *Akros*. I liked your 'short sequence of
unhappiness (not you!)' when you first sent me it, and it takes
well to the page. And thanks for the touching 'Hand held'
addition. Have you done anything more with prose? 'Light

Industrial' makes good reading, perhaps especially with its third-page venturing into the edges of Iain Sinclair country. More, I think!

I hope you are still enjoying the full 8A. Lay the kitchen table with this Japanese paper –!

Best as ever | Eddie

Gilgamesh was never performed, because of artistic disagreements within Communicado Theatre Company. Price's *Marks & Sparks* was published by Duncan Glen* (1995). 8A was the number of the Prices' new flat in Staines.

Drew Milne, academic and poet

4 January 1996

Dear Drew

Thanks very much for your letter of 20 December. The £200 cheque has been duly received and I've taken up your suggestion of writing to Andrew Brighton to see if he can squeeze a reimbursement for travel.

I look forward to anything you produce on Veronica Forrest-Thomson. I don't know if I can help you much with the 'socio-political' bit. I suppose her family would be described as ordinary middle-class west-end Glasgow, and she had a good traditional education with Latin and Greek, but – there are always buts with her! – although she was brought up in Glasgow she was apparently born in Malaya, and I don't know when the family left and whether she could have any memory of it. Had her father business there, or was he part of the postwar British administration trying to make sense of things after the colony had been retaken from the Japanese, or maybe he was in the army? At anyrate it was a very disturbed time, with many Malays having no desire to resume the British colonial yoke and with lots of communist infiltration from China. All this may be irrelevant, except in the most roundabout of ways. My first contact with her was when she was 17, in her last year at school. (I've been

looking at her letters which date from February 1965 to
August 1974.) She wrote me an amazingly mature letter
about a talk she had heard me give on the Third Programme,
about concrete poetry, and how she thought this was 'the
first healthy development in poetry since the war' (she even
referred to Apollinaire and <u>that</u> war), a poetry which showed
'responsibility towards the exploration of language instead
of the usual egotistical watered down angst-dichten which
seems to monopolise the Third Programme readings.' In
June 1965 she came to one of my readings, sat in the front
row, and asked searching questions, following this up with
a letter where she talked about Ian Hamilton Finlay and
his Wild Hawthorn Press, compared our two approaches,
wondered whether she should send work to Finlay but 'would
be apprehensive about committing myself to one label – this
is apt to inhibit individuality', and decided to send poems
to me instead, for an opinion; I of course replied, and our
correspondence grew from there. It was correspondence
more often than meetings, since of course you will know
she went to study at Liverpool not Glasgow University, and
took a First there in 1968 before going on to Cambridge and
research. But even before she left Scotland for Merseyside,
she was well aware of the new stirrings in Scottish writing
(post-MacDiarmid, post-Scottish-Renascence) around
1960, and (to answer your question) yes, she was influenced
by me and to a lesser extent by Finlay, though she enjoyed
the internationalism and innovation of Finlay's magazine
Poor.Old.Tired.Horse., which was surprising and spunky and
paradoxical in a very unEnglish (but really quite Scottish and
Bakhtinian) manner. Her interest in language, and her interest
in science (her Cambridge thesis was to be on 'Science and
Poetry'), are both very Scottish (I certainly shared them), and
although she left Glasgow and Scotland she kept in touch and
was eager to hear what I thought of – oh, everything.
Her three Liverpool years are the ones I know least about;
perhaps you may be able to find some contact at the university
there.

Her parents' address, by the way, is still in the current
Glasgow telephone book, if you felt like getting in touch:
{details supplied in original}.

Do let me know if there are any other details I can help with.

All the best for 1996 | Eddie

Milne had organised a reading series by innovative poets at the Tate Gallery in October-December 1995, and had helped push for payment. He was now working on the poetry of Veronica Forrest-Thomson*.

Peter Manson, poet and editor

8 April 1996

Dear Peter

The enclosed may seem an unlikely submission to *Object Permanence*, but I thought it might interest you. It is a translation from the Latin 'Altus Prosator' of St Columba (c.520–597) and is the earliest Scottish poem which ought to stand like a dragon at the beginning of our anthologies! And Columba, by the way, will be celebrating his quatuordeciencentenary next year (597–1997). It could be described as an experimental poem. It is alphabetic, and is written in an exotic and innovative postclassical Latin, influenced by the strange and often obscure *Hisperica Famina* ideas about diction (and influencing them in turn) which flourished in Ireland and which Columba no doubt brought with him to Iona. It pounds along on strong sweeping rhythms punctuated by mid-line rhyme and assonance. I have tried to reproduce as many of its effects as possible. Even non-believers may expect to find just the tiniest frisson of anxiety – I think – in what is truly an astonishing poem.

With best wishes | Eddie

Manson co-founded *Object Permanence* in Glasgow in 1993 to publish experimental poetry. The abecedarian 'Altus Prosator' ('The Maker on High') appeared in *CT*: 389–93 (1996), and in a slightly different version from Mariscat Press in 1997. 'Hisperica Famina' ('Western Orations') were rhetorically heightened poems in Hiberno-Latin, using arcane lexis.

27 August 1996

Dear Steven Small

Thank you for your letter of the 23rd. I shall be happy
to give a talk on *Cyrano* as you suggest, before one of the
performances. When is the play going on? Do you have any
dates in mind at the moment?

I shall try to answer your questions for the study pack,
though could I just say that you will find some material also
in the introduction I wrote when the text of the play was
published by Carcanet Press in 1992, and you may want
to quote from that. Will you be able to have copies of the
paperback available for sale during the production of the play?
Anyhow, here goes with your questionnaire:

1. I didn't work from a translation, but direct from the
French text. I used the edition by Patrick Besnier (Gallimard,
Paris, 1983) which has good background notes.

2. In this case, line by line, since I had a three-month
deadline, and had to fulfil a quota of lines every day! Three
months is not a long time to translate a full-length play, so I
had to clear the decks and get on with it, leaving other projects
aside. This pressure, however, was probably a good thing, since
it enabled me to develop a certain drive and impetus. The play
was in my mind constantly, even emotionally.

3. The Scots has a Glaswegian base, but it is only a base, and
the language is used freely and inventively to meet the wit and
inventiveness of the original. I also used English for one or two
of the characters, by way of contrast.

4. You must ask Rostand! I kept as close as I could,
using metre and rhyme as he did, and always trying to find
equivalents for his special effects. To meet the requirements
of the company, I amalgamated two characters into one, and
added a nuns' song. Is that loss or gain? Others must judge.
One 'gain', I think, is simply the fact that a Scottish version,
which might have been considered unlikely, proved possible,
and indeed to work very well.

5. I enjoyed working with the company. Although writing

is inevitably a solitary activity, I had already collaborated with drama companies (e.g. the Medieval Players, TAG Theatre Company) and with composers (Thomas Wilson, Kenneth Leighton, and most recently Tommy Smith the jazz saxophonist). There is a particular thrill in seeing something you have written given a further life on the stage.

6. Very!

7. Make 'em laugh, make 'em cry – maybe the old adage is the best answer.

Yours sincerely | Edwin Morgan

Small was writing a pack on *Cyrano de Bergerac* for schools visiting the Royal Lyceum Theatre, Edinburgh. His seven questions were: 1. Which translation did you work from and why? 2. How do you tackle a translation? Do you do it line by line? 3. What variety of Scots accent did you translate into, i.e. urban Scots, rural or what? 4. What do you feel the play lost or gained in translation? 5. Theatre is a collaborative art form. As a poet I imagine you work very much on your own – how difficult was it working with a company? 6. Were you satisfied with the final production? 7. Why do you feel your version has been so popular?

Iain Bamforth, poet, doctor and critic

29 December 1996

Dear Iain

Our letters are rather like elephants' memories, they may take a long time spacing themselves out but they are never forgotten. I ought to have answered your very welcome May letter ages ago, it didn't get lost or anything like that, but the fact that I knew I <u>would</u> answer it probably eroded the spur of guilt – anyhow, here we are, just escaping the shame of writing 1997 above! I was much interested in what you wrote about being a doctor in Strasbourg and was trying to work out whether it was better or worse than being a doctor in Scotland (or England), but I didn't get very far with comparisons, our own health service being in such a state of flux, as I'm sure you know. Many of the changes – 'fundholding', group practices, greater use of nurses, patients not being allowed to call their own doctor out at night (shades of Kafka!) – have still to work themselves through, and the <u>cui bono</u> needs a fair-sized question-mark. The image of the healer with his black bag has also to contend (at least in America and the Netherlands) with the picture of Dr Death, scurrying accoucheur of suicides, apparently unprosecutable (they've tried) despite being from one point of view a serial killer. Perhaps a white bag, or a red bag, or a tartan bag, or a bag sponsored by a fertility clinic, would be more reassuring. – My thoughts were in fact on fertility rather than death earlier this year when the BBC commissioned a 20-minute poem on the subject of human conception, which I wrote for two voices (sperm and egg) and which was broadcast in June. The heroic voyage to reach the egg was virtually a species of science fiction, though based on the facts as far as I understood them. – Heroic journeying makes me think of your parasites, fascinating essay that, and I'd say both comprehensible and suggestive, even allowing for the fact that my five years in the RAMC in the Middle East and a general interest in biology might predispose me a bit in its favour; when you were speaking of the Guinea worm I was dying for you to mention MacDiarmid's poem about that creature, 'To a Friend and Fellow-Poet', where he describes the wonderful uterine extrusion through the mouth as being just how 'we poets deliver our store' and 'by the skin of our teeth flype ourselves into fame'. It's a poem that makes as good a case for science-into-art as you could wish for. – I found the Kafka and <u>crise de foie</u> essays, though different in tone, both highly readable, and I look forward to a collection of medical essays. Will you bring in Chekhov – Astrov – Sakhalin? (Lawrence called Chekhov a willie-wet-leg but he was really describing himself.) I notice you mention the word 'livery' but not 'liverish' which I remember from earlier days being quite commonly used to denote someone who was bad-tempered but the bad temper probably had a physical cause. I think the spleen comes next – 'Spleen and Ideal: Why the Spleen is not Splenetic in French Symbolist Poetry'.

I only quite recently bought your *Open Workings* and have read it through but not closely. It's really very good, both with things that are striking (in one mode) and things which are moving (in another). I understand what you say in your letter about Orc and Urizen! You are right. There is a fine delve into human as well as geophysical (and verbal) experience. The poems that struck me most forcibly are 'Doing Calls on the Old Portpatrick Road', 'Between the Rhins and the Machars', 'The Fever Hospital', 'Boy', and 'A View of Luce Bay', plus (need I say) the splendid concluding Rabelaisian list. I hope you will be able to settle into a doctoring regime that will leave you with enough time and energy to write. It can't be easy. W.C. Williams said he used to have to scribble poems on prescription pads between patients – but he didn't give up his general practice.

Carcanet managed to bring out my *Collected Translations* recently, despite their being bombed out of the Corn Exchange. I have a new poetry collection in their hands, *Virtual and Other Realities*, pencilled in for October or November 1997. It has a 50-poem sequence, plus *Beasts of Scotland*, a suite of ten poems written for jazz setting by saxophonist Tommy Smith. I'm not sure if you are interested in jazz, but if you are, let me know, and I can send you a copy of the CD. I am still working on *Gilgamesh*, a play for Communicado Theatre Company, and this will keep me busy in the new year.

Best wishes to you and your multilingual family – | Yours ever | Eddie

Now in private practice in Strasbourg, Bamforth had sent essays on medical and cultural themes. He linked 'Parasites or, the Future of a Metaphor' to Kafka's world-view. MacDiarmid's poem appropriates detail from parasitologist Sir Patrick Manson's *Lectures on Tropical Diseases* (1905); 'flype' in Scots means to turn inside out. Carcanet Press published Bamforth's *Open Workings* in 1996. EM had used the Orc and Urizen analogy from Blake to encourage him towards more directly emotional expression in poetry.

Tommy Smith, jazz saxophonist and composer

FAX   29–1–1997
To: Tommy Smith
From: Edwin Morgan, 19 Whittingehame Court, Glasgow
G12 0BG

Mon cher Tommy en France: Voici le first poem de *Planet Wave*:

IN THE BEGINNING [if we want a date, say 20 BILLION B.C.]

Don't ask me and don't tell me. I was there.
It was a bang and it was big. I don't know
what went before, I came out with it.
Think about that if you want my credentials.
Think about that, me, it, imagine it
as I recall it now, swinging in my spacetime hammock,
nibbling a moon or two, watching you.
What am I? You don't know. It doesn't matter.
I am the witness, I am not in the dock.
I love matter and I love anti-matter.
Listen to me, listen to my patter.

Oh what a day (if it was day) that was!
It was as if a fist had been holding fast
one dense packed particle too hot to keep
and the fingers had suddenly sprung open
and the burning coal, the radiant mechanism
had burst and scattered the seeds of everything,
me, you, Andromeda, the dog next door,
out through what was now space, out
into the pulse of time, out, my masters,
out, my friends, so, like a darting shoal,
like a lion's roar, like greyhounds released,
like blown dandelions, like Pandora's box,
like a shaken cornucopia, like an ejaculation –

I was amazed at the beauty of it all,
those slowly cooling rosy clouds of gas,
wave upon wave of hydrogen and helium,
spirals and rings and knots of fire, silhouettes
of dust in towers, thunderheads, tornadoes;
and then the stars, and the blue glow of starlight
lapislazuliing the dust-grains –

I laughed, rolled like a ball, flew like a dragon,
zigzagged and dodged the clatter of meteorites
as they clumped and clashed and clustered into
worlds, into this best clutch of nine
whirled in the Corrievreckan of the Sun.
The universe had only just begun.
I'm off, my dears. My story's still to run!

Dear Tommy

I wanted the first poem to be quite strong, so it is probably
a bit longer than the other poems will be. But anyhow you can
let me know what you think.

Since we talked last Wednesday, I have been smitten by
grave doubts about whether I could carry out my part of the
performance at Cheltenham as you outlined it. There are two
problems. One is that a poem is a poem, and it is difficult to
read it with conviction if the impetus is to be broken up by
stops and starts. But the other matter is the one that gives me
cold sweats when I think about it. I have no training in jazz
(or indeed in any kind of music) and find it extremely hard
to follow any line or structure in a jazz piece – all the more
so when a 12-man band is playing round about me. Coming
in with my words at the right moment would be fairly nerve-
racking and would tend to drain away the natural confidence
you have when you read your own work in public, by yourself.
The more I think about it, the more impossible it seems. How
would it do if I recorded all the poetry beforehand, and you
with your technology could then insert what you wanted at the
points required? I am sure I can have the poems done in plenty
of time for this to happen.

I thought it best to set out these doubts right away and not

leave them till later. Sorry to download problems onto you –
but they are real!

Best as ever | Eddie

Planet Wave, a sequence of ten (later twenty) poems on the theme
of time for Tommy Smith's jazz orchestra, was commissioned by the
Cheltenham International Jazz Festival (*New Selected Poems*, 2000:
168–79; *A Book of Lives*, 2007: 23–43). Later performances allayed
EM's doubts. They had performed together on *Beasts of Scotland*
(1996) and would work on *Monte Cristo* (1998) and *Sons and Daughters of Alba* (*Cathures*, 2002: 57–62).

David Shuttleton, *academic*

15 March 1997

Dear David

Thank you for your letter of 26 February, and I have been
thinking about my contribution to the conference. Neil
McMillan's abstract sounds like an excellent subject – I haven't
been in touch with him yet but must do so. Encouraged by
your remark that several contributors are 'taking off from issues
of identity experienced by themselves', I thought I would
do something similar, trying to trace such development as I
am aware of, in acts of writing, in relation to the pressures of
sexual identity; I would refer to various indirect methods (e.g.
my translating the poetry by the gay German writer Platen, my
first-person use of a gay icon like Edith Piaf); I would bring
in the wartime Middle East experiences as you suggested;
and to add a dash of chiaroscuro I would like to discuss
briefly some gay themes or incidents in my non-gay Scottish
contemporaries (e.g. Gibbon, Trocchi, Leonard, McIlvanney,
Kelman, Welsh). Perhaps some such title as 'Transgression in
Glasgow: A Poet Coming to Terms'.

A poetry reading would be fine if you can arrange this. The
panel on Sunday morning might be ruled out by my having to
catch an early train back to Glasgow.

Jocelyn Brooke: yes indeed! An old favourite of mine. I

have almost all his books. An RAMC man like myself! Very
good at sweaty shirts open to the waist.

All best wishes | Eddie

Shuttleton and colleagues at Aberystwyth had organised a confer-
ence emerging from their interdisciplinary seminars. Neil McMillan,
researching at Glasgow University, would discuss 'cross-writing'
(speaking for the opposite sex) in novels by Alan Warner and Chris-
topher Whyte*. Shuttleton had encountered Jocelyn Brooke's work
while researching literature of the Second World War, in which
Brooke, like EM, had served in the RAMC.

Richard Price, poet, editor and librarian
(handwritten)

23–4–1997

Dear Richard – St George's Day, which I mention only
because my dentist this morning, apropos of nothing, said 'It's
St George's Day' as he was doing painful things to my upper
central teeth, was it meant to take my mind off it, or was the
Dragon of Decay being given a frontal attack? Anyhow, I'm
glad you followed your <u>down</u> letter with an <u>up</u> postcard. I
can assure you I have gone through these troughs too, when
either nothing seemed to be happening or if it was happening
no one seemed to notice. But head down, PATIENCE and
FORTITUDE, il faut tenter de vivre as Valéry said, time
will tell (though there are some near squeaks, like Hopkins
– supposing he hadn't had Bridges, black figures with pursed
lips could have made a deathbed bonfire of all his vanities –).
I like your idea of writing about Staines and the rurban, go
for it. There's <u>so much</u> in life that is not written about, and
film and video can't do everything, we need words. I hope you
like Hopper's packaging factory – I do! – Well, I have 'done'
Cheltenham with Tommy Smith and his band of 12. Strange
experience reading the 10 poems on a high stage, standing <u>very</u>
close to my microphone, surrounded by such explosive waves
of sound (planet waves), but it went well, and the *Scotsman*

sent Kenny Mathieson their jazz reviewer, who gave it an
excellent write-up. The BBC recorded it for Radio 3, no date
decided yet. – I enjoyed the lively *Southfields* mix – Hikmet,
Aygi, Meyrink, Riach, Tannahill, Pulp. And my thanks to Paul
Gordon for his diligent and encouraging piece (yes, I think I
<u>am</u> a storyteller). Carcanet, by the way, have my next collection
planned for November, that's the *Virtual & Other Realities*
one. I shall be interested to hear how you and Raymond get on
with your 'Settlement'.

Thanks for all those White Horses. I haven't seen any of
them in the flesh/chalk. <u>Uffington</u> is splendid. 'The White
Horse Poems' – somebody has probably done it.

Love to Jackie and Katie, and | best as ever – Eddie

EM identified strongly with Gerard Manley Hopkins, partly because
of his own early lack of book publication. The 'rurban' was Price's
coinage for 'between places, light industrial', focusing on the
Thames in Staines. He was planning a sequence called 'Settlement'
with Raymond Friel, one of his co-editors on *Southfields 3: City and
Light*. Paul Gordon, a Glaswegian psychotherapist and writer now
living in London, had contributed '"In Full Sight": The Poetry of
Edwin Morgan'. Price's postcard was of the White Horse of Uffington.

Kenny Ireland, *director*

FAX
Kenny Ireland   30–4–1997

Proposed Scots version of Racine's *Phèdre*

There are various English translations of *Phèdre*, but as far
as I know, there is no version in Scots. This is the situation I
want to change! At first sight it might seem that the attempt
to put this high tragedy – generally claimed as the greatest
of the French classical tragedies – into colloquial Scots is
quixotic. I believe, however, that this is not the case, and the
translation I have done so far, has helped to convince me that
the job can be done, and indeed should be done. My main

aim is to produce a version which will be speakable by actors and communicable to audiences, and in particular I want to ensure that the passion and conflict of the original – which are powerful and persuasive despite the formality of Racine's language – come across to a modern audience in a way that could well surprise them. Whether concealing or confessing emotions, these characters can get right under our skin. In making them speak Scots (it is Glaswegian-based, but not narrowly local) I have not thought to update the setting or the characters and I have kept the original names. This seemed to work with my version of *Cyrano*, and I think it will work here too. As Racine is extremely niggardly with stage-directions, a modern director has a very free hand in sets, dress, lighting, etc. I think it should be 'Greek' in some sense, and there should be an awareness that it is a seaside town (since the sea later takes part in the action). As regards dress, possibly the less the better, to bring out the strong erotic charge the play undoubtedly has.

I have occasionally used an unfamiliar word, like 'corrieneuchin' in the list of characters. As this word means 'intimate conversation', corrieneuchin-freen is a very neat equivalent of the French 'confidente' or English 'confidante'. But of course if this is felt to be too obscure, we can easily fall back on 'confidante'. I have no desire to impose barriers!

Attached is my version of the first two scenes of the first act.

Ireland was Artistic Director of the Royal Lyceum Theatre Company in Edinburgh. After the success of his translation of *Cyrano de Bergerac* into Scots, EM had discussed the possibility of using the same medium for a classical tragedy, and was encouraged to send a proposal and version of some scenes. These won a commission for the complete play.

Peter McCarey, poet and translator

27 June 1997

Dear Peter

I enclose a contribution for Gael's birthday book. It's a slightly mysterious poem which I hope may appeal to him.

'What's the Hisperica Famina?' You may well ask. The innococerncy of such an anstrept voprositation subpenesemes the vehodehiscence of the responsibolium. Basically it is a long poem (prose poem? manual? jeu d'espirit? exemplary riddle?), though the term is also used generically of the kind of writing the poem is the apex peak crest spigot and plum of, composed in 6th/7th-century Ireland in exotic postclassical Latin infiltrated by Greek Hebrew Arabic Old Irish and the author's own neologisms. We may note, one scholar says, that it comes from the same country as *Finnegans Wake*. It bristles with so many cruxes, not to say cruces, that one would be reduced to crutches to escape its clutches. It has been roughly translated, but not with any real attempt at rhetorical equivalence. For a lottery-sized carrot, one might have a go –

I do agree with you about *Faust* Part 1. Goethe-awe seems to be a part of sage-awe, and there's something wrong about that. Even *The Master and Margarita* has some penetrations denied to Goethe, and Bulgakov is a sort of anti-sage.

'Assiduous, bad dancers', yes. A week ago I saw *The Winter's Tale* at the new Globe on Bankside. Leontes just delivered his lines to, or rather at, the audience with what he no doubt thought was the right loudness of voice and largeness of gesture, but it was uninward and unpersuasive, you simply did not believe what he said. It is a wondrous play, and when it is done badly you wish you were somewhere else.

I look forward to your Glasgow visit next month.

Yours with hisperic famination – | Eddie

McCarey edited *A Gathering for Gael Turnbull* (1998) for Turnbull's* 70th birthday. EM's 'My Moriscos' (*Cathures*, 2002: 67) refers to Turnbull's skill in morris dancing. McCarey had doubted a publisher's comparison of Goethe's *Faust* Part 1 to Shakespeare and Dante.

In Mikhail Bulgakov's satirical *The Master and Margarita* (1928–40, published in a censored version in 1967) the Devil visits the Soviet Union. EM would shortly publish *Demon* (1999). McCarey had commented on the mysterious difference between dancers and non-dancers.

Drew Milne, academic and poet
(handwritten)

20–12–1997

Dear Drew

Thanks very much for your domestic-aesthetic-pastoral 'diversion' which seems to fit the writing of Christmas cards. Whether you refer to the vena cava, which I recall from my medical days, I'm not sure, but the heart's need or meed of blood/love doesn't seem far away, no farther than the round earth's imagined corners we send our cards to. I ought also to have acknowledged your excellently probing conference paper on 'The Performance of Scepticism', which I found particularly interesting on Finlay and Beuys. I've spoken to fierce defenders of the latter, but my own view veers towards the 'reactionary charlatan who mystifies art and politics' assessment you mention. I see you (like others!) have come up against the rock of IHF's refusal to have what could, depending on the light, look like a nasty political tooth either drawn or filled. I think a title like 'Adorno's Hut' is cheating a bit, if he is unwilling to defend the implications. As for o**↯↯**o – well, he has said that he <u>likes</u> to make people angry – and this again leaves the critic waving a crutch and trying not to fall down. The clear element of play – there's verbal play of course, but I really mean playing with the reader's/spectator's reactions – is still something that asks for investigation in his work. I'm not sure that the pleasure he takes in disconcerting is totally congruent with the 'classicism' which has enabled him to tutor his reactions to atrocities, whether Roman, French Revolutionary or Nazi. The protracted death of Patroclus in <u>The Iliad</u> is given by Homer without comment. Is Homer a brute? I don't know! Who can read Homer's mind? Mehr Licht please.

I hope you are enjoying Cambridge. Fenlike and miasmous after bracing Brighton, but more intellectually stimulating, is that the picture?

All the best in 1988 – | Eddie

Milne was teaching in Trinity Hall, Cambridge, and editing *Parataxis: Modernism and Modern Writing*. The 'diversion' was 'The eclipse of the ear' (1997) and his conference paper appeared in *act* (art, criticism, theory) no. 3, *Endgames* (1997). EM's response to Joseph Beuys and to Ian Hamilton Finlay's* later work seems negative on the whole. In the 1980s, IHF's interest in the architecture of Albert Speer led him to incorporate the SS double lightning bolt insignia in artworks. 'Adorno's Hut' is a dissonant construction of a neoclassical temple in wood and metal.

Nicholas Johnson, poet and publisher

10 January 1998

Dear Nicholas

My apologies for taking so long to get round to your questionnaire – Christmas and its various distractions intervened. But anyhow I enclose a few thoughts now with this letter. It was good to hear from you, and your letter reminded me of that excellent evening with Roy Gael Carl and yourself.

The British Council has asked me to give some readings in Poland, so I shall be off to Warsaw Kraków and Katowice from 20th to 24th of this month. (Fur hat and rosary, an atheist friend recommends.)

I hope you will enjoy your Edinburgh visit in February – I'm sure you will. Your idea of a talk on Sean Rafferty sounds good, and I've been trying to think of someone you might write to in Glasgow. Perhaps the most likely place would be the big new Waterstone's ('flagship') bookshop which has a cafe and regular literary events, though they tend to be linked to some event or publication (but not always). The address is 153–175 Sauchiehall Street, Glasgow G2 3EW. Try writing to

Bob McDavitt who deals with events and publicity, and even if he couldn't give you a slot he might be able to suggest some other venue. Mention my name of course if you want.

All best wishes to you in 1998. | Eddie

SITE – ODYSSEY – PUBLIC

I am sometimes referred to as a 'Glasgow poet', and I could hardly reject the label, if only because I was born in that city, have lived there most of my life, and have written about it fairly frequently. When I began bringing Glasgow into my poetry in the 1950s/1960s there was an element of challenge and the exploration of a place that had had hardly any serious poetic manifestation before that; in fact there was a distinct pleasure in feeling and showing that this was a place (of widespread ill repute!) well worth probing at every level of poetic activity. As the city was in the throes of a violent demolition-and-rebuilding programme, extensive and bristling with social consequences, there seemed all the more reason to give the place a voice. However, I called one of my books *From Glasgow to Saturn*, and the fact is that no matter where you live nowadays, you are surrounded by the media and by science and its fruits, and if you are interested in such things, as I am, you will see no contradiction in writing one day about Gorbals housing and the next (or even the same) day about a moon landing, and from there it is a short step to hallucinating the city itself, presenting it in science-fiction terms, giving it a future or an imagined past. My imagined Glasgows were not vague, and I think the real-izing, the making real, of even an 'unreal' place has always been important to me, with the corollary that place itself must be important. (I don't agree, for instance, with those who say that space probes will do the job for us, that we don't actually need to be there.)

2001 and *Star Trek* show that the idea of an odyssey is as popular as it ever was, and Joyce's *Ulysses* proved its power in terms of the novel. But the novel and cinema between them seem to have drained a lot of that power from poetry. *Maximus* and *The Cantos* are odysseys in broken boats. *Omeros* humps along labouring in all its fancy paint, but most passengers sidle off at the first port. Silliman and Hejinian write good quasi-odysseys. Dorn and Griffiths are in that area too. But whether would you read *Gunslinger* or watch *Paris, Texas* or *Yol*? Cocteau's 'poésie du cinéma' is very beguiling. Still, poets have to try! The best odysseys are mental as well as physical, and verbal as well as mental. Wordsworth compressed all this very memorably in his couplet about Newton, 'a mind for ever / Voyaging through strange seas of thought, alone' – a man in a boat, possibly one of the early arctic explorers. Sitting at a table and covering a sheet of paper with mathematical symbols, or strapping yourself in for a rocket journey to Mars – if the former can be made physical, the latter can be made mental, and both lie in wait for their Homer.

Reading to an audience is good, because writing is such a solitary activity, and a reading at least temporarily unites the poet to the rest of humanity – three of them, thirty, three hundred, but at anyrate some! Reading it aloud to an audience is also to some extent a useful test of whether there is something in the poem that could have been put better. And often, even if there is no immediate reaction, you sow seeds. I don't believe that 'poetry makes nothing happen.'

Johnson had sent a questionnaire on 'Site – Odyssey – Public' in poetry ('site' meaning 'place') to assist him with a paper. The 'excellent evening' was a poetry reading with Carl Rakosi, touring the UK in 1997, aged 94, last survivor of the Objectivist group of American modernists. Johnson's Etruscan Books published Rakosi's *The Old Poet's Tale* (1999), and he also edited and published the neglected Scottish modernist Sean Rafferty (Carcanet Press, 1995 and Etruscan Books, 1999). Roy Fisher* and Gael Turnbull* also read at the event.

16 February 1998

Dear Bob and Lawrence

Thanks for your call-to-arms of the 10th! I do apologise
for not having answered your earlier letter, but I have to admit
that my heart sinks when I see a long questionnaire, and I tend
to put it at the bottom of the pile in the hope that eventually
it will not be answerable. Basically, I don't think it is the job
of authors to talk about their own work in this way. Once a
thing is written and in print it's in the public domain and
out of the author's hands. In my own case, I don't have fixed
or programmatic views about what I do or why I do it, and
therefore I am very reluctant to make 'statements'. I am too
ondoyant et divers. Please take the following as a sort of sketch
toward an answer and no more.

Since most written or printed poetry already has a visual
element, it is probably wrong to regard visual or concrete
poetry as a totally new departure. A page of *The Faerie Queene*
looks different from a page of *Paradise Lost*, to say nothing of
a page of *The Waste Land*. These things hit the eye right way
and affect our reading of the work concerned. What 'visual
poetry' does is foreground and specialize and extend and
sharpen something which has always been there. The sense
of something truly different seems to arise when the poems
either cannot be spoken aloud or can only be spoken in such a
way as to miss a good deal of what is clearly there on the page.
I have poems which are purely for the eye and which I don't
attempt to voice or perform (the photocopioids); I have some
which are meant primarily to be heard, even though they are in
print ('Shaker Shaken', 'The Loch Ness Monster's Song'); and
I have a fair number of poems which I regard as visual poems
but which if pressed I would perform reluctantly, and warning
people about what has been missed out (e.g. the pun on <u>shah</u>
and <u>chat</u> in 'French Persian Cats Having a Ball', the shape of
'Siesta of a Hungarian Snake' and of 'Pomander'). Since most
of these visual poems clearly do have a verbal interest, there is
a subterranean appeal to the inner ear and its unspeaking voice,
and I am sure this is what people recognize to be a part of the

total effect. Probably there is no such thing, physiologically speaking, as a wholly unvoiced poem!

I don't at the moment have any unpublished examples to give you, so I'm enclosing 'Shaker Shaken' as a linear oral piece and 'Alien's Message' as a visual unperformed piece.

Best wishes for the publication! I hope you will be able to make something of this contribution.

Eddie

Cobbing, a London-based sound poet, and Lawrence Upton were co-editors of a Writers Forum publication examining the relationship of visual and verbal elements in poetry, both on the page and in performance.

Peter McCarey, poet and translator

G120BG731998

Dear Peter

Many thanks for your end-of-the-year letter, which arrived at a somewhat clouded time, when I had had a letter telling me I had been awarded the T.S. Eliot Prize for Poetry and learned the next day that the letter had been sent in error – it took a little while to recover from that dashing of expectations. Fortunately I had something to look forward to at the end of January, a reading tour of Poland arranged by the British Council, which in fact went very well, with readings and/or seminars in Warsaw, Kraków, and Katowice. I met my translator Andrzej Szuba, and also the poet Piotr Sommer. At Kraków I was asked whether I would like to visit 'Auschwitz or the salt mines', so I chose the former: it's a museum now, quite hard to get to, and on the particularly icy day I was there, with almost no other visitors, it was as grim as you would want it to be. I also explored the Palace of Culture and Science in Warsaw, which after half a century has become a sort of period piece; it's even bigger than I thought it was, but very much used for concerts and exhibitions – a computer show was on when I was there and you could hardly move through the throng. – I was pleased that Richard has arranged for you to present your *Trattoria* at the BL next month; I imagine there should be a good audience, and you'll have a chance to inspect the glories of the new venue (but perhaps you've already seen them?). I think the revised version of the essay holds together extremely well (and you tracked down Filene-Finlay!). Does the BL publish, or help to publish, these lectures? – And the syllabary! Eia popeia. First fruits of the epopee. Very sparky, sir. The only way round one is through another, yes indeed. It reminded me at times of Charles Bernstein, but I don't know if you're into him at all. I looked for your original tabulation but couldn't find it among your letters, which is annoying, as I'm usually pretty careful. Maybe you could send a copy sometime. Your last lowsing of the louse suggests a fertile field for further from-to tergiversations. – You ask about Venuti: he's Lawrence Venuti, American translator and theorist, author of (amongst other things) *The Translator's Invisibility: A History of Translation* (1995), where he argues for 'foreignizing' as against 'domesticating' translations and claims there's been an Anglo-American colonizing agenda of recent years, making all foreign texts too readable/fluent/smooth, so that *Aeneids, Iliads*, and *Odysseys* all sound as if they'd been written by the same person. He has a point, though he pushes the case to some bizarre lengths.

I believe we are both to be at the SPL in Edinburgh on 24 April to deliver Gael's tribute. It should be a good occasion and I look forward to it. I understand we are all still successfully lip-sealed!

All the best | Eddie

EM had been mis-awarded the T.S. Eliot Prize for *Virtual and Other Realities* (1997). Researching for his essay 'Translator Trattoria', McCarey had discovered the Filene-Finlay, a 1920s device for simultaneous telephonic translation at international conferences. Richard Price* had invited McCarey to lecture on translation at the British Library [BL]. McCarey's *Syllabary* is a series based on random generation of words containing all the sound syllables of English, used as a stimulus for poems containing them. It now has its own website (www.thesyllabary.com).

Nicholas Johnson, poet and publisher
(handwritten)

30–3–1998

Dear Nicholas

A belated thank you for your February letter and the two readers. They are very attractive books and I'm very pleased to have them. (Your essay paper however was not in the envelope! – If you still have a copy I'd be glad to see it.) Since your letter came I've been busy with rehearsals and performances of my *Planet Wave* with Tommy Smith and his band. We played in Glasgow Edinburgh and Stirling and got pretty good audiences. I hope a CD will emerge from it eventually but there's no definite word of this yet. I may be doing something else with Tommy later in the year. He's touring Sweden at the moment – gets around. Somehow I can't think of the Swedes and jazz, but I'm probably wrong.

I am glad you enjoyed the Edinburgh visit, despite that silly review. I saw Gael and Jill in Glasgow recently and they were both in good form. I'll be seeing Gael again in Edinburgh in April. In the meantime I am trying to get some thoughts together for the Edinburgh Science Festival, where I've been asked to give both a reading and a lecture bringing poetry and science together. As the lecture is due to be printed later in a book on the subject, I must not hum and haw but deploy my thought-cohorts in as well-armed formations as I can get mustered/mustard! Miroslav Holub is to be another of the speakers, and I am looking forward to seeing him again – we both read some years ago in Toronto.

I hope all goes well with you in creamy Devon. Daffodils and magpies everywhere here. A sort of sense of – well it can't quite be spring yet, in Scotland, though at least the clocks have gone forward. I use the active verb because I have a clock which changes its hour by itself while I am asleep. It receives a signal from the National Physical Laboratory at Teddington. Poetry and science.

All best wishes | Eddie

The 'something else' after *Planet Wave* was ten songs for the theatrical musical *Monte Cristo*, based on the Alexandre Dumas novel, and performed in Edinburgh and Glasgow in Autumn 1998. At the Edinburgh Science Festival on 18 April 1998, EM would meet Mark Smith*, as described in 'After a Lecture' (*A Book of Lives*, 2007: 91). His lecture appeared in *Contemporary Poetry and Contemporary Science* (2006), edited by Robert Crawford*.

Colin Nicholson, academic

7 May 1998

Dear Colin

Thanks for your 'progress report' – you seem to be forging ahead with vigour!

The Blake epigraph is from *Visions of the Daughters of Albion* (lines 53–57) and I admit it wouldn't be easy to find. I thought the theme of that poem, freedom v. slavery, both physical and mental, would meet 'Memories of Earth' quite well, and particularly the lines I quoted. Blake has always been one of my favourite authors.

'The Mill' is probably difficult, though I like it. I'm not sure that I would ever want to interpret it very far by myself (I do, however, look forward to seeing what you make of it). The speaker is plural and is probably something like 'me and my friends', within a markedly erotic and it would seem transgressive context. Puritanical angel and sensually liberating devil re-enact an ancient seesaw. But it isn't quite as straightforward as that. Hail baffles the grindstone, and that might be a Blakean metaphor for the happily bouncing intransigence of the poem – over to you!

I hope you have a good trip to Yugoslavia. I am in the midst of another ploy with Tommy Smith: I've written ten songs for tenor voice, to be accompanied by Tommy's music and the Paragon Ensemble. The voice is Tommy's uncle, Jeff Leyton. *Monte Cristo* is for late-night performances at the Traverse during the last week of the Festival. More details later.

Best as ever | Eddie

'Memories of Earth', with its epigraph from Blake, appeared in *The New Divan* (*CP*: 330). 'The Mill' was in *From Glasgow to Saturn* (*CP*: 248). Nicholson's analysis of this poem's subversion of moral binaries is in his *Edwin Morgan: Inventions of Modernity*: 108–109.

Mark Smith, friend
(handwritten)

18–7–1998

'Old men ought to be explorers'
                    (T.S. Eliot)

'And to be young was very heaven'
                    (Wordsworth)

Dear Mark

Here are a few thoughts in answer to those parts of your letter we didn't talk about on Thursday. Whether they'll reach you in time for our Monday meeting depends on the postal service!

Pound's categories: where would he place himself? He was certainly an <u>inventor</u> and I think he'd have wanted to claim that. You could almost say he 'invented' T.S. Eliot. He didn't quite invent <u>imagism</u> but he certainly defined and spread it and made it significant. Perhaps a <u>master</u>? – well, with all the qualifications we were talking about: brilliant/hateful, clearsighted/'mad', central/eccentric, etc. Like a damaged stick of rock, he hasn't got MASTER all the way through; sometimes it's MONSTER. But there's no sweeping him under the carpet – he's <u>there</u>.

Eliot and WW2: by that time he had become a great English patriot, and for all his dislike of Russia as an ally he supported the war effort and regarded 'Little Gidding' with its reference to air-raids and English history as his contribution to the cause. Why stay after WW1? – I don't think he would ever have returned to America. He fell out with his family when he married, and he had committed himself to 'Europe', which for practical purposes meant London. E.P. and Thomas/Stevens/

Roethke/Hardy? – Hardy he admired, but he hadn't much to do with the others. More concerned with <u>Basil Bunting</u> – there's another name for you.

Blake. Ah Blake, 'Auguries of Innocence', great stuff. That grain of sand. I think I would agree with your thoughts about eternity being made up of infinities, though I also think Blake's mind was working, in a sense, the other way, towards the infinitely <u>small</u> (an idea I explore in my 'Memories of Earth'). He sees the sand-grain as a world, or even as a universe. If you could enter it (as we might today with electron microscopes) you would find as much detail as Hubble would give you in the other direction. Although there were microscopes in Blake's time, it is quite a prophetic thought: the beauty and mystery of the universe can be seen, in Blake's mind, in the infinitely tiny as well as in the galaxies.

Would Blake have put up with Pound? Maybe for an afternoon! There would have been some points of contact (their 'outsiderishness'), but they were political opposites, and I can see Blake propelling the American bodily out of the house (as he did with some others).

Colour of the outside of the universe? Oh you are a hard man. Does it have an outside at all? If we believe Hubble, the universe is not black but black plus grey white yellow red blue green orange and violet. If it's expanding, it's not expanding like a blown-up balloon, so there's no surface for there to be an inside and an outside, is there? It can only expand, <u>if</u> it's expanding, into something compatible with itself, and we think of that as 'space', and probably black. (And remember all the masses of dark matter, or anti-matter, which so far we have found no way of seeing at all.) If Shelley is right, the 'outside' is <u>white</u>. 'Life, like a dome of many-coloured glass, / stains the white radiance of eternity.' How about that?

Your lightning-struck cable-dangler? Won't he already be burnt black before the bolt strikes? 'After the first death, there is no other' (D. Thomas). I'm sure you have a hidden thought about this which you will reveal on Monday over a Purdey. I look forward to hearing it. And to seeing you about 7pm.

Yin and yang be with you. | Eddie

AENEAS WENT TO ITALY FROM MACEDONIA

MARK WENT TO ITALY FROM CALEDONIA

Smith, a 24-year-old student with whom EM fell in love at the age of 78, came from the same Lanarkshire working-class background as John Scott (but was not Catholic). He was keen to educate himself in literature. Their relationship is described in the 'Love and a Life' sequence of *A Book of Lives* (2007). At this point, he was on his way to Italy to work on a youth project for disadvantaged children. Purdey is a health energy drink, containing ginseng. The final lines in capitals were written vertically down the sides of each sheet of paper in EM's original.

Tommy Smith, jazz saxophonist and composer

FAX   21–7–1998
To: T. Smith
From: E. Morgan

A SONG FOR GLASGOW

There's a city I know where the story is told
Of how its streets are paved with gold.
O no they're not!
O yes they are!
Its pavements are rich with gold.

No it's not London and it's not Paree,
It's where the Clyde rolls down to the sea.
O no it's not!
O yes it is!
And the Clyde sings to the sea:

People are the gold of this city of mine,
Not bought and sold, that's straight down the line.
O no it's not!
O yes it is!
And they sing it straight down the line:

We shall shine in a story that's never been told.
We shall build a city that's both just and bold.
O no you won't!
O yes we will!
It will shine both just and bold.

Dear Tommy –

   Here are some first thoughts on our SONG – see what you
   make of them –

Avanti! | Eddie

For the 'Lines of Language' element of an arts project for senior
pupils in Glasgow schools, EM was commissioned to write 'a song
about the city', to be performed at school concerts or assemblies
and also by a new schools' choir at the switching on of the city's
Christmas lights.

Colin Nicholson, academic

24 July 1998

Dear Colin
   Thanks for yours of the 21st. I have the answer to your
query about the Goddesses. The sequence was written in a
burst of activity in the week from 6 to 14 September 1982 –
very emotional experience – tears on the page as I finished the
last one – perhaps in a Zeuxippe c'est moi mood celebrating
my university retirement of 1980. I am now confused about
the poems and seldom include them in a reading. Have been
brought to almost (but not quite) assume that because they are
never talked about or selected for anthologies they cannot be
as good as I thought they were when I wrote them.
   I like the idea of your 'recent, current, and unpublished'
chapter. Maybe you could print the 'Pieces of Me' as an
appendix! It would be a selling point for the book, though
if your volume was to be used in schools I could foresee

problems with one or two 'improper' pieces (unless I'm being oldfashioned). I am enclosing a couple of items very relevant to that chapter. 'The Death of Enkidu', published very recently in a magazine, is from my second version of *Gilgamesh* which I still hope Communicado will someday put on. The ten *Monte Cristo* songs are still unpublished, and I haven't sent them anywhere for publication. Most of the *Demon* poems have now been snapped up by magazines/anthologies, but I have no plans yet for publishing the sequence as a whole (as I would like it to be).

Best as ever, and avanti! | Eddie

EM skirts around the legal problems he ran into with *An Alphabet of Goddesses* (CP: 464–77). In his enthusiasm, he borrowed phrasing from the exhibition catalogue, including text by Robert Graves, and was forced to pay copyright fees. Some 'Pieces of Me' were republished in *Dreams and Other Nightmares* (2010). His full second version of *Gilgamesh* appeared in *Long Poem Magazine*, Issue 5, 2010/2011: 3–23.

Mark Smith, friend
(handwritten)

18–8–1998

Παντα γαρ τολμητεον
  (For all things are to be dared)
        – Plato

Dear Mark

I have been thinking a lot about your Ascom-pager in the intervals of various distractions such as (a) being dragged by a friend to see *Armageddon* – advanced jingoism + advanced technology + sentiment as thick as treacle, and (b) getting some thoughts in order for the Book Festival tomorrow. Your letter said things that moved me, and said many things that make me want to say many things in return.

Your opening paragraph on youth and age, and does age bring patience and serenity? Well, I think I have patience, but

I don't find much serenity! Sailing into calmer waters, writing *Tempests*, composing last quartets, taking a deckchair into the garden – no, that doesn't seem to be me. Maybe I should add <u>yet</u>, for who knows? But at the moment I seem as open to the stimulations of change as I ever was. There have to be moments of serenity of course: watching the sky from my window, admiring the flight of a gull as it slices across, or one of the sunsets we've both seen here. But openness to change: yes, the two of us have that. Stimulation for the forward step. Avanti! You certainly stimulate me. Do I stimulate you? I hope and think I do.

I enjoyed your rhyming lines about the desires of the imagination – washing your hands in antimatter – getting to those states that defy prediction and theory. You got the beat there! Imagination must by definition lead towards the unexpected, even if it's only Wordsworth's 'Something evermore about to be', but I agree with you that <u>dealing</u> with unexpectedness is poetry's territory. And yes, I have no doubt that the mind can be, has been, will be stretched out into areas of unimagined if not unimaginable potential.

Maybe this leads back to your earlier query about mathematics and poetry. I have been looking at one poet who did try to bring the two together, in some of his work: Velimir Khlebnikov (1885–1922), a Russian Futurist who had ideas about the periodicities of historical events and used mathematics in writing about this. He was almost obsessed by numbers –

> Numbers, eternal numbers, sound in the beyond;
> I hear their distant conversation. Number
> calls to number; number calls me home.

– That's from a long poem with prose inserts, called *Zangezi* (trans. here by Paul Schmidt), and I'm enclosing a copy of one passage where he brings in some equations. I wonder what you make of it? The hero, Zangezi, is virtually the poet himself, but presented as a prophetic shamanistic figure (figure!) wandering through the world with / or <u>for</u>) amazing adventures.

Now for: Q1. Yes, Pushkin's winter poem <u>is</u> strictly metrical, a six-beat line rhyming in couplets, alternately feminine and masculine, thus in the opening line:

Zimá. Chto délat nám v derévne? Ya vstrecháyu

But for all the regular basis of the form, he makes the lines very supple and gives the impression of a speaker going through a range of thoughts and feelings about the boredom of a winter day in the country and how the boredom can be *d i s p e r s e d* ————— !

Q2: Hopkins did try to get the 'The Wreck of the Deutschland' and 'The Loss of the Eurydice' published in *The Month*, a leading Catholic journal, but they were both rejected, and we know that he was disappointed. His friends offered to place his poems in secular journals, but he wouldn't allow this, since as a Jesuit priest he accepted that 'all that we publish must be seen by censors first' (letter to Canon Dixon). But in other letters he made it clear that he would want to be published someday, somehow – the poet in him cannot help crying out. All that was published in his lifetime was 'Three Triolets', short comic pieces, and even these were in a religious journal, *The Stonyhurst Magazine*.

You asked if you could 'ask me something personal'. Yes, Mark, anything, and I will do my best to be open with you, and answer it. I regard you as a good friend, so you must feel free to speak your mind and ask what you want. As regards poetry prizes (and especially <u>that</u> one), it was obviously a psychological shock to be buoyed up one day and shipwrecked the next; but I have always believed in simply going on writing, regardless of recognition or the lack of it – I have enough trust in my poetry to do that – so you'll no have to kick my erse. You hope (you say) that I can confide in you things I wouldn't mention to anyone else. Yes, I can. I know you are not gay, and I don't want to embarrass you, but I have come to be very attached to you over those four months, and I hope I can say that without annoying or offending you. Whatever unexpected (unexpectedness again!) warp in the continuum got our paths to cross at the Science Festival, it certainly arc'd and sparked, and I still have a vivid image of you coming forward to speak to me. Well, there it is. Let us go on, in Italy or Scotland. I have a sense of the curtains being drawn back, and my god what vistas are possible – you are addressing those 'sanctities' you speak of, moving onto a new stage of life and discovery, making decisions yet leaving s p a c e s for an unknown future to touch and astonish you. Be astonished! The water's deep. The clouds race. Even nature, which you say is unchanging, changes, though you can still love it. That hill you took the Loch Sheil photo from was once not there and will no doubt sometime again not be there. 'The hills are shadows', as Tennyson said (and he knew about geology). I liked very much what you said about Glenfinnan and other towers. And yes, your rhyming lines about the mountains and the loch <u>are</u> metrical! (and attractive). I seem to have stopped writing in paragraphs. All things flow, as the old Greek said.

New paragraph at last. I was touched by what you said about your black African girlfriend. I admire that kind of openness and it was good that nothing bad came of it, despite prejudices which I am sure are still all around. What relationships lie in wait for you, I wonder, in Italy or elsewhere? I'm sure you will deal with them with your good openness and directness, at the same time keeping something that is only yourself and never allowing it not to grow. I hope in any case (– this is beginning to sound autumnal and farewellish – bah! –) that we shall always keep in touch, and that you will tell me about your doings and froings, and that the lines between us will remain powerfully charged and even give off as much blue smoke as you like.

Until Saturday at 1pm –

I remain | yours (yes, co-pilot, I like that – | engines
    revving –) | Ed.

PS you asked about corrections. I see only one* – on p.1, <u>embarassed</u> should be <u>embarrassed</u>. That's a tricky one (like the much misspelt <u>accommodation</u>).

*sorry, two. <u>Vaccuum</u> (p. 3) should be <u>vacuum</u>.

'That which cannot be, is not.' (Avvakum)
    – True, or false?

'You cannot eat a fish with a Latin name' (Morton Feldman)
   – True, or false?

No, I don't know which poet wandered on & heard the
timeless nightingale. Certainly not Emily Dickinson!
   – And I also don't know 'about next May' – tell me tell me.

The pager was presumably an idea to maintain contact. Smith
initially studied mathematics at university, before realising this was
a wrong direction. At the Edinburgh Science Festival in April 1998,
Smith approached EM with some poems for comment. The tower
at Glenfinnan (to which he had recently cycled) is a monument to
the 1745 Jacobite rising. (The three final quotations were written
vertically along the pages' margins.)

Mary McCluskey, Artistic Director, Scottish Youth Theatre

28 August 1998

Dear Mary McCluskey

Thank you very much for your letter, and for sending the
Cyrano programme and the excellent production photograph.
I enjoyed the production and must congratulate you and
all concerned for giving a new look to the play. I was there
with a couple of young chaps in their twenties, and they had
not known the play before; they simply took it as it came,
and liked it a lot. It took me longer to adjust to the changed
genders, simply because I knew the play so well with its
original characters, but it worked on me as it went on, and I
found myself happily accepting the changes. There are, in any
case, sexual ambiguities lurking in the play, since the historical
Cyrano was himself gay, and I'm sure there are whole aspects
of the play that could be brought out in different ways by
different directors. I thought the battle scene and the final
scene were particularly effective at the Cottier. I hope the cast
enjoyed themselves; they seemed to!

   With thanks and best wishes | Yours sincerely |
      Edwin Morgan

McCluskey directed a Scottish Youth Theatre production of *Cyrano de Bergerac* at Cottier's Theatre in Glasgow's West End. As the company included more female than male actors, she switched the gender of the main characters, with a female Cyrano and male Roxanne. The identity of the 'couple of young chaps' is unknown.

Marshall Walker, academic and friend
(handwritten)

8–9–1998

Dear Marshall

Good telephone talk that, even allowing for the f a ding (Gould must have been casting spells). I have passed on your message to Hamish. Hamish and family, by the way, all enjoyed *M. Cristo*, and several people have phoned to say the same, so maybe I was hypercritical about the balance, or lack of it. Maybe the days of seamless webs, like the days of wine and roses, are over. And the *Scotsman* review is more positive than the *Herald* one. The *Herald* is a bit unfair about the songs: I wasn't trying to write 'my' poems, as in *Beasts* and *Planet Wave* (poems which would stand up by themselves in a book), but simply songs to be sung by someone else within a context. Perhaps the chap who shouted out 'Bloody brilliant!' at the end of the first night's performance was right after all!

I enclose four of my ongoing Demons.

Avanti, etc. | Eddie

EM produced the lyrics for ten songs for *Monte Cristo*. Hamish Whyte* was, with Walker, a literary executor. Walker was collating a biographical record of EM's literary activities, as in the following example.

EM – DOINGS, COMINGS & GOINGS etc – 1998

20–24 January: British Council tour of Poland, giving
readings & taking seminars in Warsaw, Krakow, and Katowice.
(Included visit to Auschwitz which resulted, later on, in the
poem 'The Demon at the Frozen Marsh'.)
29 January: 'Celtic Connections' reading with Stewart Conn in
Glasgow Royal Concert Hall.
3 February: Reading at Univ. Strathclyde.
13 February: Talk + reading to students at RSAMD.
16 February: Reading at Cumbernauld Theatre.
18 February: Reading at Lady Margaret Hall, Oxford.
2 March: Reading at Lornshill Academy (Clackmannan).
4 March: Reading at Clutha Vaults, Glasgow, plus talk to
writers' group.
6 March: Performance of *Planet Wave*, Stevenson Hall,
RSAMD.
12 March: *Planet Wave*, Queens Hall, Edinburgh.
13 March: *Planet Wave*, MacRobert Centre, Univ. Stirling.
19 March: Reading at Tynecastle High School, Edinburgh.
24 March: Reading at Langside College.
18 April: Lecture + reading at Edinburgh Science Festival.
29 April: Reading at Univ. Aberdeen.
12 May: Reading at Bellarmine School, Glasgow.
16 May: Reading at launch of new 'book town', Wigtown.
1–4 June: Bournemouth.
5–8 June: London.
19–22 June: Resident poet at St Magnus Festival, Orkney.
4 July: Reading at Caledonian Bewery, Edinburgh. [Brewery–
what a drunken typist!]
15 July: Reading at Scottish Universities International
Summer School, Pollock Halls, Edinburgh.
27–31 July: Readings & discussions at John Hewitt Summer
School, Carnlough, Northern Ireland.
19 August: Edinburgh Book Festival – reading at 'Authors for
Breakfast' plus taking part in panel discussion in afternoon on
'Translating Plays for the Theatre'.
26 August: Reading at Arvon Foundation, Moniack Mhor.

1 September: First night of *Monte Cristo*, Traverse Theatre,
Edinburgh. I was in audience, not on stage; took bow on stage
at end.
5 September: Talk on writing poetry to writers' groups at
Lochgelly.
6 September: Talk on Spenser's *Faerie Queen* to Open
University students, Baird Hall, Glasgow.
8 September: I typed this!

Peter McCarey, poet and translator
(handwritten)

                                        G12 0BG 13 12 1998

Dear Peter
    (This must be the discreetest of Christmas cards – no
message, even using lemon juice.) I was glad to get your
October letter, which among other things asked if it was OK
to quote me on translation; and the answer is yes of course.
I look forward to seeing the published essay. And yes, I have
Double Click, nicely printed as usual by D. Glen. The poems
have an epigrammatic look, but they probe and pick at the
mind more than epigrams do, and I like that. I like particularly
the two in the centrefold (and that is perhaps why they are
there?). Oh, and you also queried if I'd <u>really</u> never written
a novel? I've really really not, and I doubt if I could, though
that's probably a bit defeatist. '<u>Anyone</u> can write a novel.' At
the moment I'm writing poems about – or more strictly from
or by – a demon. And I've promised to translate a remarkable,
little-known Latin poem on The Battle of Bannockburn,
written by an English priest who was there. Mariscat aim to
publish this, in time for the new parliament next year!
    Iain Crichton Smith's death was quite sudden, though it
was known that he had throat cancer. He had been due to give
a reading in London on the South Bank, and they asked me
to step in, talk about Iain, and read a selection of his poems,
which I did. I knew him for over 40 years, knew him much
better than I knew Norman or Sorley or George McB. He had
a wonderful sense of humour, and was even able to joke about

the time he spent 'in the loony bin'. Holub is another loss: he died not long after we had been talking together during the Edinburgh Science Festival. And Bill Aitken, Robert Blair Wilkie – it's been a grim year.

Did you know that Wigtown has been launched as Scotland's Book Town, on the Hay-on-Wye model? Will it work? I don't know. You certainly need a car to get there.

I shared the Stakis Prize for Scottish Writer of the Year with James Kelman. Cheque and gold medal handed over at a big bash in Bellshill (where there's a new Stakis hotel). The ceremony, with endless references to the magnificence of Stakis sponsorship, was enlivened by a fire-alarm (small kitchen event, apparently) which had us all trooping out into the night in our finery. Fire-engines arrived quickly; efficiency all round. I was sorry Jim Kelman couldn't be there – he has a year as visiting professor in Texas – but he had been videoed, and was there in spirit, reminding us of oppressed writers in Turkey, which he visited recently under Amnesty International. Myself, I'm in two minds about highlighting individual writers and artists in this way. What about the thousands of unknowns who have no lobby, no one to speak for them – not thousands but millions, in history?

For aw that an aw that, best | wishes to you all in 1999 – |
    Eddie

McCarey's *Double-Click* was published by Akros Publications (1997), and EM's *Demon* by Mariscat Press (1999). With the Scottish Poetry Library and Akros, Mariscat would co-publish *Metrum de Praelio apud Bannockburn / The Battle of Bannockburn* by Robert Baston (2004). Miroslav Holub (1923–98) was a Czech poet and immunologist; Bill (W.R.) Aitken (1913–98) a librarian and literary scholar; and Robert Blair Wilkie (1913–98) the curator of the People's Palace on Glasgow Green.

Hamish Whyte, publisher, poet, bibliographer
(handwritten)

G12 0BG 19–1–1999

Dear Hamish

Thanks for card overstamped *Royal College of Physicians and Surgeons of Glasgow*. Everyone has to advertise! The Gilmorehill event went very well – a full house, despite the weather and the ticket price. Bill Paterson did a good Tarzan cry and breast-beating. The buffet was cold nibbles and a glass of wine. I thought they might have stretched to hot sausages on sticks, for a winter's night. (That's something I'm very partial to!) – Geddes is really most interesting, and his best poems ought to be far better known. Do let me know if you ever come across his books in secondhand catalogues. I have *In the Valhalla*. The versatile chap even wrote *The Babes in the Wood: A Cantata for Schools and Classes* (music by John Kerr) which I'd love to see. – Pages 62–63 of the *Cyrano* will be fine.

And the rain it raineth every day.

All the best | Eddie

Glasgow University's Gilmorehill Centre for Theatre, Film and Tele-vision, in a former church, was celebrating the installation of two stained-glass windows featuring lines from 'Ten Theatre Poems' (*CP*: 355ff.) and 'Five Poems on Film Directors' (*CP*: 362ff.). Readings by actors Bill Paterson and Hannah Gordon included an excerpt from Edgar Rice Burroughs' *Tarzan of the Apes*. James Young Geddes (1850–1913) was a radical poet, autodidact and businessman from Dundee, whose Whitmanian poetry challenged Scotland's Victorian industrialism. The extract from *Cyrano de Bergerac* would appear in *Into Glasgow: Translations and Responses* (Mariscat, 2006).

30–1–1999

(I have that picture of you stretched out
on the grass beside Keats's grave –)
    This living hand, now warm and capable
    Of earnest grasping, would, if it were cold
    And in the icy silence of the tomb,
    So haunt thy days and chill thy dreaming nights …
                                        (Keats, from a late fragment)

My dear Mark
    Your two good letters came almost together – the slow one
of the 14th took a fortnight. I think you are right about the
Leopardi tape, but it is the usual broadcaster's fear of scaring
off the listener with anything too meaty, or those shark's jaws
you mention. At least the poet got an airing, and that's rare
enough here! If only we had <u>his</u> voice – and Keats's – both
with regional accents –
    I was greatly interested to read about your visit to the
cemetery. That cat – scary! – must have been some sort
of guardian spirit of the place, reminding you not to take
anything for granted, least of all peace and meditation. It is
good to know that Severn is given his proper and dignified
spot. His conduct was exemplary, and his account of the last
days is very moving. How many would have done what he did?
Keats had studied medicine and knew at an early stage what
was happening to him. I'm sure he must have, deep down,
known his value, but his consciousness of never being able to
fulfil his potential (plus of course the bad reviews and 'cockney'
attacks) (how could a vulgar surgeon's apprentice from London
ever write great poetry?) (plus the useless Fanny Brawne) led
inevitably to those dark 'writ in water' thoughts. Well, his
reputation, like that of the Romantics, remains high. You asked
for questions. Does writing your name in water, once done,
remain somehow for ever in the fabric of this universe, simply
because it has been done and not just thought about, despite
being rippled out of visible existence a moment later?

Rilke, Neruda: both great, though in very different ways. Rilke, as far as I know, did not get the Nobel Prize. His work deserved it, I agree. Perhaps we can say it does not have 'committee appeal'! His extraordinary self-concentration and solitariness (especially when he was writing the *Duino Elegies*) must have been one of those 'if I don't do it my own way I'll never do anything' impulses – a huge risk – solipsism, self-destruction – but he was proved right in the end. (Mind you, what would he have done without all those wealthy lady-friends?) (how, my dear Mark, would you like a <u>castle</u> to live in, with servants, to say nothing of marvellous views?)

Rilke could never have enjoyed, or even wanted to enjoy, the kind of audiences Neruda and Mayakovsky commanded, and yet Mayakovsky at least was in many ways a 'solitary' like Rilke. To get a 'non-poetry' audience probably requires either a revolutionary, heavily politicized situation or forms of entertainment (Morgan and Tommy Smith – or possibly that other Smith rapping with his friends down by the river?). I am glad Neruda made you have a second take on Stalin, by the way. It's how often forgotten, or not even known, what a heroic figure he was to people in the west, and I don't mean the left wing, it was general, during the war. Those who see him only as a 'monster' are cutting out a part of history, and that's not good. It's easy, but it's not good.

Questions – oh yes, M. Ondaatje. I haven't read the *English Patient* book, though I saw the film, and didn't greatly enjoy it, apart from the desert photography. The only book of his I have is *Rat Jelly*, a collection of poems which doesn't pulse very strongly for me, though it has an animal strangeness and undercurrentishness and can be interesting.

[Snow coming] In the Highlands I have seen a snowplough in the garden/forecourt of a house, so presumably the driver does not have to 'go to' his work?

I am enclosing Logue's Homer as promised. What do you think he (i) gains and (ii) loses through his method of translation?

Also enclosed, some samples of Stanyhurst, Marlowe, Golding – sorry I have no Sandys. Marlowe's Ovid is included in the Penguin book of his *Poems and Translations*. Whether this is still in print I don't know, but it might be.

I shall add to the package a copy of my *B. Letters*
review, plus two Pushkin translations I made for this year's
forthcoming bicentenary book. The two poems, as you will
see, are very different in style, but so they are in the original –
remarkable fellow Aleksandr!

I finished my *DEMON* sequence and passed it on to
Mariscat (Hamish Whyte). A copy will fly to you on black
leathern wings in due course. Most books have dedications,
and I've dedicated this one 'To Mark', but if you don't like the
idea just let me know. It will be a limited edition of 250 copies.

Oh, I nearly forgot: you wanted my *Essays*. The book is long
out of print, and I have only one spare copy which I must keep
for emergencies. I'll look out for a secondhand copy.

Now you look after yourself and give me all your news,
which I love to hear. Be nice to cats. Don't fall into graves –
rivers – anything!

Yours as ever | Ed

Sitting by Keats's grave in Rome, Smith had been scared by a cat
leaping on to his shoulders. He had become interested in Elizabe-
than translations, particularly Arthur Golding's *Metamorphoses*. The
'B Letters' review is of Ted Hughes'* *Birthday Letters*: 'The jagged
crystal', *The Dark Horse*, Winter 1998–99. *Demon* (1999) was dedi-
cated 'To Mark' rather than 'To M.S.', as the customary initials might
have been mistaken for those of Michael Schmidt*.

Colin Nicholson, *academic*

20 March 1999

Dear Colin

Thanks very much for letting me see the two essays. I
must say I'm greatly impressed by them, and (if the author
himself can be a judge) they show much insight into what
the poems are doing. I particularly admire your commentary
on 'Memories of Earth', which is a poem that has had very
little scrutiny before. The opening of the science fiction essay,
however, raises a point you may have to deal with if there's

still time! Your Hafiz is not my Hafiz! Mine is the great 14th-century Persian poet whose *Divan* is one of the classics of that country. There are references to his life and work scattered through my sequence (e.g. the early death of his son). I can assure you that I had not heard of Ibrahim Hafiz, which is a pity, since he would fit in so neatly with my sojourn in Egypt, and I can understand why you must have seized on his name. But no, he is not the man. Will you be able to rewrite the opening sentences, or perhaps add a note giving my disclaimer? Sorry about this!

There are a couple of points to be corrected in the *Sonnets* essay. On p.6, the last two lines of the Pilate quotation should read:

> and washed his hands, and watched his hands, and washed
> his hands, and watched his hands, and washed his hands.

The alternation between 'washed' and 'watched' is quite important in really focussing the obsessive activity, as if in close-up; it's a question of guilt more than of indecision (at least as I read it). The other point is in the notes at the end of p.14: the Mariscat Press is in Glasgow, not Edinburgh (it's situated in Mariscat Road in Pollokshields, supposedly from Mary [Queen of Scots]'s cat – she has associations with that area!).

Do let me know if you need these copies back. If not, I shall be very pleased to keep them.

All the best as ever | Eddie

Nicholson had sent EM copies of critical essays on his science fiction poetry (for the *Yearbook of English Studies*) and *Sonnets from Scotland* (for Marco Fazzini's planned anthology, *Alba Literaria: A History of Scottish Literature*, Amos Edizioni, 2005).

Hamish Whyte, *publisher, poet, bibliographer*
(handwritten)

G12 0BG 15–4–1999

Dear Hamish

Thanks for Hans Arp: I think it's great. Tom is a man of surprises. I am enclosing copies of Colin's two essays – I'm sure he wouldn't mind you seeing them. Some interesting stuff there, I think. My stick is back in the umbrella-stand, I'm glad to say. I have forged ahead rapidly with Doktor Faust and am now typing out the whole play, due at TAG by the 22nd. The entire middle part, Acts 3–4, is new, and will I hope help to give the play some cohesion. Strange to think that after writing about a demon for a year I'm accidentally in demonland again – Next time I'll send you an angel card –

All the best | Eddie

For *Into Glasgow: Translations and Responses* Tom Leonard* had translated 'I am a horse' ('Ahma Hoarss') by Hans Arp. The collection, with a Preface by EM, appeared in 2006.

Richard Price, *poet, editor and librarian*
(handwritten)

20–5–1999

Dear Richard – Another orchid for you, virtually <u>animal</u> this one, watch out! I have to thank you for that nice Bushy Park (are there any non-bushy parks?) photo of Katie and you on bicycle-built-for-two – She looks quite secure and happy! Thanks also for the offprint on Gunn's plays: you make a good and careful case, and I know how wrong it is to write off unseen/unperformed plays, though I think I still wait to be convinced; but anyhow it's good to call attention to them, and maybe some director will take it further. My own *Faustus II* is just about complete (it's complete, but little bits of rewriting required). TAG will be starting it off at the Citizens, then touring around Scotland. I'm glad you liked the shark. It was the one I myself thought came nearest to standing by itself without the music. Poetry-and-music had a big sound in Aberdeen at the weekend, when Tommy Smith and I rolled out our *Planet Wave* once more. You may have seen Magnus Linklater's comment on the performance in today's *Times*. (I was reminded of your remarks on performance in your last letter. I think it's fine as long as you don't let it become addictive – after even the finest audience has dispersed you have to go back to a little room and a little table and some sheets of A4 and without any encouragement or feedback [a cat, an orchid in a pot?!] quietly write your next piece. Maybe the public/private contrast is a productive Bakhtinian dialogism, ho ho.) Peter Forbes did want a review of your book, gave me 700 words, which I have now sent off to *Poetry Review*, so I suppose the next number – ?

Best as ever | Eddie

EM had bought various postcards of orchids, and also two plants, at an Orchid Weekend in Glasgow's Botanic Gardens. His *Christopher Marlowe's Doctor Faustus* (1999) was a new version commissioned by TAG Theatre Company (Theatre About Glasgow). 'The Bearsden Shark', one of a series of songs written for a local choir, was published in *Dreams and Other Nightmares* (2010). EM had recommended Price's *Perfume & Petrol Fumes* (diehard publishers, 1999) to Peter Forbes of *Poetry Review*.

Hamish Whyte, publisher, poet, bibliographer
(handwritten)

G12 0BG 22–8–1999

Puzzle: find the cat (more than one, actually). I'm posting this just before having lunch with Richard at the Cul de Sac. Sorry I couldn't join you in Waterstones yesterday. You'll be pleased to know that my lecture is virtually and virtuously finished. Raindog is enthusiastic about *A.D.* (I) but wants to have one scene rewritten, so that will be my priority after Wednesday.

Malcolm is taking drawing lessons. Mark, just back from
looking after autistic children in Italy, is off on a new project
tomorrow, helping disaffected teenagers in Bridgend (Wales).
Two loves at my age, isn't it absurd? But they both help me
in different ways (Mark's not gay) to be positive and look
forward, so bless them.

Till Tuesday – | Eddie

The postcard showed a Bristol tattoo artist, Les Skuse, but was
chosen more for the cat images, which EM and Whyte exchanged
frequently. Richard Price* was visiting Glasgow. EM was completing
his 'Scotland and the World' lecture for the Edinburgh International
Book Festival. His relationships with Malcolm Thomson and Mark
Smith* are described in *Sweeping Out the Dark* (1994) and *Love and
a Life* (2003), later in *A Book of Lives* (2007).

James Campbell, literary journalist and critic
(handwritten)

24–9–1999

Dear Jim
    It is always good to hear from you. Eddie Linden was on
the phone to me too, congratulating me on resurrecting Helen
Adam, whom he met (he says) in New York when she was old
and frail. The lecture (copy enclosed) caused quite a stir (big
audience of 400), and *The Scotsman* splashed the event as 'news'
rather than as a cultural item. I enclose, for your interest, a
copy of all this. I came across Helen Adam's name through my
interest in the Beats in the late 1950s, and of course she was in
Donald Allen's anthology *The New American Poetry*. I now
have most of her books. She was quite unknown in Scotland,
which I suppose is why the lecture startled many. I'd love to
see her ballad opera, *San Francisco's Burning*. The Edinburgh
Festival ought to put it on – or more properly it should be in
Glasgow!
    I have another jazz collaboration with Tommy Smith
coming up: a series of songs for next year's Glasgow Jazz

Festival, some sort of story-of-Scotland theme, not yet worked out.

I thought the four poems made a really good page in the TLS, and I've had quite a few appreciative comments. The seagull is the favourite. As I think I suggested to you, the six poems I sent were all a direct reaction to a medical problem I didn't spell out. There's always such an element of doom and dread attached to the word cancer that at first I tried to keep it confidential – but not now. I think I've managed to take it on board, and adjust my life as far as I can. It's prostate cancer, and the treatment at the moment is monthly injections (in the stomach, ouch!). I'm reasonably okay. There's a loss of stamina, and I get rather easily tired. But, I am still writing away as usual. I am determined to enjoy my 80th birthday in April 2000!

All best wishes – | And keep well! – | Eddie

Campbell, an editor at the *Times Literary Supplement*, shared EM's interest in Beat and other counter-cultural writers. EM's four poems relating to his first intimations of cancer are in *Cathures*, 2002: 45ff. On Eddie Linden, editor of *Aquarius*, see letter of 18 June 1978. EM's 'Helen Adam' (*Cathures*: 62) became part of *Sons and Daughters of Alba*, commissioned for Glasgow Jazz Festival 2000, in partnership with Tommy Smith*.

Hamish Whyte, publisher, poet, bibliographer
(handwritten)

1–10–1999

Dear Hamish
Speaking of CDs, I got Mahler 2, which I hadn't heard for years, and it all came back to me very strongly (especially on my Bose!) – the end really shakes you (and it seems more Russian than German).

I'm sorry I don't have a *Columba* score, only the libretto. I asked Moira Meighan, but she doesn't have one either. However, she suggested I contact Jo Leighton, the composer's widow, which I did. She has a score, but says it's a vast book which she really couldn't lend out. Her suggestion is that Christina go to the Reid Music Library, 12 Nicholson Square, Edinburgh, where she could certainly examine a copy of the score. See what Christina thinks about this – it's probably the best solution?

Yesterday's jab was a sore one – bled quite a bit – I've got a big plaster on. The nurse had a job pushing the thing in. 'Your skin is like a hippopotamus!' she cried.

I believe you are to join Marshall and me on the 8th? I look forward to it. We go on.

Best to Christina and Kenny – | Love | Eddie

Whyte's daughter Christina, a music student, wondered whether she might see the score of *Columba* by Kenneth Leighton. Moira Meighan, a supporter of Scottish Opera, lived nearby. Marshall Walker* made periodic trips to Scotland to discuss EM's wishes and plans. Kenny is Whyte's son, a librarian and photographer.

Richard Price, poet, editor and librarian
(handwritten)

G12 0BG 20–10–1999

Dear Richard – Here is another 'busy scene', and perhaps you have yourself toyed with a pint in the Old Toll? I love the mirrors and lights, the sleeping cowboy, the reference to H.M. the King, the accurate clothes. You could almost write the conversations (now there's a challenge).

I do agree with you about the specialness and particularity, 'exchange rates and translators'. Despite what you say about the suits, there seems to be a deeply based opposition to robotization, and with every advance in globalization (too many –tions in this sentence!) anti-global ideas and initiatives proliferate. New countries appear, despite the internet and all that. Think of vast and populous Indonesia, which is really 'Indonesia', an artificial construct like 'Yugoslavia'. Timor is only one of many supposed constituent islands with separatist desires. Will it all break up? May do! Bali is certainly not Java. And with language: (American) English is internet-dominant, but I can't see the Chinese / Japanese / Arabs being satisfied for ever with the domination. Everyone has to learn English, yes, probably. But could there not be a web of world-wide webs, an almost unimaginababel of competing Whorfian particularities? 'What can be said in Navajo cannot be said in English.' Or would that be chaos once again? Why did basic English fail? Why did Esperanto fail? Because we all want to enrich ourselves through limits to communication. Spoon-feed the devil and he will bite you.

I hope that <u>amniotic mite</u> is busy pulsing clutching and growing, Jacqui is well and Katie is sleeping. My fifth jab awaits me later today. So far all is well.

Best as ever | Eddie

EM sent this with a card of the Old Toll Bar, Glasgow. Price had written of workplace tensions between organisational co-operation and individuality in the modern world. Meanwhile, he and his wife were expecting a second child.

Alec Finlay, poet and publisher

4 November 1999

Dear Eck

Thanks for taking the poems for *Scottish Love Poetry*. Here is a short author note:

Born Glasgow 1920. Retired as Titular Professor of English at Glasgow University, 1980. Appointed Poet Laureate of Glasgow, 1999. Books include: *Selected Poems* (Carcanet, 1985), *Collected Poems* (Carcanet, 1990), *Cyrano de Bergerac* (translation of Rostand's play into Scots, Carcanet, 1992), *Sweeping Out the Dark* (Carcanet, 1994), *Virtual and Other Realities* (Carcanet, 1997, Stakis Prize for Scottish Writer of the Year), *Doctor Faustus* (revised version of Marlowe's play, Canongate, 1999), *Demon* (Mariscat, 1999).

Whatever sort of love the Dickinson poem celebrates, I love its sense of passionate abandon. Passionateness and fragmentariness link her and the Sappho of my own poem. Feeling persists through the fragmentariness, in both poets, in the most extraordinary way.

———

You ask about my health, and yes, I got some not very good news a few months ago: prostate cancer. The treatment at the moment is monthly injections which are designed to inhibit the spread of the beast. We shall see. I am feeling not too bad at all, though there's a certain loss of stamina. At least I can write!

Best as ever | Yeddie

THE PERSISTENCE OF LOVE

What is this picture but a fragment?
Is it linen – papyrus – who can say?
All those stains and fents and stretched bits, but
she was a character, even a beauty, you can see that
from the set of her head and the rakish snood
her tight black curls are fighting to escape from.
She is wearing a very very pale violet tunic
which is partly transparent, partly transluscent,
partly not there. It has slipped off one shoulder
but the shoulder has gone. The other arm has faded
to a scarcely perceptible gesture. One sandal
gleams. All the rest is conjecture.
Her name is a letter or two: Sa, Saf –
O she is all fragments. There she is though!

With John Burnside, Finlay co-edited *Love for Love: An Anthology of Love Poems* (2000). Poets were asked to present a new love poem, a love poem by another poet, and a brief comment on both. EM's 'The Persistence of Love' takes Sappho as its subject; retitled 'The Sandal', it appeared in *Cathures* (2002: 73). His other poem 'Wild Nights – Wild Nights!' was by Emily Dickinson.

2000s

(aged 80–90)

Edwin Morgan had been fascinated by time from his earliest days. Drawn towards the futuristic, he had identified himself with experiment and the avant-garde in science, technology and politics as in the arts. His cancer now promised a limited future. Yet the consultant's prognosis had offered some room for manoeuvre: six months, possibly, or six years. In any case, he determined to be as productive as his creative energy and strength of character would allow; decline into silence would come, but not yet.

Hence the remarkable list of publications from his last ten years. Some of these books, the first half-dozen or so, are continuations of his late 1990s trajectory, a pre-millennial race as various projects were driven towards completion. After 2000, the letters reveal the poet striving to overcome physical constraints. He entered the electronic age by proxy, combining the IT skills of Claudia Kraszkiewicz in Dortmund (who had set up a website devoted to his work) with the older technology of fax to engage with a new generation of readers and enquirers world-wide. The system worked like this: email enquiry to the website was printed out by Claudia and then faxed through to Morgan's big photocopy-fax machine in Whittingehame Court, where he typed a reply and faxed it back for transcription into email and onward sending. An old man's version of the internet, but it worked well enough for a time.

Increasingly frail, however, and unable to move confidently or to rise unaided when he fell, he had to give up his flat and his 'email' late in 2003 and move into a nursing home. On rare occasions thereafter, he would dictate letters or email messages, their coherence in astonishing contrast to his physical condition, weakened as he was by powerful medication and several minor strokes. The record of his letters becomes patchier, since he could not file copies as before. He remained an active correspondent as long as he could, however, and many late letters may still be in private hands. Phone calls and visits from friends maintained contact, and their letters too, despite an awareness that these might well never be answered. His elegant handwriting became spidery as he lost strength to grip the pen, an affront to his sense of self.

Chair-bound in a narrow room, Morgan nevertheless could roam in imagination. This is seen most clearly in *Tales from Baron Munchausen* (2005), a reworking of the tall tales of the retired Hanoverian eighteenth-century military man. These were commissioned for performance by Benno Plassmann, a community theatre director, who later toured in Scotland and Italy with *The Baron's Ball*. The tales are full of verve and speed with an interlacing of animal, mechanical and human energies that seems absolutely to overleap the poet's own circumscribed state. Another remarkable performance was his poem 'For the Opening of the Scottish Parliament, 9 October 2004', commissioned by the Scottish Executive after he was made Scotland's Makar or national poet in February 2004. For many people this poem, read by Liz Lochhead on the actual day, would remain the highlight of a memorable occasion. It opens *A Book of Lives* (2007), which contained several poems written out of his new life, and from the imagined lives of others too, from the Emperor Hirohito to Boethius and Oscar Wilde. This poet still had vigour, inventiveness and 'more lives than a litter of kittens', said William Wootton, reviewing the book in the *Times Literary Supplement*. It was shortlisted for the T.S. Eliot Prize and won the Scottish Arts Council Sundial Book of the Year Award in 2008.

In time the earlier *Cathures* may come to be recognised as an even stronger volume. *Dreams and Other Nightmares: New and Uncollected Poems 1954–2009*, posthumously published, revealed how very recently the poet had still been composing and translating. In one of these late 'dreams' he describes an experience of encountering poetry in translation – Norwegian as it happens – and astonishing even himself as he slept. How much he remembered and how vividly! His letters everywhere convey that sense of an astonishing mind, attuned, alert.

Book and Pamphlet Publications

New Selected Poems. Manchester: Carcanet Press, 2000.

A.D.: A Trilogy on the Life of Jesus Christ. Manchester: Carcanet Press, 2000.

Jean Racine's Phaedra: A Tragedy. Translated by Edwin Morgan. Manchester: Carcanet Press, 2000.

Attila József: Sixty Poems. Translated by Edwin Morgan. Glasgow: Mariscat Press, 2001.

Cathures: New Poems 1997–2001. Manchester: Carcanet Press, in association with Mariscat Press, 2002.

Beowulf: A Verse Translation into Modern English. Manchester: Carcanet Press, 2002.

Love and a Life. Glasgow: Mariscat Press, 2003.

Metrum de Praelio apud Bannockburn / The Battle of Bannockburn by Robert Baston. Translated by Edwin Morgan. Edinburgh: Scottish Poetry Library, with Akros Publications and Mariscat Press, 2004.

The Play of Gilgamesh. Manchester: Carcanet Press, 2005.

Tales from Baron Munchausen. Edinburgh: Mariscat Press, 2005.

Thirteen Ways of Looking at Rillie. London: Enitharmon Press, 2006.

A Book of Lives. Manchester: Carcanet Press, 2007.

Beyond the Sun: Scotland's Favourite Paintings. Poems by Edwin Morgan. Edinburgh: Luath Press, 2007.

From Saturn to Glasgow: 50 Favourite Poems by Edwin Morgan. Edited by Robyn Marsack and Hamish Whyte. Manchester and Edinburgh: Carcanet Press and Scottish Poetry Library, 2008.

Dreams and Other Nightmares. New and Uncollected Poems 1954– 2009. Edinburgh: Mariscat Press, 2010.

Hamish Whyte, publisher, poet, bibliographer
(handwritten)

19 Whittingehame Court
Glasgow G12 0BG
25–1–2000

Dear Hamish

Back from Prestonfield, which was very comfortable,
coal fires, peacocks on the lawn, but food heavy and
unappealing – perhaps that's what you get in country houses.
The deliberations went more smoothly than I had expected,
and I think we have come up with a reasonable list of 14. I
deplored the shortage of literature entries, but no one quite
seems to know the reason for it. I enclose a copy of Kennedy's
Kompleynte.

Thanks for the crayfish. I may well do something with the
critters. Are we so sure that they are baddies? People eat them
and make them into soup (quasi lobster bisque).

I've been having a hard look at my diary, and I really
think I shall have to give Friday 3 March a miss – I'm sorry.
I already have three readings lined up for that week, and two
consecutive Cathedral evenings is just too much, if I am going
to get my writing done.

I suppose you would see the attack on me in yesterday's
Herald by Patrick Reilly. I have sent in a short and I think
moderate reply. It was a strange public outburst from someone
who was a colleague at the university and (I thought) a friend
(how wrong can you be?). There seems to be a new militant
Catholicism abroad in Scotland: first MacMillan, then
Winning, now Reilly. I wonder what Jim and Donny think
about it all? – I certainly look forward to next week's lunch!

Love and peacocks – | Eddie

EM had been on a panel adjudicating the first Creative Scotland
awards. A.L. Kennedy complained that writers and publishers had
not been made aware of them. The crayfish appears in 'Clyde-Clean',
Cathures (2002). The Glasgow Cathedral millennial event was 'St
Mungo's Fire', organised by Whyte* and Donny O'Rourke*. Patrick

Reilly, a retired university colleague and Catholic traditionalist, had criticised *A.D.*; Catholic composer James MacMillan had spoken of Scotland's residual sectarianism at the 1999 Edinburgh Festival; and Cardinal Thomas Winning had argued against the Scottish Parliament's repeal of Section 28, a 1980s piece of legislation that aimed to prevent the promotion of homosexuality in schools. EM checked out the views of younger Catholic writers, such as O'Rourke* and McGonigal*.

Michael Schmidt, publisher, poet and critic

27 January 2000

Dear Michael

I enclose a bit of verse for your Commonplace Book. I am sorry I shall miss the celebrations on 11 July. On that day I shall be louting low in borrowed robes in Edinburgh, receiving a D.Litt from Heriot-Watt University.

Have a great party! | Yours ever | Eddie

I ought to write this in Nahuatl
And shake my feathered Aztec rattle
To celebrate our Mex-man's trek
Through Hinksey, Cheadle, and the wreck
Of a bombed office in wet Man-
chester, maturing his long plan
Of luring words like flocks of birds
To settle bookwards, readerwards
And oh – why not – eternitywards!

His publisher had asked for a contribution to a Commonplace Book as part of the thirtieth anniversary celebrations for Carcanet Press. 'Louting low' in Scots means to bow respectfully (here to receive the academic hood).

Mark Smith, friend
(handwritten)

15–2–2000

My dearest Mark

Your letter – of dreams and books – set me thinking about what dreams I had had lately, but I drew a blank. Daydreams yes – thinking as I sit in a chair about how my play (just finished No 2 of the trilogy – looking good, as the American astronauts say) might develop – without taking notes – I like to leave it in the mind, where it doesn't disappear, or at least so I trust myself. Your remark about part of you dying off and your believing in continual change strikes a chord with me too. Projects end and projects begin, and a good thing it is. I haven't been to Stuttgart but I'm sure you will find something there and make use of it. Energy, that's the great bazazz. You have it, I have it. Even the jellyfish wrapping its sting round a cross-Channel swimmer's legs has it: you don't have to be an aurora borealis. From Stuttgart to Swansea will be a red shift. Enjoy both, and give my warm regards to Ian Bell if he is still there. What will your Glasgow project, or Projekt, be?

I see you have been ferociously reading. Yes, I have Les Murray's *Conscious and Verbal*, good title and good book. The Manchester bombing poem is particularly relevant because of the Carcanet connection. I haven't seen their new office yet. My *New Selected Poems* is due out in April and I'll send a copy to your address when you have one.

I didn't realize I was exposed on the Internet, but since you already know something of my recent problems I am enclosing photocopied bits and pieces of the two nodes of conflict – Section 28 and the *AD* play. Life has been fairly hectic, as you can imagine. The sniping and griping is still going on. I just put my head down and get on with writing.

Hesse's poetry I don't know. Maybe you'll come across it in Deutschland (*Gedichte*, 1957). It's been described as 'limited in range and essentially Romantic', but I know you will make up your own mind! *Steppenwolf* is the only one of his books I have.

The repaired Hubble is poised to do great things. Oh I

can't wait. More images please. More million-mile towers of
gas and dust and budding stars. And speaking of smaller-scale
buds, my orchid in its pot which I thought wouldn't bloom
again has joyfully exuded five buds of which the fattest has just
today (Valentine+1) split open to wink at me with its beautiful
spotted dye. Love is everywhere.

Dentist tomorrow for my abscess. Then my next stomach
jag the following day. Apart from that, the Chekhovian
watchman goes round at midnight with his ricketie and cries
'A frosty night and all's well!'

Look after yourself. | Love | Ed

Mark Smith was in Germany on a three-month youth project, before
enrolling in Swansea University to study English and Italian. The IRA
bombed Manchester city centre in June 1996, damaging Carcanet's
offices. EM was interviewed on the Section 28 repeal by the Scottish
press, which had also misreported *A.D.* as portraying a gay Jesus.

Alec Finlay, poet and publisher

1 April 2000

Dear Eck

Thanks for the letters and books. I'm sorry I'll have to forgo
the Schwitters, but do have a Schwittzing good time. The
monthly injections do seem to be effective so far in preventing
the little monster from spreading in the way it would like to,
but the reduction in physical stamina is frustrating. Anyhow,
on we go!

Regarding *The Order of Things* (good title), here are a few
suggestions for you to think about: Canedolia, Starryveldt,
Bees' Nest, Opening the Cage, The Tower of Pisa, Interview,
Caliban Falls Asleep in the Isle Full of Noises, Blues and Peal:
Concrete 1969. For others poets, what about Dunbar's Ane
Ballat of Our Lady?

The pocketbooks are handsome, and you are now indeed
in the 'real' book world. More power to your elbow. My only
regret is that there are too many spelling misteaks. In looking

through the books I spotted about a dozen. I always think it's sad when nicely produced books have texts that don't stand up to the externals. Is there no EAGLE-EYED person over there in New Stret who would scan the proofs without fear or favour?! (You see it's catching: I can't even spell Street.)

Best from the west – | Yeddie

Finlay was organising an evening of sound poetry to commemorate the sixtieth anniversary of the arrival of Kurt Schwitters in Scotland by boat, having made his escape from Nazi Germany via Norway, before internment on the Isle of Man. *The Order of Things* was a planned Pocketbook anthology of sound, concrete and pattern poetry.

Marshall Walker, academic and friend

FAX (handwritten)   2–5–2000
To: Prof. Marshall Walker, Dept. of English
From: Edwin Morgan

Dear Marshall

  My feet are in fettle . fleecy and fluffy
  Sheep are shorn .   shoes are shipshape

    (sometimes, though not always,
    attributed to Cædmon)

Thank you for the slippers, which are just fine. I shall cut a dash when I pad across the landing to the rubbish chute. The Botanic Gardens party on the 27th went very well – readings by Tom Leonard and Ron Butlin particularly entertaining, two amazing new pieces by Tommy Smith, and all the while an under-susurrus of blackbirds. As the lights slowly came on under the dome, the birds must have wondered whether it was evening or morning – but they sang just the same.

  Best wishes and love to Stephanie | and yourself – Eddie

A thank-you fax for the seventieth birthday gift of a pair of slippers is combined with a vignette of a celebration event in Glasgow's Botanic Gardens, organised by Hamish Whyte*.

Hamish Whyte, publisher, poet, bibliographer
(handwritten)

G12 0BG   3–5–2000

Dear Hamish

Carlton George Windows Rooftop Restaurant is duly booked for 1pm tomorrow, so prepare for 'stunning food' (rock cakes?) and 'relaxed elegance' (a New Divan?).

Yesterday was a perfect day for Morven and me to have a picnic lunch at the Lake of Menteith. We sent a card to Tommy and Laura to remind them of their wedding. The ferryman's voice was clear across the still waters. We fed crumbs to an inquisitive wagtail which wagged with renewed vigour.

I await my inquisitor from Dortmund!

Till tomorrow | Love | Eddie

Morven Cameron was an old friend, taught by EM as a young lecturer. Tommy Smith* and his wife Laura were married on an island in the Lake of Mentieth near Stirling. The German research student was Claudia Kraszkiewicz*, who would later set up the Morgan website.

Michael Schmidt, publisher, poet and critic

25 July 2000

Dear Michael

I hope perhaps you will receive this just before you leave these shores. I know Chiapas very well. No, I haven't been there, but it looms large in the novels of B. Traven, one of my favourite writers. So look out for those bandits, banded tigers, jaguars, muchacho. But enjoy yourself, and hasta luego and all that.

Yes, it has been a remarkable year, and it's no deid yet. Can I keep it up? Can you keep it up! Rehearsals of *A.D.* appear to be going well (I've seen two). Robyn and Hamish and I have been wrestling with the proofs of what I hope will be a good read as well as a performance text. I am glad you think it is the fifth gospel! Not one for Oberammergau, I reckon.

I have survived two more D.Litts., at St Andrews and Heriot-Watt. The St Andrews event took three days – they believe in the long arm of tradition there – and I was somewhat exhausted at the end of it. Stamina is not my strong point now, but apart from that, and problems with steps and stairs if there's no handrail, I have to confess to being in good spirits and happy enough to receive my monthly jags or jabs if they keep the jabuar from prowling through the rest of my body. I have been writing more lyrics for Tommy Smith which have just been performed at the Glasgow International Jazz Festival. You may have seen in *LRB* some of the Easter poems I wrote for BBC television. So we continue, we go forward, thankfulness is all!

I would relish a card from Yucatan.

Yours as ever, from these Jesus-haunted Courts – | Eddie

Schmidt was going on holiday to Mexico, his first visit to Yucatán and Chiapas for more than thirty years. The lyrics were for *Sons and Daughters of Alba*, and some appear in *Cathures* (2002). The reference to the 'fifth gospel' is a response to Schmidt's rhyme in the previous letter: 'Matthew, Mark, Luke, John and Edwin, / Bless the bed that I lie on and in.'

Michael Schmidt, publisher, poet and critic

22 August 2000

Dear Michael

A little query for you when you return bronzed and bandit-free from Chiapas and environs.

Hamish Whyte would like his Mariscat to publish a collection of my Attila József translations. They are generally thought to be the best, but of course at the moment they are hidden away in the *Collected Translations* and I would really like to have them in a separate volume. There are 25 in the *CT*; there are 14 'fragments' in the Morning Star pamphlet; and there are about 20 uncollecteds in various magazines. How would you feel about the *CT* translations being included in a Mariscat volume?

I write between events at the Edinburgh Book Festival!

Best as ever | Eddie

On the matter of 'sharing' publications, Schmidt wrote: 'of all the publishers in the world, I suppose Mariscat is the least uncongenial for sharing purposes'.

Richard Price, poet, editor and librarian
(handwritten)

25–9–2000

Dear Richard

Judith Palmer phoned just before I popped this book into its jiffybag. The world is all linked! She wants me to write things on the back of an envelope – *spontaneous things* – for an exhibition of Poetry International. And of course she mentioned you. As you will see from the enclosure, *A.D.* is at last <u>out there</u> as well as on the page. I saw the three plays on Saturday, to get the full effect. The whole thing is spectacularly done as a multi-media show, which will not please everybody, but it's moving and thrilling and I liked it. The audience, largely young, stood and whooped at the end. Then it was backstage for champagne, hugging and kissing of the cast, autographs and <u>all that</u> – theatre is theatre! Anyway, I hope you enjoy the book, without the light-show and the rock-vibration. – It was good to meet Peter en famille in Glasgow, and since then I've been writing a reference for him to ensconce himself for a while at Bellagio, the Rockefeller retreat on Lake Como (looks enticing I must say) where he hopes to ride his Syllabary into the sunset.

Paolozzi v. Gormley? I'm not so sure! What I mean is that I'm not sure why I don't really take to Eduardo as warmly as you do, but I don't! The Gormley angel is crude but strikes a chord. People don't fix a football strip on Paolozzi's Newton. Why should they, you may say. Well – is that the primitive North as against the sophisticated British Library?! I think I sense something <u>destructive</u> about E.P., something that actually opposes the idea of sculpture. – These are random thoughts.

There's a possibility that *Gilgamesh* is readying himself to burst from the cuneiform onto the boards, in a joint production by the Edinburgh Lyceum and Theatre Babel which specializes in ancient and heroic resuscitations. The Tramway would again be the venue. All depends on <u>funding</u>, but if the Arts Council sees its duty (that's one way of putting it) the city of Uruk would rise again in Glasgow in January 2002. Can we all live that long? Where's Nostradamus?

Love to all at Staines. I hope the new arrival thrives – |
   Eddie

Judith Palmer was Chair of the Poetry Society's General Council. *A.D.: A Trilogy of Plays on the Life of Jesus* (2000) ran from 20 September to 7 October 2000 at the Tramway, Glasgow. On Peter McCarey's* *Syllabary*, see letter of 7 March 1998. Price had written on Eduardo Paolozzi for *Edinburgh Review* 104 (2000).

Michael Kerins, storyteller

31 May 2001

Dear Michael

PERM POEM

Come all ye freenly folk tae Perm.
Toddle fae toon or flit fae ferm.
We'se gie ye oor bit skeely germ
Of poetry an whit we term

Ferlies, tales as lang's yir erm!
We'll no can come tae ony herm
Praisin the richt auld city o Perm!

Enough of that. Or too much! It's a pity the Russian
pronunciation of Pyerm makes the rhyme slightly imperfect, or
impyerfect.

I'm enclosing some Russian translations, poems by
Mayakovsky, Voznesensky, and Pushkin. Just use whatever may
strike you as suitable.

I hope you and Ewan have a great trip. Send me a postcard
if you have a moment.

Love and all best wishes | Eddie

Kerins, a writer and storyteller, was going on a storytelling tour to
Perm with Ewan McVicar and had asked EM for some of his transla-
tions of Russian poetry to perform there.

Michael Kerins, storyteller

14–Jun–2001

FAX (handwritten)
Page 1 of 1
To: Michael Kerins   G69 9NB
From: Edwin Morgan   G12 0BG

Michael –
   Alastair Paterson, who is organizing tomorrow's reading in
the Dumbarton Library, phoned to say he would collect me
in his car and also take me back home after the meeting. So I
won't need to take up your kind offer to drive me home – but
many thanks for the suggestion. Speaking of cars, here's a little
story for you. Sitting in the forecourt at Whittingehame Court
off and on during the last week has been a fine sleek grey and
black HEARSE, ominously waiting for who? Much muttering
and twitching of curtains. It turns out that a young chap in one
of the flats who is not short of a bob or two has bought the
hearse and is going to convert it into a classy stretch limousine,

big enough to take his <u>canoes</u> when he goes canoeing. O the variety of human experience!

Love and best wishes | Eddie

Increasingly EM needed help with travel to reading events that he still wanted to attend.

Richard Price, poet, editor and librarian
(handwritten)

29–7–2001

Dear Richard

Yes, Italy is not all sweetness and light. The carabinieri are not the gentlest of order-keepers. Already since Genoa protests have erupted in Berlin and London; to say nothing of Etna! Is it the beginning of something big? How spontaneous is it? Drumming in the street seems to suggest the ballot-box is not perceived to be a deliverer of golden things. We shall see, we shall see.

I didn't go to the Vermeer party because there were huge queues and also because I had seen the Vermeers in Amsterdam (wonderfully beautiful) and didn't fancy running the gauntlet of all that School of Delft. Vermeer – Brueghel – Bosch – Grünewald – these are just about my favourite painters, a fairly 'northern' bunch, don't you think?

My Mark, the mysterious Mark, is a guy in his twenties whom I met three years ago at the Edinburgh Science Festival. He came to ask a question after I had given a talk on science and poetry. Even from a few yards off I was hit by that old bolt, that coup de foudre, and I was shaking (like Sappho) as he began to talk to me. I never thought it would happen again at <u>that</u> age. But there it is. No rules in this life. He's not gay, but we've had quite an intense relationship for three years now. He knows my feelings ('Never seek to tell thy love' wrote Blake, but sometimes you have to –) and takes them in his stride. And speaking of strides, he is very fit and physical, plays football, goes running with weights on his ankles, and cycles from Motherwell (where he lives) to see me. What else? He has a sudden dazzling smile which makes you think all things are possible.

You are right about poetry needing more 'bite' and less omniscience. You can supply it. Bite them in Edinburgh! See you soon I hope.

Best as ever | Eddie

Price had returned from a brother's wedding in Siena, noting both civic beauty and street protests. EM had visited London and seen the Tate Modern, instead of the exhibition of Vermeer and the Delft School at the National Gallery.

Mark Smith, friend
(handwritten)

G120BG 4–9–2001

My dear Mark –

You like old postcards so here is one. I am looking at your Botticelli card and thinking about what you say about Venus. If she is pregnant, it must be because she is the mother of all, what Lucretius called at the beginning of his great poem *alma Venus*, nurturing/nourishing Venus, *hominum divumque voluptas*, delight of men and gods, coming with the primavera to renew the life of things, producing, reproducing, generating through love. O it is a supreme picture! (And isn't Mercury, with his splendid leg – going all the way up – a Pasoliniesque figure from an unmade film?) In a way it is your card too, if you are ringiovinando, and how moved I was by what you said about your second life and the casting off of the casing and the melting of hardness into feeling. Everyone is different, but I couldn't but be reminded of my thirties (the 1950s) when I lived in a shell because I was afraid and ashamed to let people know how unhappy I was, and when the shell broke in the following decade and I shook myself and stepped out into the sunshine, it seemed amazing and unexpected though I could see the causes – love, music, science, a new time. The // (forgive the somewhat manky card, genuinely old!) rather trite saying that you are as old as you feel does have some truth in it, if you gaze into your specchio and know that it is not telling the whole truth. Thomas Hardy has a good poem on the subject. It will tell the whole truth <u>some</u> day, but we don't talk about that! I'm well aware of the slow but inexorable decline of the body, especially when I'm climbing a stair or falling in the snow and being unable to get up without help. Each morning I say, Well, that's another day, I can still swing my legs off the bed and stand up! But when I'm writing poetry, writing letters indeed, talking to friends, I don't feel any age in particular. Without you I would be invecchiando, I can tell you that, hermano.

Early morning cities have a peculiar magic: your Florence, my Naples, Wordsworth's London, Crane's New York – or this from Lyn Hejinian:

> When I was 14 I went to Spain. One early morning in Seville I left the hotel (of which I remember nothing but deep gloom) and walked into the exhilarating but devastating sunlight that seemed to hover, to cascade, to penetrate like some philosophical quandary. Could fate exist without us?

// What you say about the rhythm of cities – all cities – even Athens, see this card! – is true, like Wordsworth's 'all that mighty heart is lying still' (and he hated cities, so it's an acknowledgement of their power). Lyn Hejinian takes it a step further, through the contrast of the dark gloomy enclosed buildings and the almost supernatural brightness outside which both exhilarates and devastates; I thought this was a <u>southern</u> thing, but then I remember something similar about Leningrad, where the space and the icy shining can be just as powerful.

Coriolanus: One critic says of the hero 'No one would die alongside Coriolanus, much less for him'. But I recall when I was talking about the play at the College of Drama (now RSAMD), and pointing out the problems of an unsympathetic hero, one student with his eyes sparkling said 'I would follow him to the ends of the earth!' I have never forgotten that moment. What does Mark think?

Onward! | M

This letter, written over three poem-cards from Openings Press, responds to a card of Botticelli's *La Primavera*. EM's 'ringiovinando' should be 'ringiovanendo', rejuvenating. Lyn Hejinian was a favourite avant-garde writer. The Coriolanus question had come up on Smith's English course in Swansea.

Hamish Whyte, publisher, poet, bibliographer
(handwritten)

G12 0BG 21-9-2001

Dear Hamish – Glad to hear Christina was safely stowed. No bikers in Stratford? Too late in the season no doubt. – I think the József front cover picture will do very well, also the Times New Roman, and the idea of his handwriting plus my typing on back cover. Obviously the sample wouldn't do, since it looks as if the typing was a translation of the poem above, which of course it isn't. It's not one of the poems I translated, but have done so today (copy enclosed!). It's last in a sequence of 7 sonnets called 'My Homeland', an angry condemnation of 1930s social conditions, and one of his last poems. Fortunately he didn't live to see his warning about Germany unheeded! – It's busy busy busy this week. Yesterday a *Scotsman* interview which will be appearing a week on Saturday (29th) mit Foto. Today a photo session with Rory Smith (winner of schools P.O. competition), due to appear in *Herald* magazine on 29th. The *Scotsman* wanted a poem so I gave them 'Lunardi'. On Sunday Ron O'Donnell comes to take more snaps, for the NPG installation. And by the way, Claudia and Hartmut will hit Scotland at October's end to see 'my' exhibition, and I expect they'll be looking for us too! – Did you know another of those Continental Markets will be filling St Enoch Square next week, Thursday–Saturday? – I think you should just post the demons. I hope Elinor's show goes well and she manages to keep soople.

Is it 12 next Friday and we don't book? Will Gerry be there too?

Love | Eddie

And yet, my souls starts up in fear, cries out
at thought of exile from the Magyar land –
dear Homeland, hold out still a welcoming hand,
keep me, I am loyal, never doubt!

A shuffling bear in chains, its big head bowed –
to me this demonizes what should be free!
I am a poet – let your gauleiters see
my pen's not to be tampered with or cowed!

For *Attila József: Sixty Poems* (2001), Whyte had located a manuscript
version of a poem. Gerry Cambridge* was typesetting the book.
'Vincent Lunardi' (*Cathures*: 20–21) describes the pioneering Italian
balloonist's flights in Glasgow in 1785. Photographer Ron O'Donnell
and painter Stephen Campbell were organising an EM exhibition
at the National Portrait Gallery in Edinburgh. Elinor Kirk, a former
student at Glasgow University, was about to perform a one-person
show based on EM's *Demon* at the Byre Theatre, St Andrews.

Hamish Whyte, publisher, poet, bibliographer

G120BG16-10-2001

ATTILA JÓZSEF

He was chirpy and gallus, but a right cunt
to those that tried to blitz his truth
He loved to eat, squishing such fruit
as God himself might weigh and cut.
He sported a Jewish doctor's coat
that made his relatives cry out
Oh-no-for-chrissake-scarper-scoot!
He called Greek orthodoxy a stunt:
stiff with priests all pity-proof.
From east to west he was bad news –

okay, so what, fucksake cheer up!

Dear Hamish
    This is a freeish (but not misleading) version of the poem

you culled from the internet. Its title is one he used for several poems.

I got my impression, both upper and lower, taken today, and the big extraction session is planned for Monday 22nd. At the same time she will put in a temporary <u>bridge</u> (not plate), as she says a plate would be hard to fix so I am to guard and pamper my canines and tell them to remain robust and loadworthy (I'm sure there's a German word for that).

Stirling tomorrow if all goes well. After which I really look forward to Saturday at 78 St V – will book for three at 1pm.

Love | Eddie

Whyte had found another untranslated poem by Attila József, although it was not used in the forthcoming collection. 78 St Vincent Street was a favourite restaurant, and EM and HW would be joined by Gerry Cambridge* who was typesetting the book.

Richard Price, poet, editor and librarian
(handwritten)

30–10–2001

Dear Richard

The enclosed is really coals to Newcastle, but perhaps you haven't seen it? If you have any tame cryptographers prowling the BL stacks, turn them onto p. 172. Or try it yourself – some lazy day – if ever – surrounded as you are by every adjunct to cryptosophizing – I'm sorry, no prizes are offered! – I'm pleased that you like 'Pelagius', it's one of nine similar-length poems I have now completed, Glasgow poems I call them, running from the great heretic's time to the end of the 20th century – I'm really excited by them. I had known about and been drawn to Pelagius for a long time, and like the accidental link with myself, his name being simply a Latinized Morgan, a Welsh seafarer, born somewhere between Wales and Strathclyde, which of course I take to be Glasgow! The nine poems will be in my next Carcanet book, planned for this time next year when I demit the laureateship, sling the baton to – who? or even whom? – Tomorrow I have a visit

from Claudia and Hartmut: they came over from Dortmund
to see 'my' exhibition at the National Portrait Gallery in
Edinburgh, a rather striking 'tribute' by artist Steven Campbell
and photographer Ron O'Donnell, on till February, so you
may have a chance to see it (see me sitting next to a skeleton
on the subway, for instance). – The so-called war on terrorism
(ridiculous phrase) goes on its bloody way, and it doesn't look
as if any number of bombed children will deflect America
from the very mistaken path it has chosen, understandable
though the choice may be. I hated Bush's use of the word
cowardly to describe the Twin Towers assault: anything less
cowardly would be hard to imagine. The Americans seems to
have a great blank in their minds where understanding of what
other peoples think and feel ought to be. Par for the course
for empires, I suppose! – I look forward to your 11:9 book!
Any word from Michael-of-the-Carcanet yet? He has not said
anything about my *Gilgamesh* sent quite a while ago! – My
injections continue, and appear to be holding the fort. My
dentist relieved me of four teeth last week, so I am eating very
gingerlilily; good thing I like porridge?

Love and best wishes to you and the family. Ellen sounds a
joy. Hold that foot too –

Eddie

EM had sent a book about the British Library, where Price worked.
The Glasgow poems were published as 'Nine in Glasgow' in *Cathures*,
this title being an ancient name for Glasgow. Price's short story
collection, *A Boy in Summer*, appeared from 11:9 publishers in 2002.

Kate McGrath, journalist and director

FAX   17 Dec 2001
To: Kate McGrath
From: Edwin Morgan

1. *What was the best thing you saw in 2001?*

The film *Blackbirds* by the young Iranian director Samira

Makmalbaf. When so many movies today try to dazzle us with the wow factor of digital manipulation, it was hugely refreshing to watch this directly moving and humorous story of itinerant teachers with blackboards on their backs searching for pupils in the wildest parts of Iran.

2. *And the best thing you heard?*

A CD of *Russian Film Music*, played by the Russian Philharmonic Orchestra. Evocative, thrilling, sentimental, these pieces are a reminder of a great period of film-making, and composers like Shostakovich and Prokofiev did not disdain to write them.

3. *For what, more than anything else, will you remember 2001?*

The Twin Towers. Instant television made this an extraordinary event from so many different angles: the sheer quasi-fictional spectacle, the mind's horror at imagining those trapped or throwing themselves from windows, a sense of startled wonderment at the accuracy and boldness of the operation.

4. *What are you looking forward to seeing/hearing in 2002?*

A Requiem in Trondheim Cathedral on which I have been collaborating with a Norwegian composer.

5. *What's your new year's resolution?*

To keep taking the tablets!

> Dear Kate: Separate letter on its way!
> Yes, I still have a few copies of the medieval plays.
> Good to hear from you!

Eddie

Working as an arts journalist in Edinburgh before going on to co-found Fuel Theatre in London, McGrath had faxed EM an end-of-year questionnaire for *The Scotsman*. A daughter of playwright John

McGrath, she asked about EM's work for the Medieval Players. The composer was Ståle Kleinberg and 'The Trondheim Requiem' is in *Cathures* (2002: 63–65).

Michael Schmidt, publisher, poet and critic

9 January 2002

Dear Michael

Thank you for your good news of the 2nd about *Gilgamesh*. I shall possess my soul in patience till 2003/4 (I hope the former!). I realise the book will be 'something of a risk' but perhaps the trade/market will be in a more favourable mode after this year. Howard Hodgkin now: I am very glad you find the idea attractive! I do not unfortunately have any direct line to him, being merely a long-term admirer of his work. But he might be tempted to be financially kind to us if we consider the link between his coming out publicly as gay and the fact that *Gilgamesh* may be claimed as the world's earliest gay poem? In answer to your question, yes, I do have a particular picture in mind. It is *In a Hot Country* (good title to begin with), date 1979–1982, owned by Ann and Don Brown of Washington DC, reproduced on the jacket of Andrew Graham-Dixon's *Howard Hodgkin* (Thames & Hudson, 1994), and having as its central image a fat pink arrow which is most luscious and sexy. It would sell the book (he said). I once happened to be in London at the time of a new Hodgkin exhibition, hoping possibly to pick up a tiny picture at less than exorbitant cost, but I discovered that the entire exhibition had been sold before the doors were opened to the public! O that poetry was like that! Anyhow, let us press ahead –

Best new year wishes and love – | Eddie

The Play of Gilgamesh, EM's dramatisation of the ancient Sumerian epic, was finally published in 2005. Its cover image was the Queen of the Night relief, 1800–1750 BC, from southern Iraq, thought to represent either Ishtar, the goddess of erotic love and war, or her sister Ereshkigal, ruler of the underworld.

Alec Finlay, publisher and poet

FAX   14-1-2002

Dear Eck

I well remember that Stonypath visit: I thought it was
splendid that someone would call his cat Albers instead of
Mog: and I appreciated the strong tea, as I am not an Earl
Grey man. Your reminding me of it sparked off batch of
random Sixties recollections. A policeman flashing his torch
into an Edinburgh cellar at 2a.m. to see if anything more
improper than a poetry-reading was going on. At a gathering
in Tom McGrath's house in Glasgow a joint being passed
around, and as it approached me Tom grinned and said
'Moment of truth!', probably expecting I would decline, but I
took a drag and passed it on. Taking poetry to the people in
Exchange Square in Glasgow: moderately successful? – with
no microphone and against a strong wind and a few boozy
interruptions. During the truly scary Cuban Missile Crisis of
October 1962, wondering if as an army veteran I would be
called up again, and if so, what could I do, or would it be too
late to do anything? Joining the Bachelor Clan, one of the
earliest semi-public gay organizations in Scotland, and having
a partner who went wild on poppers – oh those times!

But to give more than a brief flavour, I would have to
say the whole decade for me was a period of liberation. I
could almost date my life from 1960 instead of 1920. I was
productive in poetry; I was in love; I was fascinated by space
exploration; popular music came of age and was a huge
delight; films (film has always meant a lot to me) – *La Dolce
Vita, L'Avventura, Andrei Rublyov, 2001, The Gospel According
to St Matthew, The Colour of Pomegranates* – burst across
the imagination; and even an enormous negative like the
Vietnam War (which seemed to go on for ever) released such
powerful jets of human concern that it made the decade an
unforgettable gouge on the parchment.

Yes, I go along with the idea of a Scottish Spring. It was
genuinely a time of beginnings, a time of openings, and I
always felt that those who left Scotland then – e.g. Kenneth
White, Douglas Dunn – were too impatient and should

have stayed. New international configurations – Scottish-American, Scottish-Russian, Scottish-Brazilian – appeared. New genres like concrete poetry and sound-poetry challenged a fair amount of opposition. I remember Hugh MacDiarmid growling in 1970: 'I'd hate an Ian Finlay poem on my gravestone.' Publishers like Wild Hawthorn, Migrant, Eugen Gomringer, Hansjörg Mayer encouraged Scotland to see the world and the world to see Scotland. My *Sovpoems* (1961) paid tribute to Russian writers from Mayakovsky to Yevtushenko, and my *Starryveldt* (1965) was in a sense a defence of concrete poetry, showing it at work on themes of politics and science as well as on semantic reconstruction and linguistic play. At the same time I was writing poems about Glasgow which an ongoing drama of social and architectural change virtually demanded. I did not see anything paradoxical in pursuing these varied poetries. I was not bound by dogma. I wrote what I wanted to write. I knew the time was ripe to do new things. Unconventional sinners – I was one myself – haunted 'Glasgow Green', and were they justified? If they were, even to the slightest degree, then that poem was a breakthrough. You will gather that I was more Times Square than wild hawthorn. I was more in tune with Ginsberg's *Howl* and *Kaddish* and the Kerouac of *October in the Railroad Earth* than with the Black Mountain poets favoured by your Dad and Gael Turnbull. It did not matter. Both groups of American writers were needed. We had a double benefit.

You mention R.D. Laing and Alex Trocchi. Laing I didn't know, but I knew Trocchi quite well. He fits your title very neatly, as apart from biography he nods back in several of his books to the Hogg of *Confessions of a Justified Sinner*. I remember him first of all as a student at Glasgow University at the time when I was a young lecturer in the English Department. What was he? Brilliant, wayward, charming, alarming, passing exams on Benzedrine, starting up a pig farm shortly before his finals. Everyone knew he would make his mark sometime, somehow, somewhere. *Young Adam* (1954) and *Cain's Book* (1960) are still read and are still going to be read. His public spat with MacDiarmid at the 1962 Writers Conference is part of the whole mythology of the Sixties, and was an unplanned happening not unlike the planned 'happenings' of the time, but it was also a defining moment in Scottish culture, peculiarly galling to MacDiarmid whose *Collected Poems* had just been published after years of neglect: a new era was in fact breaking out of the closet. I shared the table (and microphone and whisky) with Alex at that meeting, and remember it vividly. I didn't see him frequently thereafter, but we kept in touch, and I was one of the five Scottish recipients of his 30-odd *Sigma Portfolios* (1964–1967) – the others being Hugh MacDiarmid, Tom McGrath, Kenneth Whyte, and your Dad. This 'invisible insurrection of a million minds', as the portfolios were planned to be, cheaply cyclostyled and now a rarity on the market, comes across as a paradigmatic Sixties phenomenon, with its emphasis on revolt, liberation, alternative lifestyles, anti-universities, and worldwide cultural networking. Was all this swept away? Not quite. These are strange half-derelict sites which are today revisited and re-discussed. I can see Alex cocking a quizzical eyebrow and looking down his long nose at those who talk of his 'failure', his few novels, the silence of his later years. He sometimes looked devilish, and there are some who thought he <u>was</u> devilish. I don't know. I retain a certain affection for him, probably because I knew him when he was young. I acknowledge him as a Glaswegian risk-taker. He ripped the tent-flap apart – I don't want to see it – oh yes you do – look – look –

– All the best from the west | Yeddie

Finlay was publishing *Justified Sinners* in his Pocketbooks series. Because EM lacked the energy for lengthy writing on 'a Scottish Spring' in the early 1960s, they hit upon the idea of a letter covering this theme, written as if in reply to one recalling a visit by EM to the family home at Stonypath, as described in his poem 'To Ian Hamilton Finlay' (*CP*: 154).

FAX   5-3-2002
To: Claudia Kraszkiewicz
From: Edwin Morgan

Dear Claudia
   Thank you for your fax and emails of 28 February. Perhaps
you could email the 'mysterious' Tony Mathieson as follows:

Dear Tony Mathieson: Thank you for your honest and
solicitous enquiry about the Robin Jenkins book. All is above
board. Last year I decided I had to do something to lighten
the load on my shelves, and passed on a lot of my books to
secondhand dealers. You may well come across others! Best
wishes to you. Edwin Morgan.

   You asked for my Celan translation – here it is. It was
published with others in Alex Finlay's *Irish* (Morning Star):

> Give me the right of way
> to stalk your corn and enter your sleep,
> the right of way
> to cross your sleep-track,
> the right to slice peat
> in the glen of the heart,
> tomorrow.

   And now you are deep in divanland! I shall try to answer
your questions. I think I first came across the word divan/
diwan when I was in the Middle East during the war. I
was interested in the way in which the word had developed
divergent meanings – sofa, assembly, collection of poems –
and particularly the last of these. I liked the idea of a book of
poems which was not a narrative sequence but where there
were many mini-narratives with connections all the way
through, a collection of poems which were sitting 'in divan' and
talking to one another from which the reader/listener must
piece together what he wants to piece together. *The New Divan*
was meant to be the equivalent of a long poem, but without

the reader being driven along by narrative linearity (wow).
Yes, I read Goethe's *Westöstlicher Divan* in the Penguin edition
of his *Selected Verse* (1964) which has a prose translation by
David Luke at the bottom of each page. Hafiz I read in various
translations: Justin McCarthy, *Ghazels from the Divan of
Hafiz* (1893); Walter Leaf, *Versions from Hafiz* (1898); Arthur
Arberry, *Fifty Poems of Hafiz* (1947); A.J. Alston, *In Search of
Hafiz* (1996). I also read Jalaluddin Rumi and Omar Khayyam
and other Persian poets, all in translation, although I do know
something about the language and its metre and rhyme. Good
luck with your comparisons!

Tommy Smith is pleased with the first four poems I have
given him to set for 'Planet Wave Part 2'. Six more to go! Busy
summer ahead!

Absolutely no sign of summer here – wild winds and
deluges of rain. Congratulations to Borussia Dortmund on
reaching the semi-final!

> I return your besten Wünschen and look forward to your
> next fax! | Eddie

Mathieson had found EM's signature in a second-hand copy of *A
Land of Innocence* by Robin Jenkins and wondered if the book had
been stolen. Alec Finlay* was extending his work with Paul Celan's
'Irisch' (Morning Star, 1977), including a version from CK. For her
thesis chapter on 'The New Divan', she had sent a series of questions.
Borussia Dortmund was her football team, passionately supported.

Richard Price, poet, editor and librarian
(handwritten)

25–3–2002

It's a fine book, Richard – frosted, melted, and marbled! I shall
treasure it. I had to take a glass to see what was under *diehard*,
it looked like figures, a date? but no, it was a ghostly *p o e t r y*
– the publishers have done an excellent job, no more than the
poems deserve, and I agree with you, the collection has links
and hinges and 'critical mass'. I enjoyed your walled orchard

too, with its cinnamon and bramleys (I remember that too!) and its last line.

M.S. did at last reply about *Gilgamesh*, and (I have to tell you) with enthusiasm. No immediate publication, but he would like to do it in 2003/4. He must be serious, as he asked me if I had any ideas about cover design – oh yes I have. I'd like Howard Hodgkin if it's not too expensive. Meanwhile he is forging ahead with my *Cathures* which he has scheduled for November. I think it should be quite a strong book. No word yet on who will step into the Laureate's Mercurian sandals in October. I hope they do at least continue it.

Poems continue. I am well into my new sequence for Tommy Smith, *Planet Wave Part 2*, which is ten poems carrying <u>things</u> forward – things, history, man, the globe, the universe, oh what not – from Copernicus to now and beyond – pouncing on moments where I hope something thrilling can be distilled or projected. It heaves, it grows! Nothing published yet.

Do you know Theatre Jet in London? They have commissioned me to write adaptations of some Japanese <u>Kyogen</u> plays – the comic interludes that lighten the solemnities of <u>No</u>. So I must brace myself, or unbrace myself, to slip into <u>farcical mode</u> as soon as spring comes. Perhaps it is a good thing, as my last medical checkup at the Beatson showed some problems. A farce or two will help to keep my head above water. And speaking of heads, my sculpted head will shortly be unveiled in bronze, along with <u>herms</u> of Liz Lochhead, Iain Crichton Smith, and Hugh MacDiarmid, at Edinburgh Park (a business park outside Edinburgh), and the plinth will be carved with a new poem for the occasion. I enclose a copy for you interest. We are all hovering between one world and the next –

Love to all, and on we go – | Eddie

Price's new collection was *Frosted, Melted* (diehard, 2002). Liz Lochhead would succeed EM as Glasgow's Poet Laureate in 2005. Both parts of 'Planet Wave' appear in *A Book of Lives* (2007). The sculptor of the 'herm' portrait bust was David Annand, and the poem 'A human head...' opened *Dreams and Other Nightmares* (2010).

Claudia Kraszkiewicz, researcher and teacher

Dear Students

Thank you very much for your fax about my poem 'O Pioneers!'. I am glad you found it interesting, and I admire your diligence in working out what might be the right questions to ask. The poet, of course, cannot always tell you the answers! Writing poetry is not a cold-blooded activity, and many things fly into one's head during the course of composition which resist being reliably pinned down afterwards. However, with that proviso, I shall try to answer some of your queries as I go through your letter.

I don't know Cather's novel. The title was suggested to me by Walt Whitman's poem 'Pioneers! O Pioneers!', which has both a real and an ironic relation to my poem. I have never used editors, and a poem usually bristles with changes made in the manuscript; I prefer to keep it on one page rather than have separate drafts. I have not seen the actual tunnel inscription, but when I read about it I thought there was a poem there. I enclose a not too good photograph, which was printed above my poem in an anthology called *Things Working*, ed. Penny Blackie, Penguin English Project, Penguin Books, 1970. I don't know if the inscription still survives; I hope so! As regards interpretation, the poem is possibly simpler than you suggest. What started it off was the fact that William Sharp's trouble with the spelling seemed prophetic of the endless delays in getting the tunnel made – more than a century in fact. The idea began sharply but soon began to be blunted, as the changes in the man's name and the permutations of '1880' as time wears on are meant to indicate. You are right, of course, in pointing out Sharp's desire to make his mark on history; it is a graffito that is both interesting and historic, since it was made by a workman and not by a sculptor. The asterisks, by the way, act as a sudden dislocation, pushing the action into a far future, with the tunnel idea at last being given up in favour of a grand bridge (which was in fact proposed by some people, but regarded as impractical.)

The poem is printed in my *Collected Poems* (Carcanet Press,

Manchester, 1990 and 1996).

Thanks again for writing, and my best wishes to you all in Minnesota.

Yours sincerely | Edwin Morgan

Ten Advanced Literature students at Marshall School in Duluth, Minnesota, had sent a series of questions on his 'O Pioneers!' (*CP*: 189) to the website, and this reply would be forwarded to them via Claudia Kraszkiewicz. Willa Cather's prairie novel was *O Pioneers!* (1913).

Karen Mountney, Programme Officer, Scottish Poetry Library

FAX   23 July 2002

Poet interview questionnaire   Scottish Poetry Library Please return by 9 August

1. *Where do you get your ideas for poems from?*
   Sometimes from things that happen to me or to people
   I know; sometimes from items of news in newspapers or
   radio or TV; and sometimes a line or a phrase flies into my
   mind and I couldn't say where it came from.

2. *What's the most unusual place you've ever written a poem in?*
   Walking along Piccadilly on a hot day in London, I 'wrote'
   the poem in my head, memorized it, and put it onto paper
   when I got to the place where I was staying.

3. *Who are your favourite poets?*
   I have always read a lot of poetry, but I don't really think in
   terms of 'favourites'. I like different poets at different times.
   However, poets I do happily go back to would include
   Whitman, Donne, MacDiarmid, Hart Crane, Edward
   Thomas.

4. *Why did you decide to write poems?*
   It's a mystery! I began writing when I was at school, and

it must have been because I loved words and language and enjoyed some of the poetry we had to read (and often learn by heart) – Tennyson, Shelley, bits of Shakespeare, bits of Milton.

5. *What do you like best about being a poet?*
The possibility of giving unexpected pleasure to other people.

6. *If you weren't a poet, what else would you be?*
I would probably be a carpet designer. When I was sixteen I had the chance of becoming an apprentice 'slab boy' at Templeton's Carpet Factory on Glasgow Green. I didn't take it up, but have often wondered what my life would have been like if I had. There are many forks in life where you have to choose which way to go, and you can't do everything!

7. *What or who has had the greatest influence on your poems?*
I have no idea. Cinema? Glasgow? *The Faber Book of Modern Verse* (1936)? Falling in love?

8. *Can you recommend three poems I should rush to the Scottish Poetry Library to read?*
Tennyson: 'Ulysses'
Iain Crichton Smith: 'Owl and Mouse'
Kathleen Jamie: 'The way we live'

9. *What top tips would you give to aspiring young poets?*
Read poetry. Write about things that really interest you, whatever that may be. Try out regular forms as well as free forms.

10. *If you could visit anywhere in the world or universe, where would you go and why?*
One of Jupiter's moons, Io, which has active volcanoes and gives out radio waves that we can detect here on earth. Perhaps it is sending us signals? I want to know more!

Developing the Scottish Poetry Library website for young people aged 10–14, Mountney had sent this questionnaire for EM to answer by fax.

Marshall Walker, academic and friend
(handwritten)

29–9–2002

Dear Marshall

Books flying about everywhere – here is another; another advance copy, to be launched with *Cathures* at Borders on 20 November. Your letter (16 September) and Villa-Lobos disc received with thanks – I enjoyed your account of the composer who seems very good but very patchy. – Yes, I'm sure my 'Blind' refers to the same woman you refer to. She always gathers a crowd, some of them visibly moved. It's the unsentimental clarity that does it. – You are wrong about our chronology (too many Brazil nuts?): we are listed not to October 1999 but to July 2001! I enclose an update, and of course I have a copy of the last list if yours has been chewed up by the computer. – Scaffolding still round Whittingehame; we hope to see an end to the whole dusty racket next month.

See you in November – | Eddie

EM sent a copy of the Carcanet *Beowulf*. Walker had asked whether 'Blind' in *Cathures* referred to a singer he had seen in Glasgow's Argyle Street. He included a tape of his own radio programme on composers. The maintenance scaffolding on Whittingehame Court formed the backdrop to *Love and a Life* (2003).

Goings & Comings & Doings etc

2001 (cont.)
9 August: Reading at SUISS, Pollock Halls, Edinburgh
14 August: Reading at Edinburgh Book Festival with Don Paterson. Panel discussion later same day with D. Paterson et al.
17 September: Reading at Coatbridge Library.

28 September: Speak at unveiling of Gerry Loose inscription on Kirklee Bridge.

29–30 September: With Colin & Kulgin at Frenich.

1 October: Reading at Geordie's Byre, Ayr.

4 October: Reading for National Poetry Day at Byre Theatre, St Andrews.

5 October: BBC interview on World War II women's poetry.

17 October: Photographed by Ron O'Donnell at Stirling Castle.

25 October: Press Day for EM exhibition at National Portrait Gallery, Edinburgh.

31 October: Recorded poems for Tommy Smith at Tillietudlem.

14 November: Reading of Italian poetry translations at Scottish Poetry Library.

29 November: Reading for Society of Authors at Waterstones, Glasgow.

30 November: Reading of József poems at National Portrait Gallery.

7 December: Reading at James Hamilton Academy, Kilmarnock.

10 December: Reading at Reid Kerr College, Paisley.

2002:

24 January: Reading at launch of *Nomad* magazine gay number.

4 March: Reading at Paisley Central Library.

4 April: Unveiling of herms of Scottish poets at Edinburgh Park.

5 April: Someone called Linda Grieve phoned to say she had an embroidered picture I made during the war – my mother had had it & must have given it to someone who had passed it on – all very strange – LG was going to give it back to me – but never did – never communicated again – all very odd & disappointing. I would have liked to have the picture – a bird in a tropical forest.

9 April: Scaffolding begins to go up at Whittinghame Court for major repointing of brickwork. The noise, the dust!

20 April: Reading of Hungarian translations at Glasgow University.

26 April: Reading at Scottish Literature Department, G.U.

5 May: Reading at St Mary's Cathedral.

11 May: Reading at 'G12' (James Arnott Theatre).

24 May: CT scan at HCI hospital, Clydebank.

15 June: Reading for medical group at Caledonian U.

19 June: Bone scan at Western Infirmary.

28 June: Tribute evening to EM at RSAMD.

15–15 July: With Colin & Kulgin at Frenich.

25 July: Started new cancer treatment with Dr Fullerton at Gartnavel.

6–7 August: Reading at Pittenweem Festival (Kellie Castle).

11 August: Reading at Edinburgh Book Festival with Don Paterson.

12 August: Reading at SUISS, Pollock Halls, Edinburgh.

14 August: Lecture on contemporary Scottish literature for *Scottish Left Review*, at Stand Comedy Club, Edinburgh.

13 September: Read my poem for David Daiches's 90th birthday with a group of his colleagues & friends at his home in Edinburgh.

22 September: Interviewed at home by American film-maker for a documentary on life of George Bruce.

30 September: Reading at Edinburgh Writers' Club.

1 October: CT scan & bone scan at HCI hospital, Clydebank (now called The National Health Waiting Times Centre! since it was taken over by National Health Service).

Peter McCarey, poet and translator
(handwritten)

4–12–2002

Dear Peter

It was good to hear about your Campos performance in Geneva – indeed just to know that he is still a performer! – and your tantric days in Kyoto – was it silence, stillness, occasionally a whack with a stick? Did you ever read Alexandra David-Neal's *With Mystics & Magicians in Tibet*? Hard to believe, and yet in a sense hard not to believe. I've been doing nothing so interesting. Travelling about has become too difficult. Events in Glasgow and Edinburgh I can manage, but

that's about it. Did you know there was a West of Scotland
Dowsers society? I gave a reading there – they asked me
presumably because I have a poem called 'The Dowser' – but
I was able to tell them I had actually dowsed with a twig on a
farm in Co. Wicklow many years ago and (perhaps) persuaded
myself that the twig moved. However, not being too mobile
means one can sit and write, and I've finished a 50-poem
sequence which is largely autobiographical and possibly not
publishable (Hamish Whyte and I are talking about it), and
also a translation of Robert Baston's Latin poem on the Battle
of Bannockburn – I don't know if you've come across it. He
was a Carmelite friar sent by Edward to celebrate English
victory, but was taken prisoner and could only be ransomed if
he wrote his poem celebrating England's defeat! Let modern
poets not complain about difficulties.

Syllabary installed in the Tate Modern: oh yes, you should
work on that. It's a great gallery and would be the right place
for such an imaginative work. I'm still computerless but get
lots of emails on my website set up for me by Claudia in
Dortmund – she faxes them through and it's really quite quick.
Did I give you it before? – www.edwinmorgan.com

Best as ever | Eddie

McCarey had heard Augusto de Campos* and his son perform
sound/concrete poetry in Geneva. On a WHO visit to Kyoto he
had visited a Tantric Buddhist monastery. *Metrum de Praelio apud
Bannockburn / The Battle of Bannockburn* was co-published in 2004.
The Syllabary installation was suggested by Richard Price* and Alec
Finlay*.

Mark Smith, friend
(handwritten)

8–1–2003

My dear Mark
   (You asked for a thistle: this is the best I can do.)
   Thank you for the five cards. Florence is now in my

hands – everything from cloisters to comfort stations. We've had hard frost here and I haven't been out on the slippery streets. Through my GP I've started the process of getting a home help and a pager alarm, and when the social services arrive to assess me I shall also ask about the walk-in shower you mentioned. I was very <u>down</u>, but am coming a little up. It's a moment of adjustment, and it's quite hard – when you know you are no longer independent – as I was brought up to be – and have to have help. My night on the floor was strange. As I was dragging myself about, trying to claw myself onto some furniture, but without success, I also at times was looking down on myself from above and thinking What a poor creature scrabbling there, is that the best you can do, I thought the species was Homo erectus, get up man! And I wouldn't have been able to phone if my telephone hadn't had a built-in microphone so that I didn't have to lift the receiver. Such little things! Anyhow, anyhow, here we are, and I have your letter which I have read many times. I also have another card – //
My gratitude to you is more than I can say, though something of it is in the poems. You gave me a new lease of life, and without you there wouldn't have been the last book or the recent sequence. I am very glad that you accept the sequence, and of course we can discuss details of it when you are back in Glasgow. Hamish is keen to publish in time for my birthday on 27 April, but he says he can start the preliminaries now and if necessary make changes later. We already have ideas for the cover design –

This picture shows an older Cairo than the one I knew, but the domes and tombs and the brooding air of decaying but still powerful grandeur are still what I remember, among all the rackety additions and the teeming streets, about which you already know – !

// Can you love Cairo, and Florence and now Bilbao? I haven't lived in the last two, but I think I have a net that sweeps up all three. Cairo, if you include its pyramids and domes and modern skyscrapers, and discount all the clutter and cacophony, joins hands with Bilbao, and Florence is the odd man out with its traditional acceptability. Yet Florence unmistakably vaut le détour. I do hope the new Scottish Parliament with its so-called upturned boats will turn out to be at least a mini-Guggenheim. Will you be at its opening, or will your restless spirit be on the move 'somewhere in Europe' – or America – or Brazil where Marshall Walker's new lady-friend comes from? And you want to take your restlessness out beyond the grave, beyond the ash-furnace? You want the stars? You want 2001, with or without a black slab? I couldn't agree more that the universe is so wonderful it would be the greatest of fates to explore it galaxy by galaxy – and it may be a multiverse, how about that – and never come to rest. But is it not more wonderful that this should happen, in the future, to living beings rather than to dead ones? I don't feel that particular desire for – next card! // personal immortality because of the feeling that if a few poems survived it would be enough – I'd be in the poems – anything else would be a defying of the law of death. I also have the stubborn irrational belief (but is it wholly irrational) that everything we do is somehow written into the fabric of the universe and cannot be destroyed even if it cannot be accessed. 'The moving finger writes, etc.' It may be a terrible thought that we have only 'one moment, in annihilation's waste' but if that moment was somehow, somewhere being preserved – No, I doubt if it would satisfy Mark! // Here is a card for partying. You said you were a great partyer. Ecstasy now if not hereafter. If the present Iraq madness continues and debouches into war, will those who are not called up become apocalyptically hedonistic or will they do a Tom Leonard and write about the horrors?

It won't be long till you are here and we can talk. Hasten the day!

Love | Eddie

EM responds over five varied postcards to five received. He had fallen in his flat late one evening and, unable to rise, lay on the floor till morning, thinking it too late to call a neighbour. In *Love and a Life* (2003) Mark Smith figures alongside others whom EM had loved.

Kulgin Duval, *book dealer and friend*
(handwritten)

2–2–2003

Dear Kulgin

Thank you for the fine card, the very perjink skaters,
and the Himalayan views. I was sorry to hear about Joan's
blindness, which must be particularly awful for her. If I still
have her address I must send her a card and her niece can
read it to her. I miss Morven a lot. I knew her for many years
(she was one of my first students) and always enjoyed meeting
her, her conversation – and her <u>cooking</u> – like Colin she was
a splendid cook! I have written a poem about her which will
be in my next book, due out in late April. You shall have a
copy! Your very kind suggestion that I might stay with you for
a few days, and that Colin might drive me there and back, I
would gratefully take up. I find public transport quite difficult
now, and take a taxi if I have to go into town. I have lost a bit
of self-confidence since my fall – though I now have a pager
alarm and don't feel quite so vulnerable at home. The bruises
have almost said goodbye! Tomorrow the social services will
be paying me a visit, to see if I can get a home help to do some
shopping for me. I also want to replace my bath (I daren't
lie or sit in it, as I couldn't get up, all I can do is <u>kneel</u>!) with
a walk-in shower. If the social services can't do it, I'll make
arrangements myself and pay what has to be paid.

Did you know that Peckhams in the Central Station has
been taken over by Marks & Spencer? Will it be as good?
Probably not!

No black-faced monkeys here – squalls of sleety snow
sweeping across the Campsies. You are much better off where
you are!

Best of love and good wishes to Colin and yourself – |
Eddie

From his house in Kerala, Duval had sent pictures of Trisul mountain.
Joan Tebbutt was a calligrapher and book-binder whom EM had
met at Frenich. Duval also referred to the recent death of Morven

Cameron, whose poem did not appear in *Love and a Life*, but was published in *Dreams and Other Nightmares* (2010).

Maggie Fergusson, biographer

1 March 2003

Dear Ms Fergusson

Here are some answers to your questions.

1. I first became aware of GMB's work during the 1950s, and followed it closely, in both verse and prose, from *Loaves and Fishes* onwards. I was attracted by the clean-cut style and by the Orkney settings which were fresh and original at that time. Later, I became less satisfied by the repetitiveness of his work, or what I saw as the restricted canvas of a few central themes and references of which he became too fond.

2. Glasgow was a bigger place, and poets did not congregate in one or two chosen pubs like the Edinburgh 'Rose Street poets'. I visited Rose Street once or twice, but I was never attracted by that hard-drinking scene. In any case, along with Tom Leonard and others I was concerned to put Glasgow on the contemporary literary map.

3. MacDiarmid was always criticised for this or that, but I think there was a general acknowledgement that he had made a real breakthrough in the 1920s, and things were never going to slip back again. On the other hand, when it came to the 1960s he was himself obstructive to the new wave of writers that included Ian Hamilton Finlay, Alexander Trocchi, and myself. Hero he may have been, but there was an edge to our admiration for him.

4. I may have met George sometime when we both happened to be in Edinburgh, but if so, I have no recollection of it. I met him in Stromness in the 1970s (1972?), and of course at the Festival in 1985, and got on very well with him. I was not totally surprised by the revelations in his autobiography about drinking and depression, as I always felt that the absence (as far as I know) of any close relationship in his life, with either women or men, suggested a loner's lack,

a loner's darkness, which all his cosy and couthy journalism about the local community could not quite hide. On my visits to Frenich we often talked about George; Colin's view (and I agreed with him) was that George was fundamentally gay, but totally closeted and inhibited and possibly in denial to himself about it. Commentators have studiously shirked this particular nettle, but I think a serious biographer ought to grasp it.

5. Yes, George hated cultural chit-chat and I'm sure he was glad when the festival was over!

6. Yes, we talked about these things, but although we were natural opposites we accepted each other's position with humour and goodwill.

7. Who can predict? I think people will always enjoy his clarity, his storytelling, and the whole background of an anciently inhabited group of islands. I am less sure of the ritualistic, often simplistic Catholic element of his work (all those threes and sevens, candles and prayers). I am inclined to think that his stories will stand the course better than his poems. But he is certainly a part of that creative generation, and he is an original.

Do let me know if I can be of any further help.

With best wishes | Edwin Morgan

I don't know whether you have seen the enclosed poem, but I thought it might interest you.

Writing her biography of George Mackay Brown, Fergusson asked for EM's impressions. He suggested she send specific questions. In summary, these asked for: 1. EM's first impressions of GMB's work. 2. His view of the Edinburgh poetry scene and its rivalry with Glasgow. 3. The effect of MacDiarmid on the image of poetry/poets in Scotland, and whether EM's generation saw him as a hero. 4. His first meetings with GMB, and reaction to revelations in his autobiography. 5. His reaction to GMB's claim of dreading the St Magnus Festival. 6. Whether their contrasting views of progress were discussed. 7. GMB's place in the canon of Scottish literature. (The poem was 'Orkney 1985', dated May 1997 in the MS Morgan Manuscripts Catalogue, University of Glasgow Library.)

23–4–2003

Dear Gerry

You said you liked the colour, so here it is again! I can keep
one eye on the green, and one eye on the foaming blossom.
Thank you for the 'blue sky, green grass' booklet which is
splendidly fresh in its detail and shows how much can still
be done with that old 'a day in the life' trope (is it a trope?
– Milton would know – ah, L'Allegro!). Kevin Masson's bee
makes a striking cover. Thanks also for the proofs – all seems
well at last. You have the rhyme-improved second line of
'Freeze-Frame', and I think you will have been able to add the
date of composition at the end: September–November 2002?
Since we're not having any blurb, it's useful to have at least the
date.

I hadn't seen the GMB picture. It certainly is the man,
almost frightening in its realism – relentless – and therefore
missing something of his mischievousness – but a masterly
portrait. I think I could have done without the crescent moon
through the window.

Yesterday was my last radiotherapy session (for the
moment anyway), and now I have to wait till my doctor gives
his assessment. The process is painless, but the trekking back
and forward to hospital every day is tiring and a nuisance
in practical terms (but I shouldn't complain – one of my co-
radiotherapees had to travel daily from Oban). I still have
some pain. The radiographer says helpfully that 'it usually
gets worse before it gets better'. I must keep the carrot of that
better firmly in my sights!

Isn't it a nice irony that if democratic voting returns
in postwar Iraq, the people will very possibly plump for a
fundamental Islamic state? That pilgrimage to Kerbala, with its
flailings and breast-beatings, was a remarkable sight. Oh the
twists and turns of history!

The house is full of dust. The men have now installed my
walk-in shower and the bath has gone to the bath's graveyard

– actually broken up and binned. New tiling on floor and wall, shining tough glass screen, electric shower, a new life?

All the best as ever | Eddie

Cambridge was typesetting *Love and a Life*. *Blue Sky, Green Grass* (2003), a 600-line poem on 'one day in the life of Lawthorn Primary School' in Ayrshire, came from his residency there as writer and naturalist, and incorporated the children's work. The postcard portrait was Erik Hoffman's *Nightfall – Portrait of George Mackay Brown* (Aberdeen Art Gallery and Museum).

Norman McBeath, *photographer*

28 April 2003

Dear Norman

Thanks for your letter of the 22nd. I am very pleased that your poets' portraits project is moving forward towards book and exhibition in 2004. It will be excellent if the Scottish National Portrait Gallery take it on.

Here is a 'statement' as you ask:

Why is poetry important to me? It is a very ancient art which has gone through many metamorphoses but survives because of its power to move people's emotions in unexpected ways. A good poem delivers first surprise – 'I've never seen those words brought together like that before' – and then assent, which may give joy or sadness but above all a sense of satisfaction and finality – no other way of putting it would do. And the poem has a strange means of retaining its power, despite the loss of surprise, so that even if you revisit it years later it can still catch your heart. Is it good for you? Is it good for society? Without offering proof, I'd give a yes to both questions.

And here is a signature: *Edwin Morgan*

With best wishes | Eddie

McBeath had taken EM's portrait in May 2001 for a planned photo-graphic study of poets. Working towards a launch coinciding with National Poetry Day, he had asked the poet for a brief statement on why poetry was important to him.

Richard Price, poet, editor and librarian
(handwritten)

G12 0BG   11–5–2003

Dear Richard – Artist's books everywhere! This is not a proper letter but just to let you know that I would be delighted to have lunch with you on Monday 2 June. 1pm? Shall I book at No78 (St Vincent Street)? I shall take a taxi so there will be no problem. I have now fallen getting onto as well as getting off a bus, and I can't help feeling fate is trying to tell me something – so I only use buses in emergencies and when I am not carrying anything.

  You are right: if my dress sense is offbeat, put it down to colour blindness. I am a red-green colour-blinder, the commonest kind of achromatopsiac (now there's a good word). I know because I have been tested. Shortly after I began lecturing, a member of the Psychology Department who was interested in perception came to the English Department looking for achromatopsiacs. I thought (from my schoolboy art classes) that I might be, and volunteered for the Ishihara test, an elegant book of colour plates where arrangements of dots are read to give different numbers by normal and colour-blind people – very convincing. I hope the B.L. has the Ishihara book, printed in Japan? He also tested me with skeins of silk. With a pale green one in my hand, I confidently said 'Pink!', to the gasps of my colleagues. I think my memory of the moment underpins the Chinese poem I sent you. Did you know that 10% of men are colour-blind, but <u>almost no</u> women? Now there's a <u>real</u> difference between the sexes, but what does it mean? Any further Hommes/Femmes thoughts? (And I agree with you about Verlaine, remarkable stuff.)

  From my red-green workshop – | Love | Eddie

Chan Ky-Yut, a Chinese-Canadian artist, had asked Price to collaborate on an artist's book, and had also invited EM, who wrote this letter on a flyer for an exhibition of artists' books from across the world, together with ex libris prints, *Five Continents – Ex Libris*, at the Glasgow Print Studio Gallery in May–June 2003. EM sent 'The Challenge' in response to Chan Ky-Yut's blending of calligraphy and colour.

The Challenge

Don't ask me about colour: your pale pink
Might be pale green, your dark purple deep blue
For all I know; but I bless your black ink
Twirling and tying a character or two
And how should I not bless the sudden flash
Of yellow godly and visible like a mandarin
Sleeving himself into a coat to cut a dash
Among the shadows. So what's out, what's in?
You move like a fish and no answers come
Beyond the pleasures who could ever explain
As the swift cursives, water, finger, thumb
Sweep space into shapes and half make rain
That never falls on roofs that never thrum:
Challenge of smoke-paths in the weather-vane.

(For Chan Ky-Yut) March 2003

Ken Cockburn, poet and editor

26 June 2003

Dear Ken

Thanks for your letter of 23 June. I have put together a 'top eleven' poems for your forthcoming SPL anthology:

W.S. Graham: The Visit (*Uncollected Poems*, 1990, but written in 1978)
Norman MacCaig: Praise of a Man (*The Equal Skies*, 1980)
Tom Leonard: right inuff (*Ghostie Men*, 1980)

Liz Lochhead: Mirror's Song (*Dreaming Frankenstein*, 1984)
Iain Crichton Smith: Owl and Mouse (*The Exiles*, 1984)
Jackie Kay: Close Shave (*The Adoption Papers*, 1991)
Don Paterson: An Elliptical Stylus (*Nil Nil*, 1993)
David Kinloch: Envoi: Warmer Bruder (*Paris-Forfar*, 1994)
Graham Fulton: Cream of Scottish Youth (*Knights of the Lower Floors*, 1994)
Gael Turnbull: Whin (*A Rattle of Scree*, 1997)
Richard Price: Motorcruisers (*Scape*, 2002)

See you on 5 July. All best wishes | Eddie

With Robyn Marsack*, Director of the Scottish Poetry Library, Cockburn was editing *Intimate Expanses: XXV Scottish Poems 1978–2002* (2004), and asked EM to list his top ten poems between those years.

Christopher Whyte, poet, novelist and academic

28 June 2003

Dear Christopher
    Your letter upset me – obviously – but it will not stop me communicating with you or welcoming you if you come to pay me a visit, as I hope you will. I had not thought of your silence as deliberate, but rather to be explained by your being busy with the combinations of academic work and your own writing, plus trips abroad. I think it is a pity that you did not come out with what you call your 'gripes' a bit earlier; your brooding – it seems to me – has led you into getting things well out of proportion.
    I remember the occasion that seems to have rankled most with you, but I don't remember saying the things you attribute to me, and certainly not any 'gleeful malice'. This may merely confirm for you my insensitivity, but on the other hand it may be thought to indicate your own over-reaction (as you confess to being 'over-sensitive' in these matters) to something said unguardedly in the course of a social meal. As I don't now recollect the argument that was going on, whether

you were saying that no one is any better for having read the Authorized Version – I can't comment any further. But if you were offended, you should have said so, either then or shortly thereafter. It is not good to let things fester.

Grand Old Man of Scottish letters? I think not! I am old, and I am a man, but grand is not my style, never was, never will be. I am no Goethe. If you get to my age and are still writing reasonable stuff, clearly people will be interested and will interview you and write about you, but this is curiosity more than adulation. If you think I relish adulation, or worse still seek it out, you don't know me! I am very well aware of the whole precarious and provisional nature of reputation. The only thing that matters is to be able to leave at least a few poems that will be remembered and read with pleasure, and who can guarantee that? – unless perhaps they are hammered into the fabric of the universe (actually I believe that) and will someday, somehow be able to be accessed. If you saw the hostile review of *Cathures* in *Stride* magazine, you would know that I am as vulnerable to criticism as any other writer. And I think when you have read the enclosed book you will find it transgressive enough to resist the clutch of establishments. (And it is a plain text, with no blurb or hype or recommendation.)

My problems now are physical – how to get from A to B. I am fairly unsteady on my feet, and the cancer has spread from the prostate to the bone, giving me a great deal of pain in hip and right leg. I had a course of radiotherapy recently, which may have helped. The Social Services are good, and I have a home help who does my shopping for me once a week. After I fell in the house one night, couldn't get up and lay on the floor till morning, I got myself a personal alarm which hangs round the neck and would summon assistance if pressed.

Four novels on your stocks! – I long to see them. You are splendidly prolific. I hope we can talk about that and many other things. Let me know when you would like to come to Whitt. Ct.

All the best | Eddie

Socialising with several Glasgow poets, when Whyte described the sense of alienation from the English language that led him to write in Gaelic, EM declared that his own sense of entitlement to it came from the King James Version of the Bible. Whyte detected an anti-Catholic bias in the remark. He also felt that EM had moved from an outsider role to that of Grand Old Man of Scottish letters. EM enclosed *Love and a Life* (2003) to refute this charge.

Judith Chernaik, writer and arts organiser

5 August 2003

Dear Judith

Thank you for your letter of 1 August. I do indeed remember *Carnival of the Animals*, and very enjoyable it was, at St John's Smith Square.

I have had another look at 'Fossils', and would be happy to have it included in the anthology. It might work as it stands, but I wonder whether the 'ammonite' reference would be too difficult for that age-group, even though they certainly grow up with the names of the dinosaurs. Suppose we were to change the last two lines to:

Where shall we find you, animals all?
You'll hear us roaring at the carnival!

I believe this would be an improvement, but see what you think.

It would be a pleasure to have a tape of the music, as you suggest.

All best wishes | Eddie

Fossils

Dinosaur egg! Dinosaur egg!
We'll hatch you yet. Say please! Beg!

Jurassic Park! Jurassic Park!
Watch their jaws shine in the dark!

Iguanodon! Iguanodon!
Shambles erect in the London dawn.

Triceratops! Triceratops!
Rattles his bones until he drops.

Tyrannosaurus! Tyrannosaurus!
REX REX REX is all his chorus.

O giant ammonite, where have you been?
I've been to the carnival and stolen the scene.

Edwin Morgan

Originator of *Poems on the Underground*, Chernaik had asked EM
some five years previously for a poem to accompany *Carnival of the
Animals* by Saint-Saëns. Publishers Walker Books were now inter-
ested in combining a book and CD, aimed at 5–11-year-old children,
and there was the chance to alter the poem.

Claudia Kraszkiewicz, researcher and teacher

FAX   20-Sep-2003
To: Claudia Kraszkiewicz
From: Edwin Morgan

Dear Claudia – I'm out of hospital after a month, and back
home briefly. I shall be leaving Whittingehame Court and
going into a nursing home within the next fortnight or so –
will send you details as soon as I hear. This will mean no more
faxes! You will have to answer emails by yourself, or ask people
to write to me at my nursing home address. A pity, but it
cannot be helped. I am not very mobile now, and will have to
be looked after.
     To answer your last email of the 18th:
Maria Sankus: no readings in prospect, but perhaps you could
tell her about my CD, where she would at least hear my voice.
Joyce Graham: The quotation about the hen is not by me but
by Norman MacCaig – I don't remember the title of the poem.

<u>George Hand</u>: No, I don't know him!

Thank you for sending Dortmund sunshine. Some of it got through, mixed with showers, today!

All best wishes | Eddie

EM had to leave his large fax-photocopier behind. Marion Sankus was a 17-year-old school student. The misquoted line is from 'Summer Farm' by Norman MacCaig. George Hand from Arizona had heard EM's 'Strawberries' (*CP*: 184) on the radio and wanted the reference.

James McGonigal, academic and poet

Lyndoch Nursing Home
69 Schaw Drive
Glasgow G61 3SB
14-1-2004

Dear Jim

Just to keep you in the picture.

Not long after you left yesterday, one of the male nurses whom I get on with very well popped in to see how I was doing. I thought I'd never have a better chance to mention the nocturnal problem, and told him I wasn't feeling too brilliant after a sleepless night caused by all that shouting in the corridor. I didn't want to make an official complaint, but if he as an insider could do anything… He said he knew about the problem; others had made the same sotto voce complaint. He said he'd speak to the Matron, Joyce, but warned that it was a delicate matter, involving the woman's family and relatives if any change of regime was contemplated. We'll have to wait and see. Actually, last night was relatively peaceful, so perhaps my words have had some effect – but I won't bet on that!

Doris has given me the first of my new stronger morphine tablets. 'They may make you sleepy.' Oh well, I've at least got this letter written.

Best as ever | Eddie

EM agreed to go into a care home in Bearsden, near where his father lived as a child. This unhappy time of readjustment came to an abrupt end some seven months later when the home closed with minimal warning.

David Kinloch, poet and academic
(handwritten)

21–2–2004

Dear David

It is curious how often things come in clusters. When your poem arrived, I had been reading Orhan Pamuk's Turkish novel *My Name is Red* and Robert Irwin's fascinating *The Arabian Nights: A Companion*, both of which seem to provide an unexpected but relevant background. At the same time I was eating a tangerine which was a gift from the taxi driver who drove my English *Telegraph* interviewer to the nursing home and who enthusiastically suggested some questions he might (and did?) ask – something very Glasgow about the incident, bizarre but touching. Anyhow, it was a thoroughly juicy tangerine, as tangibly exotic as the other parts of the cluster. I think I had advised you to try a big hotel, but Crail must have been a sound choice. I took to the poem right away, the colour, the detail, the physicality, the strange but touching relationship, the history – but I shall go back to it many times, richly calligraphed as it is.

I'll be delighted to see you again whenever you are free.

All the best | Eddie

Kinloch had visited EM in the nursing home, and afterwards sent a poem for comment: 'Baines His Dissection', later published in *In My Father's House* (2005).

James McGonigal, academic and poet

Lyndoch 13–6–2004

Dear Jim

I'd be glad if you could bring one or two things from the house, the next time you come: one of the folding Perspex chairs from the kitchen (behind the door); the big scissors hanging on the wall cupboard near the kitchen door; and two books from the study (shelves on the left side) – Allen Ginsberg's *Howl* and Lyn Hejinian's *My Life*.

I wonder if Ian Bruce has managed to find out yet whether the new people want the house <u>completely</u> cleared, including kitchen appliances?

All the best | Eddie

EM needed extra chairs to accommodate visitors to his single room. He continued to write, including 'For the Opening of the Scottish Parliament, 9 October 2004' (*A Book of Lives*, 2007). Ian Bruce was his lawyer, overseeing the sale of the flat at Whittingehame Court.

James McGonigal, academic and poet
(handwritten)

CC 19–11–2004

Dear Jim

A couple of things.

I have received McTear Auctioneers' cheque for £346.82, for sale of the household goods. It isn't much, but I had no huge expectations, having gone through this process with my mother's effects a long time ago. By far the most valuable item was the Doulton chamberpot; if you still have any chamberpots lying about, don't throw them away! I don't know whether this cheque has to be declared for next year's income tax – I'd have thought not – but would you ask Andy McBean about this? And also, do we have to declare the amount of the house sale? In case it has to be declared, the McTear cheque is dated 17-11-2004.

My watch has started stopping again, if I can put it that way. I've stopped wearing it, as it's just too unreliable. From what your jeweller said, do you think it's worth taking it back, or should I just keep it in my drawer?

Looking forward to seeing you soon | Eddie

CC is Clarence Court care home in Glasgow's West End. When his flat was sold, EM's books went to Glasgow's Mitchell Library, and his art works and papers to the University of Glasgow. Apart from a few gifts to friends, the house contents were auctioned. His watch was activated by wrist movement, and a sedentary life now caused it to wind down. Andy McBean was EM's accountant, and an executor of his will.

Russell Pearson, cousin
(dictated letter)

Clarence Court
1 December 2008

Dear Russell

Many thanks for your recent letter, giving me the sad news of Tom's passing. I'm very sorry to hear that, but relieved too that he had such a short time in hospital, and little or no pain. As you say, he lived a full life in Tasmania. I'm sure that many will miss him, yourself most of all.

I find it difficult now physically to write: my hand refuses to grip the pen properly and the handwriting is hard to read. Sometimes, as now, I ask a friend to type things out for me. It is a real frustration, not to be able to reply promptly and easily to friends. Many people still do write. Recently I have been considering buying a computer and trying to master the new language of email.

Painkilling drugs dull much of the discomfort I would otherwise feel, but have the side-effect of making it harder for me to concentrate for longer stretches of time. And occasionally I doze. However, on the positive side, I am quite well cared for here.

Please do keep in touch, even though I may be slow to respond. I appreciate it.

With every best and warm wish – | Eddie

Russell and Tom Pearson, two elderly cousins living in Tasmania, shared a house and an enthusiasm for golf, and kept in touch with EM through Christmas cards and the occasional letter. This reply was mainly dictated.

Anthony Gardner, editor, Royal Society of Literature
(dictated email)

16 December 2008

The Poet Laureate

Even if the role of Poet Laureate were not to be continued, I think that we'd have to invent something similar. Some people are put off or confused by the title itself – what is a 'Laureate'? But they would accept it more readily if we had another name for it. I don't know what exactly that name should be, but the word 'laureate' seems somehow rather precious and old-fashioned. It would be better if we could get back to the old idea of being given, simply, a laurel wreath. That would be the final reward for all your labours. There's nothing there to draw the poet into many years of effort, working for monetary or political gain. No, simply the realisation: I am this person, and I wrote these good poems, and I'm being given an abstract recognition in the form of this very charming floral wreath – which I now put on.

In these post-devolutionary days, of course, we have to differentiate between the Poet Laureate and the Welsh or Scottish national poets. In Scotland, this role is sometimes known as the National Makar, or maker. The Laureateship now has to strive to indicate that it is not simply an English appointment, by re-emphasising its 'British' credentials. Such anxiety may indicate that it is in fact a political role, by particular appointment to The Queen (capital T, capital Q). While this is true, it does not satisfy the people of Scotland, who are, I think, quite certain of a movement in politics and society that is developing towards a very different way of looking at things – a Scottish as compared to an English way. The two nations (if we want to use that term) are still closely attached, but moving away from that towards some kind of separation, although there may be argument about what degree of separation there should ultimately be. So if we could find a less obscure and less 'defensive' way of describing the post of Poet Laureate, that would be better.

On another level, it would also be good to remind people that poetry still exists and has a role. We do require some person who can provide a kind of clarion call to the country, or a warning voice for a change of direction, if that is necessary. I think people would not disagree with the idea that we need a spokesperson for the nation, or for individual nations within Britain, and that this could even be a useful role. The Laureateship needs a commanding presence, then, and certainly not someone tied to any narrow party version of truth. Culture involves many things, and I am thinking here about something historical. When Hungary in the middle of the 19th century was struggling to get out from under the Russian or German yoke, Petőfi, a very strong poet, and a young man too, published a remarkable, short and vehement poem, 'Nemzeti Dal', or 'National Song', which was instantly celebrated. It was a reminder that a national poetry should not be involved in clinging to any particular political idea, or writing for money, and it is certainly not to be seen as a passing gift (whether granted by a queen or anyone else). Rather, poetry at this level should remind people that if they want to achieve something in the world, and to really be taken seriously, then they need to show the world what they stand for. And surely those who are best equipped to articulate this are good writers, and this includes poets.

Edwin Morgan

Andrew Motion was to demit office as Poet Laureate in 2009, and Gardner, who edited the annual *Royal Society of Literature Review*, contacted EM as the Scottish equivalent for a statement on the Laureate's role. Answering a different survey of poets' preferred choices for Poet Laureate at this time, EM suggested J.H. Prynne.

Garry McGregor, Edinburgh LGBT Age Project
Co-ordinator
(dictated email)

7 July 2010

The LGBT Age Project

The first thing I think about, as a gay nonagenarian, is of being one hundred! On a more serious note, in my case the worst thing is mobility – or the lack of it – not being able to go out or to meet people. A lot depends on your health. Being very old is fine if you are not in too much pain. I have experienced pain over the last few years.

I would be good to have someone to talk to about this. I do not mean 'tea and a chat' with the old women who outnumber the men in the care home where I now live. Old women and old men don't generally get on well. Interaction and attraction between the sexes is *usually* over by our advanced stage. You can't artificially make people enjoy talking to each other.

The most important thing now is to see things clearly, and to discuss things openly with one person or group. This is where the LGBT Age Group will be very helpful. If the problem can then be dealt with, fine. If not, it must be coped with. There are also positives about old age, of course, if you are not hospitalized. Age encourages you to think about your condition, and to see if it can be made any better.

It is also quite important for old people to have contact with younger people. In my care home, the age range is from 72 to 102. In my experience, I get on better with younger people than with those of my own age. This can be a chance to look back over your life, and to convey that experience to younger people. Such contact might be difficult to organise: you need a room, space – freedom from the demands to do this or that. But telephone contact with an interested listener can also work well.

A young friend of mine died recently at 50 years of age. He once told me he was glad that he was not my age. But if it comes to the worst, there is nothing to be done except to 'calm the mind', taking an oriental approach to life. My own advice at ninety years of age is not to expect too much – but definitely to expect something!

Edwin Morgan

The Edinburgh LGBT Age Project aimed to set up a helpline for elderly gay people who might be living in isolation, and asked for some comment that could be used in publicising the new service in the local media. This response was dictated and sent, almost verbatim. The friend who died was Bobby Craig, who figures in the final poems of *The New Divan* (1977) and in 'Love and a Life', in *A Book of Lives* (2007). The poet himself died six weeks later.

Further Reading

Biography
McGonigal, James, *Beyond the Last Dragon: A Life of Edwin Morgan* (Dingwall: Sandstone Press, 2012)

Selected Critical Studies on Edwin Morgan and his Context
Bell, Eleanor and Linda Gunn, eds, *The Scottish Sixties: Reading, Rebellion, Revolution?* (Amsterdam: Rodopi, 2013)

Crawford, Robert and Hamish Whyte, eds, *About Edwin Morgan* (Edinburgh: Edinburgh University Press, 1990)

McGonigal, James, *The Poetry of Edwin Morgan*, Scotnotes series (Glasgow: Association for Scottish Literary Studies, 2013)

McGuire, Matthew and Colin Nicholson, eds, *The Edinburgh Companion to Contemporary Scottish Poetry* (Edinburgh: Edinburgh University Press, 2009), 'Edwin Morgan', pp. 97–110

Miller, David and Richard Price, *British Poetry Magazines 1914–2000. A History and Bibliography of 'Little Magazines'* (London: The British Library and Oak Knoll Press, New Castle, DE, 2006)

Morgan, Edwin, *Nothing Not Giving Messages: Reflections on His Work and Life*, ed. Hamish Whyte (Edinburgh: Polygon, 1990)

Nicholson, Colin, *Edwin Morgan: Inventions of Modernity* (Manchester: Manchester University Press, 2002)

Riach, Alan (ed.) *The International Companion to Edwin Morgan* (Glasgow: Scottish Literature International, 2015)

Watson, Roderick, *The Literature of Scotland: The Twentieth Century* (Basingstoke: Palgrave Macmillan, 1984, 2007), 'New Visions of Old Scotland', pp. 203–15

Whyte, Christopher, *Modern Scottish Poetry* (Edinburgh: Edinburgh University Press, 1996), 'The 1960s', pp. 120–48

Scottish Literary Review, 4:2, Autumn/Winter 2012, Edwin Morgan Special Issue (Glasgow: Association for Scottish Literary Studies)

Index

Names in bold are the correspondents selected for this book, and a page entry in bold signals where a letter to the named person can be found. MS Morgan references after names refer to the Edwin Morgan Papers in the University of Glasgow Library (see explanatory note at the end of this index). Page entries not in bold signal references made to this person in letters written to others. Names not in bold refer to writers and artists mentioned in the letters, with page references.

MS Morgan references relate to the Edwin Morgan Papers in the Department of Special Collections, University of Glasgow Library. The majority of his letters were filed by Morgan in either named correspondent files (which have been assigned the prefix (MS Morgan D) or in a series of general, chronological files (MS Morgan T). Researchers are welcome but should get in touch in advance of a visit.